MASTERPLOTS II

POETRY
SERIES
SUPPLEMENT

9

Poet-Z
Cumulative Indexes

Editors

JOHN WILSON   **PHILIP K. JASON**

Project Editor
MCCREA ADAMS

SALEM PRESS

Pasadena, California   Hackensack, New Jersey

Editor in Chief: Dawn P. Dawson
Managing Editor: Christina J. Moose
Project Editor: McCrea Adams   *Production Editor:* Yasmine A. Cordoba
Acquisitions Editor: Mark Rehn   *Manuscript Editor:* Douglas Long
Research Supervisor: Jeffry Jensen   *Research Assistant:* Jun Ohnuki

∞ The paper used in these volumes conforms to the American
National Standard for Permanence of Paper for Printed Library
Materials, Z39.48-1992.

Library of Congress Cataloging-in-Publication Data
Masterplots II. Poetry series. Supplement / edited by John Wilson
and Philip K. Jason.
    p.   cm.
    Includes bibliographical references and indexes.
        1. Poetry—Themes, motives. I. Wilson, John, 1948-
    II. Jason, Philip K., 1941-
PN1110.5.M37   1992
809.1—dc20   91-44341
Supplement   CIP
ISBN 0-89356-625-X (set)
ISBN 0-89356-628-4 (volume 9)

First Printing

PRINTED IN THE UNITED STATES OF AMERICA

LIST OF TITLES IN VOLUME 9

LIST OF TITLES IN VOLUME 9

MASTERPLOTS II

POETRY SERIES

THE POET'S COURAGE

Author: Friedrich Hölderlin (1770-1843)
Type of poem: Ode
First published: 1801, as "Dichtermuth"; collected in *Gedichte*, 1826; English translation collected in *Poems*, 1943

The Poem

Friedrich Hölderlin's "The Poet's Courage" consists of seven four-line classical hexameter stanzas that examine the relationship of the poet to nature, lament the loss of the poet to natural forces beyond the poet's control, and exhort the reader to take both courage and caution from the poet's costly struggle. The poem begins by posing a rhetorical question to the reader, asking if the reader understands that human beings are kin to all that is alive and asserting that humans exist ultimately to serve "Fate." Based on these assertions, the poem directs the reader to travel without fear though life.

This idea of accepting "all that happens there" continues into the second stanza as the reader is once again provided with affirmations that neither harm nor offense should be found in the progression of that which must be. The images of the third stanza support this representation of human existence in service to nature's larger forces, in the "quiet near shores" or over "silent deep/ Water" through which the "flimsy/ Swimmer" travels. The fragile poet loves to be among these living, teeming creatures, and it is this union that makes possible the poet's song. Moving from the general human condition to that of the poet in particular, the fourth stanza establishes the relationship of the poet to all "those alive, our kin" for whom "we sing his god." The poet is developed as nature's spokesperson, one who exists in a "glad" state, open and "friendly to every man." Additionally, the idea of trust is introduced and carried into the fifth stanza, in which the poet, the "brave man . . . trusting, . . . makes his way" only to be dragged below the waves at times; thus submerged and overwhelmed by the forces of nature, he falls mute.

After the poet's death, as the sixth stanza explains, his "lonely" groves lament the loss of "Him whom they most had loved" even though he died with joy and gladness. His message has not been lost, though, since a virgin, an appropriately uncorrupted listener, often still hears his "kindly song" in the "distant boughs." Ironically, the song of nature sung by the poet is now echoed by nature after the poet's loss. The last stanza presents a final image of "a man like him," another poet who passes the place where the forces of nature submerged the first poet and who contemplates this "site and the warning." As the poem concludes, however, this warning does not deter the other poet from his task since the final line explains that the poet, "more armed," walks on. "The Poet's Courage" provides a cautionary example for the reader and for those poets who trust all and speak for nature: While nature may overwhelm and silence a single voice, other voices will draw on that courage and continue the refrain.

Forms and Devices

Hölderlin's modernity lies in his reliance on particulars, on the invocation of a person or thing, while more conventional poets have felt obliged to present a sequence of arguments or metaphors. Hölderlin's poem "The Poet's Courage" proceeds by flashes of perception or allusion, true not to the laws of argument but to expressions of feeling and thought. From the first two stanzas' spirited illumination of the human traveler who ought to vanquish fear and thoughts of defense in the light of Fate's directing hand, the poem moves into the particular images of powerful nature in contrast to the precarious position of the poet who is at one with nature yet is overwhelmed by the magnificent forces to which he gravitates. This extraordinary combination of concrete imagery and visionary breadth, this fusion of spiritual intensity and sensory details, gives the poem its impact. Hölderlin provides glimpses of water images (quiet shores, silvery floods, the silent deep, overwhelming waves, and teeming sea life) then carries the trusting poet under, swallowed up by the very object of his devotion. The reader is thrust into the company, then, of the virgins and the other poets who observe the first poet's passing and learn from his song.

"The Poet's Courage" relies on the personification of nature: The wave is "flattering" when it draws the poet below, and his "lonely" groves "lament" his loss. This representation of nature further reinforces Hölderlin's notion of the poet's union with nature, especially since his song can be heard "in the distant boughs." The poem describes all of nature as "our kin," and by recognizing, developing, and trusting this close relationship with nature, the poet is able to sing for "Each of them . . . his god." Even the trees echo the poet's song, and the site of his passing carries a warning.

In addition, the poem's structure reveals Hölderlin's admiration for classical Greek poetry since his experimental verse forms are adapted from the fifth century Greek poet Pindar. Even in translation, his lyric rhythms pull the reader like a forceful current guided by laws of the form but flowing with an energy of their own. Hölderlin's use of inversions, too, creates the illusion of antiquity ("Glad he died there"), as does the creation of the lost poet as the vanished classical tragic hero whose fatal flaw (his trusting union with the very nature with which he is one and of which he sings) is also his priceless gift.

The inversions also serve to create a sense of suspension since Hölderlin often builds a series of clauses and phrases preceding a concise, emphatic, main statement. For example, the third stanza's construction defies sequential syntax, opening with three prepositional phrases that increase the intensity of the eventual subject, which is further suspended in the inversion "travels the flimsy/ Swimmer." These radical departures can lead to ambiguity, but Hölderlin himself asserted that "much greater effects can be obtained" via the use of these devices.

Themes and Meanings

In his tragic odes, especially "The Poet's Courage," Hölderlin's pantheism, his desire to be at one with the cosmos, continually comes up against his awareness not only of the essential differences between humans and the rest of nature but also of the isolation into which individual people are precipitated by their consciousnesses. The poet who possesses the great gift of knowing, of being at one with nature, suffers alienation from the rest of humanity, those who do not have the courage or the vision to recognize and embrace this relationship. In the fifth stanza, the poem describes "One such brave man" who stands apart from the masses and who is mourned in his passing not by his fellow human beings but primarily by the forces of nature and the virgins who have been uncorrupted by the general human retreat from nature. This tragic poem, then, provides a metaphor of an intellectual point of view that can be none other than the awareness of being at one with all that lives and an assertion of the courage that is required to embrace that awareness. This representation of the tragic is mainly based on what is monstrous and terrible in the coupling of God and humanity, in the total fusion of the power of nature with the innermost depths of humankind. Hölderlin said, "There is only one quarrel in this world: which is more important, the whole or the individual part," and, in "The Poet's Courage," his message is clear: Individuals who acknowledge their place in the whole of nature, who sing of the union with joy and trust, will eventually cease to exist as individuals, becoming one with the whole and surviving only in the message that they have fused with nature.

Hölderlin bases his vision on a belief that nature, history, and art are part of a larger scheme that transcends individual existence; he speaks as a poet-seer, looking forward to the possibility that opposites can be harmonized. In addition, Hölderlin, who believes that the poet's mission is to educate through art, emphasizes the value of the poet's work. This air of the heroic poet, this tone of noble idealism and exalted transcendence, permeate the poem. Ultimately, the poet must make the great sacrifice and cultivate this marvelous, mysterious knowledge even though these gifted individuals come to grief. They are heroes, these poets, who represent humanity's honorable and hazardous attempts to ennoble itself, and their fate is shrouded in a heroic, tragic atmosphere.

The feeling in much nature poetry seems to derive from the conviction that something is to be found in nature that is absent from civilized urban life. In "The Poet's Courage," however, Hölderlin goes beyond the assertion of nature's grandeur, release, beauty, and ability to inspire, into an emphatic representation of nature as a power asserting itself and expressing itself in manifold forms, a power at once material and spiritual, comprehending all creation. This power of nature is so all-encompassing that once poets reach this awareness they cease to exist, and it takes a special kind of courage, "The Poet's Courage," to seek that awareness.

Kathleen M. Bartlett

PORPHYRIA'S LOVER

Author: Robert Browning (1812-1889)

Type of poem: Dramatic monologue

First published: 1836, as "Porphyria"; collected as the second of two poems titled "Madhouse Cells," in *Bells and Pomegranates, No. III: Dramatic Lyrics,* 1842; subtitled "Porphyria's Lover" in the collected edition of *Poems,* 1849

The Poem

"Porphyria's Lover" is a sixty-line poem of irregular iambic tetrameter with an *ababb* rhyme scheme, a pattern which continues through the poem's twelve five-line divisions. It is believed to be Robert Browning's earliest study in abnormal psychology. It is perhaps more accurately termed a soliloquy or an inner monologue than a dramatic monologue, since it identifies no specific auditor. The term "dramatic" more aptly describes many of Browning's later poems, in which the tension arises from the drama that builds as the speaker unwittingly reveals himself to a specifically identified listener present in the poem. The fact that Browning called the poem "dramatic" is probably explained by his reaction to reviews that had ridiculed his earliest work as too subjective. After these, he insisted that readers see his poetry as objective by distinguishing between his personal self (the poet) and the voices of his fictive speakers in his monologues. He did not want critics to think these created speakers expressed the poet's personal emotions.

The title leads one to expect a love relationship, perhaps two lovers in a cozy cottage retreating from the storm described in the opening lines. However, the perceptions reported by the speaker (the "lover") soon alert the reader to his unbalanced perspective. This speaker attributes attitudes and willful actions to the wind: It is "sullen," it has torn the elm trees "for spite," and it has tried to "vex the lake." These opening lines reveal the speaker as fearful, as a passive listener, and as one who seems to project his own emotions onto the external world. He appears to be an unreliable reporter.

He then describes the entrance of Porphyria, whose actions and words contrast with the speaker's passivity: She has "come through wind and rain" to "shut the cold out and the storm." She then warms the cottage, an action that the speaker has lacked the will to perform for himself. He seems to lack any awareness that he has a will or a voice of his own: He reports that his arm and his cheek are placed by Porphyria around her waist and on her shoulder. He seems to experience himself as being without an active, directing center of his own being, since he has only "debated" possible action, being too engrossed in his own feelings to initiate action. When he can finally act, prompted apparently by a drive to preserve the moment of Porphyria's surrender to him, he murders her by strangling her with her own hair. In the remaining lines, the speaker clinically describes opening Porphyria's eyelids, loosening her hair around her neck, kissing her dead cheek, and propping her head on his shoulder in an act that mimics her earlier placement of his head. As he had projected his own attitudes and emotions onto the external storm in the opening lines, he concludes by attributing his murderous act to Porphyria's "utmost will" and "one wish." The final line suggests a complete lack of conscience in the speaker: "And yet God has not said a word!"

Forms and Devices

Browning's forte and his principal formal strategy in this early poem is a monologue through which an unaware speaker reveals character disorders. It is the speaker's diction and syntax as he reports his perceptions and inferences that reveal his moral character. The first four lines are simple, flat, four-measure statements, end-stopped and regular in meter until the spondee of line 5, "heart fit." After the speaker's personification of the wind, which suggests his own helplessness and suppressed emotions, the ambiguous grammar of the emphatic spondee suggests both a heart ready to break and a heart that is having a fit. Lines 6-15, which describe Porphyria's movements, are correspondingly more fluid, with enjambment and midline clause breaks. The effect is a contrast between Porphyria's action and the speaker's unmoving passivity. Lines 15-30 show the speaker overcome by Porphyria's presence. He has lost even the weak "I" of line 5 and has become so dissociated from himself that he reports his inability to reply to Porphyria's call as "no voice" being heard, as though he is outside himself listening. The word "displaced" (line 18) suggests the displacement of the speaker's center of being, a kind of moral paralysis. This self-alienation continues with the speaker's sense that Porphyria is the one who moves his arm and head. The word "stooping" (line 19) is, again, grammatically ambiguous, this time as a dangling modifier, since the speaker, not Porphyria, is the one who must bend over to reach her shoulder (line 31 shows that he is the one who must look upward). Lines 22-25 seem to indicate the speaker's judgment more than Porphyria's "murmuring," as they continue his merging, or confusing, of their identities.

Still seeing himself through Porphyria's eyes, the speaker regains his sense of "I" in lines 31-35, but the descriptive phrase "happy and proud" is ambiguous, referring either to "I" or to "her eyes." He feels that he has become her god or idol, although he is in the position himself of the worshipper, looking up as his elation further severs his swelling heart from his debating judgment. Lines 36-41 reveal the speaker's intense need to capture the moment, to possess Porphyria permanently in a kind of aberration of an erotic consummation, the act of strangulation reported in the emphatic first half of line 41. The speaker's certainty that she "felt no pain," which he repeats, is further evidence of a bizarrely delusional personality. The simile of the bud mocks epic grandeur and, through grammatical ambiguity again, may refer to the speaker or the dead Porphyria, just as the laughing blue eyes may be his own or his hallucinative perception of hers. With Porphyria reduced to an unthreatening corpse and after having asserted his will by murdering her, the speaker is able to act part of the role of a lover as he kisses her dead cheek. It is clearly a demented lover, however, who takes possession of the corpse and interprets its expression as "glad" that its "will" is fulfilled since his love is "gained." Use of the passive voice is significant throughout the poem, indicating a speaker who cannot feel responsible for what he does. Is the "one wish" (line 57) a "darling" wish because it is hers, or is it the wish of her "darling," the disordered speaker? Does the speaker await, during and after the night vigil, blame or commendation from God?

Themes and Meanings

This poem enacts the behavior of a distorted personality and mocks, pointedly, the attribution of the capacity to love to such a personality. Browning would not have used the term "schizophrenic" because it did not come into psychiatric parlance until the twentieth century. He could, however, present the disordered thinking of one suffering from personality dissociation, experiencing alienation from self and from what is normally perceived as reality, exhibiting inappropriate emotion and behavior, and unable to feel responsible for his emotions or his actions. This "lover," so dubbed ironically, obviously cannot love or even affirm himself as an autonomous being who could generate love. In Browning's moral perspective, this speaker would be another jealously possessive and tyrannical male similar to the duke who speaks in the more widely known poem "My Last Duchess." The theme is a frequent one in Browning's poetry.

A possible additional thread of meaning may be derived from the knowledge that the poem was first published with another poem, "Johannes Agricola in Meditation," and that the two poems were later grouped under the heading "Madhouse Cells." Browning clearly believed that both poems represented forms of madness. Johannes Schneider (Agricola) was associated with German religious reformer Martin Luther, but they did not agree on all points of theology. He was the founder of the Reformation sects of antinomianism, a belief labeled heretical by the orthodox because it taught that those among the elect (that is, those predestined for salvation, according to some forms of Calvinism and Wesleyanism) could not sin regardless of the apparent evil of their acts. The periodical in which Browning first published the two poems, the *Monthly Repository*, was edited by W. J. Fox, who was a friend of the Browning family and who rejected Calvinist ideas of election in favor of Unitarianism. Either he or Browning prefaced the poems with a note explaining that antinomianism maintained that God would not chastise one that he had chosen to save even if that person broke the moral law by committing murder or other heinous crimes. This context of early publication seems to offer the best explanation of the final line of the poem. Browning's characterization of his speaker as a lover can thereby be read as his satiric exposé of a religious fanatic so convinced of his predestined salvation that he feels himself to be beyond divine retribution for his murderous act and subsequent necrophilia.

Carolyn F. Dickinson

THE PURSE-SEINE

Author: Robinson Jeffers (1887-1962)
Type of poem: Lyric
First published: 1937, in *Such Counsels You Gave to Me and Other Poems*

The Poem

"The Purse-Seine" is typical of many of Robinson Jeffers's short poems. As is characteristic of lyric poems, the poet shares his personal experiences, thoughts, and opinions directly with the reader, using beautifully rendered scenes of nature to illustrate his point. It is written in Jeffers's unique verse form: a type of free verse with very long lines. The poem's twenty-four lines are divided into four unequal stanzas. The first stanza presents a scene of commercial sardine fishermen working with a particular kind of net known as a purse seine. The reader is told that this kind of fishing must be done at night when there is no moon so that the schools of fish can be located by their phosphorescent glow. Thus readers are presented with the image of a small boat at sea in nearly total darkness. The narrator then focuses in more closely with a description of the lookout man pointing out a group of fish. The helmsman circles the boat around the fish, setting the net. The bottom of the net is pulled closed, or pursed, and the trapped fish are hauled aboard.

The second stanza is a more artistic interpretation of the same event. The poet begins with a disclaimer, "I cannot tell you/ how beautiful the scene is" and then proceeds to describe it. He says it is a "little terrible" as well as beautiful because of the panic of the trapped fish as the net tightens. The beauty is in the phosphorescent glow that the fish make as they swim and thrash, churning the water into a "pool of flame." Then, in contrast, sea lions slowly rise from the darkness of the sea, separated from the sardines, their normal prey, by the net. A mention of the night studded with stars closes the scene, locating the activities described within the context of the entire universe.

The third stanza shifts to a new scene in which the narrator describes the view of a city from a hill at night. He tells the reader that the lights of the city remind him of the fish in the net. He explains that because humanity has become cut off from nature and has become dependent on the artificialities of the cities, each individual is helplessly trapped by whatever future civilization has to offer. According to the narrator, the shine of the city is the same as the glow of the fish, indicating that the net of doom is tightening around it. He predicts that "inevitable mass-disasters" will come in a few generations: Civilization will decline through political repression, revolution, or anarchy. In the final short stanza, the narrator, now identified as the poet by speaking of "our verse," asks if the reader can blame him for writing poems that are "troubled or frowning." He claims that his poem "keeps its reason" instead of becoming hysterical about such predictions of doom by accepting the fact that "cultures decay, and life's end is death."

Forms and Devices

One of the most striking aspects of the poem is the verse form. Jeffers has been praised and criticized for his unusual verse form consisting of long lines that seem to be divided arbitrarily. Some lines in this poem are twenty-two words long and take up three lines on the printed page. The lines are without rhyme, and often the rhythm is not immediately apparent. It is not quite free verse, however, and the poet himself claimed to use a system of meter and stress suggestive of the rhythms of the tides and the blood, and the patterns of everyday speech. Many critics have attempted to discover the key to this system by counting accents and lines; however, the structure of the poem seems to be driven by its meaning and the sound of its words rather than by an arbitrary, mathematical arrangement of syllables and stresses.

Jeffers's short poems usually involve the description and interpretation of a particular experience. From this basis, he goes on to comment on the experience and use it as a symbol or an analogy for some aspect of the human condition. "The Purse-Seine" follows this pattern, describing the capture of the fish and comparing it to humanity's entrapment by civilization. Jeffers's lessons are rarely left hidden: The messages are stated quite clearly. The instructional or moralistic nature of the poem is achieved through the unique narrative voice that Jeffers uses. It becomes obvious that the poet is speaking directly to the reader, especially by the time the poet refers to his own verses in the last stanza. He also speaks plainly, describing the scene in conversational language and then bluntly stating that he is comparing the purse seine net to the confining civilization of the city. The poet's tone is prophetic and admonitory, warning humans of the doom that awaits them if they follow their present course.

Jeffers is able to take this "moral high road" without offending the reader by his use of a distant perspective: He becomes an omniscient narrator as well as an individual speaking to the reader. He describes the fishing scene from an indefinite point of view that even knows the actions of the sea lions in the deep, dark water. He observes the city from a specific place on a nearby hill but also from a great psychological distance. He speaks of humanity as "them" rather than "us." This perspective gives his opinions and warnings some validity: Readers are led to believe that he can see things that they, mired in the immediate present, cannot see. The poet's conversational tone also helps readers to believe him. He uses words rooted in science and politics that readers may not be accustomed to hearing in poetry: phosphorescence, interdependence, government, and anarchy. He speaks directly to readers, saying "I cannot," "I was looking," and "I thought." At the same time, he disarms readers with beautiful descriptions of nature and metaphors of fish as rockets and cities as galaxies of stars.

Themes and Meanings

Jeffers was as much a philosopher as a poet, and no discussion of his work would be complete without mention of his philosophy of Inhumanism. This perhaps unfortunate term, coined by Jeffers himself, is often misunderstood. It has nothing to do with cruelty or meanness, though those human failings are common in his long narrative poems. Instead, it refers to a detachment that allows the poet to step outside the human condition for a more cosmic viewpoint. The poet's way of dealing with the suffering and other negative aspects of humanity and modern civilization is to see them in the context of geological or cosmological time and space. From the perspective of billions of years and the infinite distances of the universe, humankind is really a brief and perhaps not very important phenomenon. This cosmic viewpoint is underscored by the images and metaphors used in the descriptive passages in the poem. The phosphorescent fish are described as rockets and comets, and the first scene ends with the walls of night and the stars, which places the small, confined world of the fish in the net in the context of the limitless expanses of space. The city, too, is described as confined and even claustrophobic, yet it is compared to the light not only of stars but also of galaxies.

Inhumanism is the key to another of Jeffers's major themes: the beauty of the natural world. The poet is in awe of what he calls in the title of another poem "divinely superfluous beauty." This is beauty that exists for its own sake, usually unseen by humans, from the starry wheels of the galaxies to the phosphorescent glow of the fish in the sea. He even finds beauty in the violence and apparent cruelty of nature. In other poems, he praises the violence of weather and the sea, and the ferocity of hawks; in "The Purse-Seine," he praises the seemingly cruel work of catching fish. The fishermen in this poem are not part of the city and civilization; rather, they are making their living close to nature and are not condemned for killing the fish any more than the sea lions would be. They are part of the pattern of life and death and thus contribute to the beauty to be found in the natural world. From this detached, Inhumanist viewpoint, the poet sees the tragedies of civilization and its estrangement from nature, as well as its eventual decline into chaos and darkness, as acceptable or even beautiful. These things all play their small parts in the inevitable evolution of the grand ways of the universe.

Joseph W. Hinton

QUEEN-ANN'S-LACE

Author: William Carlos Williams (1883-1963)
Type of poem: Lyric
First published: 1921, in *Sour Grapes*

The Poem

Written in non-metrical verse, "Queen-Ann's-Lace" is a single-stanza, twenty-one line poem. Its title suggests it is about the common field flower also known as the wild carrot. A wide, white flower about a hand's width in size, Queen Anne's lace contains scores of tiny blossoms and, in the center, a dark spot. In *I Wanted to Write a Poem* (1958), William Carlos Williams said that he used "straight observation . . . in [his] four poems about flowers, 'Daisy,' 'Primrose,' . . . 'Queen Ann's Lace,' and 'Great Mullen.'" He "thought of them as still lifes . . . . [and] looked at the actual flowers as they grew." Indeed, the poem's speaker might be observing a field of Queen Anne's lace as the sun's rays touch it.

The poem's opening line, however, announces a much different subject: the white-ness of a woman's body, which the speaker contrasts briefly in the first three lines with "anemone petals." He finds "Her body is not so white," "nor so smooth—nor/ so remote a thing." Then, throughout the remainder of the poem, he compares her body's whiteness with a commonplace "field/ of the wild carrot." With this comparison, there is "no question" of too much "whiteness," for at each flower's center rests "a purple mole."

Initially, the wildflower exerts its power, "taking/ the field by force," not allowing the grass to "raise above it." In the second half of the poem, however, the woman's body responds to her male lover, "a blossom under his touch." "Wherever/ his hand has lain there is/ a tiny purple blemish." Ultimately, his touch erotically transforms and purifies her (and the whole field of Queen Anne's lace), first into "a/ white desire," then "to whiteness gone over." Just as such a field of wildflowers would respond to the light and warmth of the sun and could not live without them, the woman responds to her male lover.

Clearly, Williams moved well beyond his "straight observation" of actual flowers, the still life which was the starting point for this poem. Rather than being simply a poem about a flower, "Queen-Ann's-Lace" represents an intense human experience, a moment during which the poetic imagination transforms straight observation of a common wildflower into a sensuous—and sensual—moment of awareness. Focusing, at this point in his career, on the essence of physical things, Williams later explained, "Emotion clusters about common things, the pathetic often stimulates the imagination to new patterns."

Forms and Devices

At the time Williams wrote "Queen-Ann's-Lace," he had been, for several years, a member of the Imagists, a small group of early twentieth century poets that included

Ezra Pound, H. D. (Hilda Doolittle), John Gould Fletcher, Amy Lowell, and Wallace Stevens. Rejecting Romantic idealism and Victorian moralism, the Imagists advocated, instead, the use of common speech and concrete images, the freedom to choose any subject matter, and the need to create new rhythms. "Queen-Ann's-Lace" exhibits all of these principles. With only one word that might puzzle some readers ("anemone," a flower in the buttercup family), its language is simple. The poem, furthermore, presents, in detail, an image of a common wildflower that most readers have already experienced or easily can. Likewise, its subject is not the typical rose of Romantic and Victorian poetry but a wild carrot and a woman's body, both energized with sexual meaning.

Although Williams begins the poem with a simile that contrasts the whiteness of a woman's body with the anemone, it is mainly through metaphor that he transforms his straight observation, his still life, into a dynamic field of action that reveals the life and energy hidden in Queen Anne's lace. To create this dynamic field, Williams uses a central metaphor: Her body "is a field/ of the wild carrot taking/ the field by force." He then extends the analogy throughout the remainder of the poem. Forceful, but *not* "white as can be" and certainly *not* virginal, the woman (and the flowers) respond to the lover's caresses with increasing intensity marked by changing color. Thus, instead of the "remote" whiteness of anemone petals, "Wherever/ his hand has lain there is/ a tiny purple blemish," then "a/ white desire," and finally "whiteness gone over."

While the poem's movement from beginning to end may seem circular, from "white as/ anemone petals" to "whiteness gone over," it is actually spiral. It does not return to where it began but moves to a different plane. The "white desire," the "pious wish to whiteness gone over" are not "remote"; they depend upon the lover's touch, just as the transformation of the flower depends upon the poet's subjective observation and interpretation. As critic Peter Halter notes in *The Revolution in the Visual Arts and the Poetry of William Carlos Williams* (1994), "Throughout his life Williams was to remain diffident with regard to too facile use of metaphors and similes, but throughout his life he was to use them as a poetic device for making the energy in things manifest."

In "Queen-Ann's-Lace," as in many of his other poems, Williams does not employ traditional metrical or stanzaic patterns. As critic Stephen Cushman notes in *William Carlos Williams and the Meanings of Measure* (1985), Williams's prosody is "based not on time, accents, sounds, or recurrent phrases, but on lineation" marked by enjambment (run-on lines). Thus, to create the "new rhythms" called for by his fellow Imagists and his own particular form of "free verse," Williams systematically used enjambed lineation, carrying rhythmical and grammatical sense from one line to the next without pause or punctuation. As a result, the lines of "Queen-Ann's-Lace" often do not begin or end as the reader might expect. Only three of six sentences, for instance, begin at the start of a line, and only three end at the conclusion of a line. Likewise, only eight of the poem's twenty-one lines end with pauses or stops; conversely, eleven lines contain one or more internal pauses or stops. Ultimately, however, the dominant run-on lines of Williams's non-metrical verse establish rhythm between lines and connect line to line.

Because enjambment appears so frequently in Williams's poetry, its absence—a change in the fundamental pattern—becomes noteworthy. In "Queen-Ann's-Lace," the last four lines are end-stopped, not enjambed. Significantly, these lines describe, in a series of images, what the poet's "touch" has caused the field of flowers to become "white desire, empty, a single stem,/ a cluster, flower by flower,/ a pious wish to whiteness gone over—/ or nothing." Arresting and emphatic, the punctuation and rhythm here parallel each striking, powerful, and discrete image. These effects would be blunted if the images were broken up and carried over from one line to another.

Themes and Meanings

In his personal epic, *Paterson* (1946-1958), and in several other places, Williams writes, "No ideas but in things," declaring that the poet's role is to perceive and express through "immediate contact with the world" the objects which surround him. The poetic imagination can make a poem of anything, even a field of common wildflowers. Precisely such a poem, "Queen-Ann's-Lace," appeared in *Sour Grapes* (1921), a book of verse whose title reflected Williams's mood at the time, one filled, as he writes in *I Wanted to Write a Poem*, with "disappointment, sorrow. . . . [for he] felt rejected by the world." This very positive poem and several others like it in *Sour Grapes*, however, embody his delight in physical things, and his ability to discover their hidden beauty. Beginning with straight observation, he transforms the wild carrot and makes a poem which is a woman.

In *Poets of Reality* (1969), critic J. Hillis Miller observes that "Queen-Ann's-Lace" also admirably represents "Williams's power to charge a whole scene with sexual meaning," a "constant mode of his relation to the world" that is demonstrated throughout his work. Indeed, the poem reflects the relaxed sexual mores of the 1920's in the United States, for Williams openly depicts the flower-woman's sensual arousal and rapture under the sun-poet's touch. The poem does not, on the other hand, embody the era's new freedoms for women (for example, the right to vote guaranteed by ratification of the Nineteenth Amendment in August, 1920). Displaying his opposition to such freedoms, Williams portrays the woman and the flower in "Queen-Ann's-Lace" as both earthbound and submissive. In contrast, the sun and the man that touch them are unrestrained and dominant. The flower may thus prevail over "the grass/ [which] does not raise above it" and take "the field by force," but it blossoms only wherever the male sun's "hand has lain." Likewise, the woman can only respond to the man's erotic touch, which fulfills her "pious wish to whiteness," purifies her, and makes her more than "nothing." She (and the flower which represents her) may be lovely and sensual, but she owes her existence to the poetic hand and imagination that created her.

Joseph M. Nassar

THE RAISING OF LAZARUS

Author: Rainer Maria Rilke (1875-1926)
Type of poem: Lyric
First published: 1934, as "Auferweckung des Lazarus," in *Späte Gedichte*; English
translation collected in *Poems, 1906 to 1926*, 1957

The Poem

Rainer Marie Rilke wrote his only novel, *Die Aufzeichnungen des Malte Laurids Brigge* (*The Notebooks of Malte Laurids Brigge*, 1930, 1958), in Paris in 1910. It left him emotionally drained and unable to write much in the ensuing years. He travelled to North Africa and Egypt, then to Italy and Spain. From Toledo, where he studied the art of El Greco (1541-1614), Rilke moved further south for the winter to Ronda. It was there that he wrote "The Raising of Lazarus." Surrounded by beautiful landscape, he enjoyed six weeks of prolific writing in early 1913. The poems he wrote in Ronda are among his best but were not published together during his lifetime. Rilke had come to the conclusion that only cohesive groups of poems should be published, and he was already working on his *Duineser Elegien* (1923; *Duino Elegies*, 1930) at the time, which would eventually become a cycle of ten complex poems. In June of 1913, he would publish his cycle on the life of Mary, *Das Marienleben* (*The Life of the Virgin Mary*, 1951), which he had written in January of 1912.

Rilke was raised in the Roman Catholic Church, and much of his poetry shows a deep Christian influence. *Das Stunden-Buch* (*The Book of Hours*, 1941) was a major early work, written in 1899, 1901, and 1903 and published for Christmas of 1905. Its three books, *Vom mönchischen Leben* (*Monastic Life*), *Von der Pilgerschaft* (*Pilgrimage*), and *Von der Armut und vom Tode* (*Poverty and Death*), treat Christian themes in a traditionally devout manner.

Something happened to change Rilke's outlook. "The Raising of Lazarus" is so boldly secular that it hardly seems to have been written by the same poet. Rilke had, in the interim, read the works of the Danish philosopher and religious thinker Sören Kierkegaard (1813-1855), who was critical of conventional Christianity and emphasized the importance of individual choice.

To see just how far removed Rilke's poem is from the only account of the miraculous raising of Lazarus from the dead in the Bible, it is helpful to read John 11 for comparison. Verse 25 is the one most often quoted, where Jesus said: "I am the resurrection, and the life." Rilke has chosen to cast the event in a different light, with a post-Freudian focus on how Christ felt about what he was doing. And he leaves out God the Father altogether.

Much remains unsaid in "The Raising of Lazarus." Rilke assumes the reader will recognize the unnamed main character as Jesus Christ, who has already amply demonstrated his ability to heal the sick. It is useful, when reading the poem, to recall, from John 11, what happened before the scene Rilke portrays and the consequences of that scene. Christ deliberately delayed coming any earlier, and his raising of

Lazarus was the ultimate provocation for the Pharisees, who then were determined to have him put to death. Rilke is fascinated with the individual who, following the dictates of an inner necessity, avoids an easier route and subjects himself to the stress of a supremely challenging task.

Forms and Devices

The poem itself deals only with the actual raising of Lazarus in Bethany. Narrated in the third person, it elaborates greatly on the Biblical observation that Christ "groaned in the spirit, and was troubled" (John 11:33). His reluctance is evident from the start, as is his critical detachment from humanity: "people need/ to be screamed at with proof." He briefly entertains the hope that at least his friends Martha and Mary, Lazarus's sisters, will believe in advance that he can bring Lazarus back to life. But not even they see his arrival in Bethany as the solution. Rilke effectively uses direct quotation so that we may hear, with Christ, what he has to contend with: "you come too late."

The next step is essentially a violation of nature and goes against Christ's own inclinations. Two extremely short sentences describe his intensely emotional reaction: "In anger" and "He wept." Even on the way to the grave, he has serious reservations. But as Christ begins to walk, Rilke's sentences begin to flow: eight verses before the full stop at "Move the stone!," then through to the end of the poem without a break. Since English sentences tend to be shorter than German ones, the contrast in Rilke's sentence lengths is not always retained in translation. In the original German, the syntactic units mirror the content. They show Christ stop and gather his energy, then set in motion a process that even he is unable to stop.

In the Bible, Christ talks briefly with God, then calls Lazarus to come out. Rilke's dramatic poem relies more on gesture than on words for its effect. He introduces the silent and suspenseful raising of Christ's hand, then the tightening into a claw, which in the German literally applies suction to the grave ("ansaugen"). Then he creates tension in the reader by revealing that Christ fears he might accidentally be raising many more than Lazarus, that "*all* the dead might return/ from that tomb."

Rilke keeps us in suspense and expands his rhyme scheme as the tension builds. The basic scheme of the poem is rhymed quatrains, but, at the last, Rilke makes us wait for a fifth verse before the rhyme, before Christ has the reassurance that he has raised only one and the life of the common people can go on as usual. The nightmarish elements of uncertainty and doubt make reading the poem an emotional experience.

Rilke's interest in existential questions places him outside expressionism in literary history, yet "The Raising of Lazarus" has much in common with the work of Rilke's expressionist contemporaries, whose influence cannot be ruled out. It was written in 1913, during a period of protracted inner crisis for Rilke that coincided with the unrest felt by many artists, particularly the expressionists, prior to the outbreak of World War I. Its unique approach to the familiar Bible story concentrates on Christ's inner feelings, giving precedence to subjective reality, as did the expressionists. Rilke's poem shows Christ strongly resisting what he must do, an attitude in keeping with the father-son conflicts in expressionist literature. And finally, in common with the innovative expressionists, Rilke uses the form itself as a means of expression: A basic pentameter propels the poem, and the lack of division into stanzas mirrors the inexorability of Christ's undertaking.

Themes and Meanings

Prior to writing "The Raising of Lazarus," Rilke had gone to Toledo for several weeks to see more works by the famous Spanish painter El Greco. The poem has strong visual components and the feverish intensity of El Greco's later works, even though El Greco is not one of the artists who painted the raising of Lazarus. The shocking moment Rilke captures so well is the moment of Christ's uncertainty. There is so much tension in his hand that it clenches like a claw as he begins to work his miracle, unsure of how it will end. This is Christ the man, not the god. The terrifying uncertainty he experiences is something everyone feels when doing something dangerous or unfamiliar for the first time.

Rilke's empathy with the figure of Christ, as he describes him, extends beyond the moment to Christ's whole situation. Even those closest to him do not understand him. They force him to defy nature in order to prove his deity but are incapable of grasping the continuity of life and death so evident to him. At the same time, there is a conspicuous absence of communication from above, from God the Father.

Christ's alienation in the poem is strikingly similar to that of the equally freely re-interpreted Prodigal Son in Rilke's autobiographical novel, *The Notebooks of Malte Laurids Brigge*. The final paragraph of the novel reads: "What did they know of him? He was now terribly difficult to love, and he felt that One alone was able for the task. But He was not yet willing." Both Christ and the Prodigal Son are misunderstood. Both contend with the excruciatingly difficult task of being true to their own natures, which place them quite apart from the average person. Rilke's extraordinary accounts of these biblical characters results from his identification with aspects of them, and they become representations of elements of himself. He was convinced that he must write and became frustrated when he could not do so. His works were produced at great personal cost. He could not live with other people for any length of time but needed human contact, and this led to a most unsettled lifestyle. Rilke's life is testimony to the difficulty of living with a creative gift that consumes the artist. His portrayal of Christ in "The Raising of Lazarus" focuses on the agony that accompanies the possession of exceptional powers.

Jean M. Snook

READING LAO TZU AGAIN IN THE NEW YEAR

Author: Charles Wright (1935-   )
Type of poem: Meditation
First published: 1990; collected in *Chickamauga*, 1995

The Poem

"Reading Lao Tzu Again in the New Year" is a poem of middle length (forty-seven lines) written in free verse. The title is somewhat misleading, since neither Lao Tzu nor whatever work of his Charles Wright has been reading is mentioned in the poem. Instead, the reading of Lao Tzu's poetry and his view of nature seem to trigger a meditation on the end of the year and the absences or emptiness in nature and humankind. The speaker of the poem is the same speaker who appears in all the poems of *Chickamauga* and Wright's next book, the Pulitzer Prize-winning *Black Zodiac* (1997). He is an aspect of Wright himself, a seeker of some ultimate truth, some "essence," who never seems to find the answers he is seeking. Instead, in this poem, the search sets in motion a meditation on "essence" that deals primarily with time and the winter landscape. The poem is divided into three distinct sections and has a clear movement and development. The first two sections portray the world as dead and the speaker close to despair. The third section shifts from this gloom to affirmation.

The poem begins with the "Snub end of a dismal year." The focus is on winter and the dying of nature rather than on any suggestion of renewal provided by the new year. This sense of endings is further defined and intensified in the description of the landscape. The sky has an "undercoat of blackwash," and in his dead world the speaker must "answer to/ My life." The tone is morbid, nearly despairing. A new year may be beginning, but "nothing will change hands." There will be no revelation, only repetition.

The poem then meditates upon cycles of rising and falling: "Prosodies rise and fall./ Structures rise in the mind and fall." The speaker thinks only of "failure," and nature seems cut off from its own parts rather than being a unified and healing system. There is a more hopeful shift at the end of the second section, as all the "loss" the speaker sees becomes a "gain."

The last section of the poem is more description than meditation. It is "Four days into January," and tiny grass is growing "under the peach trees." The birds are singing, and the speaker now sees the place of humankind in a more hopeful light. People may be "between now and not-now," but they are "held by affection." They are connected by bonds of feeling, not merely adrift in a world of failure and dead ends.

Forms and Devices

One of the most important devices of the poem is Wright's use of free verse. It is not a free verse that arbitrarily breaks lines; there is, instead, a clear integrity of the line. Wright also sets one line off against another by indenting some lines far toward the right margin. He thus creates a counterpoint between lines, adds asides that comment on the previous line, and makes forceful caesuras between lines.

Wright uses a number of traditional poetic devices in the poem, but imagery is clearly the most important. There are images of emptiness or diminishment in the first section—the "dwarf" orchard and the sky with its "undercoat of blackwash." It is the "snub" end of a dismal year. There is also an interesting allusion in the first section: "this shirt I want to take off,/ which is on fire." These lines allude to the shirt of Nessus, which caused Hercules to go mad after putting it on. In that fit of madness, he killed his wife and children.

The second section continues the negative imagery. Failure "reseeds the old ground"—a brilliant image that reverses the renewal of "seeding" into a cycle of failure and hopelessness. The rest of the second section is more statement than imagery: "Prosodies rise and fall./ Structures rise and fall." There is, once more, a cycle that does not renew but only repeats. The references to prosody and structure are literary and suggest the problem of creating a meaningful poem in the midst of a meaningless cycle.

Images of nature follow these statements, but they are negative also. "Does the grass, with its inches in two worlds, love the dirt?/ Does the snowflake the raindrop?" Things that should be closely connected into structures instead have their parts cut off from each other; everything and everyone is isolated. There seems to be no solution to this problem, because "those who know will never tell us." The "word" that should illuminate instead "leads us another step from the light." At the end of the second section, however, the poem turns from its depiction of despair to the beginning of affirmation: "Loss is its own gain./ Its secret is emptiness." The "dark selves" of the poem move as "the tide moves." The acknowledgment of emptiness and the movement of self and nature together seem to point a way out of the dilemma.

In the last section, the images of nature are connected, in contrast to the isolation of the first section. "The grass grows tiny, tiny/ Under the peach trees." Although the growth is tiny, it does provide some hope, and the speaker seizes upon that hope. Birds are singing, and nature is growing; only humankind is isolated "between now and not-now." Yet even that displacement is "held by affection." This tenuous affirmation is supported by the poem's final, significant image: "Large rock balanced upon a small rock."

Themes and Meanings

The first important theme in the poem is that the change of the year does not produce change or renewal but a seemingly endless cycle: "Old year, new year, old song, new song." Nature is part of this repetitive cycle. The references to literary elements in the poem are worth noting, as they are also caught in an unrenewing cycle. "Prosodies rise and fall./ Structures rise in the mind and fall." The change in prosodies does not give the poet a useable metrical system but a sense of chaos in the displacement of existing systems. The imagination of the poet is caught in this dead end as well; Structures may rise in the mind, but then they disintegrate. Furthermore, words—and thereby the naming and placing of objects, the most elemental tools of the poet—do not provide an instrument for vision but take one further from illumination.

The "emptiness" of the second section is an important thematic shift in the poem. It reflects not a repetitive cycle but a closure. Although it does not provide renewal, it is a step toward change and a way out of the endless cycles of the poem. The "loss" that has filled the first two parts of the poem is now a "gain." Wright does not explain this paradox; he simply asserts it as a truth. In addition, there is a freedom of movement here that has not been seen earlier in the poem: Our "dark selves" move like bodies of water being moved by the tide. The darkness that has been so much a part of the poem is also altered in the last section as "Sunlight sprays on the ash limbs." The image finally proclaims an illumination of the dark world and dark selves.

The place of humankind, for which the poet has been looking since the beginning of the poem, is discovered and asserted at the end. The phrase "We're placed between now and not-now" seems at first to be merely a description of human displacement; people can never live truly in the present, only between two states. However, Wright adds another line to this formulation. People are also "Held by affection." Both words are important: "Held" suggests human contact and being sustained, while "affection" suggests the feelings, bonds, and gestures of everyday life. With this assurance, this balance, the speaker can stop his metaphysical speculations about humankind and nature. Where he is in time becomes less important than being "Held by affection." The last image is also important: "Large rock balanced upon a small rock." The differences are brought together in an equilibrium that closes the poem.

James Sullivan

READING THE BROTHERS GRIMM TO JENNY

Author: Lisel Mueller (1924-   )
Type of poem: Meditation
First published: 1967; collected in *The Private Life*, 1976

The Poem

"Reading the Brothers Grimm to Jenny" is a forty-six-line poem arranged in four stanzas. Jacob Grimm and his brother Wilhelm were well-known nineteenth century German collectors of fairy tales. As the title indicates, the poet is reading these fairy tales to her daughter Jenny. In later collections, the poem includes the subtitle "Dead means somebody has to kiss you," which shows that Jenny is young enough to form her image of death from a fairy tale, specifically from the story of Snow White, who was awakened from deathlike sleep by a kiss. Although the poet seems to be addressing the child, she is not speaking but thinking the poem while reading fairy tales aloud. In fact, the poet is arguing with herself. By implication, she is also arguing with her contemporary American peers, many of whom disapprove of fairy tales for children in the belief that they present a false picture of life.

In the first stanza, the poet contrasts Jenny's "black and white" world, in which things happen by magic, with the poet's "real world," which functions by negotiating ("gray foxes and gray wolves/ bargain eye to eye") and by doing what it takes to survive ("the amazing dove/ takes shelter under the wing/ of the raven to keep dry"). In the second and third stanzas, the poet asks herself why she lies to the child by allowing oversimplified fairy-tale values to seem real when she knows that one day Jenny will have to live in the adult world and "live with power/ and honor circumstance." In the fourth and final stanza, however, the poet recognizes that the creative power of belief can transform the world and says that she learns this "once more" from the child.

The poem is full of references to magic, including the stories of Snow White ("Death is a small mistake/ there, where the kiss revives"), Cinderella (who had the nearly impossible task of sifting lentils from cinders), Rapunzel (upon whose hair a prince climbed the tower in which she was imprisoned and whose pitying tears cured him after he was blinded), and birds that "speak the truth" (found in many fairy tales). In this magical world, life is divided into "kingdoms of black and white," both commanded by the mind; in the adult world, however, the "foxes" and "wolves" are gray and so are the values, and the mind must cope with power and circumstance outside the self. The conflict between childhood and adult views of the world and the conflict within the poet-as-mother about what she should teach the child creates and sustains tension throughout the poem. The recognition of this conflict allows transcendence of it at the end to become a credible answer to the question.

Forms and Devices

The imagery of the poem is vivid and physical: "you shoulder the crow on your left,/ the snowbird on your right." At the same time, imagery of equal intensity evokes scene after scene from fairy tales. Common metaphors (clichés) in this poem show how deeply fairy tales have become ingrained in everyday life. The reader is led to see the gray foxes and wolves not only in their metaphorical senses of clever (foxes) and devouring (wolves) people and not only as a mixture of good and bad (gray) but also as actual gray-haired businesspeople and politicians negotiating and making compromises.

When read aloud, the poem sounds like a ballad, yet the balladlike rhyme and rhythm are not arranged visually in traditional four-line stanzas; rather, they are set into four long stanzas: The first and fourth are of fourteen lines each, suggesting the fourteen-line sonnet, a reflective form that traditionally poses and then answers a question. Like the sonnet, this poem asks and answers a question. Unlike the sonnet, the question is not asked until the second stanza and is answered in the fourth and final stanza. The second and third stanzas have nine lines each. This symmetrical arrange-ment of stanzas further reinforces the idea of an ordered world. The progression of the poem is not narrative like a ballad but is an argument that makes use of ballad meter and rhyme to reinforce one side of the argument. As long as the poem deals with the magical and with the belief that everything is simple, the lines are end-stopped (their thought does not carry over to the following line) or the rhyme and meter themselves compel the stop: "gray foxes and gray wolves/ bargain eye to eye,/ and the amazing dove/ takes shelter under the wing/ of the raven to keep dry."

When the poet begins to recognize that the child's "truthful eyes" and "keen, attentive stare/ endow the vacuous slut/ with royalty," the lines spill over onto the next lines; then the form returns to the more structured end-stopped lines, even though the poem has shifted to include the idea of a less simple adult world. The rhymes begin with true rhyme (white/right, through/roo-coo), followed by slant (consonant) rhyme (wolves/dove, innocence/circumstance) and assonant (vowel) rhyme (climb/binds, is/insist/bliss), eventually returning to true rhyme (see/key/be). This variation would also be found in a ballad. In this poem, the variation helps to prevent a sing-song effect, and the return to true rhyme reinforces acceptance of the magical view.

Themes and Meanings

The central issue of the poem is the conflict between the way things are and the way they should be. This is a conflict as old as the human hope for a better world. Realists refer to it as "reality versus illusion"; idealists refer to it as "the real versus the ideal." Mueller sums up the realist view in the lines "Jenny, we make just dreams/ out of our unjust lives." However, the poet is not content with labeling them only as dreams; instead, she finds that the ideal can serve a creative purpose: "Still, when your truthful eyes,/ your keen, attentive stare,/ endow the vacuous slut/ with royalty, when you match/ her soul to her shimmering hair,/ what can she do but rise/ to your imagined throne?" The poet sums up her balancing of the real and the ideal in the lines "And what can I, but see/ beyond the world that is// the world as it might be?" The poet recognizes that this is more than a conflict; it is a juggling act. With nothing but the fairy-tale ideal, a child is ill-prepared for the real world, in which there is no absolute right or wrong. On the other hand, with nothing but the real world in its present state, there is no hope for anything better. It is a temporary balancing, one that Mueller has undertaken in many of her poems. In this one, she relieves the didacticism of her conclusion—that people expand their limits when someone sees a creative possibility for them—by referring to it as something the child teaches her "once more."

Poets are especially concerned with balancing the real and the ideal, knowing that these are also the literal and the imaginative and that poetry needs both. Mueller's concern with the real and the ideal is made more poignant by the knowledge that she and her parents escaped from Adolf Hitler's Germany and took refuge in the United States in 1939. She grew up all too aware that the world is no simple fairy-tale existence. Yet many of her poems are filled with the fairy tales of her childhood, and her work shows that, despite discouragement, it has remained important to her to help make "the world as it might be." The intensity of her use of fairy-tale characters and motifs reflects the fact that, growing up in Germany, her idea of fairy tales differs from the American view that such tales represent mere wishful thinking. Rather, she inherits the European view that fairy tales, like myths, vividly present stock characters and situations people meet in everyday life, and she takes their power seriously, even though she recognizes their simplicity.

Helen Shanley

REAPERS

Author: Jean Toomer (1894-1967)
Type of poem: Lyric
First published: 1923, in *Cane*

The Poem

"Reapers" is a short poem of eight lines in iambic pentameter rhymed couplets, a form sometimes referred to as heroic couplets. It appears as the second piece in Jean Toomer's *Cane*, a collection of short stories, sketches, and poems intended to show the beauty and strength of African American life. The poem is spoken by a first-person narrator, but this narrator neither enters the action nor comments on it. This is typical of the work collected in *Cane:* The narrator usually selects particular details to present to the reader but trusts the reader to interpret the details wisely. Only rarely, and usually in prose pieces, does the narrator guide the reader more directly.

The eight lines divide neatly into two sections, each representing a different vision. In the first four lines, black field workers sharpen their scythes with sharpening stones. When they are finished, they place the hones in their pockets and begin cutting. The men are silent; the only sound in the scene is the sound of the steel blades being ground against the stones. The narrator, standing far away (physically or emotionally), dispassionately reports what he sees. In the second four lines, the narrator turns his gaze to another field or another day, and the silent black men are replaced by a machine, a mower, drawn by black horses. The mower has run over a field rat, which lies among the weeds bleeding and squealing. The mower blades, stained with the rat's blood, continue on their path.

Forms and Devices

"Reapers" is divided into two sections, two scenes, with no commentary from the narrator to help the reader interpret their meaning. That the two are meant as separate pieces is clear, both because of the fact that the only lines that are end-stopped are the fourth and the eighth and because of the pointed similarity of the openings of the two sections: "Black reapers" and "Black horses." However, the two pieces are closely linked; Toomer has not written the poem in two separate stanzas but as two pairs of paired couplets. The meaning lies simply in the contrasts between the two parts, and the poet uses careful arrangements of sounds in the two scenes to emphasize those contrasts. In the first scene, silent except for "the sound of steel on stones" and the suggested swishing of blades through grass, the poet uses repetitive sibilant sounds as seen in the phrase just quoted and in the second line: "Are sharpening scythes. I see them place the hones." The sounds and rhythms of the poem echo the sounds of the scene and direct the reader toward hearing the scene as peaceful and steady.

By contrast, the second scene features a noisy machine and a "squealing" rat, and the sounds of the lines are harsher, with consonants standing side by side to create cacophony. In line 6, the words "field rat, startled, squealing bleeds" must be read one at a time; the ending consonants of one word and the beginning consonants of the next word do not run well together and thus cannot be read aloud smoothly. The consonants in this section are more explosive. For example, the hard *c* of "continue cutting" is not found at all in the first section, and the insistent near-rhyme of "bleeds," "blade," and "blood" can only be intentional. Before turning to writing, Toomer had considered becoming a musical composer, and all of his poetry reveals a deep concern for the musicality of language. Critics have often commented on the lyrical cadences of his poems about natural beauty such as "Georgia Dusk" and "Evening Song" (also from *Cane*). "Reapers" is an example of his use of the same ear to echo the sounds of men and machines.

Themes and Meanings

For Toomer, one of life's essential truths was that industrialized society had ground humankind down, destroying people's natural goodness and sense of community. As industrialization increased, the world became more chaotic. In "Reapers" and in the longer *Cane* from which it is taken, Toomer explores the dichotomy between humans and machines and, by extension, between the human and the subhuman or nonhuman qualities of people. Humans can feel and care, they can make moral choices, but machines cannot. "Reapers" demonstrates this truth by setting two scenes side by side: a scene of men working in a field and a scene of a mowing machine. In the first scene, all the work is done by humans with hand tools. Notably, it takes more than one reaper to do the job; doing work by hand requires more workers and therefore builds or sustains a community. Toomer pointedly calls these men reapers rather than mowers or cutters. They are reaping, or cutting and gathering, with a purpose: to provide food.

The machine, on the other hand, is a mower cutting weeds. It is driven by two horses; the human driver, if there is one, is not seen and does not appear to be directing the action. Instead, the narrator presents only a mindless machine pulled by mindless animals with no sense of purpose and no human sensibilities. A machine cannot react to a squeal of pain or a stain of blood. It does not know what it destroys, and it would not care if it did know. Toomer believed that people who harm or oppress others do so because they have given up their human qualities and have become like machines.

The pessimistic tone of "Reapers" is typical of the section of *Cane* in which it appears. Just before "Reapers" is a short story, "Karintha," about a beautiful and innocent child of the South who is ultimately destroyed by the sexual mistreatment of the men around her. "Reapers" is followed by another poem, "November Cotton Flower," and a short story, "Becky," both about victimized and defeated women. Throughout *Cane*, images of machines and factories always hint of decay or destruction. For Toomer, modern life—and particularly modern Southern rural life—was doomed unless humankind would turn its back on mindless industrialization and reclaim its humanity.

Cynthia A. Bily

THE RELIC

Author: John Donne (1572-1631)
Type of poem: Lyric
First published: 1633, in *Poems, by J. D.: With Elegies on Author's Death*

The Poem

"The Relic" is a lyric poem consisting of three stanzas of eleven lines each. As with numerous other English Metaphysical lyrics, the stanza form and rhyme scheme are unusual and perhaps unique. The pattern of five rhymes in each stanza is *aabbcddceee*, while the meter of lines is complex and somewhat irregular but basically iambic and effectively supplements the poem's thematic development. The four weighty iambic pentameter lines that conclude each stanza reinforce a change of tone from flippant or cynical to serious.

John Donne relies heavily on a first-person speaker who comes across as both worldly and spiritual, each quality being carried to an extreme. At the beginning, the speaker projects himself into the future when, long after his death, his bones are disinterred to make room for another burial. The macabre image of a disturbed grave contrasts with another more pleasant image. The grave digger, Donne asserts, will discover a bracelet of bright hair about the bone of the speaker's forearm. The hair represents the mistress, the "she" of the poem, just as the bones represent the speaker. Once the remains have been discovered, the perspective shifts from the speaker to the grave digger. The sexton may leave the grave without further disturbance, thinking that the "couple" is a pair of lovers who used the device of the hair so that at Judgment Day their souls might meet at the grave and enjoy a visit. This conceit is understood only if the reader knows the medieval and Renaissance conception of Judgment Day in which believers thought that souls would go about seeking their scattered body parts at the time of the Apocalypse in order to reunite them and experience the resurrection with both body and soul intact.

The second stanza introduces another possibility more in keeping with the poem's title. Donne suggests that the sexton may do his work during a time when "misdevotion" rules, that is, when worship includes the adoration of relics. If that happens, he will take the bones and the hair to the bishop and the king, who will make them objects of adoration. The woman's hair will remind a later age of Mary Magdalene, and the speaker's bones will suggest "something else." After they have become relics, they will be credited with miracles performed during their lives, and people of the later period will want to know what miracles they performed. At the stanza's close, the speaker promises to explain them. The third stanza represents the speaker's view of the miracles they accomplished, expressed for the enlightenment of a later age. He asserts that they loved well and faithfully but that their love had nothing to do with differences of sex. Their constant love was instead entirely chaste, subdued, and so mysterious that they themselves did not understand it. At the conclusion, however, another abrupt shift in thought occurs, changing the poem into a compliment. The speaker asserts that he would surpass all language if he told "what a miracle she was."

Forms and Devices

The devices of "The Relic" are complex and intricate, with brilliant imagery and characterization. The macabre beginning and cynical tone suggest a poem that will conclude with wry pessimism or cynicism. Instead, the lyric offers a positive affirmation upholding the value of love. Personification is perhaps the most ingenious device that the poet employs. Objects such as the grave are personified, but Donne goes beyond his normally strained meanings by making the bones represent the speaker's character and the wreath of hair represent the mistress. While the first-person speaker sees his bones becoming his character in a later age, he also retains his own authorial persona, asserting that his address in "this paper" (the poem) will explain the miracles they have wrought to the audience. The speaker's alteration between a tone of hard worldliness and a spiritual, idealistic side creates a vivid, dramatic contrast. The grave digger also becomes an important personage in the poem, for he reacts to what he sees in different ways. Even a generalized audience is conjured up as the two lovers become objects of devotion, adored by "All women . . . and some men."

The work reveals the typical obscurantism of Metaphysical poetry, including allusions to esoteric ideas and outmoded concepts such as the more extreme Renaissance concepts of the Apocalypse and the practice of removing bones from graves after a time and placing them in a charnel house in order to make room for a new tenant. Yet some allusions remain obscure to modern scholars. The reference to the chaste mistress as Mary Magdalene has led scholars to conjecture that the mistress may be Magdalene Herbert, Donne's patron and the mother of the poet George Herbert. What Donne means by having the speaker refer to himself as a "something else thereby" cannot be clearly ascertained. Another crux occurs in lines 29-30 ("Our hands ne'er touched the seals/ Which nature, injured by late law, sets free"), a passage that has puzzled critics and editors for many years. The lines clearly proclaim that their love was chaste, but the precise meanings of the metaphor "seals" or the personification "nature, injured by late law, sets free" remain elusive. A possibility is that Donne had in mind the innocent sexuality of Eden before the Fall contrasted to a later time of law when human sexuality became laden with the concept of sin.

The lyric is, above all, a poem of sharp contrasts. In an early analysis, poet T. S. Eliot refers to the intellectual agility required of the reader, using the alliterative sixth line ("A bracelet of bright hair about the bone") to illustrate the point. The imagery exerts special demands and offers special rewards. The initial image, a bracelet, is pleasant, and the phrase "of bright hair" that follows, though unusual and unexpected, still represents something pleasant. The completion of the image lends further surprise, even astonishment, for the expected "about the arm" veers into the macabre "about the bone." The reader finds it necessary to adjust the normal and expected responses to conform with the juxtaposition of diverse images. The entire poem places exceptional demands upon the reader yet offers pleasant surprises. The stanzas themselves illustrate the need for shifts in perspective. As they begin, the worldly speaker offers cynical asides, sardonic references, and a tone of hard realism. In the course of each stanza, a transition to a contrasting idealism or a suggestion of idealism occurs by way of conclusion.

Themes and Meanings

Although its title suggests a religious poem, "The Relic" is in reality a celebration of platonic love and a poem of compliment. The poem's pervasive religious diction and imagery establish a framework for celebrating a platonic relationship between the poem's speaker and his mistress. However, the complexity of both religion and love as themes invites multilevel meanings and ambiguities, and the poem is fraught with these. Donne is at his most ingenious and obscure as he develops the tropes and witty hyperboles of the lyric.

In his numerous songs and sonnets, Donne offers extremely varied treatments of love as a theme, from the most cynical and blatantly sexual to the most idealized, platonic form. "The Relic" employs a highly charged religious context to celebrate an ideal, chaste love. In the poems that reflect a positive attitude toward love, whether sexual or ideal, Donne frequently depicts the love as unique, special to the speaker and his mistress, even arcane and elevating, and apt to be misunderstood by ordinary people. The love celebrated in "The Relic" is mystical; not even those who share it can understand it. This hieratic view of love is implied by the sexton, who is puzzled by the remains he discovers, and then by the speaker's urge to explain it to a later age. The thinly veiled implication is that people in the later age, like those in the present, will be incapable of understanding the lovers' virtue because they cannot approach it.

It is a tribute to Donne's imaginative genius that he derives a transcendently noble theme from an initial, macabre image. In this regard, "The Relic" represents a sharp contrast to its companion poem "The Funeral," which employs similar macabre imagery. In "The Funeral," Donne uses the device of a woman's hair and a recently deceased corpse as a kind of consolation for unrequited love. The speaker, who proclaims that he will be discovered dead with a wreath of her hair about his arm, protests that he intends to bury some of her because she would have none of him. In contrast, the speaker in "The Relic" celebrates a long-enduring, chaste love that is comforting but too mystical to be fully understood.

Stanley Archer

RENASCENCE

Author: Edna St. Vincent Millay (1892-1950)
Type of poem: Narrative
First published: 1912; collected in *Renascence and Other Poems*, 1917

The Poem

"Renascence" is a narrative poem of 214 metrical lines split into nine stanzas of varying length. Although it literally means "rebirth," the poem's Latinate title carries different connotations than does its English equivalent. The title "Rebirth" might have led readers to expect a poem with a strongly earthly or physical aspect. Edna St. Vincent Millay's title, in contrast, suggests that the poet is about to speak of more elevated matters, possibly spiritual or cerebral. The poem does start on a purely physical level, although it soon leaves that plane behind. The persona of the poem, or narrator, tells of a moment when she looks around and becomes sharply conscious of the landscape around her: mountains, trees, a bay, and islands. "These were the things that bounded me," she says of them. Seeing them as boundaries, however, sparks a mental crisis. The world suddenly feels disturbingly small. In her heightened and anxious state, even the sky seems near enough to touch. She reaches for it and finds herself swept into a visionary episode.

Initially, she enters a paradoxical state: She becomes all-seeing and all-feeling but does not lose her sense of individual being. She gains a godlike perspective that gives her such a wide view of human suffering that it threatens to overwhelm her merely human reactions: "For my omniscience I paid toll/ In infinite remorse of soul." She experiences the deaths of a thousand people by fire and sympathetically finds herself perishing with each of them even as she simultaneously stands apart as an individual, mourning for all. She similarly experiences the death of another group of unfortunates caught in an accident at sea: "A thousand screams the heavens smote;/ And every scream tore through my throat." The weight of her universal compassion soon grows so great that it presses her into the earth: "Into the earth I sank till I/ Full six feet under ground did lie." In this state of spiritual extinction, she feels the weight leave her. She welcomes the soothing earth: "Deep in the earth I rested now;/ Cool is its hand upon the brow/ And soft its breast beneath the head/ Of one who is so gladly dead." Above her, she then hears the sound of rain, which reminds her of life and its simple joys. She regrets missing not only the rain but also the sun that follows rain: "O God, I cried, give me new birth,/ And put me back upon the earth!" At this outburst, a torrential rain washes her from the grave and restores her: "I know not how such things can be!—/ I breathed my soul back into me." She finds herself back within the world of physical limitations, a return filled with joy: "Ah! Up then from the ground sprang I/ And hailed the earth with such a cry/ As is not heard save from a man/ Who has been dead, and lives again." She also possesses insight she had not been given before:

> O God, I cried, no dark disguise
> Can e'er hereafter hide from me
> Thy radiant identity
>
> . . . .
>
> I know the path that tells Thy way
> Through the cool eve of every day;
> God, I can push the grass apart
> And lay my finger on Thy heart!

The poem concludes with a twelve-line coda in which the narrator affirms her new understanding, which relates the limitations of the outer world to inner dimensions. The world, she says, is as wide as the heart and as tall as the soul. She then issues a caution against weakness in either: "But East and West will pinch the heart/ That cannot keep them pushed apart;/ And he whose soul is flat—the sky/ Will cave in on him by and by."

Forms and Devices

To make this transcendent episode vivid, Millay uses a vocabulary consisting of common, concrete words. She expresses the onset of the vision in terms of touch and hearing: "Infinity// Held up before my eyes a glass/ Through which my shrinking sight did pass" and "Whispered to me a word whose sound/ Deafened the air for worlds around." When her poetic persona then experiences omniscience, Millay describes the visionary's subsequent remorse as a physical burden: "And so beneath the Weight lay I/ And suffered death, but could not die." The weight pushes the visionary into the earth, which Millay describes in starkly contrasting but earthy terms: first as the dusty confines of a grave and then as the calming hands and bosom of a comforting mother. Paradoxes, in fact, help convey the visionary's successive states of disorientation. Her omniscience battles with her individuality, her subsequent "death" becomes a seedbed for a renewed thirst for life, and her final, revivifying vision of the sun leads to her release from the grave by a torrent of rain. Millay's sense of tone and phrasing gives such opposing images and motifs colorful life. Her most musical lines call to mind the lyricism of English poet John Keats ("To catch the freshened, fragrant breeze/ From drenched and dripping apple-trees"). In contrast, her sometimes morbid concerns, bold imagination, and deceptive simplicity suggest the influence of American author Edgar Allan Poe. Her lines contain many elements to be found in the work of her contemporaries, including preoccupations with exoticism and deep sentiment. Yet Millay combines unabashed lyricism with unflinching statements to give to "Renascence" distinct freshness and vivid life.

Millay composed "Renascence" in rhymed couplets of iambic tetrameter: Each line contains four feet, or pairs of syllables, in which the accent generally falls on the second syllable. Although the majority of lines observe this regular pattern, the poet demonstrates flexibility from the outset. Her opening line begins with a trochee: "All I could see from where I stood." The typical reader will place stress on the first syllable of the first foot. In the last three feet of this four-foot line, the stress falls regularly upon each second syllable. She demonstrates another kind of metrical flexibility in the fourth couplet of the first stanza, where she shortens the lines by a syllable: "Straight around till I was come/ Back to where I'd started from." By this removal of the initial foot, a metrical technique known as "acephalexis," Millay achieves a quickening of pace that speeds the reader onto the fifth couplet. Insofar as the next sixteen syllables of the stanza reiterate the first words of the poem, the shortening of that preceding couplet also helps give the repetition a certain weight of inevitability.

Themes and Meanings

"Renascence" is a poem about limits. In the course of the poem, the visionary persona, who may or may not have been Millay herself, moves from experiencing limits as stifling and constricting to experiencing them as liberating and as the measure of one's spiritual being. Despite the extraordinary nature of her experiences, the visionary narrator goes through tribulations common to many: People often grow dissatisfied with their circumstances, wish for more, then become distressed if they receive what they wanted. The visionary in "Renascence" feels constricted by the small scope of her immediate world. She is then given an unlimited viewpoint that distresses her until she begs for relief. She finds this relief in death and burial, a situation that soon makes her yearn for life again. Only then does she realize the value of what she started with: the physical world and its natural limits. Her "renascence," or rebirth, is mental, not physical. She returns to a world identical to the one she initially abandoned but sees it through new eyes.

"Renascence," one of Millay's youthful works, asks the perennial questions of youth: What is the meaning of existence? What does it mean to be an individual? Is there anything special about being "me" as opposed to being anyone else? Millay approaches these questions by imagining an ideal soul who looks around and sees only "normal" reality, which seems confining and unsatisfactory. She then imagines that soul dwarfed through contact with the greatness of a universal soul. In learning insignificance, the individual soul gains the perspective necessary to appreciate significance. The soul then values the world as it is given, even if it is no more than a constricted spot surrounded by mountains, woods, a bay, and islands.

The world is worth living in, Millay seems to say to her readers. However, it is worth living in most for those who understand what the visionary in the poem has come to see: that the limitations that appear to be outside are actually inside. "The heart can push the sea and land/ Farther away on either hand," she says, "The soul can split the sky in two,/ And let the face of God shine through." Moving beyond limitations, especially those imposed from within, constitutes genuine rebirth.

Mark Rich

REPRESSION OF WAR EXPERIENCE

Author: Siegfried Sassoon (1886-1967)
Type of poem: Dramatic monologue
First published: 1918, in *Counter-Attack and Other Poems*

The Poem

"Repression of War Experience" is an unrhymed poem in three stanzas. Along with the poem's publication date, the title suggests an unwillingness or inability to recall or accept experiences undergone during World War I. In using the clinical word "repression," Siegfried Sassoon might well be making direct reference to the book *Die Traumdeutung* (1900; *The Interpretation of Dreams*, 1913), in which psychoanalyst Sigmund Freud pointed out that although a person may not fully register traumatic experiences at the time they occur, repressed memories always return to haunt the sufferer. Because Sassoon speaks through the persona of an English soldier rather than in his own voice, "Repression of War Experience" is not a lyric but a dramatic work. As is true of all dramatic monologues, the voice of the persona dominates the poem.

In the first stanza, the soldier is at home in England on a summer night. He lights some candles and watches as moths flutter around the flames, wondering why they seek that which will kill them. Almost immediately, however, he finds that the moths trigger memories of his own wartime terrors, thoughts that he has "gagged all day." In the second stanza, the longest of the three, the mood changes as the soldier gives himself instructions on how to behave: He resolves to maintain control by lighting his pipe and seeks solace in nature by wishing for a rainstorm "to sluice the dark" with "bucketsful of water." Needing a more immediate solution, however, he gazes at the books lining the room but becomes unnerved by the sight of a huge moth bumping against the ceiling, which leads him to think about the garden outside the house; he imagines ghosts in the trees, not of his comrades lost in battle but of an older generation, "old men with ugly souls" who stayed at home to die slow, natural deaths. In a final effort to pull himself together, the young man reassures himself that he is far away from the war. In this last stanza, however, the soldier imagines that he hears the ominous sound of muffled guns on the front lines in France. They are sounds he cannot silence.

Forms and Devices

Since Sassoon describes warfare from the point of view of one who has actually experienced combat, those who have fought in any war or who know somebody who did can easily identify with this poem. Like the war poetry of Edward Thomas, Ivor Gurney, and Wilfred Owen, all of whom fought in World War I, Sassoon's poetry has been widely read. As Patrick Quinn points out in *The Great War and The Missing Muse* (1994), Sassoon, together with these other poets, helped swing the opinion of the literary establishment in England against the war. It is easy to see why Sassoon caught the attention of the English public. Utilizing a technique of documentary realism, the poet uses the slangy language of the barracks: "jabber," "O Christ," and "bloody war." Initially, too, the poem focuses on familiar images that could have been found in any house in England at the time the poem was written: candles, moths, a pipe, roses, and books. However, the poem is more than a factual journalistic record. Sassoon also uses dramatic irony, a device essential to any dramatic monologue: Caught at a critical moment, the soldier unintentionally reveals more to the reader than he realizes.

Unlike most dramatic monologues, which are addressed to an audience, the soldier in this poem is talking to himself. At times, the soldier addresses himself as "you"; at other times, he speaks in the first person. In Freudian terms, the soldier's use of "you" seems to suggest that his superego, his commonsense self, is speaking, whereas the use of "I" implies thoughts emerging from deep inside, the Freudian id, site of the repressed memories of war. Conflict exists between these two parts of the soldier's psyche. Sassoon makes this conflict clear through the device of juxtaposition. In the first line of the poem, for example, he juxtaposes the image of the candles the soldier lights with the moths flying into "liquid flame." Then, to show that the soldier associates these moths with his fallen comrades, Sassoon juxtaposes an image of the war itself. In this way, the poet implies a comparison between the suicidal moths and the soldier's mates who "blunder in" and become engulfed in gunfire at the battlefront in France. A final juxtaposition ends the stanza: The soldier's superego admonishes, "It's bad to think of war," but his id reasserts itself in the young man's fear of losing control of "ugly thoughts" and being driven out "to jabber among the trees."

Sassoon continues this pattern of juxtaposition in the second stanza. Just after the soldier lights his pipe and remarks, "Look, what a steady hand," he must "count fifteen" to regain control. Next, Sassoon juxtaposes the soldier's thoughts of the delights of a possible rainstorm with the possible delights offered by the books lining his shelves, a connection that the soldier himself cannot accept. Instead, he bites his nails and lets his pipe go out, unable or unwilling to read "the wisdom of the world/ . . . waiting on those shelves." Then, as if to show that the soldier's id is winning its struggle against the superego, Sassoon juxtaposes the image of the suicidal moth bumping and fluttering against the ceiling with a second image generated by the id rather than a cautionary admonition from his superego as was the pattern in the first stanza, a nightmare vision of ghosts that the soldier thinks he sees lurking in the trees outside. However, it is the final series of implied comparisons of this stanza that dramatizes the extent of the young man's angst: He first identifies these ghosts as "horrible shapes in shrouds" and then, confusing this nightmare with reality, asserts that the shrouds cannot be those that envelop the bodies of his fallen comrades because his comrades are "in France."

In the final stanza, the soldier's hold on reality snaps completely. Although his superego briefly reasserts itself to reassure the young man that he is "summering safe at home," the remembered sounds of muffled gunfire trigger his primal trauma: the fear of death on the battlefield. Feeling this fear just as intensely as if he were still at the front, he says, "I'm going stark, staring mad because of the guns." By concluding on a characteristic note of savage irony, Sassoon shows that the young soldier, far from achieving a therapeutic, Freudian breakthrough, is succumbing to his posttraumatic stress. The sound of the "whispering guns" cannot be quieted.

Themes and Meanings

"Repression" is a poem about the power of repressed memory. It is also a highly serious, accusatory work. As Erich Maria Remarque wrote in *Im Westen nichts Neues* (1929; *All Quiet on the Western Front*, 1929), it focuses on a soldier who, while he may have escaped physical harm, was "destroyed by the War." By tracing this young man's failure to come to terms with his war experience, Sassoon may be suggesting that the trauma of World War I, mostly fought from muddy, vermin-filled trenches, is so great that it renders any such accommodation impossible.

This poem differs from other war poems written during this period: Thomas describes the way the war violated the natural order of things, Gurney recaptures particular scenes with painful quietness, and Owen mourns the tragedy of young men killed in battle, while "Repression of War Experience" dramatizes in a particularly direct fashion the manner in which the experience of war can inflict permanent psychic damage so painful that is must be repressed. However, the poem also suggests that the young soldier was not the only one to repress the war, implying that others, perhaps military censors, the press, or those who profited from the war—the "old men with ugly souls"—also engaged in repression, preventing the British public from becoming aware of the futility of continuous, massive bombardments by the guns that "never cease." Sassoon's sudden twisting of the reader's expectation at the end of the poem—the soldier's descent into madness, which makes the reader feel uncomfortable or perhaps even responsible for the soldier's breakdown—may suggest that Sassoon saw as his poetic mission the necessity to pierce the dehumanization and complacent patriotism of many people in England during this period. In the end, it is this poem's direct indictment of the brutal consequences of repression for both the soldiers who fought and those who sent them out to "blunder in/ And scorch their wings" that makes it so powerful.

Susan Tetlow Harrington

RETURN

Author: Czesław Miłosz (1911-   )
Type of poem: Lyric
First published: 1991, as "Powrót," in *Dalsze okolice*; English translation collected in *Provinces*, 1991

The Poem

"Return," with thematic divisions consisting of single sentences or short paragraphs, is a meditative poem whose cadence conforms more to the rhythms of prose than to those of verse. The poem is written in the first person and is autobiographical. Although the poet includes the reader in his musings, there is no doubt that the focus is on the poet's own life experiences. In fact, "Return" can be considered an emotional history of Czesław Miłosz's life in capsule form.

The poet has returned home to the places of his youth. They, like him, are ostensibly the same and yet not the same. The passage of time has changed all the important details. The man and his homeland are now "incomprehensibly the same, incomprehensibly different." Standing on the shore of a lake, the poet remembers the sufferings and despair of his younger self standing on this same shore, but the experience of many years has made him realize that such pain was not his alone but the inevitable result of living in a cruel world. However, he honors the boy and all young people who have not grown "sly," who refuse to acquiesce, and who refuse to "participate for ever."

The middle section of the poem changes in tone as the poet deals briefly with the gifts of the world, a woman's body, and the beauty of a lake, but this mood is fleeting as the poet almost immediately asks if it has all been worthwhile. Many of Miłosz's poems written outside his native Lithuania deal with the experiences and people of his past. At times these past voices threaten to drown out his own living voice, but in "Return," where one might expect the poet to be surrounded by images of the past calling to him, there is, paradoxically, silence. The ghosts of the past have left him; he is the only one standing on the shore.

The last section of the poem carries with it the implicit subtext almost always present in Miłosz's later work. To fully understand a poem, the reader must be familiar with the vicissitudes of the poet's life, such as his boyhood in Lithuania, his life under the Nazi and Stalinist regimes, and his decision to escape to the West in search of artistic freedom. For an appreciation of "Return," this background knowledge is especially important because the conclusion of the poem not only contains Miłosz's philosophical commentary on his life (and on life in general) but also constitutes a type of poetic manifesto or "life" manifesto. Miłosz's life may have been one of "chaos and transience," but poetry is "the changeless garden on the other side of time."

Forms and Devices

At first glance, "Return" seems devoid of any poetic devices or images, but the apparent simplicity of the proselike lines is deceptive. What first attracts the attention is the use of the "I" in the first lines, but as the poet begins to feel the chasm between his younger and older selves, the pronoun shifts to "you" for the boy of his youth and then to "he" and "we" as all are enveloped in the evils of the world. The "I" returns as the poet individually feels the beauty of the world, but the "I" of the older man and the "you" of the boy merge in their appreciation of the gifts of life: "Only for me" and "Only for you." While separate in suffering, they unite in joy. In the last section, only the "I" of the old man remains as he reflects on what has happened to him since he left this place so many years before.

"Return" is very representative of Miłosz's later work in its almost complete rejection of any poetic devices such as metaphor or symbol. Any attempt at versification or rhyming techniques is also absent. The two- and three-line divisions of the poem are meant to correspond to the natural flow of thought. However, also dominant in Miłosz's poetry is nature imagery, and again "Return" is no exception. What is different because of the theme of the poem (Miłosz's return home) is that all the imagery exists in the present. In other poems, similar sounds, smells, and shapes call forth correspondences to the past while the poet strives in vain, at times, to stop this sensorial stream of past consciousness. In "Return," the opposite occurs as the poet vainly tries to use the past to orientate himself in the present, but he cannot find the "traces of the lanes."

It is characteristic of Miłosz's poetry that even in the midst of the contemplation of the most beautiful landscape there is always the bitter realization of the evil inherent in the world that beauty covers. Even in "Return," in the contemplation of a beloved, often longed-for sight, the image of the cruel demiurge who created a "pitiless" world of "chaos and transience" appears. The poet sets apart the concept of this horror by twice repeating the question "How can it be?"; it is the only repetition of the poem. For Miłosz, this evil deity is the poetic icon for the dark side, "the imperfect Nature" of his philosophical dualism; the "perfect Nature" that his poetry has tried to find is symbolized by the "changeless garden on the other side of time."

Themes and Meanings

"Return" is a poem about a poet and the meaning of his life and work. Therefore, many of the important themes of Miłosz's poetry are at least touched upon in the poem. Miłosz is a Metaphysical poet. The greater part of his work in the West has been autobiographical, in which the quintessential challenge has been the question of identity. Miłosz has used his own personal experiences as stepping stones in his examination of the value of human existence. In "Return," this exploration of meaning is linked to another recurrent theme: the analysis of one's life as it approaches its conclusion. Miłosz does not aggrandize the episodes of his life or emphasize hardships or problems. If anything, he deprecates his own history: "Somehow I waded through; I am grateful that I was not submitted to tests beyond my strength." His, he ironically states, has been "a blindly accomplished destiny."

Many critics have spoken of the conflict inherent in Miłosz's worldview; the poet himself calls this metaphysical dilemma his "ecstatic pessimism." This seeming contradiction of terms is colored by the Manichaeanism inherent in Miłosz's philosophy. The world can be beautiful; the poet is fascinated by this beauty, but he knows that it is always contaminated by evil. His pessimistic evaluation in "Return" of the importance of his own life is linked to this same duality. As a poet he re-creates beautiful images, but, given the autobiographical nature of his work, a certain disappointment or dissatisfaction, even bitterness, is always present. For example, he condemns those who are trained in "slyness" but then characterizes himself sarcastically as having "grown slyly just" and praises those who have chosen suicide rather than continue participating. The mood of Miłosz's poetry swings constantly from joy to despair, from skepticism to faith, in his search for answers. The world is "horrible," "comic," and "senseless," but through his poetry, which has been both the means and goal of this search, he has validated his belief in its opposite.

Miłosz's poetry has been distinguished by the persistence of memory, by the multitude of voices, and by the different levels of time that meet and diverge in the poet's consciousness. The reader should expect the same poetic layering in "Return," but it is not there, a fact that surprises the poet himself. Always haunted by the past, he has expected it to reach out and grab him on his return; he has even chosen a favorite spot of his youth for this blending of lives. However, in this literal return to the past, he seems to have mysteriously lost the ability to emotionally and figuratively recapture it. Away from his homeland, he has always walked with those he left behind, but here there are no "troubled spirits flying by." The ghosts have brought him here, but now it is as if they have left him alone to answer his questions by himself. The insistent "I" of the poem defines his solitude and the stark loneliness of existence.

In an age that eschews personal responsibility, Miłosz has stood out as an ethical as well as a Metaphysical poet. His own life was dramatically changed by historical forces, and thus he constantly examines the role of the individual in society. To what extent can the individual accept credit for his actions? To what extent must he accept blame? In "Return," a sense of personal guilt is apparent as the poet concedes that his choices have led him away from the real world. Did he have a choice?

Charlene E. Suscavage

RETURNING

Author: Linda Pastan (1932-   )
Type of poem: Lyric
First published: 1981, in *Waiting for My Life*

The Poem

"Returning" is a free-verse poem of twenty-one lines divided into three seven-line stanzas. The title raises some key questions about the poem: Where is the main character of the poem (a woman identified only as "she")? Where is she returning from? Where is she going? On one level the answers are easy. Linda Pastan employs an extended analogy, based on a parachutist returning from the sky to "the coarser atmosphere of earth," to present this returning. It is more difficult to decide to what other process the parachutist's descent provides an analogy. The first stanza sets up this analogy and brings the parachutist from the clouds down to treetop level. The second stanza awakens the subject's eyes and nose to the sensations of this coarser life of earth. She smells the pines, and her husband starts to "swim" into view. In the final stanza, the parachutist lands in her garden and pushes the chute aside, signaling the end of the flight. In the last three lines, the poet likens the discarding of the parachute to the way "she pushed the white sheet/ from her breasts/ just yesterday."

The first line ("She re-enters her life") provides a clue to the nature of the analogy. The subject has been away from her normal life, perhaps in an altered psychological or physical state. In fact, the place she has been seems to suggest a Platonic ideal: Apparently, it has a very fine atmosphere as contrasted with "the coarser atmosphere of earth." In this other reality, she experienced "the sensual shapes of clouds" whereas in her "life" she finds only "cloud-shaped trees." Furthermore, the shapes of the trees are deceptively inviting, for the soft leaves are "transitory" and the branches are "sharp." Indeed, the place where the poet has been is clearly more pleasant than her normal world. Stanza 2 presents a dawning earth consciousness as the smell of pines pierce "the surface of memory" and a vision of the speaker's husband "starts to swim/ back into sight." Stanza 3 identifies both the duration and quality of the poet's flight: "brief but brilliant." All of this suggests that the speaker is "returning" from a sexual climax.

Forms and Devices

The understated effectiveness of Pastan's poem is quite remarkable. She conveys the sexual experience so discretely that it could be completely missed. Except for the last three lines, it appears only as distantly reflected in the "sensual shapes of clouds" and the "silky" texture of the parachute. The lofty imagery used to describe the ecstatic state, in other words, is quite separate from any hint of the physical mechanisms that play a large part in producing that state. The major device of the poem is an extended analogy between the descent of a parachutist and the experience of a woman after sexual climax. In that sense, this poem is like a miniature allegory with one kind of experience described through the language of another kind of experience. Understanding one thing in terms of another is a traditional technique of poetry, whether in simile, metaphor, analogy, or allegory. The use of an extended and consistent simile or metaphor through the whole poem is less common.

Pastan's choice of imagery is quite interesting. Through most of the poem, the parachutist is pictured against a natural backdrop: clouds, trees, branches, leaves, pine scent, and a dark lake. Against this backdrop, the husband "starts to swim/ back into sight" at the end of stanza 2. In stanza 3, the garden provides an interesting transitional image of nature under human control. It is also described as "their" garden, the woman's and her husband's, and seems to indirectly allude to the mutuality of the sexual act. This leads to the final, completely human image of the white sheet juxtaposed with human breasts. The image of breasts, often associated with fertility and nurture, works well with the garden and the possibility of procreative sex.

Themes and Meanings

"Returning" is a poem about the aftermath of an ecstatic moment, presumably a sexual climax. The experience is so intense and pleasurable that it must be considered otherworldly rather than a part of the poet's ordinary life. It also appears, at least at the climactic moment, to be a solitary experience. It is only as the woman floats down to the harsher realities of the earth that her husband starts to come into view. However, this is also a poem about a meaningful relationship: The woman lands in the garden that she and her husband cultivate, plant, tend, and harvest together. It is a product of partnership with a "brief but brilliant" interlude of solo flight. The poem is not particularly erotic, but it is highly attentive to the senses of the subject as she passes between states of being. The association of sex with flight has been used in poetry before, but Pastan's particular use of a falling parachutist to illustrate the subject's return to her ordinary life is striking. Falling through the air in a parachute must necessarily be an exhilarating but brief experience. The poem is also unusual in being situated around the transitional moments rather than being firmly rooted in one state or the other.

Although the ecstatic experiences are achieved by different means, two other well-known poems provide a comparison to Pastan's passage between the worlds of the ecstatic and the ordinary. In John Keats's "Ode to a Nightingale," the poet, on the "viewless wings of Poesy," flies away to the land of the sweetly sad singing of the nightingale, a fairyland where the Queen-Moon sits on a throne surrounded by "all her starry Fays." He indulges in the "soft incense" of seasonal plants and fruits, but all too quickly he is recalled to his ordinary reality, not sure if his experience was a vision or a "waking dream." Likewise, in Robert Frost's "Birches," the poet escapes the "pathless wood" of his normal life for a brief time by contemplating and then climbing a birch tree. After an ice storm, the birches, sun shining through their "crystal shells" of ice, provide an extraordinary vision of beauty, raising the poet out of his ordinary self. The birches also provide an escape from this life by serving as a ladder "*Toward* heaven." For Keats and Frost, like Pastan, the ecstatic experience is brief but brilliant. They live in the ordinary reality of this life, where branches are "sharp" (Pastan), "one eye is weeping" (Frost), and "men sit and hear each other groan" (Keats). Their brief escapes give them a chance to gain perspective on this life and give them a toehold in another world even as they return to this world.

Scott Moncrieff

RING OUT YOUR BELLS

Author: Sir Philip Sidney (1554-1586)
Type of poem: Lyric
First published: 1598, in *Certaine Sonnets*, which was included in *The Countess of Pembroke's Arcadia*

The Poem

"Ring out your bells" is part of a miscellaneous collection of thirty-two sonnets and songs. This song is divided into four stanzas, each composed of six lines of verse and four lines of choral refrain. The speaker's opening request, addressed to his neighborly audience, suggests the ancient custom of tolling church bells to announce a local death. It also establishes the common funereal experience and the solemn tone for this poetic monologue about the death of love. The speaker distances himself from his own abstract emotion, the idea of love, by personifying it (giving love human attributes and treating it as if it were a real person). In this way, the concept of love, separated from himself, becomes a fictive character whose death is cause for his initial request. When love is viewed as a separate individual, the speaker can complain bitterly about his frustration and misery, the causes for love's infection, sickness and death, and his haughty mistress's abusive and capricious cruelty. Thus, there are three characters in this dramatic song: the speaker, his absent mistress, and love.

The idea of death, a universal event, introduces the situation and allows the speaker to appeal to a reader's sympathetic responses. When he urges his listeners to action—to ring the church bells, openly express grief, wail sorrowful songs, and read thirty requiem masses—the speaker clothes another commonplace occurrence, a romantic dispute and separation, with the mental anguish normally associated with death and funerals. Other experiences familiar to some readers are the paradoxical conflicts and frustrations in some love relationships. In the first three stanzas, the speaker elaborates on the misery, scorn, and rejection love endures when honor and loyalty are considered to be worthless virtues. He portrays love dying on a bed built from his mistress's foolish and overweening pride; wrapped in a burial shroud of disgrace; valued, even in her last testament, with false worth and censure; and finally entombed in the lady's cold, stony heart. Ironically, the inscription on love's tombstone will reveal that the lady's glancing eyes once shot arrows of love at the speaker, creating instant love between them. This magical, first-sight love, an old Elizabethan belief, is similar to what William Shakespeare developed with his star-crossed lovers Romeo and Juliet.

The first three choral refrains, identical in their four lines, echo the lover's plaints about his proud mistress's scornful, frenzied behavior. Also, the fourth line repetitively recalls a prayer drawn from church rituals. The fourth stanza abruptly and radically shifts perspective. The speaker announces his error with a phrase similar to a biblical comment, "Love is not dead, but sleepeth" (Matthew 9:24). Actually, love and his mistress are just deliberating on a reward worthy enough for him. With his reversed attitude, the speaker praises his mistress. His reawakened love helps him turn his scathing accusations into self-scorn and mockery for his earlier comments. Despite the speaker's jubilation, the song's final line paradoxically repeats the religious prayer that concludes the first three refrains, "Good lord, deliver us."

Forms and Devices

Sir Philip Sidney was a poetic experimenter, synthesizer, and innovator in poetic theory and forms. He sought new ways to use and revitalize old literary traditions and conventions such as those popularized in Petrarchan and Platonic love poetry. Petrarchan love sonnets featured aristocratic and courtly lovers who complimented and manipulated an idealized mistress with extravagantly flattering metaphors, images that implied parallels between two ostensibly different things. For instance, some facial features of an iconic mistress might be suggestively likened to stars, roses, pearls, or cherries. Platonic love originally described an aristocratic code of chivalrous devotion to a married lady or to one of superior social rank. Through time, the chaste nature of this old bond was sometimes abused. In courtships in which lovers were not given favors or awards, the discontented petitioner agonized, complained, and pled repeatedly to the untouchable lady who refused him. In "Ring out your bells," the speaker's catalog of grievances typifies him as a Platonic lover whose courtship has been soundly rebuffed. In rebellion, his thoughts turn dark when his virtues or lofty aims are not rewarded in some way.

Simple patterns of imagery support the synthesis of Petrarchan and Platonic traditions. The speaker implies an analogy between love's tomb and the mistress's stony heart and suggestively equates love's eyes with the love darts in the epitaph. Even the mistress's unpredictable behavior resembles the manners of the aristocratic coquettes depicted in Petrarchan sonnets. However, one extended metaphor dominates most of the content. Throughout the song, the implied analogies between the banality of a broken romance and the heartbreak of death are determined and reinforced by the funereal and religious wrappings associated with the death metaphor.

Sidney's interest in prosody, the metrical structure of verse, relates to his stylistic strategies to match rhythms and words. Just such a metrical innovation introduces the fourth stanza. Sidney dramatically stops the rhythmical pattern of iambs when his phrasing and meter dictate a pause underscoring his speaker's changed perspective. The startling statement, "Alas, I lie," in iambic meter (one unaccented syllable followed by one accented syllable), is followed by a trochee (one accented syllable followed by one unaccented syllable), "rage hath this error bred." The accentual stress on "rage" also emphasizes and intensifies the trochaic pattern in the ensuing line: "Love is not dead." Repetition of this same trochee, along with "but sleepeth" in the next line, allows Sidney to match sound to the sense of the verse. Although he does not mention this song, William A. Ringler, in the introduction to *The Poems of Sir Philip Sidney* (1962), writes that several of Sidney's sonnets "bring a new rhythm into Elizabethan verse . . . the first regularly sustained accentual trochaics in English" until the 1590's.

Themes and Meanings

"Ring out your bells" is a poem about the subject of love. However, it is the hidden driving force of desire behind the various forms of love that Sidney explores through the filter of his own experiences and feelings. Sidney's personal world included the political arena in Queen Elizabeth's court. There, he and others sought the monarch's royal favor, which could give them government employment, financial rewards, or honors testifying to their worldly worth and virtue. Additionally, these courtiers courted noble patrons who could help arrange an aristocratic marriage for them or help support their political, military, or literary endeavors. Sidney had direct experience with frustrated desires in his attempts to solicit more than temporary governmental or military appointments from Queen Elizabeth.

The flattering compliments of Petrarchan love sonnets aimed at courting a lady's favors arise from the same ambitious urges of desire as the hyperboles (conscious exaggerations) used to court a queen or a noble. There is little difference between practices. Furthermore, when the Platonic lover suffers and rages about his mistress's scorn and rejection of his worth and faithfulness, his misery underlines the desire behind his egoistic self-love. Feelings of worth, honor, and personal identity grow from the self-validation gained from recognition or reward for deeds accomplished. Human courtiers such as Sidney felt equally discouraged and frustrated when their valiant efforts were rejected.

Sidney's literary world evidences another of his own literary desires, an altruistic wish found in his great love for poetry. At the heart of Sidney's book *The Defence of Poesy* (1595) is his defense and definition of what poetry is, what it can or should do, and how to write it to accomplish this lofty goal. Moreover, when he viewed the poetry of his own time, Sidney was not happy with the poetic abuses he saw. As Ringler observes in his introduction to *The Poems of Sir Philip Sidney*, Sidney "set out to be a Daedalus to his countrymen, to teach them rules of right writing, and to provide them with models to follow." This idealistic aim underwrites his effort to achieve an example of good poetry with a deeper level of meaning. In "Ring out your bells," Sidney works within the traditions and conventions of love poetry. However, he rejuvenates them by showing what a few changes can do to hackneyed concepts and images. His double vision, the extended metaphoric comparison of love's trivialities with the solemnity of death, transforms the Petrarchan/Platonic single-vision lyric into a brief model of a mock-heroic romance. This second point of view indirectly points out the comical exaggerations, trivialities, stupidities, and abuses. Ironically, the final prayer might well express the poet's own desire: "Good lord, deliver us" from poets who abuse poetry.

Betsy P. Harfst

ROMANS ANGRY ABOUT THE INNER WORLD

Author: Robert Bly (1926-   )
Type of poem: Narrative
First published: 1967, in *The Light Around the Body*; revised in *Selected Poems*, 1986

The Poem

"Romans Angry About the Inner World" begins with a question, and the rest of the poem is an attempt to answer this question: "What shall the world do with its children?" It was written during the Vietnam War as one of the blatant antiwar poems Bly collected in *The Light Around the Body*, but the contemporary conflict is placed in the historical context of ancient Rome, which—once the parallels are understood and the distant past conflated with the present—makes the present terror even more horrific.

The poem is built around a series of parallels between "executives" and "executioners." At first these terms seem to suggest a contrast, but the reader quickly realizes that Bly intends to associate them with each other: The "executioners" of ancient Rome have become the "executives" of contemporary society. The present-day executives, like their ancient Roman counterparts, are unaware of the "leaping[s] of the body" or of any of the ways that one can "float/ Joyfully" toward the "dark" positive places in the psyche.

The central section of the poem describes the execution of Drusia by the Romans. The Romans believed that Drusia had "seen our mother/ In the other world"—that is, that she was a member of the mystical cult of the Magna Mater, or Great Mother. This cult appeared in very ancient times, and its members were persecuted by the Romans. Members encouraged the development of the speculative side of consciousness and celebrated the archetype of the feminine. Drusia was therefore regarded as dangerous, and she was tortured and then killed by the Romans.

The other world that Drusia has seen is the "inner world" of the poem's title; the contrast between the "inner" and "outer" worlds is important in terms of Bly's political and psychological theme in this poem. The significance of such contrasts is made clear in the epigraph to the book, which is taken from the writings of Jacob Boehme, the seventeenth century German mystic who based much of his philosophy on the notion of the "two worlds." Part of the epigraph reads: "For according to the outward man, we are in this world, and according to the inner man, we are in the inward world." Bly, following Boehme, develops his dichotomy in terms of the contrasts between the inner and outer worlds and between the masculine and the feminine sides of the psyche. The contrast is between the Romans, who "had put their trust/ In the outer world" and women such as Drusia, who have put their trust in the inner world. The Romans want Drusia to "assure them" that they have put their trust in the right place, and when she refuses to do so they kill her.

After they have tortured and killed Drusia, the Romans dump her body onto the ground. Immediately, and almost miraculously, a light snow begins to fall. It covers

Drusia's "mangled body," and the murderous executives/executioners are "astonished" and withdraw. The poem ends with two vivid and somewhat enigmatic images that attempt to define the significance of the contrast between the inner and outer worlds.

Forms and Devices

"Romans Angry About the Inner World" consists of a single stanza of thirty lines written in free verse. In lieu of more conventional poetic devices such as rhyme and meter, Bly relies on rhythm, juxtaposition, imagery, the dichotomy of the "two languages" (the epigraph from Boehme continues, "Since then we are generated out of both worlds, we speak in two languages, and we must be understood also by two languages"), and especially on the kind of "deep images" for which Bly is famous. These devices control the movement of the narrative and establish a meditative mood complementary to the theme.

In many essays and in various interviews Bly has described and defined what he means by "deep images." They are images that stress feelings and that "trust" emotional states of mind without excluding the intellect. They often "leap" from one thing to another in the same way that the mind "thinks in flashes"; they merge inward "reality" with outward reality; they are filled with spiritual energy and are psychologically accurate even though, when first described, they often seem to be irrational. Bly discusses these deep images in terms of the contrast between "inwardness" and "outwardness" in his essay "Recognizing the Image as a Form of Intelligence" (1981), in which he argues that a deep image can join Boehme's two worlds together. Therefore, "when a poet creates a true image, he is gaining knowledge; he is bringing up into consciousness a connection that has been forgotten."

"Romans Angry About the Inner World" ends with two deep images, both of which are attempts to describe the way in which the inner world relates to the outer world. In the first of these images, Bly compares the inner world to "a thorn/ In the ear of a tiny beast!" that the thick fingers of the executives are unable to pull out. That is, the inner world is something inside themselves that the executives wish to renounce but cannot. In the final image the inner world is called a "jagged stone/ Flying toward us out of the darkness." Putting aside safe, distanced references to the dastardly practices of the ancient Romans or to the anonymous evil-minded executives of the twentieth century, Bly implicates himself and his readers: The inner world, like a premonition of some inevitable cataclysmic event or impending apocalypse, is coming toward *us*.

Themes and Meanings

In his essay "Leaping up into Political Poetry" (1967) Bly writes, "America . . . may become something magnificent and shining, or she may turn, as Rome did, into . . . the enemy of every nation in the world [that] wants to live its own life." "That decision," he says, "has not yet been made." He adds that "a true political poem is a quarrel with ourselves"; it is "a sudden drive by the poet inward" that attempts to "deepen awareness."

Just as the whole of "Romans Angry About the Inner World" depends upon the question posed in the first line, the poem's theme is Bly's attempt to answer this question. It is not a question to which any explicit answer can be given, and for this reason, before he turns to consider it in terms of our own time, Bly first establishes a historical context for it. In terms of ancient Rome the context consists of showing what should not have been done—and thus, by way of contrast, suggesting what might be done now. That Bly chooses his historical example from ancient Rome is important. Readers may be reminded of a number of parallels between ancient Rome and twentieth century America: Rome was a major political power, it was prosperous and powerful, and it maintained what was regarded as an "enlightened" empire. Still, Rome fell. Bly seems to suggest that unless Americans learn from Rome's example, they may well be doomed to a similar fate. The poem is a warning against the destruction that the people of the United States face unless they change their ways.

But how is such a change possible? "What shall the world do with its children?" Children are the world's hope for the future. They are innocent. They have not been trained as either "executives" or "executioners." They are still open to the inner world of the psyche, filled with mystery and illumination. There seems to be a hint of a biblical passage in Bly's reference to children. Jesus said, "Suffer the little children to come unto me, and forbid them not: for of such is the kingdom of God. . . . Whosoever shall not receive the kingdom of God as a little child, he shall not enter therein" (Mark 10:14-15, King James Version). Bly's image of the "thorn," combined with the fact that the Romans persecuted Christians, makes it seem as though Bly is developing his theme through a religious thesis, even though he is thinking of it in a universal context.

The "jagged stone/ Flying toward us out of the darkness" at the end of the poem appears to be a harbinger of some imminent destruction about to visit the world and, no doubt, to change it as drastically as the fall of the Roman empire changed the ancient world. The Romans were "angry about the inner world" and sought to suppress it, but we should not be. Rather, we should welcome the inner world as children would. Thereby we may see to our own, and the world's, salvation.

William V. Davis

THE ROSE

Author: George Herbert (1593-1633)
Type of poem: Lyric
First published: 1633, in *The Temple*

The Poem

George Herbert's "The Rose" is a lyric and meditative poem first published as part of his collection *The Temple*, a group of poems written as a record of a man's efforts to recognize and follow God's will; it was also intended to guide and comfort others. "The Rose" has the musical and cyclical qualities typical of many poems in the collection as well as many of Herbert's hymns that appear in the Anglican hymnal. Its eight stanzas of four lines each have a rhyme scheme of *abab*. Every line begins with a beat and continues in three iambic feet. Three stanzas—1, 5, and 7—include two lines ending in feminine rhyme; that is, the second-to-last syllable receives the beat, and the unaccented syllables rhyme. These three sets of lines come to bear the important message of the poem: The rose offers pleasure, it purges, and it claims repentance.

The poem is also something of a meditation that takes the form of a dialogue with self or an imagined questioner. The speaker explains his reasons, either to a friend or to himself, for adopting the life he has chosen. His decision to give up his life in order to be more useful reflects a submission to God's will. Pressed, in the first line, to take more pleasure in life, the speaker responds that he wants no more pleasure than he has apportioned to his "strict but welcome size." Pleasures, he explains, do not exist. They are only griefs in disguise. He offers the rose as a symbol of all that is beautiful in the world to explain his point. The rose, he notes, is fair and sweet, but its beauty is accompanied by pain: It is thorny, and it pricks. This discomfort must be borne by the admirer of the rose. If the rose symbolizes all "that worldlings prize" and ultimately causes pain, it is clear, by extension, that all other worldly joys also bring suffering. With suffering comes repentance, and, while repentance cleanses, it also rends the spirit, just as "physick" (medicine) rends the body.

The speaker thus prefers health over the cure. He refuses the offer of worldly pleasure, yet he refuses it gently ("fairly"). Surprisingly and paradoxically, however, he ends by accepting the rose. Through analysis of the rose as representative of life's pleasures, he has seen his reason for rejecting it. Yet as he explains his choice, he recognizes more clearly the beauty of his own preference for the simple, godly life. This life now comes to be best represented by the rose. In its simple, incomparable beauty, it is unlike the worldly pleasure of life even if it does provide an instructive metaphor for it. Thus, the rose comes to represent the simple, beautiful, and accessible gift that he accepts.

Forms and Devices

"The Rose," like all of Herbert's poems, has an orderly, clever, and paradoxical form. Using simple words, Herbert constantly invents new forms that appropriately reflect the ideas being explored. His poems use all the repetitive devices (particularly rhyme, alliteration, assonance, consonance, and repetition of words and phrases), as well as meter and form, to convey meaning. The shaping of some poems to reinforce the literal meaning shows the importance he attaches to the form itself. The form also reflects the perception of an orderly universe, which is revealed through close observation, analysis, and a metaphorical habit of mind.

Herbert's poems present an artistic formulation of the analysis of a conflict. The result is often a dialogue. The Socratic dialogue was, for the classically educated person of the seventeenth century, the way to explore a topic in order to understand it. Herbert uses the dialogue repeatedly in his poems, achieving both clarification of an issue and the intimate tone for which his work has been so admired. The participants in the dialogue are sometimes an unnamed questioner (as in "The Rose"), sometimes two aspects of self, and sometimes God and self. Through this technique, readers sometimes hear the voice of the tired, angry, or lonely Christian with whom they identify. At other times, readers hear the voice of Herbert's gentle, loving, and caring God. This intimate voice draws readers into the poem, creating an emotional response that creates, in turn, a tension with the more aesthetic response prompted by the carefully contrived form. While "The Rose" does not create the highly emotional response of some of Herbert's other poems, it does illustrate the technique. The speaker draws the reader into his thought process and his final jubilant celebration of his own choice by offering the rose as a symbol of it.

Herbert also writes from a metaphorical habit of mind. In the tradition inherited from medieval times, sixteenth and seventeenth century writers expected to see correspondences in an orderly world. This way of viewing the world was not unlike the contemporary manner of seeing metaphors, but it differed in degree. For them, metaphor became a symbol or emblem reflecting complex meaning and values. The rose acquires complex meaning: The beauty and the pain that comes from seizing it represent the delight of seizing the pleasures of the world and the attendant pain of this action. Herbert shows, through the rose, that beauty and pleasure do have a cleansing and redemptive effect, but this is an effect that this seeker of the good life does not enjoy and that can be avoided by choosing a path different from the path of pleasure and delight that the rose has come to represent. The rose then accrues a meaning that is similar to the emblematic meaning of Christ's cross.

Themes and Meanings

The theme and meaning of this poem point to Herbert's life, in which poems ultimately became prayers and prayers became poems. His early life of high hopes, high achievements, and thwarted ambitions prepared him to write poems about people's attempts to align themselves with God's will. Born into a good family, Herbert was well-educated and brought up to expect a court position. He served as a tutor and as the University Orator at Trinity College in Cambridge, England, positions meant to prepare him for such a career. However, he saw his plans fail to materialize with the deaths of those influential friends who would have recommended him. He then began, later in life than most, to pursue Holy Orders. This was not a completely new direction for him, for he had been influenced by his mother, who encouraged him to pursue a religious life. However, his decision to become the parson at the country church in Bemerton, England, at age thirty-five did require a change in his life. His poems of the struggle to accept God's will and recognize His love for man were written during the four years he was pastor at Bemerton before his death at age thirty-nine.

"The Rose" could serve as an introduction to Herbert's task of describing humankind's inner conflicts. He commits himself to the ascetic life, a life not lacking in its own kind of beauty. In its description of the speaker's resolution to turn away from the inviting pleasures of this world and focus on the "size" of self, it speaks to all humankind. Through the internal conversation explaining the speaker's choice, the poem offers a reaffirmation of a spiritual decision.

While some readers of devotional poets have preferred the more spontaneous verses of Herbert's disciple Henry Vaughan or the more impassioned poems of John Donne, Herbert's admirers appreciate the subtlety of his wit and the sincerity of his voice, both of which are evident in "The Rose." The manipulation of the rose itself to symbolize first what he rejects and then what he accepts shows the nature of his wit and his appreciation for paradox. Indeed, all of his poems are informed by that major paradox of Christian teaching: In order to save one's life, one must lose it for the sake of Christ. The carefully designed artistic form and the clearly realized, particular voice of this ardent pilgrim create poems that express both the universal truth of humanity's relationship with God and each person's struggle to accept God's love and will. Typical of Herbert's work, this poem demonstrates the correspondence between form and meaning. "The Rose" encloses the totality of its meaning through the order, the voice, the dialogue, the symbol, and the paradox.

Bernadette Flynn Low

ROUTE

Author: George Oppen (1908-1984)
Type of poem: Meditation
First published: 1968, in *Of Being Numerous*

The Poem

"Route" is a long poem in free verse consisting of fourteen sections, each structured differently. The title indicates that the poem describes a series of journeys: the narrative of the poet's own life, the process of creating poetry, travel by car and other modern forms of transportation, and the voyage of humankind itself from the promise of human chromosomes to a fast-approaching apocalypse. Although the poem is written in first person and includes autobiographical material from George Oppen's life, most of "Route" is a philosophical meditation that considers multiple points of view and the perspective of "we" rather than "I."

The first section presents a series of ancient, elemental materials ("the beads of the chromosomes," "sources," "crude bone," "the mass of hills," and "the sun") that the speaker tries to link to a contemporary moment of individual perception ("Your elbow on a car-edge/ Incognito as summer"). The speaker says that the motive for writing this kind of poetry, which is made up of separate and distinct images, is to "achieve clarity." The second section describes the importance of this clarity as a "force" that human beings experience as shared rather than "autonomous," despite the fact that even the objective world is discontinuous and constantly changing like a "house in moonlight." Next, the speaker develops the idea that the "thing" should not be reduced to "nothing" and that even the act of looking out a window at the world should be done without egotistical emotions. Then the speaker argues that words themselves are also things and are not "transparent" and have ethical implications for "those in extremity." He also claims that people actually understand reality best in the state of boredom because then they are truly able to experience time.

There is a radical change in tone from the fourth to the fifth section as the poem moves from dreamlike images to a journalistic prose account. It reports a story about the suffering of French people forced to hide in individual holes during much of World War II in order to avoid being drafted into the German army and depicts information Oppen actually received while serving as a soldier and translator. The sixth section returns to lines of verse but continues with a meditation on the nature of war, although, as elsewhere, abstract concepts are presented through concrete relationships. The section concludes with things that are so simple ("there is a mountain, there is a lake") that they are often misunderstood.

The eighth section explores how humanity's view of modern life has been changed by the automobile. Although cars are "filled with speech," it is the man whose car has crashed who "sees in the manner of poetry." In the next section, the speaker compares the countryside that is driven through to a historical context, but he presents history in personal terms, including an allusion to the suicide of Oppen's mother when he was a child. The tenth section continues this roadside perspective as a way to understand a poetic perspective that is composed of scenes rather than symbols and that is, by definition, finite rather than infinite.

The twelfth section views the larger human-made landscape of "sheetmetal," "concrete," and "gravel," which is modern but is haunted by time and related to the fruit of the biblical Tree of Knowledge. In the thirteenth section, it becomes clear that the roadside landscape has already supplanted traditional public urban architecture, which was built so that people could entangle themselves "in the roots of the world" or to provide "shelter in the earth." In the final section, the speaker predicts cataclysm for his culture like that experienced by the American Indians. In the conclusion, however, the speaker refuses to abandon his civilization, even if it is doomed, and affirms the reality of this world as it approaches its end.

Forms and Devices

Oppen is considered to be one of the founding Objectivist poets, and he uses a succession of objective images to achieve the poetic effects of "Route." The Objectivists were a diverse group launched by Ezra Pound, who believed that poetry should rely on images rather than metaphors, and influenced by William Carlos Williams, who asserted that there should be "no ideas but in things." Because Oppen believed in the importance of giving realism to the thing described in his poetry and not merely treating the image as a vehicle for a more abstract or intellectual concept, he avoids relying on metaphors. A careful reading of "Route" shows few metaphoric constructions, even when the logic of the poem would seem to demand it. Sometimes the poem juxtaposes images or words without making the relationship between them completely clear, so that the reader may wonder whether or not a phrase such as "Reality, blind eye" is a metaphor. Sometimes the poem isolates the image from the rest of the text so that it can have greater impact as a moment of perception such as the "sea anemone . . . filtering the sea water through its body." Although the poem opens with a simile comparing chromosomes to a rosary, much of the poem uses association by proximity rather than association by comparison, so that it is not just the images themselves that are poetic, but the sequence of images: "And beyond, culvert, blind curb, there are also names/ For these things, language in the appalling fields."

Oppen defines poetic experience primarily in visual terms with his "moving picture," but "Route" is also a poem that functions on an auditory level, although the speaker would seem to be diminishing the importance of song by saying, "Let it be small enough." In many ways, "Route" is not a poetic poem: It includes a long section of narrative prose, and it is structured more as a meditation than a lyric. Nonetheless, although the poem is in free verse, its music appears in the use of repeated refrains such as "We will produce no sane man again" and "All this is reportage." Oppen also builds rhythm by repeating grammatical constructions ("of invaders, of descendants/ Of invaders"), metrical patterns ("into gravel in the gravel of the shoulders"), and words ("Clarity, clarity, surely clarity is the most beautiful/ thing in the world,/ A limited, limiting clarity"). The most striking lines use simple diction in extraordinarily complex clauses (both grammatically and musically): "These things at the limits of reason, nothing at the limits of dream, the dream merely ends, by this we know it is the real."

Themes and Meanings

Oppen argued that he was trying to bring greater realism into poetry, although his realism was philosophical realism rather than the sociological or psychological realism that most readers would associate with the term. Many of Oppen's ideas about how human beings perceive the world moment by moment were derived from and influenced by the twentieth century German philosopher Martin Heidegger. Other concepts in "Route" that also appear in Heidegger's work include time as a dimension of being, boredom as a way to experience reality, the importance of "things" in themselves rather than just as they relate to ideas, the belief that language is not a transparent medium for ideas, and the conviction that the relation of human beings to the earth is in crisis.

Oppen is also responding to moral questions raised by the historical events of World War II and his personal participation in combat. Although Oppen was a well-known pacifist for most of his life, in "Route" he tries to understand his time as a soldier in Europe. His enlistment could be easily understood in ideological terms: Oppen was a leftist Jew and a confirmed anti-Nazi. "Route," however, presents more complexity. The speaker in the poem sees the war in terms of "madmen" who "have burned thousands/ of men and women alive," but he also realizes that they were "perhaps no madder than most." A series of rhetorical questions about war are raised in the sixth section, but the poet does not presume to answer them. In talking about the war, the speaker suggests that the truth is both "perfectly simple" and "perfectly impenetrable" and suggests that truth is not necessarily moral.

"Route," like the larger book in which the poem appears, *Of Being Numerous*, compares the isolation of people as autonomous individuals with solitary perspectives to communal responsibilities to act ethically toward other people and the world. Perhaps nowhere in the poem is the existential dilemma of isolated individuals more poignant than in the wartime story about men living alone in holes in the French countryside for years, even while snow fell, even at the cost of sacrificing the safety of their families. The men's decision to enter their lonely holes is not presented in idealistic or nationalistic terms, but the story is important because these are men who made an ethical decision not to fight while Oppen made an ethical decision to fight. The abstractions of pacifism, therefore, prove unimportant to both combatants and noncombatants.

Elizabeth Losh

RUBY TELLS ALL

Author: Miller Williams (1930-   )
Type of poem: Dramatic monologue
First published: 1985; collected in *Imperfect Love*, 1986

The Poem

"Ruby Tells All" is a sixty-four-line, five-stanza poem written in blank verse. The title of the poem establishes both the occasion of the poem and the confessional nature of the piece: The speaker in the poem is a woman named Ruby, who recounts some of the major events in her long life and reflects upon what life has taught her. One of the strongest features of the poem is the voice of Ruby, an unwavering and direct voice that characterizes her and establishes her position in society.

"Ruby Tells All" is an appropriate introduction to Miller Williams's work because Williams frequently writes poems that are dramatic monologues: works in which a character directly addresses an audience in such a way as to unintentionally reveal some substantial insight or show some important aspect of his or her personality. As is the case with many of Williams's dramatic monologues, in "Ruby Tells All" the speaker is identified in the poem's title. While there is little interaction between speaker and listener in the poem, some critics have maintained that Ruby is telling her life story to a customer at the coffee shop where she works. Support for the assumption that Ruby is speaking to one of her customers comes in the second stanza, in which Ruby says, "I've poured coffee here too many years/ for men who rolled in in Peterbilts."

In the first stanza Ruby tells about her childhood; in the second she explains how difficult it is as an adult to tell truth from lies. In the third stanza she recounts a major event in her adult life, and in the fourth stanza she discusses old age and sums up her thoughts about what is important in life. Finally, in the final stanza, she considers what she might do to reestablish a connection with her long-lost daughter.

The poem begins with a recollection from Ruby's youth. As a child, she was told that "crops don't grow unless you sweat at night," and she explains that in her childhood she felt as if she were especially important because she thought "that it was my own sweat they meant." This stanza indicates Ruby's connection with life and with the process of growth. However, with the passing of childhood comes the loss of "everything that's grand and foolish." One of the losses brought about by the end of childhood is the ability to discern truth from lies. The second stanza deals specifically with Ruby's inability as an adult to tell truth from falsehood.

The third stanza focuses on the most important event of Ruby's adult life: a love affair with a married man, an affair that produced a daughter. Although Ruby feels that, "Given the limitations of men, he loved me," the man disappears, leaving her to raise her daughter on her own. Ruby has apparently been a good mother; she loves her daughter, and she says that she "raised her carefully and dressed her well." At the time of the poem, however, the daughter has grown up and moved away. Ruby does not know where she is.

The fourth stanza contains Ruby's reflections on old age, especially her growing awareness of the passage of time and the inevitability of her own death, as well as her opinions about men and their natures. She assesses what does and does not matter in life. In the fifth stanza she laments the fact that she has lost touch with her daughter and wonders what she could do or say to bring her daughter, if she is still alive, back into her life.

Forms and Devices

"Ruby Tells All" is an excellent example of Williams's tendency to write about ordinary people in ordinary language. Ruby's diction characterizes her as a working-class person, but even though her language is ordinary, Ruby is able to achieve extraordinary insights about life. The most important formal aspect of the poem is its meter; it is written in blank verse (unrhymed iambic pentameter). Iambic pentameter is the most common pattern in English poetry, and its rhythm appears naturally in English speech and writing. Therefore, iambic pentameter is a suitable meter for a poem that is "spoken" in the voice of one character.

The formal meter of the poem is, however, in juxtaposition to Ruby's diction. Her common diction is especially apparent in stanza 2, in which she says, "I wouldn't take crap off anybody/ if I just knew that I was getting crap/ in time not to take it." In addition to juxtaposing Ruby's common diction with formal meter, Williams uses juxtaposition to close the poem by mixing her philosophical musings with personal ones. When contemplating what she might tell her daughter if they should meet again, Ruby wonders if she should say "that against appearances/ there is love, constancy, and kindness" or that her fingers hurt at night and she has dresses she has never worn. The juxtaposition of philosophical concerns with ordinary ones is indicative of Williams's ability to write powerfully about common people who have uncommon insights about life.

In "Ruby Tells All," Williams employs repetition and metaphor to highlight the poem's essential concerns: an assessment of what matters in life and the notion that life is composed of loss and change. For example, the clause "Everything has its time" appears twice in the poem, once in stanza 3, in which Ruby discusses the loss of the man who fathered her daughter, and again in stanza 4, when she speculates about growing old. Also in stanza 4, the word "don't" is repeatedly used to help characterize the negative natures of men. Moreover, in the final stanza, three lines begin with the words "maybe that"; the repetition of these words introduces a catalog of Ruby's alternatives concerning what she might tell her lost daughter.

The poem is also informed by metaphors that promote its thematic concerns. The first metaphor occurs in stanza 1 when Ruby notes that "We lose everything" and that everything "becomes something else." Reversing a commonplace observation, she says that "one by one,/ butterflies turn into caterpillars." The second important metaphor occurs in the fourth stanza, in which she comments on men and their natures. According to Ruby, "What's a man but a match,/ a little stick to start a fire with?"

The varied line length of the first, third, and fourth stanzas is another formal element in the poem. The first stanza, which deals with Ruby's childhood, is fifteen lines long; the third stanza, which deals with her adult life, is sixteen lines long; and the fifth stanza, which deals with her old age, is seventeen lines long. Each stage of her life is, therefore, marked by a longer stanza.

Themes and Meanings

"Ruby Tells All" is a poem about coming to terms with the nature of life, deciding what matters in life, and dealing with the inevitability of death. Ruby believes that life is characterized by loss and change, and she believes that, in the end, some things matter "slightly" and some things do not. According to Ruby, people "lose everything that's grand and foolish," and everything "has its time." Everything, of course, includes Ruby herself, who mentions that she feels "hollow for a little while" when she reads the obituaries in the newspaper and finds that someone younger than herself has died.

Ruby's thoughts about the passage of time and about death and dying lead her to make assessments about what is important in life. For her, dying matters, pain matters, and being old matters, but men do not matter. Indeed, Ruby believes that men have limited natures and that they live by negatives such as "don't give up,/ don't be a coward, don't call me a liar,/ don't ever tell me don't." She assumes that her daughter has learned these lessons about life and men, and at the conclusion of the poem she lists some of the other life lessons she might offer her daughter. Indeed, her thoughts about her lost daughter are evidence of her desire to stay connected with the human community as long as possible given the inevitability of death.

Dave Kuhne

THE SADNESS OF BROTHERS

Author: Galway Kinnell (1927-   )
Type of poem: Elegy
First published: 1980, in *Mortal Acts, Mortal Words*

The Poem

In seven stanzas of free verse, Galway Kinnell, the first-person narrator, remembers his lost brother, who died twenty-one years before. Kinnell creates an imaginary reunion he and his black-sheep brother might have in their fifties if they could meet. His brother had run off years ago, after his dream of being a pilot failed; he wandered around and eventually died as an exile from his family. Kinnell imagines that they meet and hug, and that his splintered family momentarily is reunited.

The poem is divided onto 5 sections, beginning with the surfacing of a subconscious memory of the brother that Kinnell experiences as "a mouth/ speaking from under several inches of water." This resurrected corpse of a memory brings an ugly image of the lost one as "wastreled down" with "ratty" eyes. In part 2, old photographs of World War II airplanes and of a tractor left by his brother trigger Kinnell's memories. He remembers that his brother's soaring dream of being a pilot was shattered when he "washed out" of pilot training in 1943. Kinnell's brother, broken by this failure, became a wanderer for twelve years until he died in an automobile crash in the Wyoming desert. In part 3, the poet sees himself and his lost brother as both possessing traits of their unsuccessful father, Scotty. He remembers his father's walk and "jiggling" knees, his beliefs in "divine capitalist law" even though he was starving, and his half-failures both in war and civilian life. Also, he remembers, with some nostalgia and gentle humor, the whole family sleeping in one bed because of the cold and their poverty; when one turned, they all had to turn. This reminder of unity and warmth ends when the poet states that Scotty's life "revealed not much/ of cowardice or courage: only medium mal." The father, even though he shared his wife's dreams and "bourgeois illusion," remained only a "medium" man with some evils and weaknesses who, like the lost brother, was not successful.

At the beginning of part 4, the narrator shifts to the present tense and imagines his dead brother with him at his present home. Kinnell describes the fears he might experience in reuniting with the prodigal brother who had become a stranger. He fears that his brother might be obnoxious, want "beer for breakfast," or criticize his family's "loose ways/ of raising children." Kinnell then recalls the rebellious, snarling, and gangsterlike behavior of the black-sheep brother as a teen. Then, in contrast to the snarling teenage image, Kinnell remembers his brother being six years old and innocent, ecstatically waving to the family from the "rear cockpit" of a "Waco biplane" as his dream of being a pilot began.

The last part starts with Kinnell rejecting the fears and, in his imagination, lovingly embracing the lost brother. The brothers stand together in the doorway reunited; both are humanized as Kinnell ends by saying, "we hold each other, friends to reality,/ knowing the ordinary sadness of brothers."

Forms and Devices

Kinnell is a confessionalist poet—that is, he writes about his own personal experience and tries to transmute it and depict it as universal human experience. True to his Whitmanesque roots, he writes in free verse and creates vivid, emotive images through repetition, analogies, irony, and poetic catalogs as he weaves his elegiac "reunion" in this poem.

In the second section, for example, Kinnell moves from the outside world of physical memorabilia—photos left by his brother—inward to the mental images formed in his own memory. Such inward motion may represent one step toward the mental reunion found at the poem's end. Kinnell begins and ends this part of the poem by mentioning the odd photograph in the box, one of a farmer sitting on a tractor and gazing at his fields. The poet repeats the words "photograph" or "photographs" three times and implies a whole cluster of images of planes when he catalogs and lists names of World War II airplanes: "Heinkel HE70's, Dewoitine D333/ "Antares," Loire-et-Olivier H24-2—." Each plane presumably had a photograph, so many photographs are implied. By listing the plane names and exact model numbers, Kinnell reveals his brother's expert knowledge of World War II aircraft. The repetition of names also underscores the brother's obsession with flying.

Ironically, the brother's flying dream was dashed at the point it possibly could have been actualized in life—he went to flight school only to find that "original fear/ washed out/ all the flyingness in him." Apparently, the lost dream destroyed the brother, who was unable to create another viable dream and "only wandered/ from then on" until he died twelve years later in 1955. At the end of this section, Kinnell transforms the snapshot of the farmer on a tractor from a physical image into mental images within "the memory of a dead man's brother." In this very personal stanza, the poet "confesses" his struggle with memories of his sad and unfulfilled brother's death and imaginatively gathers his lost brother into his living memory through repetition and the catalog of old photographs.

Kinnell creates complex and affecting images. The opening simile reads, "He comes to me like a mouth/ speaking from under several inches of water." The image is complex partly because it operates on both visual and aural (hearing) levels and partly because it generates several different associations. On a visual level, the image functions as a form of synecdoche (the use of a single part to stand for the whole or to evoke a more complex whole). Since a mouth is closely associated with a face as a whole, the image can be of a whole face, perhaps a corpse's face, emerging from the deep. If the face is underwater, it is not quite clear and is wavering in appearance, perhaps a whitish blur in dark water. On the aural dimension, a mouth speaking from underneath water produces indistinct or burbling sounds—one imagines something just below hearing trying to bubble through to the surface. The sound is not yet understandable but becomes audible. The complex images of stifled talk and indistinct sounds linked to a bleary image of a humanlike entity striving to surface is an evocative and apt representation of a repressed memory trying to break through to a person's consciousness. It also is a memorable and somewhat frightening way to begin a poem about the power of memory to both recall and re-create the dead brother.

Themes and Meanings

Kinnell's "The Sadness of Brothers" is part of a series of long confessional poems about both mortality and different members of his original family. He writes about his mother's death and its effect on him in "The Last Hiding Place of Snow," also published in the volume *Mortal Acts, Mortal Words*. Even though he writes of death in "The Sadness of Brothers," he does not seem particularly morbid. Instead, he seeks to overcome death, at least for a moment, by using the power of language to re-create a reunion with the dead brought to life in a poem. By writing such poems, Kinnell seems to believe that he can existentially protest seeing the dead as wholly separate from the living, since those who are gone can be brought back and immortalized in a work of art. The dead can regain life in the memory of the living.

Kinnell is by no means a unidimensional or wholly dark poet; he also writes well about human joys and about life in a family. Even in *Mortal Acts, Mortal Words*, he pens lighter poems; one is about his own son, Fergus, and is entitled "Fergus Falling." Kinnell also talks about his relationship with his first wife in "After Making Love We Hear Footsteps" and "Flying Home." Earlier in his career, he wrote political poems protesting the savagery of the Vietnam War, and his most famous early poem, "The Bear," apparently was conceived in a southern sharecropper's house while Kinnell was working for a civil rights group. Kinnell is deeply humanistic and a poet of many parts and moods.

David J. Amante

SAINTS IN THEIR OX-HIDE BOAT

Author: Brendan Galvin (1938-   )
Type of poem: Dramatic monologue
First published: 1992

The Poem

Saints in Their Ox-Hide Boat is a book-length dramatic monologue that owes much to both the traditions of epic poetry and the traditions of hagiography, or the study of saints' lives. The speaker of the poem is Saint Brendan the Navigator, who is relating the tale of his famous voyage that may have taken him as far as North America. Brendan tells his story to a young scribe who sets down his words. The interplay between Brendan's story and his discursive comments to the scribe constitutes an ironic commentary on the poem itself, which is both the history of a voyage and the history of the poem's composition. The title of the poem refers to the voyage made by a group of Irish monks led by Brendan on a type of pilgrimage called, alternately, "white martyrdom" or "blue martyrdom," as Galvin explains in his introduction to the poem. A "white martyrdom" was a pilgrimage by a monk in the general sense, while a "blue martyrdom" was specifically a pilgrimage by sea. Abandoning their monastic lives and "every heart-softening face," the monks in the poem embark on a sea voyage in an ox-hide boat called a curragh. The title, with its plural "saints" and singular "boat," suggests a substitution of the smaller community on the boat for the larger monastic community in Ireland.

Although the characters in the poem are monks, the poem is in many respects a poem of sailors and the sea. It begins with Brendan relating sailorly advice: how to embark safely on a sea voyage, what time of year is fortuitous for sailing, and what kind of sailors to take along. The last is of particular importance, and Brendan includes a long list of the different sort of people one ought not to select. He wants, instead, "a few with sense/ long on muscle." He tells the young scribe this, Brendan says, because he knows the boy was raised "among fields and hills." Galvin really is conditioning the reader, however, to understand the demands of the sea and to illustrate Brendan's thought process as he begins to assemble his crew. Most of Galvin's readers, like the young scribe, are not familiar with the nautical concerns Brendan describes. Galvin wants to make clear, as he said of the monks in his poem, that "these men were both religious contemplatives and hardy sailors." Like all good poets, Galvin creates his own ideal readers by educating them about his subject.

Preparations for the voyage, the "blue martyrdom," occupy a significant portion of the poem and provide many comic moments. The sailors are a superstitious lot and are quick to interpret natural occurrences as good or bad signs that will affect when they depart. For example, on the first attempt to leave, Owen, the most superstitious of the sailor-monks, interprets a dream about a flock of sheep on a hill. He questions Martin, the monk who had the dream, about whether the sheep were going up the hill or down, since the former—according to Owen—would mean good luck for a journey, while the latter would spell bad luck. Brendan mordantly observes that "next he'd be interpreting our sneezes." After discussing several other omens, including the crow of a rooster and an upset chair, Owen announces, "—No good will come of our dipping a single oar"; the trip is postponed. The next day, one of the sailors, Diarmuid, sees a hopping raven, considered a good omen. Brendan is hopeful, but then Conor tells of hearing a wren, which Owen believes cancels the good omen. After much discussion, the trip is again postponed. On the third day, one of the monks boards the boat from the left side, an act that Owen believes will bring terribly bad luck, but Brendan insists that they leave and even threatens them with physical violence.

The actual journey, when it finally begins, is decidedly not like other great epic sea journeys, and it contrasts particularly with the *Odyssey.* Homer's epic is filled with mythical creatures: Circe, Cyclops, Scylla, Charybdis, and gods and goddesses in human form. By contrast, Brendan's description of his voyage is pointedly realistic, and he seems more interested in relating the practical concerns of embarking on such a voyage than he is in relating the spiritual dimension of it. Once again, Galvin uses the character Owen and his superstition to contrast with Brendan's common sense. When the monks hear seals barking in the fog one day, Owen wrings his hands, crying that it is the "howling and slobbering" of damned souls. Brendan's realistic attitude is an important counter to Owen's superstition, because the latter's ideas often "found soft nests in his brothers'/ minds." Through contrast to Owen, it is clear why Brendan has become the leader of a growing group of monks. Owen is more closely allied to the pagan era fast receding into the past, while Brendan is helping to found the Christian future of Ireland.

Throughout the journey, natural phenomena undercut the supernatural. The monks witness an island floating in the air, for example, but Brendan correctly interprets it as "another trick of the sea." (Galvin provides a few explanatory notes to his poem, and he explains this natural phenomenon as an atmospheric disturbance called the Hillingar effect.) Often, the conflict between natural and supernatural explanations leads to comedy. For example, Owen tells the other monks about the magical clay on the island of Inishdhugan that has the ability to drive away the lice that have been plaguing them. The monks land and barter with Dhugan, the island's chief. They sprinkle the clay about the boat liberally, only to discover that it does not work at all; indeed, Brendan suspects that the clay made the lice "double their coupling." Similarly, Owen sees yellow eyes glaring at them from an iceberg and screams that Brendan has brought them "where souls/ are conducted after death." Brendan considers joking ("I hadn't recalled dying"), but instead responds with the measured explanation that the yellow eyes are those of an owl.

Along with the humor, Galvin provides realistic description of what such a voyage must have been like. Even as readers laugh at the monks with their lice or at Owen's superstitions, they realize the discomfort and fear the sailors must experience. Galvin provides some graphic details about their life on the curragh: The monks eat their meals in the dark so they will not see "what's already eating what we're supposed to eat." More often, they do not even have food and must subsist on very small rations.

Brendan prefers the days when the sea is rough, because only then do the seasick monks not complain of their hunger. Sickness runs rampant. One monk, Diarmuid, is swept overboard, and even Brendan finally succumbs to a feverish vision. Along with these obvious stresses on the monks is the stress of the mundane "memorizing the same/ five faces over and over" as they float day after day on the sea.

Forms and Devices

Saints in Their Ox-Hide Boat has two main antecedents, one of which was the book *The Brendan Voyage* (1978), written by Tim Severin about his re-creation of Saint Brendan's journey in the curragh. Some of the realistic details of Galvin's poem come from this source. The more important of the sources was a historical document, the *Voyage of St. Brendan*, which contains the legends, written in Latin, that the Brendan of the poem dismisses as exaggeration. That text gave Galvin material that his more realistic Brendan could deride and caution his young scribe to avoid. The Latin text probably also provided Galvin with inspiration for the many figures of speech he includes that are typical of writings about saints' lives and of epic poetry. He uses hyphenated epithets that are nearly Homeric in their intensity; warriors are "iron-chested ones," for example, and the sea is a "seal pasture where every angel-haunted/ abbey stone sinks out of memory."

Galvin's poetic imagery is likewise rich, and his use of metaphor noteworthy. Within the space of a few lines, Brendan describes humans as no more than a "clutch of fish bones," describes the Irish islands as a "stone beehive," and discusses his monastic vows as a forgoing of the "lit/ eye of a woman and the poured-milk/ turn of her neck." In just these few metaphors, Galvin illuminates Brendan's theology, the Irish geography, and the devotion required when one takes monastic vows.

Although the poem is nominally a dramatic monologue, and the entire poem is related by Brendan to the young scribe at the monastery, Galvin energizes his poem with exchanges between Brendan and others. At several points Brendan directly addresses the young scribe, giving his narrative a conversational tone. He reminds the scribe repeatedly to write the story down just as he tells it, with no embellishment. When commenting on the younger monks who accompanied him on the voyage, Brendan takes a moment to comment on the scribe's youth as well. On other occasions, Brendan relates dialogue and disputes between the various monks, particularly his ongoing dispute with Owen. Galvin indicates reported language without quotation marks, instead using dashes to distinguish them from Brendan's other description. The trip to the island of Inishdhugan is one such extended passage. The description of the monks' interaction with the canny old pagan, Dhugan, is notable for the amount of reported language given by Brendan. The passage has Dhugan asking riddles of the monks, followed by their often comic responses:

> —Well, riddle me this then. I move
> what cannot move itself. Though none can
> see me, all bow down to me. What am I?

—God! One of the brothers whispered behind me.

—Yes, God! the others encouraged.

—Almighty God, I answered smiling at
the thought I'd cornered him now.

—The wind, he answered with a smirk.

By having Brendan quote the other characters, as in this passage, Galvin is able to give his poem a sense of immediacy without violating the rules of the dramatic monologue form.

Similarly, the poem culminates in a conversation just as Saint Brendan has arrived off the coast of North America. In the only truly supernatural moment of the poem, an angel appears to Brendan, and Galvin intersperses the monk's words with those of the heavenly visitor. The angel, though Brendan fears he may be a devil, provides a vision of the future. He forecasts Irish warfare and division, the potato famine, and the great emigration of the Irish to North America. They will need "the sanctuary of places like this," the angel says. This section of the poem is the most technically complex, for Brendan relates the conversation with the angel but also tells the reader what his thoughts were at the time. Because Brendan did not know if the angel could "listen inside as well as out," the scene is very tense, and the interspersing of the dialogue with Brendan's thoughts dramatizes his inner conflicts, particularly at the conclusion of the poem when the angel shakes him, shouting "—Say it, man! Out with it!" This suggests that the Angel *does* know what Brendan is thinking. Galvin indents Brendan's response both to draw attention to the great statement of faith that follows and to provide a fitting sense of closure to the poem:

> O Lord
> I have loved
> the Glory of
> Your house

The poem ends with no punctuation, as if to say that Brendan's hymn of praise to God does not cease but rises upward forever.

Themes and Meanings

Saints in Their Ox-Hide Boat has as a major theme the conflict between Christianity and paganism. Galvin, in his introduction to the poem, observes that during Saint Brendan's life there existed "no clear distinction between early Christian and late pagan." Brendan is clearly conscious of the way the "old persuasion" of pagan beliefs has lasted well into the early Christian era. This persistence is particularly obvious in the early part of the poem, as the monks are stalled by the numerous bad omens. While Brendan is part of his culture and is not immune to superstition, he grows frustrated with Owen, the exemplar of the superstitious sailor. Likewise, Brendan criticizes the tendency of scribes to populate their records of saints' lives with fantastic creatures. At several points, he addresses the young monk who is recording his story, and admonishes him to write it just as he tells it, "whether you consider it/ fantastical, or not fantastical enough."

Indeed, though Brendan reminds the boy not to create things or to exaggerate the difficulties, there is much in the monk's story that is fantastic, not the least of which is the journey itself. The idea of a group of monks traveling in a curragh and reaching the shores of North America seems unbelievable, though it is a journey that has been re-created in modern times.

Perhaps most difficult to understand is why Brendan went on the voyage at all. Indeed, Brendan himself questions his motives, wondering if it was pride that led him to embark on the "blue martyrdom" or if it was an honest attempt to find God. Brendan recognizes, too, it might partly be to escape the "hammering and dust" that accompanies the monastic community that has grown around his personality. Galvin, in his introduction to the poem, explains that abbots often found their desire to "maintain a small community" subverted by their own charisma. The society on land has become oppressive to Brendan, and he believes that he must "break from that abbey's yoke" to contemplate and come closer to God. It is ironic that so many retreat from society to Brendan's monastery in order to find God but that the leader himself needs still more seclusion. Brendan mulls over the question of his own motives, as he says, "without arriving at a solid answer." After Diarmuid is swept overboard, he labels himself a "gambler with souls not my own." It is in part this sort of honesty and self-effacing criticism that makes Galvin's Brendan so sympathetic a character. When he describes "fishing/ for Diarmuid's soul with my prayers," the reader feels the sense of loss and culpability that Brendan feels. Similarly, when Brendan orders the scribe to "make me no miracles. I am no saint," his honesty is so convincing and so appealing that he seems a saint in spite of himself.

Finally, then, the poem is about exactly what it says it is about: a pilgrimage to find God. Because Galvin has presented Brendan throughout the poem as a realist, not prone to exaggeration or to flights of fancy, the most fantastic element of the poem, Brendan's vision of the future, seems believable. The scribe need not fabricate a miracle: Brendan provides him with one by describing the appearance of the angel, who says that North America will one day be a "sanctuary" for the Irish. Fittingly, the poem ends with words of Brendan that affirm his faith and, ironically, his sainthood.

Joe B. Fulton

THE SEAFARER

Author: Unknown

Type of poem: Meditation

First published: A.D. 960-980 in the Exeter Book; collected in *Seven Old English Poems*, 1966; lines 1-99a translated into English by Ezra Pound, in *Selected Poems*, 1957

The Poem

The unique copy of "The Seafarer" is found in the Exeter Book, a manuscript anthology of Old English poetry assembled about A.D. 975, although many of the poems, including "The Seafarer," may have circulated in oral versions before being written down in the form in which they now exist. The poem's Christian message would seem to rule out any date earlier than the seventh century, when the Anglo-Saxons were converted; at the other extreme, it may have been composed, at least in the form in which it survives, around the time that the scribe copied it into the book in the second half of the tenth century. The 124-line poem is untitled in the manuscript, and its author is unknown. The best-known translation is that of Ezra Pound, whose rendering of the first ninety-nine lines has been widely admired on its own merits by readers with no knowledge of the original.

"The Seafarer," like most Old English poetry, is characterized by textual problems, abrupt transitions, and apparent inconsistencies in tone and structure that combine to render any modern interpretation tentative and subject to revision. Earlier scholars frequently read the poem as a dialogue between an experienced sailor and a young man who has not yet been to sea, dividing the text into alternating speeches (though with little agreement as to where these speeches begin and end). More recently, the critical consensus has come around to the view that the poem is a monologue by a single speaker, a religious man who has spent a life on the sea and is now meditating on his experience of life on Earth and contemplating the afterlife in Heaven.

The poem begins with the speaker's remembrance of the hardships of his past life on the sea, focusing especially on scenes of solitary voyages undertaken in harsh winter weather. He contrasts his lonely and difficult seafaring existence with that of the dwellers on land who enjoy the comforts and pleasures of social life. At about line 33 of the poem, the seafarer resolves to return to the sea for another voyage, evidently to a distant land. He then shifts from personal experience to more general remarks in the third person about how seafaring men are different from landsmen, drawn more strongly to wander than to share in their admitted prosperity and the beauty of the land, especially in spring and summer. The seafarer then briefly returns to his personal thoughts about the voyage he is planning.

At about the midpoint of the poem, he explicitly makes the point that life on the land is sterile, fleeting, and insubstantial. In the second half of the poem, he moves away from the autobiographical discussion of his experiences and concentrates on the revelation to which they have led him. He develops at length the argument that worldly goods and honors are transient and insubstantial and that the wise man will therefore turn his mind entirely to the eternal life in the heavenly kingdom, considering not how to enjoy himself on Earth but how to prepare himself for Heaven, which offers the only true home for humankind.

Forms and Devices

Old English poetry is alliterative, relying on repetition of the initial sounds of stressed syllables rather than on rhymes at the end of lines as its structural principle. The details of this alliterative practice can be quite complicated, but the most typical form is illustrated by lines 31-32 of "The Seafarer," which appear thus in the original Old English: "Nap niht-scua, norðan sniwde,/ hrim hrusan band, hægl feoll on eorðan" ("Neareth nightshade, snoweth from north,/ Frost froze the land, hail fell on earth then"). Each line is divided into two half lines (separated by editorially provided commas in these examples), and the alliterating letters for each line (*n* and *h*) must occur in both halves. Each half line usually has two stressed syllables, and while either or (more often) both may alliterate in the first half line (the "a" line), in the second half line (the "b" line), the first stressed syllable must alliterate and the second must not.

While there are many threads of imagery throughout the poem, including those of cold, barrenness, and the progression of the seasons, the central metaphor is surely that of the ship at sea, which was used throughout classical and medieval literature in a variety of permutations to symbolize human life. The specifically Christian version of the image used in this poem typically identifies the waves and salinity of the sea with the uncertainty and bitterness of postlapsarian life on Earth and the sailor as the Christian tossed about by its various storms and waves. Perhaps the best-known example of this symbolic system is Noah's ark, which was read as a parable of the power of the ship of the church to save Christians from the floodwaters of sin. Depending upon the nuances of individual interpretation, the seafarer's ship can thus be seen as the church or his religious faith, which protects him from drowning in the sea of a fallen and sinful world, or as the ship of his soul journeying over temptation (and potential shipwreck at the hands of Satan) toward a heavenly destination. In such readings, the chaos represented by the sea of sin is contrasted with the stability of Heaven.

Other readers have suggested that the sea may also reflect a Christian baptismal image whereby the water represents the possibility of rebirth into faith, thus explaining the seafarer's decision to return to the sea. The ship motif provides a number of possibilities for further elaboration; in "The Seafarer," for example, commentators find that the sea bird in flight represents the seafarer's soul in contemplation of God, that his night-watches represent his earlier spiritual darkness, and that the sea journey represents a religious pilgrimage. These various interpretations are not necessarily contradictory and may merely reflect the poet's sophisticated handling of a complex symbol by developing more than one of its significances.

Themes and Meanings

Early scholars of Anglo-Saxon literature believed that "The Seafarer" represented an early pagan poem that had been adapted for Christian audiences by the insertion of pious formulas throughout and a moral at the end; accordingly, these scholars expended considerable ingenuity in attempting to excise the Christian elements to discover the "real poem" hidden beneath these composite overlays. Pound's famous translation, in line with this emphasis, systematically removes or downplays many explicitly Christian elements of the poem and stops before the overtly homiletic conclusion, which features some dozen direct references to God and the heavens in the last twenty-five lines.

Now, however, critics seem generally to agree that the two halves of the poem are unified by a movement from earthly chaos to heavenly order and that its coherent thematic thrust is the Christian message that the afterlife is more important than life on Earth. The poem is frequently discussed in conjunction with "The Wanderer," another Exeter Book poem that shares many themes and motifs with "The Seafarer," including the structure in which a specific treatment of biographical subject mat-ter—the plight of a wanderer or seafarer—is followed by a more general homiletic section that draws a religious meaning from the earlier material.

The sailor, as a man required to travel over a hostile and dangerous environment, had always seemed to Christian poets to be a naturally apt image of the believer's life on Earth, which should be viewed as a hazardous journey to the true homeland of Heaven rather than as a destination to be valued in itself. In this poem, the speaker seems to be a religious man (or reformed sinner) who has chosen the seafaring life as much for its efficacy as a means of spiritual discipline as for any commercial gain to be derived from it. The original opposition in the poem between landsmen and seafarers gives way to the insight that all men are, or ought to think of themselves as, seafarers, in the sense that they are all exiles from their true home in Heaven. As lines 31-32 (previously quoted) establish, the land can be just as cold and forbidding as the sea, and the virtuous, at least, should hope that they will be sojourning in this harsh world for only a brief time.

True Christian "seafarers" must psychologically distance themselves from secular life, as the seafarer of this poem has done both literally and figuratively. The poet appears to encapsulate his theme at the pivotal midpoint of the poem: "therefore the joys of the Lord seem warmer to me than this dead life, fleeting on land." This recommended ascetic withdrawal from worldly interests should enable the Christian to properly reject the comforts of life on the land as transient and seek spiritual rather than physical comforts.

William Nelles

THE SEARCH

Author: George Herbert (1593-1633)
Type of poem: Meditation
First published: 1633, in *The Temple*

The Poem

"The Search" is a personal meditation in which the author wonders why God appears to have forsaken him. The poem is structured into fifteen four-line stanzas. The rhythm of the poem is terse and staccato because each stanza's first and third lines consist of eight syllables, set off by four-syllable second and fourth lines. The first and third lines rhyme with each other, as do the second and fourth. Each stanza comes to a full stop. This structure lends a tone of driving restlessness, consonant with the searching theme.

Th poem is written in the first person; George Herbert directly speaks to and asks questions of God. "The Search" is one in a long collection of Herbert's poems called *The Temple*. All of the poems in *The Temple* are religious in theme, although many have a less mournful tone than that found in "The Search." The religious feeling Herbert speaks of in his poetry is considered to be personal and genuine to his actual experience. The reader can assume that Herbert actually felt at some time the longing described in "The Search." This fact is significant to Christian readers of Herbert, who are able to find solace and guidance in his works. Many non-Christian readers also admire Herbert's poetry, in part because of its honesty.

Herbert begins the poem by asking, "whither art thou fled,/ My Lord, my Love?" One can assume that the speaker in the poem at one time enjoyed a closeness with a personal god. His voice is not that of a first-time searcher, questioning the existence of God. At one point in the poem he begs God to "Turn, and restore me." He prays often, does not feel God's presence, yet observes how elements of nature seem to be oblivious to God's absence. The author asks if perhaps God has not created another race of humans, now favored with God's attention, "leaving th' old/ Unto their sinnes?" Of particular pain to the searcher is the possibility that it is God's desire to remain distant, as opposed to this distance being the just wages of faulty individuals. Perhaps God is distant because it is his will.

Partway through the poem, the writer's tone changes from descriptions of his pain and pining to descriptions of God's magnificence and direct entreaties to God to make himself felt. Finally, Herbert reasons that once God does choose to return, despite the once-felt huge distance, he will be as one with God because God, in his awesome power, is the only one capable of creating the distance and of closing it.

Forms and Devices

In agreement with the religious nature of "The Search," Herbert makes use of language familiar to many Christians through biblical allusions. The first stanza contains the line, "My searches are my daily bread," which directly reflects the New

Testament's Lord's Prayer, "Give us this day our daily bread." The poet implies here that his daily sustenance consists of looking for the warmth of God's presence that does not, for him, materialize. Later in the poem, Herbert speaks of a distance so huge that "East and West touch, the poles do kisse." Personification of this nature, such as having two inanimate and completely separate objects, the Earth's north and south poles, kiss each other, is a poetic device used frequently in the Bible's Old Testament. For example, in Psalms 85:10, "righteousness and peace have kissed each other."

While Herbert is considered by most critics to be one of the premier Metaphysical poets in English, his use of Metaphysical conceits is not as pronounced in "The Search" as it is in some of his other works. In his poem "Love (III)," for example, he successfully compares divine love with a waiter in a tavern. This type of imaginative and unlikely comparison is peculiar to Metaphysical conceits, and Herbert excels at them. The metaphors found in "The Search" are not as single-minded or fully developed as the example from "Love (III)," but there are intriguing images of space and distance that appear and reappear through the stanzas almost like a song's refrain. Line 5 describes the searcher's physical attitude of prayer: "My knees pierce th' earth, mine eies the skie." An arc of space is created by the line from the searcher's knees on the ground to the sky as he throws back his head in a prayerful plea. The next two stanzas reinforce the same picture of distance between the earth and sky. The poet looks to the green herbs "below" and the stars "above" to observe that God's other creations, unlike he, are cognizant of God's closeness. The next two stanzas again portray arcs of space, as the searcher is like an archer who "sent a sigh to seek thee out/ . . . Wing'd like an arrow; but my scout/ Returns in vain." Later the poet laments, "Thy will such a strange distance is,/ As that to it// . . . parallels meet." The last two stanzas resolve the poet's grief by closing the painful distance.

The poem's last images are those of the precise movements of two fencers and of the movement of space between them. The poet asks when God "dost turn, and wilt be neare;/ What edge so keen/ What point so piercing can appeare/ To come between?" These lines bring to mind the thin, narrow fencer's rapier that for all its sharpness is too dull to be able to separate God from his chosen. In contrast to the huge expanses God is capable of creating, and about which the poet has talked at length, so can God's "nearenesse bear the bell,/ Making two one." The phrase "bear the bell" is truly enigmatic; it may refer to an unknown Elizabethan expression. It is also possible that it refers to the two fencers' bodies coming together against the "bellegarde," or protective hand covering, of a fencing sword, thereby resulting in their nearness bearing "the bell," making two one.

Themes and Meanings

Like a genuine search, "The Search" is a journey: The poem begins at one place and ends somewhere else. The poet's thinking moves from painful lament to a search for an explanation and finally to a kind of peace. The first part of the poem is a passive description of the grief of separation and the searcher's attempt to rejoin his God. Close to the middle of the poem, one can see the writer's mind shift to ask from where the separation comes. The searcher's pain climaxes midway through the poem when he asks if his suffering might be God's will. The faithful searcher wins a final comforting reward, when, as expressed in the last third of the poem, he acknowledges God's greatness. The end of the poem definitely strikes a different tone from the beginning.

"The Search" reinforces a basic concept in Christianity—that when one is suffering and needful, one's immediate response should be to give thanks to and celebrate God. "The Search" is the story of one pilgrim's obedience to this directive and his resulting reward. One of the primary strengths of this poem are the sumptuous and celebratory descriptions of God's greatness. While the language is simple, the images are sophisticated. It has been suggested that even the distance felt from such a magnificent God is in itself a type of relationship with him, and the searcher does find solace in descriptions of God's greatness.

Coupled with the description of one pilgrim's personal journey toward his god can be found the image of the state of Christians as a group in relation to their God. It has been suggested that the poem describes the existential situation of humankind in relation to God—that of an unnatural and evil loneliness and grief after the exile from the Garden of Eden. The distance spoken of in the poem represents the difference between true man and woman as inhabitants of the Garden versus their faulty counterparts after the fall from grace. Thus when the poet begs of God, "Turn, and restore me," he seeks restoration to a place where the poet and humankind once were, in God's presence.

Valerie C. Snyder

SEEING THINGS

Author: Seamus Heaney (1939-   )
Type of poem: Lyric
First published: 1991, in *Seeing Things*

The Poem

"Seeing Things" contains two sections. In the first, as the poem begins, the speaker is being helped into a small boat that will carry him and other passengers from Inishbofin, a small island off the coast of northwestern Ireland, to the mainland. He mentions what he sees, smells, and hears as they are helped into the shifting boat that is sitting low in the water. They sit together in "nervous twos and threes," obeying the boatmen's commands. Although the sea is calm, the speaker suddenly becomes anxious because of the motion of the boat as the diesel engine is started. As the boat proceeds over the water, he has the experience of mentally looking down from above at the boat and passengers—as if he were in "another boat/ Sailing through air"—as they fare "riskily" to their destination.

The second section begins with a single Latin word, *claritas*, which means "clearness" or "brightness," a splendor of objects affecting the sight; it also means "clearness to the mind." The speaker, having just experienced the literal waves of the sea, now looks at water carved in stone on a cathedral facade. He describes the sculptor's lines as "Hard and thin and sinuous"; playful fish are cavorting about. The main image in the stone carving is a figure of Jesus being baptized by his cousin John the Baptist, an event which prompts the speaker to write, "The stone's alive with what's invisible." The "invisible" may refer to another occurrence in that same biblical scene. The gospel writer records that a voice from a cloud was heard proclaiming, "This is my beloved son in whom I am well pleased." After the baptism, Jesus took decisive action and embarked on his public life.

The poem concludes with a reference to an atmospheric condition. The heat of the afternoon creates wavy visible lines of heat in the air. These waves, like the waves of the sea and the water on the cathedral carving, prompt the speaker to reflect on life. He sees life as something dynamic, significant, and capable of sharp changes: The wavering air is "Like the zig-zag hieroglyph for life itself."

Forms and Devices

Although the poem is unrhymed, its cadences carry a lilting Irish rhythm in phrases such as "shilly-shallied," "nobody speaking," "but even so," "Swayed for balance," and "hurrying off." The poet uses devices such as alliteration, assonance, and consonance to approximate the quiet sounds of water on a Sunday morning—a repetition of *s*, *l*, and the short *u* sound in the lines "Inishbofin on a Sunday morning./ Sunlight, turfsmoke, seagulls, boatslip, diesel."

Seamus Heaney's use of unusual adjectives or epithets extend the meaning of the poem. He refers to *claritas* as a "dry-eyed Latin word," signifying a literal, physical condition for seeing things clearly. Then he describes the carving of Jesus as having "unwet knees," an observation that indicates how closely the poet studied the image and, consequently, why he was able to make some original associations with the water image. The "zig-zag hieroglyph" of the poem's last line unifies the poem, since it refers to all the water images and relates the zig-zag image to life's low and high points, to life's shilly-shallying (indecisive) moments, and to positive commitments.

"Seeing Things," as its title implies, is a poem about vision. The fusion of abstract and concrete, of natural and supernatural, is central to Heaney's visionary enthusiasm. Through using the image of waves and moving water in different contexts, the poet shares his vision with the reader: First, there are the literal waves of the Atlantic Ocean on which he and the other passengers—possibly schoolchildren, as the scene is based on a memory of Heaney's childhood—were gently tossed by the rocking of the boat. Because of Heaney's Catholic background and education, scriptural images remain an integral part of his work. The passengers also recall Jesus's disciples, frightened in a boat while Jesus slept. Heaney's use of mythology, or more precisely, his Dantesque vision, offers another angle of vision for the same scene: Because the passengers are sitting quietly, obeying the boatmen's commands, the reader is reminded of the mythological Charon, who ferried the dead across the River Styx to Hades.

The next image of moving water in the poem centers on a carving on the front of a medieval cathedral; there is both a "flowing river" and the movement of water as John pours water over Jesus's head. The water image here implies the exact opposite of the ferryman section, because the baptismal waters signify a rebirth, a beginning of Jesus's public life, a looking forward. The final reference to waves concerns waves of heat on a sultry afternoon, which affect vision. The poet presents an abstract pattern, a zig-zag, as symbolic of high and low points in a person's life. In "Seeing Things," the poet looks beyond the thing itself to see or understand the splendor that the thing (waves) represent.

Themes and Meanings

Heaney has commented, regarding this poem, that it is himself as a child who fears crossing the water on a boat ride to church. He has the same fear of crossing those waves as did the ancient characters of mythology. He does not rid himself of his fear and anxiety until he is safely onshore looking back at the experience.

When he arrives at the church, the story pictured on the church's facade reminds him of the water he has just crossed, but this time, instead of seeing himself as the focus, he looks at the figure of Christ being baptized. The poet meditates on this immersion in water as a deliberate choice—no fear is evident here. Moreover, this event, this baptism, separates the hidden life of Jesus up to this time from the very public life which he sees as his mission or vocation. Heaney may have in mind the differing demands of his own private and public lives. Many of Heaney's poems refer to the struggles he had after deciding to pursue poetry as his vocation, so it is understandable that this baptism makes such an impression on him.

In the last poetic sentence (the last three lines), Heaney pictures the children, himself among them, feeling the intense heat of the day. As the figure of Jesus stands up to his knees in water, he and the children are "up to our eyes" in heat waves, putting the poet in the position of "seeing things" in both a literal and metaphorical way.

Rita M. Scully

THE SEVEN-YEAR-OLD POETS

Author: Arthur Rimbaud (1854-1891)

Type of poem: Narrative

First published: 1895, as "Les Poètes de sept ans," in *Poésies complètes*; English translation collected in *Rimbaud: Complete Works, Selected Letters*, 1966

The Poem

"The Seven-Year-Old Poets" is a narrative poem composed of sixty-four Alexandrines (the classical French line of verse containing twelve syllables) arranged in rhymed couplets and in four loosely-formed stanzas of four, twelve, fourteen, and thirty-four lines respectively. Written in 1871, when Rimbaud was sixteen, it exemplifies the poet's unique vision of reality, one that depicts a young boy's yearning for creative and sensual freedom through the written word.

The first stanza expresses the child's relief as his Bible lesson comes to an end, the book being closed by "the Mother," his own, who has been reading aloud. She is self-satisfied in her religious devotion but fails to read in her son's blue eyes that his soul is "filled with revulsions."

The second stanza reveals the secrets of the child's intimate life. Obedient all day, he sometimes shows nasty habits that are symptomatic of his inability to repress his true desires. Passing through the halls at school, he sticks out his tongue, his fists clenched, ready for revolt. In the summer, he locks himself up "in the coolness of latrines," where he reflects and revels in the smells.

The third stanza continues the description of the child's activities, now in winter. In the garden, the poet lies in the dirt at the foot of a wall, squeezing his eyes until he sees visions. His only friends are raggedy children, "stinking of diarrhea" and conversing "with the gentleness of idiots." The mother, presented in the first stanza as pious, duty-bound, and blind to the rebellious nature of her son, is frightened at the sight of these children and feigns appreciation of her son's compassion for their state.

The last stanza, the longest, portrays the images that the child describes in the novels he writes, the dreams that oppress him at night, and his delight in solitude. At the age of seven, he is inspired by exotic images of "Forests, suns, banks, savannas" and reads illustrated papers depicting Spanish and Italian women laughing. He engages in sexual antics with the daughter of the workers next door, under whose skirts he sits to "bite her buttocks." He takes back to his room "the savors of her skin." On Sundays, "all spruced up," he reads the Bible, and, at night, dreams oppress him because he does not love God but rather the workers whom he watches returning home at the end of the day. As an escape from the harshness of reality, he dreams of "the amorous meadow" and "luminous" and "healthy perfumes." Finally, he seeks solitude in a bare room with closed shutters, damp and dank, where he rereads his novels filled with exotic and bizarre images of "flesh-flowers," "celestial woods," and "drowned forests." Lying on pieces of unbleached canvas, the young poet reads and dreams of sails.

The poem ends with an ellipsis, or three suspension points, indicating that the young poet's life continues, following the chronology and development indicated thus far. "The Seven-Year-Old Poets" foreshadows Rimbaud's unique aesthetics, his attempts to create innovative and shocking imagery that acts as a liberating force, as well as one that the deflates the smugness of bourgeois taste and morality.

Forms and Devices

"The Seven-Year-Old Poets" is beautiful and spellbinding in its depiction of a child who is already keenly aware of his vocation as a writer. More important, it reveals, through striking ironic juxtaposition, those secret and forbidden pleasures derived by the child in an austere atmosphere dominated by a puritanical mother. The poem begins with "And," indicating that the reader is entering a context that has already begun and that continues to develop. The mother is conveyed by "Mother," the capital letter suggesting her importance, symbolic nature, and forceful presence in the child's life. Not only is she symbolic of adult authority, but she is also the image of pious spirituality, and she is blind to her child's true soul, which is drawn powerlessly to the obscene and forbidden. She is the example of bourgeois respectability and moral rigidity against which Rimbaud revolted in his poetry as well as in his personal life.

To counter the stifling atmosphere created by "the Mother," the young child lives, at times, in another world. Hence, the juxtaposition, in the second stanza, of his actions in the school, where one would normally expect obedience and respectable behavior ("All day he sweated obedience"), and his private activities in the latrines, where he seems to relish the foulness of the air, serves to underline his rebellious nature, a nature that seeks solitude, and of which his mother seems unaware. This attempt to escape from the stifling atmosphere created by his mother is evident also in his choice of friends. He is drawn to children who are "Feeble, with blank foreheads, eyes fading on their cheeks," with dirty, sickly fingers and soiled clothing. He is attracted, therefore, to the underprivileged, downtrodden, and unintelligent; that is to say, to the opposite of the image of the perfect child nurtured by his mother. This is made all the more clear through the image of the young boy "all spruced up" and reading the Bible on those "pale Sundays of December" that he dreads. On these days, ironically, he is aware of his love not of God but of the workmen he watches return home, a love that is forbidden by his mother's religious beliefs and that echoes Rimbaud's own homosexuality.

Ultimately, the use of juxtaposition underlines the dichotomy that makes up the boy's life. He must live in the reality of Puritanism, conservative religion, and oppressive order created and reinforced by his mother but finds solace in his own reality, which is the opposite of the former. His world is one of foul smells, young sexuality, poetic inspiration, and ultimate freedom. The poem closes by evoking the cycle of his life, for he is delighted temporarily in his dreams of sails, symbolic of his quest for freedom of expression, which he achieves in his writing. The suspension points at the end serve to communicate the continuation of the context introduced by the "And" of the first line. Once the dream of sails is extinguished, the child will return to the stifling atmosphere created by "the Mother."

Themes and Meanings

"The Seven-Year-Old Poets" is a metaphor underlining the importance of freedom, in all its varied manifestations, in the life of a child who lives in an oppressive, puritanical, and hypocritical atmosphere dominated by a mother who is symbolic of such a way of life. The title, although in the plural, depicts one young boy who writes novels about his life and dreams of far-off lands, and who, in his private moments, rereads the novels he is writing while lying on pieces of blank canvas, a symbol of his life yet to be lived and the potential for the complete freedom for which he yearns.

The intolerance and hypocrisy of the bourgeois world that he witnesses are portrayed through the oppressive nature of school and church as well as his mother's feigned attempt to support her son's interest in lower-class and underprivileged children. The son's silent rebellion is further accentuated by his awakening sensuality and sexuality, which are translated by images that are both scatological ("in the coolness of the latrines/ . . . dilating his nostrils") and somewhat sadistic ("he would bite her buttocks") in nature.

It is, however, the metaphor of writing that is most fascinating, both as a symbol of the child's quest for freedom (an important theme) and as a reference point for Rimbaud's own life. Written when he was sixteen, "The Seven-Year-Old Poets" foresees the attainment of freedom in all its fullness by the adult Rimbaud in his affair with the poet Paul Verlaine (1844-1896), as well as in the revolutionary aesthetics of his more mature poetry. "The Seven-Year-Old Poets" is an eloquent introduction to his poetry and to his innovative, and, some would say, shocking imagery. More important, however, it foreshadows the breathtaking innovation practiced in his famous poem "Le Bateau ivre" ("The Drunken Boat"), a metaphor for poetic discovery in which the exotic lands and fabulous creatures remind the reader of the "flesh-flowers opened in the depths of the celestial woods" in "The Seven-Year-Old Poets." In the latter, the freeness of the form, combined with the elegance of the Alexandrine verse, are masterfully used by Rimbaud in order to create a refined and yet innovative poetic use of language.

"The Seven-Year-Old Poets" carries the reader through the intricacies of a child's perception of the world, splendid and, at times, full of despair, and ends on an uplifting note: The final image of sails, created by the canvas on which the child lies, will continue to carry him, through his imagination and writing, to foreign lands, unknown sensations, and experiences, and, ultimately, will offer the liberation from reality that he seeks.

Kenneth W. Meadwell

THE SEVENTH ECLOGUE

Author: Miklós Radnóti (Miklós Glatter, 1909-1944)
Type of poem: Meditation
First published: 1946, as "Hetedik ecloga," in *Tajtékos ég*; English translation collected in *Foamy Sky: The Major Poems of Miklós Radnóti*, 1992

The Poem

"The Seventh Eclogue" is a poem in seven stanzas, written in the classical form of the eclogue. The poem begins at twilight, in a military encampment. It soon becomes clear that the poet is a captive, confined in a stockade enclosed by "cruel wire." With the fading of sunlight, the wire becomes physically invisible. The poet knows that the constraining wires are still there even though it is night. Yet the fact that he cannot see them fills him with a visionary hope, a fantasy of escape and liberation.

The second stanza presents the imagined escape of the prisoners. References to Serbia, where the Hungarian Army was engaged fighting on the German side during World War II, make clear the poem's setting and wartime milieu. The poet glimpses a release to "the hidden heartland of home" that is actually so far away. He wonders whether his homeland, or perhaps literally his home itself, is as it once was. Might not the terrible bombing and carnage of the war have destroyed it? The stanza ends with perhaps the most striking line of the poem, "Say, is there a country where someone still knows the hexameter?" The hexameter is a six-beat poetic meter traditionally used in classical Greek and Latin verse, also used in this Hungarian poem in which the poet is deliberately evoking classical forms. By asking if the hexameter is still known in his homeland, the poet is wondering about the survival of civilization itself. Have the expressions of higher culture such as music, art, and poetry survived in war-torn Hungary, or have they been reduced to rubble in the wartime carnage?

In the third stanza, the poet describes the process of writing this very poem in the prison camp, or *lager*, the German term found in the poem. He must write when the guards do not see him, at night, and without a flashlight or book, lacking the ability even to put the correct accents (important in the Hungarian language) on the individual words. He is cut off from the outside world, receiving no mail; the camp itself is shrouded by fog.

People of many nationalities are in the camp, all imprisoned by the Germans, all wanting desperately to go home to their families. Even though they are all aware that death is nearly certain, they hope for a last-minute reprieve, a miracle. The poet compares his condition to that of an animal infested by fleas. The degrading conditions in the camp cannot last much longer, but, as the poet grimly concedes, neither can his life. The moon rises, making the wire once again visible, ending any possible fantasy of escape. The poet sees the armed guards, whose job it is to make sure none of the prisoners will get away.

In the last stanza, the poet addresses his beloved, who is back in his homeland. Despite all his dreams, he feels in his heart his separation from the woman he loves.

Her absence, as signified by the bitter image of a cigarette-end replacing her kiss, renders any continuing hope impossible, as the horrible conditions surrounding him bring the poet to a state of final, resigned despair.

Forms and Devices

An "eclogue" refers to a classical poetic form most commonly associated with the Roman poet Vergil. Eclogues sometimes involve dialogue between two characters (as in Radnóti's own "Fourth Eclogue" (1943), but they can also be a monologue such as this one. Eclogues are written in hexameter, or six-beat meter, and traditionally describe a pleasant natural scene that may then suffer calamity or deprivation. Radnóti's prison-camp setting is a particularly dire enactment of the traditional idea of the fallen or violated landscape. The first line might suggest a traditional pastoral scene, with its brooding twilight mood. But the sudden introduction of the "cruel wire" in the second line conveys the agony and emotional directness characterizing the rest of the poem. This is in obvious contrast to the conventionality and formal mood of the classical eclogue, though Radnóti is really extending the classical form, not overturning it. Indeed, Radnóti's combination of emotional power and classicism, rare in twentieth century poetry in any language, is strikingly in evidence in this poem. The classical meter and precedent help contain the suffering and thwarted hope of the poem; they explain it and give it meaning.

Radnóti uses the eclogue form not only to frame the poem but also to contribute to its meaning. In the almost inconceivable barbarism of World War II, classicism—in times of peace merely a way of expressing kinship with literary tradition—becomes an eloquent counterpoint to the barbarism and horror in which the poet is immersed. The poem's most crucial line, "Say, is there a country where someone still knows the hexameter?" exemplifies this protest against barbarism, this sense that what might seem a mere literary form is in fact the saving grace of a world otherwise lost to evil. In the original Hungarian, the line is "Mondd, van-e ott haza még, ahol értik a hexametert?" All the other words in the sentence are terse, ordinary one- or two-syllable words, and the abrupt appearance of the lofty "hexameter" shows how out of place the word is in the prison-camp milieu—and therefore how much the values it connotes are desperately needed.

The poet has difficulty even getting the poem on paper: Not only are the circumstances harrowing, but also the material necessities of writing—light, pen and paper, time, and freedom to write—are fundamentally lacking. That the poem was written at all, much less that it emerged as such an eloquent, accomplished, and fundamentally finished work, is a testimony both to the poet's talent and to the strength of his character. A sense of poetry as an earned if limited victory over barbarism is at the heart of the poem's classicism and its investment in classical forms and meters.

Themes and Meanings

As a Hungarian, Radnóti was not necessarily vulnerable to German imprisonment: after all, Hungary was Germany's ally in the war. However, Radnóti was an independent, left-wing thinker; in addition, he was a Jew. A prime target of Nazi persecution, he lived nearly the entire wartime period anticipating his own death. Although "The Seventh Eclogue" gives voice to rapturous visions of freedom, liberation, and release, the poet knew all the while that, in the real world, he would never be free to return to his home, that his life was to end shortly under the grim conditions of imprisonment. "The Seventh Eclogue" was written in the Haidenau prison camp in the mountains above the Serbian town of Zagubica, where Radnóti was imprisoned by the Germans in July of 1944. Radnóti survived countless ordeals in the following months but was finally shot by the Germans and buried in a mass grave in Hungary in the autumn of 1944.

Yet Radnóti, though recording his torment, does not surrender to it. He attempts to remain a thinker, a poet, a human being; insofar as possible, he goes on as before. This is illustrated by the fact that he had begun writing eclogues before the war, his first being written in 1938, when his own personal heartbreak and his questions about the nature of his poetry seemed far more important than external world events. Thus Radnóti displays an extraordinary consistency, persistence, and courage. He bears witness to the war and, tacitly, his own death, yet produces a poem that stands against all the suffering that he and millions of others had to endure at the hands of the Nazis.

The dialectic between imprisonment and freedom is the central motif of the poem. The poet, imprisoned, is able to attain imaginative freedom; even if the literal redemption of the captives in never achieved in life, a victory of the imagination has been won. But the poem is not credulous in its utopianism. It ends on a note of practical disappointment that the poet is still far from his beloved, who cannot be brought back to him by all the visions in the world. The poem ends on a touchingly personal note, as the presence of absence of the beloved takes precedence over the carnage and torture of the war. Yet this interior focus is part of Radnóti's overall message. The individual, he makes clear, cannot be lost amid a tumult of wars and ideologies. The maintenance of individual feelings and individual consciences, far from being a personal whim, is a prerequisite if civilization—the beauty, mystery, and classical rigor that the poem has been trying to evoke against the darkness—is to be preserved.

Nicholas Birns

SHAME

Author: Arthur Rimbaud (1854-1891)
Type of poem: Lyric
First published: 1891, as "Honte," in *Reliquaire*; English translation collected in *Rimbaud: Complete Works, Selected Letters*, 1966

The Poem

"Shame" is a short poem of twenty lines whose five stanzas are presented (in the original French) in a standard *abab* rhyme scheme. The poet makes use of an anonymous first-person voice to speak about his enmity for an anonymous other, referred to simply as "him." Alluding to a rift that has occurred between the poet and his enemy, the poem expresses vividly the poet's hostile feelings after the separation. Many critics familiar with Arthur Rimbaud's biography believe that the poem communicates Rimbaud's angry reaction after his falling out with his close friend and fellow poet Paul Verlaine.

The title of the poem "Shame" obviously refers to a feeling the poet wishes to express or evoke, but it is not immediately clear which persona ("I" or "he") feels the shame or why it is felt. By his spiteful tone, the poet would have his reader assume that his enemy, "he," should be feeling shame—presumably because of an injustice the poet has suffered at his enemy's hand. In any case, if the poet feels shame, it is well concealed behind the exaggerated and almost childish violence he would like to inflict on his enemy.

The poem begins in a grotesque and violent mood, making graphic reference to corporeal mutilation: "As long as the blade has not/ Cut off that brain/ That white green fatty package . . . ." The reader can presume that the poet here is making reference to himself, saying that as long as nobody has committed such violence against the poet, he will be thinking about taking revenge against his enemy. In the second stanza, the poet makes a direct appeal to his opponent to mutilate himself, implying that such a self-mutilation would satisfy the poet's desire for justice. The poet lists in stark, clinical detail the various body parts he believes his opponent should cut off, appearing to take joy in spinning out his sadistic fantasy ("O miracle!").

In the third and fourth stanzas the poet recognizes the futility of his appeal; he knows that his opponent will not commit such acts, that there will be no justice. In response, the poet declares that he will continue to cause trouble for his enemy as long as "he" is alive: Like a child, the poet will constantly pester "him"; like a skunk, the poet will foul "his" territory. In the last two lines of the fifth stanza, the poet seems to pull back from his vengeful mood when he summons God to have prayers said for his enemy once "he" has died. Rimbaud seems here to hearken back to his early religious instruction, rejecting finally the sin of vengeance and invoking the Christian principle of forgiveness. Perhaps, in the end, the shame is Rimbaud's for harboring sinful feelings. Then again, since Rimbaud is famous for his frequent use of irony, he may not be pulling back at all.

Forms and Devices

Rimbaud is associated with the French Symbolist movement, whose reputation for opaque language and formal complexity is well known. Since Symbolist poets tend to suggest their referents rather than openly naming them, readers should be cautious about pulling meaning too quickly from Rimbaud's deceptively simple poem. The first thing to emphasize in this light is that while the poem's visual appearance and fairly rigid rhyme scheme suggest a strict adherence to poetic tradition, the poem reads as if Rimbaud has simply strung together three more or less prosaic sentences. Unlike some of his more obviously difficult and elegant poetry, this poem seems facile, almost overly accessible. In that sense, the poem embodies a highly wrought tension between tradition and modernity, between complex poetry and accessible prose.

On a first reading, the reader is certain that the central opposition is between the poet and an "other" (perhaps Verlaine). That certainty occurs because the poem's prosaic quality and conventional grammar make this opposition so blatant. For example, the reader readily assumes from Rimbaud's grammatical distinction between "I" and "he" that these pronouns refer to two different people. To further emphasize this opposition between "I" and "other," Rimbaud brackets his appeal to his enemy within parentheses and he repeats in an exaggerated fashion the third-person possessive pronoun "his" in the second and third stanzas: "his nose," "his lips," "his ears," "his belly," "his legs," "his head," "his side," "his guts," "his death." The excessive repetition of "his" convinces the reader that Rimbaud must be referring to the body of an "other." Yet such obvious repetition suggests an indirect appeal to look for deeper poetic meaning.

Indeed, upon closer inspection, the reader begins to notice that the poem's tightly structured rhythm and its frequent uses of enjambment strategically interrupt the poem's linear syntax; they jar the natural flow of prosaic meaning and throw the reader off balance: "He should cut off his/ Nose," "his ears/ His belly! and give up/ His legs!" Whatever Rimbaud's intent, the effect of this strategic positioning of enjambment is to mark a formal division between grammatical subject and object and thus perhaps between "self" and "other" as well.

Rimbaud also strategically undercuts the opposition between "I" and "he" by subtly replacing the demonstrative adjectives in the first stanza ("that brain," "that . . . package") with possessive adjectives ("his") in the second and third. As mentioned above, the reader assumes from the sharp opposition between the first and second stanzas that the two stanzas refer to two different people and assumes, from the continued use of the possessive "his" from the second to the third stanza, that the second and third stanzas refer to the enemy, not to the poet himself. Upon closer inspection, however, the reader notices that the theme of cutting a head from the third stanza actually circles back to the idea of cutting "that brain" from the first stanza. Logically, this would suggest that the subject of the first and third stanzas are the same and thus that the poet is imagining this violence inflicted upon himself. The parentheses around the second stanza, in this case, would seem to indicate formally that the "other" actually lies within the poet.

Such a blurring between self and other is further reinforced by the poet's refusal to name the personas that figure in the poem. Rimbaud restricts himself to a highly ambiguous use of pronouns and he also relies on metonymy and simile to make reference to the poet ("the troublesome child," "the so stupid animal," "like a Rocky Mountain cat"). This poetic device of suggesting and partially naming serves to withhold the poem's concrete referents from the reader's view. In the end, Rimbaud's ambiguity undercuts our initial certainty about precisely who is doing what to whom.

Themes and Meanings

The point of interpreting should never be to make a poem unnecessarily difficult; one should not look for ambiguity where there is none. In this case, however, the poetic ambiguity is clear, and it appears to point to a deeper meaning beyond the prosaic one. One could argue, for example, that Rimbaud's soul is divided against itself and that the poem is a dramatization of Rimbaud's inner psychological turmoil. On the one hand, Rimbaud expresses his sadistic fantasy for revenge, and on the other, he expresses the punishment he should receive for entertaining such sinful thoughts. The formal strategies insisting on opposition noted above would thus serve to punctuate Rimbaud's internal conflict between his asocial desire for vengeance and the moral stricture that prohibits such a desire. "He" in this case would not refer to another person (such as Verlaine) but to the poet's alter ego, to an unconscious self-aggression outside Rimbaud's rational control. According to this scenario, the numerous references to violent acts may be an expression of a guilt complex, a masochistic fantasy whereby Rimbaud irrationally desires punishment for his errors or sins. In that case, the final lines calling for prayer more clearly point to Rimbaud's own expression of shame.

This all may seem wildly speculative unless the reader is familiar with Rimbaud's famous dictum: "I am an other." What Rimbaud means by this is that his psyche is self-divided, one half against the other. The "other," the part outside his rational and linguistic control, speaks through him in spite of himself; it expresses desires and fantasies that reason or morality cannot easily impede. Such an internal division between passion and rationality, between individual desire and morality is a traditional one that goes back as far as the Greeks. Rimbaud radicalizes the opposition by giving this "other" a name, "he," as well as by granting it supremacy. This idea of the divided psyche or the "other within" anticipates Sigmund Freud's idea of the unconscious, and it makes Rimbaud one of the first truly modern poets.

Scott M. Sprenger

THE SHAPE OF THE FIRE

Author: Theodore Roethke (1908-1963)
Type of poem: Lyric
First published: 1947; collected in *The Lost Son and Other Poems*, 1948

The Poem

In 1948 Theodore Roethke published *The Lost Son and Other Poems*, introducing the greenhouse and sequential poems that have come to define his unique style. "The Shape of the Fire" is the last poem in "The Lost Son" sequence. Roethke's long poems are explorations of psychic states, and they progress cyclically rather than in a logical linear narrative. "The Shape of the Fire" begins by returning psychologically to the awakening of consciousness in the womb. The images follow the sensory world of a child, a primordial, animistic, natural world characteristic of "The Lost Son" poems.

Roethke does not depict a comforting landscape. Images are surreal and incoherent, as shapes in a fire are. Knowledge comes from "a nameless stranger." The images of receding water and a beached boat symbolize the stagnation of the spirit. The landscape is unpleasant and threatening; even the flowers "are all fangs." However, it is a time of transition. The speaker envisions the water returning and calls, "spirit, come near." The hour of ripeness, which can result in his release from this sterile landscape, approaches. He calls for his mother to "stir" and "mother me out of here." At the end of section 1, he bids farewell to the elemental forms of nature as he is [re]born.

Part 2 begins with the child's discovery of his body. As in the beginning of part 1, the language is a childlike combination of questions and nursery-rhyme cadences. After this short, playful section, however, comes another nightmare vision, first of an adult figure, "a varicose horror," and then of another wintery landscape characterized by snakes, sticks, sharp winds, and howls. These images represent the problematic time of adolescence, with the primeval ooze and slime of sexuality. Now "the uneasy man" "must pull off clothes/ To jerk like a frog/ On belly and nose/ From the sucking bog." "Words writhe," and the light speaks in a "lewd whisper." He seems betrayed by his own body as he observes, "My meat eats me."

Part 3 provides a short hiatus in the form of enigmatic aphorisms. It provides a transition from "the journey from flesh," which "is longest," to the image of the rose, which "sways least." For Roethke, the movement and journeys that make up the events of life, are difficult and frightening. The end he seeks is stasis; the rose, which is a mystical symbol of finished perfection, serves as a guide.

In part 4, when the protagonist again regresses to a primordial natural landscape, full spiritual progress begins. This landscape is supportive and lifegiving. "Death was not" in this environment. Now the cave is not sorrowful, but sweetened with fertile rain and the sustenance of apples. Flowers are everywhere, moving into fullness, "buds at their first trembling," "wakening blossoms," a profusion of flowers, associated with love. The last section of "The Shape of the Fire" is replete with images and symbols of spiritual wholeness and fulfillment: the flowers, "the whole air!/ The light, the full sun" of illumination, and the boat, the symbol of his spirit, which is drifting effortlessly now. The final image compares the light, which enriches the spirit, with the water in a vase, filled to surfeit so that it holds the flower in an invisible yet nourishing and supportive embrace.

Forms and Devices

Roethke's poetry is most innovative in its use of animistic natural imagery and symbolism, its use of the tone and language of childhood, and its intense psychological explorations. Poems such as "The Shape of the Fire" move convincingly from preconscious lack of self-awareness to mature mystical spirituality. *The Lost Son and Other Poems* volume was critically acclaimed for the poet's immediate identification with nature. Nature is anthropomorphized: the cracked pod "calls"; the worm is "fond"; the spiders "cry." It also reflects the protagonist's moods, being frightening and menacing or loving and beckoning as he progresses and regresses on his spiritual journey.

Certain images become symbols, either universal ones, such as light, which brings spiritual illumination, and water, which brings fertility and birth, or personal symbols, such as flowers, which are identified with Roethke's childhood in his father's greenhouse and represent the instinctive urge to struggle into life. Roethke's poems are intensely subjective; few critics separate the protagonist or speaker from the poet himself. The landscape of "The Shape of the Fire" is drawn from his childhood in Michigan, "the marsh, the mire, the Void." It is "a splendid place for schooling the spirit. It is America," he wrote to Louise Bogan in an "Open Letter" (printed in *Mid-Century American Poets*, edited by John Ciardi, 1950).

Yet however personally conceived, Roethke's symbols are also universal, from the dreamlike landscapes, which are night journeys of self-discovery, to the roses, which are symbols of mystical wholeness. No matter how personal or egocentric a poet, Roethke also insisted that his poems represent a racial memory, and his imagery bears this out.

In addition, the startling language of the first segments of the poem attempts to capture the nonsense rhymes and associational, nonlinear narrative of a young child. Roethke says that "rhythmically, it's the spring and rush of the child I'm after . . . if necessary, without relying on the obvious connectives: to speak in a kind of psychic shorthand when his protagonist is under great stress" (from "Open Letter").

Roethke presents landscape as emotion, perception, memory, and dream in direct, almost abrupt, statements that give his poetry the power of immediate perception and thought. His catalogs of proverbs in section 3, like those of his mentor, William Blake, bombard one with strong images that imply a mystical knowing, which becomes more clearly delineated in the final passage. The long, descriptive lines of spiritual illumination one finds here are developed more fully in Roethke's later "North American Sequence."

The cumulative result of this poem, with its experimental childlike rhythms interspersed with adult reflection, its varying line lengths of free verse, and its enigmatic, often disconnected narrative, is to approximate a spiritual journey. The overall form of this stream-of-consciousness technique re-creates his "history of the psyche (or allegorical journey) . . . a succession of experiences, similar yet dissimilar. There is a perpetual slipping-back, then a going-forward; but there is *some* progress" ("Open Letter").

Themes and Meanings

The journey that "The Lost Son" poems represent is the universal experience of individuation. According to psychologist Carl Jung, who formulated this theory, individuation is a process of development arising from the conflict of the conscious and unconscious psychic states. A person can never be whole until both states are given equal attention and exist in equilibrium.

"The Shape of the Fire" illustrates Roethke's attempt to achieve this psychological balance by exploring both psychic states. The regression to childhood, where the line between the conscious and unconscious is blurred, is Roethke's starting point in his search for himself. His use of preconscious imagery as signposts for his own identity is what characterizes his poetry.

The dreamlike imagery represents a night journey; an exploration of the interior of the country also represents a descent into his unconscious. The water, the cave, the elemental natural images are indicative of birth, rebirth, and the depths of the mind all at once. Thus, the poem moves between consciousness and unconscious states in order to achieve this archetypal spiritual wholeness.

"The Lost Son" poems often contain initiation rituals. Parts 1-3 of "The Shape of the Fire" use the elements of initiation rites: the natural signposts; the frightening adults who guide him (the witch, the flat-headed man); the sexual rite, during which he becomes an "uneasy man"; and finally, the mysterious wisdom he receives in part 3. Initiation is an important part of the individuation process for Roethke, whose poetry is obsessed with finding himself and his place in the world.

The last two parts of "The Shape of the Fire" begin Roethke's quest for mature mystical illumination, which comes to fruition with "The Rose" in "The North American Sequence." Here he looks for a sacred time of origins, a time out of time, "further back" when he was part of nature, "mov[ing] through a dream of wakening blossoms." This part of the poem harkens back to another of Roethke's mentors, William Wordsworth, who sees the child as coming from the universal truth of God into the corrupt world of civilization. Roethke is very much a Romantic poet in his association of mystical truths with nature and his fear of the frantic pace and despoiling aspects of urban life.

Thus, for all his personal imagery and subjectivity, Roethke is primarily a poet of archetypal themes. He said of his poems, "I can feel very impersonal about them for they seem to come from a tapping of an older memory—something that dribbled out of the unconscious, as it were, the racial memory." (*The Selected Letters of Theodore Roethke*, 1968). The evocative power of a poem such as "The Shape of the Fire" resides in the transformation of personal experience through images and symbols into universal experience. If originality marks these poems, it is the originality of the great poet who can see through his experience to the collective memory of all.

Sandra J. Holstein

SHE WALKS IN BEAUTY

Author: George Gordon, Lord Byron (1788-1824)
Type of poem: Lyric
First published: 1815, in *Hebrew Melodies Ancient and Modern*

The Poem

"She Walks in Beauty" is a short poem, consisting of three six-line stanzas. On the surface it is a fairly conventional description of a beautiful woman, evidently someone with whom Byron is acquainted. The poet does not identify her by name, indicate his relationship to her, or hint as to the occasion that brought them together. (Scholars have ferreted out these matters.) Even if such information is not essential to understanding the poem, it is surprising that Byron provides so little concrete detail about the actual appearance of the woman he is describing. He does not speak of her as tall or short, slender or statuesque; he does not tell his readers the color of her dress or the color of her eyes. In fact, at the end of the poem the only specific fact the reader knows is that she has black hair.

Nevertheless, there is no doubt that the lady has made a definite impression on the poet. To him, she is beautiful in the same way that "night" is beautiful, and, as he hastens to add, he means a particular kind of night, one of "cloudless climes and starry skies." There is no threat of a storm in this imagined landscape; there are no clouds to produce even a shower. Such a night is not really dark, for, as readers are told, the sky is filled with stars. Their light is soft and subdued; similarly, the dark lady has "tender" eyes, as unlike those of less subtle women as the light of a "starry" night is from that of "gaudy day."

Byron proceeds to amplify his earlier suggestion that a perfect combination of "dark and bright" is the secret of his subject's beauty. The second stanza of the poem begins with an explicit statement to this effect: either more or less light, he insists, would have at least to some degree "impair'd" her "grace." At this point, the poet finally gives his readers a clue as to what may have triggered his response, for it appears that the lady does have "raven" hair. However, Byron does not have so specific an explanation for the brightness of "her face." He does not seem to mean that she has a rosy complexion; instead, it is her "thoughts serenely sweet," so evident in her facial expressions, that account for the impression she makes on all those who observe her.

In the final stanza, Byron continues to explore the relationship between inner and outer beauty. The blushes that appear on the lady's "cheek," her "smiles," everything on her "brow," or countenance, all reveal her sterling virtue. In the last lines of the poem, Byron sums up what he surmises: that the lady spends much of her time doing good deeds, that her "mind" harbors no animosity toward anyone, and that when love enters her heart, it is an "innocent" emotion. Byron's description of a dark-haired lady thus becomes much more: It is also his definition of the ideal woman.

Forms and Devices

Though Byron may have rebelled against tradition in other ways, his poems are generally conventional in form. "She Walks in Beauty" is no exception. It is written in standard iambic tetrameter, with alternating rhymes, a new set in each stanza. Metrically, the poem is quite predictable; there are none of the lilting anapestic variations so familiar in Byron's other works, but stately measures are appropriate for a woman who is herself so decorous. The masculine line endings and the use of end-stopped lines, alternating with lines which necessitate a pause, recall the neoclassical heroic couplet, a form Byron much admired. However, here there is no satire nor epigrammatic wit; instead, the purpose of the form is to ensure the slow progress of the poem, thus emphasizing the lady's dignity, her steadiness, and her self-control.

The poem is also interesting in the degree to which it is dominated by a single simile. Although after the first stanza the poet abandons explicit references to the night, throughout the poem he emphasizes the idea of perfect balance, not only between dark and light but also between thought and action, mind and heart.

Nevertheless, though "She Walks in Beauty" praises harmony, it has other implications as well, reminding one that, for all his neoclassical dedication to form and balance, Byron was, after all, a Romantic. To a degree, the images work to deny the poet's explicit statements, for although the pace of the poem is in keeping with its praise of tranquillity, its images stress movement and therefore the inevitability of change. Byron's lady is not posing, but walking. She is shown in motion, her hair waving, her "eloquent" face expressive as she responds to the world around her and to her own thoughts—sometimes with smiles, sometimes with blushes. These small alterations imply that just as the stars will move in the night sky and night itself turn to day, the lady will change. Only in the poem will she remain forever lovely and innocent.

Themes and Meanings

Byron's biographers agree about the occasion that inspired the poem. On June 11, 1814, Byron is said to have attended a party, perhaps a ball, at the home of a Lady Sitwell, and there to have seen for the first time his young cousin by marriage, Mrs. Robert John Wilmot, dressed in a black mourning dress adorned with spangles. Supposedly Byron wrote "She Walks in Beauty" either the same night or early the next morning.

If the account of Mrs. Wilmot's gown is accurate, it is easy to see why Byron thought of a starry night when he looked at the young beauty. Moreover, though death is not actually mentioned in "She Walks in Beauty," the fact that the lady's dark clothing was a token of mourning makes it likely that the conventional association of night and death was in Byron's mind as he wrote the poem.

This interpretation also helps to explain why Byron included the poem in the volume *Hebrew Melodies*. One of Byron's friends had suggested that the poet and a young composer, Isaac Nathan, collaborate in producing a volume of songs in the Hebrew folk tradition, and Byron agreed to work with Nathan on the collection. For that reason, a great many of the lyrics that Byron wrote take as their subject matter characters and stories from the Old Testament. Byron not only included "She Walks in Beauty" in the volume but also made a point of asking Nathan to have it appear first in every edition of *Hebrew Melodies*. The most obvious explanation is that Byron usually placed what he considered his best poem in a collection first. Since "She Walks in Beauty" is one of Byron's most anthologized poems, evidently in this case the poet's judgment was accurate.

There may also be a thematic justification for Byron's using "She Walks in Beauty" to introduce *Hebrew Melodies*. Certainly it is the depiction of an ideal woman. One has only to look at the modifiers to see why this woman would be so easy to live with: "tender," "softly," "serenely," "sweet," "pure," "soft," and "calm." It is, however, significant that the final word of the poem is "innocent." Byron's ideal may be viewed as a portrait of Eve before the Fall, appropriately placed first here, as it is in the Old Testament.

"She Walks in Beauty" is one of the few optimistic lyrics in *Hebrew Melodies*. The later poems show human beings as fallen creatures in a fallen world. What scant hope there is may come through art. For example, in the second poem in the collection, "The Harp the Monarch Minstrel Swept," King David's songs elevate humanity above its fallen condition. However, generally life is shown as essentially tragic and probably meaningless. In "Jephtha's Daughter," an innocent young woman is forced into martyrdom. In "All Is Vanity, Saith the Preacher," it is asserted that even poetry is helpless against despair.

Any discussion of the meaning of "She Walks in Beauty" should also point out how inconsistent Byron's admiration of the woman is with his own Romantic tendencies. This ideal woman has the neoclassical virtues of reason, moderation, and self-control. By contrast, Romantics value feeling above reason. Byron usually shows rebellion as proof of intellectual independence, excess as a road to truth, and passion as an indication that one is truly alive. Considering the rest of his works, as well as his life, it is ironic that Byron was so drawn to the virtuous lady he describes in "She Walks in Beauty." On the other hand, it is only human to value that which we ourselves have lost and which, unfortunately, will probably not long survive in this fallen world.

Rosemary M. Canfield Reisman

THE SHEPHERD'S WEEK

Author: John Gay (1685-1732)
Type of poem: Mock pastoral
First published: 1714

The Poem

The Shepherd's Week is a series of six poems, each representing one of the days of the week; Sunday has been omitted, ostensibly for religious reasons. The title establishes these poems as pastorals, and they do derive from the pastoral tradition. Five of the six are based on the *Eclogues* of the Roman poet Vergil, dated between 43 and 37 B.C. (English translation, 1575), which in turn were influenced by the idylls of Greek poet Theocritus, written about 270 B.C. However, though Gay acknowledges his debt to his predecessors, *The Shepherd's Week* is not a conventional pastoral. Gay substitutes the unlettered, realistic characters of his own English countryside for the usual elegant, artificial shepherds and shepherdesses who use the rural scene only as a backdrop. For this reason and because of its comic tone, *The Shepherd's Week* is customarily described not as a pastoral but as a mock pastoral.

In his prose introduction to *The Shepherd's Week* entitled "The Proeme to the Courteous Reader," Gay announces his intention: to write a "simple Eclogue" in the Theocritan mode, thus demonstrating to the poets of his age what a pastoral should be. Gay comments at length on the influence of "maister Spencer" (Edmund Spenser) and the *Shepheardes Calendar* (1579) on his own work in terms of structure and even the names of his characters. "The Proeme" ends with an explanation of his choice of language. The "Prologue," which follows, is addressed to Henry St. John, First Viscount Bolingbroke, the great Tory leader and a member of the poet's circle. Gay describes the shepherds' grief upon hearing a rumor that their monarch, Queen Anne, has died and their relief when they find that she is alive and well, having been saved by her physician, Dr. John Arbuthnot, another of Gay's friends. Arriving at court to see Arbuthnot, though he does happen to have with him the poems for Bolingbroke, Gay notes how different this world is from the one he left. Then he performs as expected. He praises the most prominent courtiers present, lauds the Tory leadership, and modestly presents his completed "Eclogues" to Bolingbroke, assuring him that if there were any possibility that his verse would interfere with statecraft, he would gladly "burn book, preface, notes and all."

Each of the six poems in *The Shepherd's Week* has its own cast of characters and its own drama. "Monday; or, The Squabble" begins with two lovesick shepherds discussing their miseries. Lobbin Clout is enamored of Blouzelinda, while Cuddy cannot sleep for thinking of his Buxoma. They decide to have a contest to see which of them can best praise his mistress in song, with the sage Cloddipole serving as a judge. Before long, Cloddipole's patience wears thin. He stops the competition without declaring a winner and sends the two shepherds off to water the neglected livestock. In "Tuesday; or, The Ditty," Marian bemoans the fact that she has lost her beloved

Colin to Cic'ly. Her error, she thinks, may be in having given Colin a knife, for superstition teaches that knives "*always sever love.*" These speculations are cut short, however, when Goody Dobbins arrives to have her cow serviced, for Marian must bring out the necessary bull.

"Wednesday; or, The Dumps" is about Sparabella's abandonment by Bumkinet, who is so blind that he prefers Clumsilis to her. Remembering how her love for Bumkinet enabled her to resist the advances of the local squire, Sparabella waxes bitter about love and finally resolves to kill herself. However, she cannot find a satisfactory method of committing suicide, and, since night has fallen, she decides to postpone any drastic action until the next day. In "Thursday; or, The Spell," another maiden is faced with the loss of her lover, but Hobnelia is a practical person who always has a remedy at hand. Throughout her relationship with Lubberkin, Hobnelia has routinely used spells to keep him in line. She explains these spells in detail, ending with a description of how she obtained a love potion for use in this present crisis. Fortunately, this time nature, not the supernatural, comes to her rescue. Suddenly Lubberkin turns up in an amorous mood, and Hobnelia, who dreads the thought of dying a virgin, is more than willing to cooperate with him.

The subject of "Friday; or, The Dirge" is not love but death. Bumkinet returns from an absence ready to "quaff a cheary bowl" with his friends, only to learn that their Blouzelinda has died. Sadly, he recalls happier days. As in traditional pastorals, nature itself is urged to grieve for the lost maiden, and Grubbinol insists that all living creatures seem aware of her death. He then proceeds to a poignant account of the scene at Blouzelinda's deathbed during which she expressed her wishes concerning both the disposition of her small treasures and her simple funeral. The shepherds do not think that they will ever cease to grieve for Blouzelinda. Then they see "bonny *Susan*" and transport her to the ale house where, with "ale and kisses," they manage to "forget their cares."

The central character of "Saturday; or, The Flights" is Bowzybeus, who, though a drunkard, is acknowledged to be the Muse's darling. Roused from his stupor by the local lasses, he pulls himself together and, obviously inspired, puts on an impressive performance. Bowzybeus sings about nature and the supernatural; he transports his listeners to a fair like the one he has just attended, with its peddlers and mountebanks; he recites the old, familiar ballads; and at one point he even intones a psalm. Then the music stops. After receiving the kisses that will be his only reward, Bowzybeus again falls asleep. Thus both the day and *The Shepherd's Week* come to an end.

Forms and Devices

Even if, as he insists, Gay intended to avoid the usual artifice in his pastoral, *The Shepherd's Week* is clearly the work of a highly self-conscious artist. For example, at the end of "The Proeme," the poet identifies the language used by his characters as his own invention. He explains that though it is certainly not what one would hear at court, neither is it any identifiable rural dialect. Some of the characters' expressions are very modern, but a good many of them are archaic. In case some future "lover of

Simplicity" should arise to translate *The Shepherd's Week* into a "modern dialect," Gay has helpfully included "glosses and explications of uncouth pastoral terms." This machinery is part of the joke, for any writer knowledgeable enough to provide it would have been able to make his language as consistent as he wished.

It is also important to note that this supposedly artless work is highly allusive. It has been pointed out, for example, that all but one of the poems are based on specific Vergilian eclogues. "Tuesday," the exception, has a contemporary model, for it was designed to fulfill the criteria for a "Pastoral Ballad" set forth by Gay's fellow poet Alexander Pope in *The Guardian*. There are also many allusions to classical mythology in *The Shepherd's Week*. For instance, the drunken Bowzybeus is clearly drawn from Silenus, one-time tutor and thereafter follower of Bacchus, the Greek god of wine. There is more to the resemblance, however, than the enthusiasm for strong drink: When he is inspired, Bowzybeus appears almost godlike. Gay does not draw his allusions only from classical sources. His characters have an ancient oral culture of their own. They quote old proverbs, as Lobbin Clout does in "Monday" when he insists that "Love is blind"; like Hobnelia, they live by spells and superstitions; and they respond enthusiastically when Bowzybeus sings the ballads they know so well. The fact that Gay does not aid his reader by footnoting his allusions while he spends so much effort on the language is still another indication of his tongue-in-cheek attitude toward his subject matter, his readers, and the work itself.

The verse form used for *The Shepherd's Week* is particularly effective for comic and satirical purposes. Consisting of a pair of rhymed end-stopped lines, the eighteenth century heroic couplet not only has the classical virtue of symmetry but also lends itself beautifully to epigram, antithesis, and comic reversals. "Tuesday," for instance, contains numerous examples of artistically satisfying parallelism, such as "In ev'ry wood his carrols sweet were known,/ At ev'ry wake his nimble feats were shown." After giving examples of Marian's inability to continue her usual tasks, Gay sums up the situation with an epigrammatic comment: "For yearning love the witless maid employs,/ and *Love*, say swains, *all busie heed destroys*." In "Monday," Lobbin Clout calls to his sweetheart in well-crafted antitheses: "Come *Blouzelinda*, ease thy swain's desire,/ My summer's shadow and my winter's fire." The funniest passages in the poems, however, are those in which the poet or his characters indulge in sentiment and then, within the space of a couplet or two, reverse the mood with a reminder of reality. Thus in the last four lines of "Tuesday," Marian stops weeping when a cow is brought to be bred. Not only does she "dry her tears," but she also takes care of business and makes sure that she is paid.

Gay's imagery, too, reflects the frequent changes of mood and tone that are meant to keep the reader off balance. For example, in "Friday," Bumkinet's "doleful dirge" provides a generalized and idealized version of grieving nature, with its "dewy sorrow," its "ev'ning tears," and its "rolling streams" with their "watry grief." On the other hand, the hogs "wallowing 'mid a feast of acorns" and the detailed description of the butter-churning process are highly realistic, as are the elements of the dying girl's will. Generally, the poet moves from idealized images to realistic ones rather than the converse. Thus in the final two verse paragraphs of "Friday," he first presents some conventional scenes in conventional language. His bulls standing with "curled brow" and his maidens at their milking might have come from any bucolic landscape. However, Gay's images soon become much less picturesque. His hogs in "sinking mire" and his moles at work thus prepare for the realistic conclusion of the poem. The description of "bonny *Susan*" in flight, pursued and captured by the shepherds, is not only more vivid than the earlier conventional imagery, but it also emphasizes the difference between literature and life. Thus, with consummate skill, Gay utilizes various poetic technique to underscore his ideas.

Themes and Meanings

Because satire cuts two ways, sometimes three or four, it is always subject to misinterpretation. However, even the most prominent scholars of eighteenth century literature admit that they are uncertain as to the purpose and meaning of *The Shepherd's Week*. There are a number of theories. It is sometimes argued that Gay's work is in large part merely a burlesque of the pastoral pattern. On the other hand, English writer Samuel Johnson and others have believed it to be a worthy example of what a pastoral should be. The moving account of Blouzelinda's death would certainly support this view. Some critics believe that *The Shepherd's Week* was intended to parody the Vergilian eclogues on which five of Gay's poems are based; others believe that it was written in order to ridicule the poet's contemporary Ambrose Philips, who had fallen out with Gay's friend Pope. It has even been argued that references to the popular songwriter Thomas D'Urfey are in fact an oblique attack on Philips.

Some resolve these critical difficulties by saying that perhaps *The Shepherd's Week* has no single target but is, in essence, just one *jeu d'esprit* after another, united in that they all reflect the poet's perception of the absurd in human conduct. Thus in "The Proeme," first Gay plays himself as he attacks the literary establishment with its "critical gallimawfry"; then he assumes the mask of unctuous piety, insisting that only "great clerks" should comment on religion and explaining that he omits Sunday from his week for religious reasons; finally, with his explanation of the language and with his footnotes, he pretends to be pedantic. By the end of "The Proeme," Gay has satirized at least three kinds of absurdity, and a careful examination of the comments addressed to the reader leads one to suspect that there is probably a fourth because anyone who would take such obsequious flattery at face value would, without question, qualify as a fool.

The contrast between rural and urban life, which is a standard theme of pastoral poems, is basic to *The Shepherd's Week*. In the traditional pastoral, however, worldly people such as those in the "Prologue" are simply transported to the country, where they spend their time brandishing their crooks, observing sheep, and composing poetry. Gay's characters, on the other hand, are country bred and naïvely unaware of the outside world. Often they are very funny, as when, in "Monday," the two lovers descend from high-flown sentiments to descriptions of food. Whenever he appears to mock his rural folk, however, Gay is once again setting a trap for his readers. If they laugh at real shepherds and shepherdesses because they think of them as a different breed from themselves, it is the urban sophisticates, not the rural innocents, who are the real fools.

Nowhere is the thematic complexity of *The Shepherd's Week* more evident than in the treatment of sex. In his "Prologue," Gay points to the gathering of wealth as the primary motivation of England's ruling classes. Indeed, their only interest in the rural population is in what they produce. Gay does not have to remind readers that among such people marriages are matters of contract and that what they call love is, like poetry, a mere diversion from "affairs of States and Kings." By contrast, Gay's shepherds and shepherdesses are refreshingly sincere. They fall passionately in love; they are miserable when the object of their affection is absent or indifferent or, worst of all, enamored of another; and when, as at the end of "Thursday," mutual desire and opportunity coincide, they couple ecstatically, without thought of the consequences. Eventually these young lovers will marry, settle down, and work toward the wisdom of the old. At the moment, however, they are simply responding to the urgings of nature.

In implicitly contrasting the artificial existences of city dwellers with the natural lives of country folk, Gay is doing what the best pastoral poems have always done. Even though he sometimes mocks the excesses of the pastoral convention and even light-heartedly laughs at his simple characters, Gay's mock pastoral was not written either as an attack on the form itself or as a satire of rural life. Indeed, the materialistic courtiers could learn much from the shepherds and shepherdesses in Gay's poem. There is much about them to admire. They are compassionate, capable of honest joy and grief, and highly practical. After their flights of fancy, they always get back to work, for whatever one's emotional condition, the cattle must be watered and the cream must be churned. They may seem ignorant, even foolish, but they know secrets that cosmopolitan readers could never comprehend: how to adjust to the rhythms of nature and how to keep their balance in success and failure, happiness and frustration, life and death. Unlike at least some of Gay's readers, they have no inflated sense of their own importance but are, instead, keenly aware of their participation in the great cycle of death and rebirth. After Blouzelinda, Susan may bring her own kind of joy, but eventually, when the songs are over and "the sun descends," one has no choice but to succumb to sleep.

Rosemary M. Canfield Reisman

SINCERELY

Author: Naomi Shihab Nye (1952-   )
Type of poem: Epistle/letter in verse
First published: 1994, in *Red Suitcase*

The Poem

"Sincerely" is a cleverly constructed seventy-nine-line poem about the art and craft of letter writing. Its author, inspired by her Palestinian-American heritage and extensive travels to Asia, the Middle East, and Central America, considers correspondence from friends, family, and strangers a fascinating subject. She begins the six-part poem by describing envelopes as "usually white and slim,/ bleached as a shell we might press to our ears." Letters, she suggests, are full of mystery, humor, pathos, and joy. Within the first few lines, Naomi Shihab Nye poses several thought-provoking questions about letters: What are their unique shapes and sizes? Where do they travel in their long journey from one place to another? What do they bring us? Most important, what do they demand from us?

As if to illustrate the answers, Nye shares brief portions of five letters, each presumably a response to an earlier epistle. The first begins "Thank you. The articles about raising children/ arrived when my child was being very difficult." Sometimes letters come with much needed advice. Unfortunately, in this particular case the narrator lost the parenting articles before she could put their helpful hints to use. Nevertheless, because she is grateful for the kind gesture, in return she encloses a brochure listing places to buy Hawaiian clothing in Texas, "should you have a need." With this exchange Nye humorously illustrates that letters provide an avenue for reciprocal sharing of a wealth of information, some useful, some fanciful.

The poem's second section opens with a letter writer's familiar apology: "I am sorry I did not answer for so long." As if to explain, the writer describes an important professional project that has consumed all her time; it involves writing to poets in sixty-eight countries asking for permission to publish their poems. This daunting letter-writing task, which costs 95 cents per letter, has prevented the speaker from penning personal letters to friends. She attempts to correct this situation in part 3 by responding to a woman who has lived on an island her entire life but who is now leaving. Ironically, the narrator longs to revisit the island, whose beauty has stayed with her since her visit many years before: "your island/ stays lodged inside me, a mint/ I turn over and over with my tongue for its endless/ flavor." It is apparent that the two writers would like to change places, just as their letters do, but they cannot.

In section 4 the speaker marvels at how the mail system permits individuals who barely met, "barely brushed one another" in the rush of life, to become friends and to share ideas, books, and cherished possessions that link their diverse communities. The final section appropriately celebrates the wonder and richness of new acquaintances who arrive by mail with a hello "so long and wide/ whole countries live inside it." These enlightening and welcome missives bring descriptions of each tree and corner in another part of the world. Ending the poem with a return to shape and size, Nye symbolically suggests that letters should be made in the shape of kites to ride "the ache of breeze" that lies between the correspondents.

Forms and Devices

Figurative language abounds in Nye's lively poem about the power of the written word. Engaging the reader's fancy, she employs personification to explore the human qualities of letters. She calls them "travelers" who journey through "slots and chutes and shelves and bags" and then, because often it is a very long and tiring journey, fall asleep in the narrator's black mailbox. When she slices open the letters with the blade of a small knife taken from "a case carved like a fish," this simple gesture "opens a far world" as news from friends and family pours forth, "cranking the creaky door of the heart." Sometimes, visited by an "impudent question," she wonders if she is equal to the task of responding. Like the words of the letters she receives, Nye's words touch and enlighten readers. Poet William Stafford has praised Nye's poetry for combining "transcendent liveliness and sparkle along with warmth and human insight." He calls her "a champion of encouragement and heart."

One reason for Naomi Shihab Nye's appeal is her skillful use of metaphor to examine gently the interplay of countries and cultures. In the third section, the letter to her island friend, the speaker compares her memory of the island to a mint, rolling around on her tongue as she absorbs and savors the flavor. This sweetness sharply contrasts with the other woman's aching desire to leave the same island. Her friend wears "the colors of the horizon inside [her] bruise," suggesting that the reality of her life is surely nothing like the speaker's delicious island memory. One of the ways readers come to understand the complexity of other cultures is by sharing stories. Nye introduces this intimacy through juxtaposed events, images, and bits of dialogue, which in a sense become for the reader an overheard long-distance conversation.

The poetic discourse of "Sincerely" consists of a series of questions, of the sort one typically asks friends in correspondence, such as "Yes, I am fine. . . . What about you?" and, in reference to a long lapse between letters, "Can you be patient?" Later in the poem, as she ponders sending a woolen doll from Chiapas to a new friend, she asks, "Do you want her?" The questioning draws readers into the epistolary exchange, and although they hear only half the conversation, they may occasionally be tempted to answer, to slip into a new role, thereby better understanding cultures outside their own experience. Nye elicits this reader response so subtly that the effect may be overlooked.

Themes and Meanings

The collection from which this poem comes, *Red Suitcase*, is filled with global travels and the curiosity and richness engendered by life's journeys. Poet and literary critic Alicia Ostriker has written that "Naomi Shihab Nye is at home in this world . . . a world that includes the Middle East and Texas, men and women, childhood, parenthood and old age, the pain of war and exile." She brings a particularly accepting and peaceful vision to her poetry that transcends political difference and transforms singular lives into global communities. "Sincerely," as its title suggests, offers an epistolary method and a truth-seeking heart for this important undertaking. Nye's favorite motif of travel is explored in new ways. As the speaker reflects upon the entire letter-writing phenomenon, she says, "Think of the waves and wires/ this envelope must cross. The mountains and muddles." It seems almost a miracle that people worldwide can connect in this way.

An important consideration for Naomi Shihab Nye is that letters (and her poem about letters) can be used to enhance global and personal understanding. Often people are consumed by their own lives—their children, their jobs, or as Nye says, "the flood of comings-and-goings." While they may not think they have the time or interest to learn about other cultures, letters provide the perfect opportunity. While letter writing may appear to be a simple act, there exists another layer of meaning beneath the words. One of Nye's earlier collections of poetry about ethnic diversity, acceptance, and peace is entitled *Words Under the Words* (1995), and "Sincerely," too, shows an emphasis on subtext, on the lives behind the words. These range from the speaker's busy professional literary life to the lonely life of her friend living "on the cliff so long,/ staring off to sea dreaming what lies/ on the other side." The island dweller believes that big U.S. cities are "what is happening." The poet's vision, however, casts doubt on the assumption that Western ways are the "right" or only ways. Never one to coerce her readers, Nye considerately packs a suitcase big enough for everyone and says, "Come along." If readers welcome new vistas and experiences, they will find her a sensitive and compassionate guide.

Carol F. Bender

SIR PATRICK SPENS

Author: Unknown
Type of poem: Ballad
First published: 1765, in *Reliques of Ancient English Poetry*

The Poem

"Sir Patrick Spens" is a well-known and popular ballad of unknown origin. The poem has many versions, with considerable variation in length and detail, as indicated in Francis James Child's extensive five-volume collection, *The English and Scottish Popular Ballads* (1882-1898), which includes eighteen versions under the title "Sir Patrick Spence." The most widely known version is a composite one with modernized spelling which appears in volume 1 of *The Norton Anthology of English Literature*, starting with the first edition in 1962.

In the most common version, the poem has eleven stanzas, each consisting of four lines, with the second and fourth lines rhyming. Even in the modernized version, the language suggests a long-ago Scots dialect that is more easily understood when the words are said aloud than when they are seen printed on the page. This is entirely appropriate and in keeping with the history of ballads, anonymous narrative songs that were preserved by oral transmission long before they were written down.

It is also typical of ballads that the historical events which might have led to the creation of the ballad are unclear. It is not known which king might be referred to in the poem or if there ever was an actual Sir Patrick Spens. Connecting details, such as why the king ordered Sir Patrick Spens to sea, where he was headed, or why the Scots lords were aboard the ship, are not given, but the stark tragedy is clear.

"Sir Patrick Spens," like most traditional ballads, relates a sad and tragic story of danger and death. The Scottish king, in Dumferline, wants a sailor to sail his ship. An old knight says that Sir Patrick Spens is the best sailor; the king writes and signs a letter, which is delivered to him as he is walking along the seacoast. At first Sir Patrick laughs at the order, then a tear blinds his eye and he asks who has done this "ill deed" to send him to sea at this time of the year (presumably winter, when the sea is at its roughest).

Sir Patrick Spens tells his men that they will sail in the morning. One man expresses the fear that there will be a deadly storm and that they will "come to harm," because he has seen an omen of danger, a circle rounding out the new moon. A group of Scots noblemen are aboard the ship when it sinks. The ladies on the shore will wait in vain for their return. They will never see Sir Patrick Spens or his passengers again. Instead, deep in the sea, halfway between somewhere and Aberdour, Scotland, there lies Sir Patrick Spens, with the Scots lords at his feet.

Forms and Devices

"Sir Patrick Spens" consists of quatrains (stanzas of four lines), with the second and fourth lines rhyming, a rhyme scheme commonly signified as *abcb*. The lines alternate between tetrameter (four metrical feet, or stressed syllables, per line) and trimeter (three feet per line). Such quatrains are called ballad stanzas. The basic meter is iambic, an unstressed syllable followed by a stressed (accented) syllable, the most commonly used poetic foot in English-language poetry. "Sir Patrick Spens" is virtually a model of the form of the traditional English ballad.

The regular meter, or beat, of the ballad is typical in that ballads were originally songs. The simplicity of the music to which they were sung not only influenced the distinctive verse form but also promoted a simplicity in the narrative itself. In addition, because they were oral, rather than written, over time stanzas were lost or forgotten, phrases altered, and details changed. Further changes were made as editors from the eighteenth through the twentieth century collated versions and selected phrases and lines they deemed most poetic or appropriate. Thus the narrative has an intense compression, a spareness that concentrates on the culmination of the action, on the heart of the tragedy.

The poem opens with an image: "The king sits . . . / Drinking the blude-reid wine." That blood-red wine is foreboding and immediately raises disturbing questions. Is the king capable of making sound judgments? Does he revel in asserting his authority? Does he understand the risk to all those he sends to sea? Imagery carries much of the drama of the story. After the king sends his letter, the fourth stanza shows Sir Patrick reading the orders. At first he laughs in disbelief, but he quickly understands its mortal import, and "a tear blinded his ee" (his eye). Nonetheless, he summons his crew. As so often occurs in ballads, some omen of death emphasizes the danger and psychologically increases the fear. An unnamed crew member laments that late the night before, "I saw the new moon/ Wi' the auld moon in her arm,/ And I fear..../ That we will come to harm."

The image of the crescent moon with the outline of the fully rounded moon was often believed to be an indication of severe storms to come, but in the poem there are no details of storms, winter seas, or a ship floundering and sinking. Juxtaposed with the image of the ominous moon, however, is an image of death by drowning. Here the poetic device is synecdoche, using a word that substitutes a part for the whole: The lords had worried about their cork-heeled shoes getting wet; now their hats float above the water.

The women will wait in vain for any of the lords or for Sir Patrick Spens, for they will "see thame na mair" (no more). The use of the age-old Scots dialect makes the entire poem, including the ending, seem more authentic; the words seem to come from the voice of the bard singer or a common person dolefully considering the inexorable workings of destiny. Deep under the water, "there lies guid Sir Patrick Spens."

Themes and Meanings

No historical Sir Patrick Spens or Spence is known. "Sir Patrick Spens" may be based on a thirteenth century historical event, or combination of events, involving a Scottish king's daughter or granddaughter being taken to or brought home from Norway. It may be a conflation of several different shipwrecks, focusing on the dangers of sailing and the supernatural omens that forewarn the doomed. It may simply be a story of suffering and loss that has no specific historical reference but is common to the human condition. Indeed, the ballad has a hauntingly universal appeal.

Many questions and themes emerge. The drowning seems needless, senseless. Yet there is at least a grudging admiration for Sir Patrick's prompt acquiescence to the king's unavoidable order and an even clearer sense that Sir Patrick's men go with him to sea because they are personally loyal and willing followers. One might wonder whether treachery was involved in the old knight's telling the king that Sir Patrick Spens was the best sailor. One might ask whether the king had an overwhelming reason to risk sending a ship to sea at a bad time of year and thought Sir Patrick was his only hope. Such concerns about human motivation have remained problematic throughout the centuries. The supernatural also continues to intrigue. Is there some unknown power that seeks to warn individuals about their actions? Is there some intuition, or some external projection of inner knowledge, that enables people to make optimal choices?

There are sociopolitical implications in the inclusion of the Scots lords, who appear in the numerous versions of the poem but are never explained. Although as in most ballads there is no editorial commentary, it is clear that Sir Patrick Spens is more admirable than the lords, particularly in the depiction of the lords as being so fussy that they did not want to get their fancy cork-heeled shoes wet even while aboard a ship and in the wry finality of their hats floating on the water. They themselves are not merely drowned with Sir Patrick but are "at his feet" in the watery grave.

A similar attitude is taken toward the ladies who sit with their fans in their hands and stand with their gold combs in their hair, waiting fruitlessly for their lords to return. These are not hard-working peasant women longing for the return of their husbands or sons. These ladies, like their lords, are pictured as the idle rich, perhaps as insensitive and demanding of others as the king may be.

These motifs do not lessen the impact of the narrative. Rather, everything adds to the impact of the loss of good Sir Patrick, to the finality of the loss of the ship and all aboard, and to the sense of events often being the result of forces beyond any individual control. At some level, the human spirit often finds itself crying out, with Sir Patrick Spens, "O wha is this has done this deed,/ This ill deed done to me"—and yet, the poem suggests, the individual continues to act, and at best proceeds with courage in the face of whatever storms may blow.

Lois A. Marchino

SIR WALTER RALEGH TO THE QUEEN

Author: Sir Walter Ralegh (c. 1552-1618)
Type of poem: Lyric
First published: 1655, in *Wits Interpreter*; collected in *The Poems of Sir Walter Raleigh*, 1813

The Poem

Written sometime between 1581 and 1587, "Sir Walter Ralegh to the Queen," a thirty-eight-line lyrical poem in five stanzas, directly addresses Queen Elizabeth I of England. The queen has perhaps criticized Ralegh's failure to write love poems for her recently as indicative of his lack of affection or passion. His poem is meant to refute such criticism and to explain that his love is indeed true and unwavering despite his poetic silence. His organizing idea is the difference between true love and false love—with his love, of course, being true and others' love false.

His initial image compares human passions to "floods and streams" to argue that shallow passions, like shallow streams, "murmur," while deep passions, like deep floods of water, remain silent because of their natures. His conclusion on the basis of this analogy is that those who speak or write much about their inner feelings of affection in reality feel no such affection. If they are very verbal and outspoken about their emotions ("rich in words"), they will be lacking in the deeper affections characteristic of a lover and will be incompetent in the true art of love ("poor in that which makes a lover"). The second stanza applies the general rule to the particular case and asks the Queen, whom Ralegh praises as the "dear Empress" or ruler of his heart, not to misunderstand the value and nature of true passion. He asks her not to think that he feels no pain at her silence or their separation just because he does not beg her to be more compassionate and to take pity on his sad state. Instead, his silence is indicative of the depths of his genuine regard. Furthermore, if he does not write love poems complaining that she misunderstands how deeply her beauty has conquered his heart, the cause is not from any absence of love on his part but from "excess of duty" or a sense of obligation to her as queen.

The third stanza explains further. Ralegh says that because he knows that he seeks to serve a perfect saint, whose returned affection all desire but none deserve, he chooses to endure pain and grief rather than reveal his feelings. His strong, passionate feelings would compel him to write love poems to her, but because she is too high above him in rank, status, and perfection, and in fact too high above all other potential human lovers, discretion, reason, and devotion make him choose to be her suitor from afar, to love in silence. This silence, he argues, betokens a deeper sorrow at the distance that separates them than words could. Though words, of course, might be wittier, they would be more superficial. As a "beggar" who cannot speak, he argues that he deserves more pity than those who openly complain about their lovelorn state. His final appeal is for the queen, his "dearest heart," not to misread his secret passion, a passion he swears is true. Ultimately, he asks for her compassion for the deep pain he hides at the same time that he asserts that he asks for no compassion. (The psychological game is like that employed in William Shakespeare's Sonnet 130, claiming not to be doing something while doing something.) Thus, in a poem that is a love complaint, Ralegh claims not to be writing love complaints out of courtesy and love for his queen. He claims that silent suffering is more indicative of love than writing a poem in which he presents himself as the silent sufferer.

Forms and Devices

Scholarly debate has questioned whether "Sir Walter Ralegh to the Queen" (sometimes called "The Silent Lover" or "To the Queen") is truly a five-stanza poem or two poems merged: "Sir Walter to the Queen" (one stanza) and "Wrong not, Dear Empress of my Heart" (four stanzas). Certainly, the first stanza differs in form from the last four. It contains four lines with alternating end rhyme (*abab*) and then a concluding couplet (*cc*), all in iambic pentameter. The remaining four stanzas have eight lines each, an alternating rhyme that changes sound sets after the first four lines (*ababcdcd*), and iambic tetrameter. However, the stanzas are unified by imagery and argument, and major Ralegh specialists argue that they belong together. Lines 1, 3, and 5 of the first stanza have variations on the iambic meter, lines 3 and 4 are enjambed, and the couplet has a feminine rhyme; such variations recur throughout the remaining stanzas.

Ralegh rhymes "prove" with "love" and "utter" with "suitor," sounds that no longer rhyme in English but that did in Renaissance England. The word "Plaints" is a shortened form of "Complaints" and refers to a special convention of love poetry—the love complaint, in which the lover complains about ill treatment at the hands of an indifferent or uncaring lover, all to win her pity and compassion and perhaps an admission of returned affection. Ralegh must be cautious here because his audience is not a real lover or even a would-be lover but the queen, on whom his fortune depends, and his poem, though privately passed around a limited court circle, was nonetheless a public statement, not an intimate, private communication.

As a literate and unmarried queen, Elizabeth enjoyed playing the witty game of love through poetry as a way to bind her courtiers to her. As a court favorite who had many enemies, Ralegh had to move between flattery and witty gamesmanship—he had to flatter, entertain, and win the queen's favor and support. The poem depends on a central image to make its argument: passions compared to floods and streams that can sweep one up in their power. Shallow, noisy streams of little force are contrasted with deep, silent channels of force and power. This comparison was a standard Renaissance image. Sir Edward Dyer's "The lowest trees have tops," for example, similarly asserts, "Where waters smoothest run, deep are the fords," and "True hearts have ears and eyes, no tongues to speak," while Sir Philip Sidney's *Arcadia* (I,127) notes, "Shallow brooks murmur most, deep silent slide away." The watery nature of the image would be connected with the Renaissance idea of the four humors that control human behavior—in this case emphasizing blood, which would motivate the lover and cause passion to overwhelm reason. It would also wittily play with the queen's nickname for Ralegh. Others called him simply "Wat," but she called him her "Water," since he sailed the seas winning booty and new lands for her. Ralegh plays his own variations on the water image and theme, managing to have things two ways: He asserts his passion in the image of deep, powerful waters but also his reason, which makes him do what duty and discretion demand rather than yield to personal feelings of love that would be presumptuous, given the difference in status between his beloved and himself.

Themes and Meanings

"Sir Walter Ralegh to the Queen" is an anatomy of love—its central theme is the difference between true love and false love: False love is hidden in a swirl of superficial verbiage; true love is painfully silent. Ralegh's argument follows traditional Renaissance themes and conventions. For instance, he emphasizes the traditional Elizabethan view of humankind as torn between passion and reason, emphasizing that his passion would lead him to write love poems (complaints), and praise the queen's saintly perfection, beauty, and glory in order to win her affection or at least to entertain her. In contrast to despairing lovelorn poetic narrators (such as Sir Thomas Wyatt in "Whoso list to hunt"), he has let reason dominate for the queen's sake. Revealing his affection openly would not only be indiscreet and subject to misinterpretation, given her high rank and the fact that so many others are also charmed by her, but would also be a denial of the depth of his true affection, which, like deep waters, is so strong that he must be silent. Another poetic convention of courtiers is exaggerated praise of the beloved, who here is acknowledged to be beyond the reach of mortals.

The poem's themes of secret love, of the despairing, agonizing lover, and of a potential for misunderstanding or public injury recur in Ralegh's poetry. They seem in keeping with Ralegh's ongoing poetic dialogue with his queen, although some modern commentators have attempted to attribute this poem to Sir Robert Ayton rather than to Ralegh. Inevitably, in such a poem, private meaning related to the daily personal conversations between the queen and her favorite would lie behind the public utterance, especially given Ralegh and the queen's love of theatrics and their long history of public performance of their interacting life roles. In "See those sweet eyes," for example, Ralegh expresses a similar sentiment and situation—the lover gazing on the "sweetest eyes" is unable to plead his case and praise his beloved's beauty because her greatness, her inexpressible merit, and his sense of duty force him into silence.

The uncertain chronology of the poem in terms of Ralegh's relationship with the queen leaves critics uncertain about the precise vicissitudes of Ralegh's career—whether he was in or out of favor—at the time this poem was written. What is known is that the poem was written to serve the needs of Ralegh's career and it fuses personal feeling with conventional arguments. Ralegh thus turns his life into art.

Gina Macdonald

SKIPPER IRESON'S RIDE

Author: John Greenleaf Whittier (1807-1892)
Type of poem: Ballad
First published: 1857; collected in *Home Ballads and Poems*, 1860

The Poem

"Skipper Ireson's Ride," a ballad in nine eleven-line stanzas, is a story told through a third-person narrator who reports on the words and actions of the poems's characters but does not take part in them. Typically, a ballad presents one dramatic or exciting episode, not a fully developed story. As the title suggests, "Skipper Ireson's Ride" focuses on one brief moment in the man's life: his ride out of the town of Marblehead, Massachusetts.

The poem opens by harkening back to strange rides from legends and fables that would have been familiar to Whittier's nineteenth century educated audience: Apuleius on a golden ass, the Tartar king Calendar's ride on a brass horse, and Muhammad's winged mule. The tone is at the same time grand and ridiculous. Soon Ireson takes his place among this strange company, for it is revealed that Skipper Ireson's ride is not on a swift horse or chariot, as might be expected. Instead, the refrain (repeated with slight variation at the end of each stanza) introduces

> Old Floyd Ireson, for his hard heart,
> Tarred and Feathered and carried in a cart
> By the women of Marblehead!

The next two stanzas take up the action *in medias res*, as the women struggle with the cart and hurl insults at Ireson. Whittier uses exaggerated comparisons to heighten the grim humor. Ireson appears as a "rained-on fowl" with "body of turkey, head of owl." The rioting women, on the other hand, are compared with the Maenads, female followers of Bacchus, as they might appear "wild-eyed, free-limbed," on an ancient vase.

In the fourth stanza the poet explains the reason for Ireson's punishment: When his ship was sinking, full of his own townspeople, he sailed away and left the crew to drown. No motive is given for this action; the poem is concerned only with the punishment itself, dealt out by women who have lost their men because of Ireson's actions. Stanza 5 mourns the wrecked ship that "shall lie forevermore" and the women who "looked for the coming that might not be." The tone of stanzas 4 and 5 is mournful, with no traces of humor.

The sixth stanza returns to the action as the cart passes through the town, and old women and men lean out of their homes cursing. Suddenly, with the seventh stanza, the tone changes again, to a peaceful and lyrical description of the beautiful Salem road. For the first time, the poet focuses on Ireson himself, who sits numbly, unaware of the beautiful flowers beside the road or of the voices shouting at him. In stanza 8,

Ireson speaks for the first and only time, crying out that he can bear this punishment from his neighbors, but he cannot bear to face God and his own guilt. The poem ends with the women deciding to leave further punishment to God. With "half scorn, half pity," they release him and leave him "alone with his shame and sin."

Forms and Devices

"Skipper Ireson's Ride" has often been considered the greatest American ballad of the nineteenth century. Part of its strength lies in Whittier's skillful juxtaposition of specific local elements—a common element in his most successful ballads—with references to the ancient world of classical poetry. The most obvious example of this juxtaposition occurs in the refrain. When the refrain is spoken by the narrator, it is in formal, educated language, but when the village women cry out the refrain, the poet presents their distinctive Marblehead dialect, and "Tarred and feathered and carried in a cart" becomes "Torr'd an' futherr'd an' corr'd in a corrt." No comment is made about the shift; the poet simply wants to reader to hear the poem told in two distinct voices.

Specific references to local geography, including the names of Marblehead, Chaleur Bay, and the Salem road, place the action of the poem firmly in the real world. At the same time, comparisons of Ireson to Apuleius or Muhammad, and of the women to conch-blowing followers of Bacchus, elevate the story to the realm of the fantastic. The women are both real-life residents of a real fishing village, surrounded by its fog and rain, hearing winds and sea-birds, smelling apple blossoms and lilacs, and also mythical creatures, the stuff of story and song. Again, the narrator does not call attention to the contrasts. This matter-of-fact juxtaposition claims for the story of Skipper Ireson a place among the greats; the rustic citizens of old Marblehead are not only poor fishing folk but also representatives of the passionate emotions that define humanity.

Those passionate emotions do not exist one at a time in the human heart. Love, hate, anger, pity, and sorrow may appear in one person all at once, especially in a time of grief. As the critic John Pickard has ably demonstrated, Whittier's sudden shifts in the poem echo the shifting emotions experienced by the surviving townspeople. Thus the focus moves abruptly in and out, backward and forward, from a wide historical overview to a direct look (but from a distance) at the feathered Ireson, from a wide-angle crowd scene to a flashback of the sinking ship, back to the crowd, then to a serene look at beautiful scenery followed by a tightly focused look at Ireson. Similarly, the background noises in the story change from "shouting and singing" with "conch-shells blowing and fish-horns' twang" to the shouted conversation between the doomed fishermen and Ireson, to the silence of the wrecked ship with only "winds and sea-birds" for sound, to the hoarse and "treble" cursing of the older villagers, to the calm beauty of the Salem road, and finally to Ireson's pitiable outcry and the women's "soft relentings." This cacophony of sound and silence, along with the shifting visual focus, keeps the reader off balance, heightening the dramatic tension.

Themes and Meanings

The meaning of "Skipper Ireson's Ride" is encapsulated in the refrain, in the central figure's transformation from "Old Floyd Ireson" in the first stanza to "Poor Floyd Ireson" in the last. During the poem, Ireson changes, or his neighbors' perception of him changes, from a man to be hated and cursed to one to be treated with scorn yet pity. The theme of a person coming to a new understanding is as old as literature, and often this acquisition of new knowledge or insight involves a journey. The journey might be a protracted one through a long work such as Homer's *The Odyssey* or Dante's *The Divine Comedy*, or a brief visit from city to country or from country to city, or even a short ride out of town on a rail. The technique of echoing a psychological or moral journey by a literal journey through space is effectively employed here.

For the characters of Whittier's New England poems, the themes of transformation and redemption, and of error and correction, were best understood in a Christian religious context. The mob of women who have tarred and feathered Skipper Ireson act from the human emotions of grief and rage, and they seek human vengeance. Their method of punishment is to humiliate Ireson, to make him (or show him to be) less than a man. Yet they are not fully human in their own actions; with the exception of the brief mournful passage in stanza 5, they are seen only as a mob, never as individuals.

When Ireson at last cries out his confession, everything changes. Instantly, the shouting stops. With his first cry of "Hear me, neighbors" there is the possibility of seeing the characters not just as mob and victim—us and them—but as members of the same community. Ireson acknowledges his guilt and points out that his shame before his neighbors can never pain him as much as his pain before God. As the women are called to remember their own relationships with God, they too are transformed. They begin to step forward as individuals, "the wife of the skipper lost at sea" or "an old wife mourning her only son." When they become individuals again, standing themselves before God, their own hard hearts start to soften. They do not reach perfect grace or perfect forgiveness, but with "half scorn, half pity" they release Ireson and give him a cloak. It is left to the narrator, not the women, to refer to the captain now as "Poor Floyd Ireson."

The poem ends with Ireson alone and ashamed. There is no moral statement at the end. The narrator reveals nothing of Ireson's motive for his betrayal of the fisherman or of what happens to him after he acknowledges his sin. Perhaps he implies that these matters are not the reader's concern, that they should remain between Ireson and God.

Whittier based his poem on a fragment of a folk song he learned from a schoolmate, expanding on that fragment with a story of his own imagining. Years after the poem was published, he learned that Ireson actually had not been responsible for the abandoning of the ship but had been blamed for it by an unscrupulous crew.

Cynthia A. Bily

SLEEPING IN THE WOODS

Author: David Wagoner (1926-   )
Type of poem: Lyric
First published: 1973; collected in *Sleeping in the Woods*, 1974

The Poem

"Sleeping in the Woods" is a poem composed of forty-eight lines of free verse that seems to ebb and flow on the page. The gerund in the title (sleeping), along with other verbals (participles and gerunds usually ending "-ing"), is common in David Wagoner's poems and notably in their titles. The first poem in the collection *Sleeping in the Woods* is "The Singing Lesson," and other titles in that book include "Talking to Barr Creek," "Beginning," "Living in the Ruins," "An Offering for Dungeness Bay," and "Raging." Discounting such nouns and pronouns as "ceiling," "morning," and "anything" that end in "-ing," Wagoner includes some forty verbals in this poem, which leaves readers with a sense of flow that may suggest progression, abundance, or change. Certainly the use of verbals keeps the poem in motion and does not allow either stability or rest, despite what the title might imply.

Wagoner is fond of confronting an undesignated character in his poems by using the second-person "you," which tends to lure readers into identifying themselves with that character while the poet remains somewhat distant as a teacher or adviser. The voice of the poet, which can even be godlike at times, may be compassionate and genuinely helpful, or it may be sinisterly ironic. Many of Wagoner's best poems (including this one) are meditative in nature, but the tone is conversational. He enjoys moving between the profound and the playful, with much of the playfulness dependent on the ambiguous nature of language. Readers must always be prepared for puns, sometimes very serious ones, almost none of which are accidental in Wagoner's poems.

In the opening lines of the poem, the speaker indicates that "you" are lost in the woods and must bed down for the night. In the third line he writes, "you have nothing," and for an instant the reader is confronted with annihilation; however, that instant lasts for only as long as it takes to read the next line: "you have nothing/ But part of yourself to lie on." Wagoner depicts the character in the poem "standing," "kneeling," "crouching," "turning over old leaves," and "going under" in the process of bedding down. The play on "going under" suggests simply crawling in under the leaves but also being ruined or overwhelmed. In this process, the person (or persona) in the poem becomes "like any animal" entering "the charmed circle/ Of the night," but the human body is awkward and not readily adaptable for such a purpose. The speaker represents the persona as stiff-necked, "One ear-flap at a time knuckling your skull."

The phrase "But now" that opens the fifteenth line indicates a second movement in the poem, in which the persona is "lying still," watching the shadows, and going to sleep ("not *falling* asleep," the speaker advises, not losing anything to the earth beneath) without a ceiling or walls. The persona is now settled down at "the place where it is always/ Light"; that is, the persona is entering a dream state, and dreams may reveal deep truths. The dream, however, may be "sunk in blood," and all night the mind might plague the sleeper with fear of being food for wild animals. The speaker teases the persona by suggesting that the persona's body ("hidebound substance") might provide food for the very low ("mites") or the very high ("angels").

Near the end of line 37, the speaker quite casually advises, "Turn up/ In time, at the first faint stretch of dawn, and you'll see/ A world pale-green as hazel." The awakening is lyrical and rejuvenating as the persona's "cupped hand" is "lying open/ . . . in the morning like a flower." It is not at all unusual for Wagoner to resort to a pun as he ends a poem: "Making light of it,/ You have forgotten why you came, have served your purpose, and simply/ By being here have found the right way out./ Now, you may waken." Whatever it was that drew the persona into the woods has been rendered trivial by the experience of having come to terms with it.

Forms and Devices

Wagoner has compared the undulating lines in this and several other of his poems to a sine wave or an expansion-contraction pulsation. Typically, readers encounter a long line with five or six heavily stressed syllables, then a shorter one of four or five stresses, and then an even shorter one of just two or three stressed syllables. On the page, these lines look almost like tercets (three-line stanzas), but they are not self-contained units; that is, the loosely constructed sentences flow over the line endings, often prompting readers to anticipate one thing at the end of a line only to be surprised by the first word or phrase in the next line. Most of Wagoner's lines end without punctuation marks (enjambment), and the sentences are often quite lengthy (one of them in this poem is nearly 170 words long and rambles over twenty-three lines). The effect of this kind of syntax and line play is to keep readers alert, but the result of being an attentive reader of a poem by Wagoner is not so often clarity as it is an awareness of the multiple meanings of words and of the events they define. The ambiguity is intentional.

The greatest risk Wagoner takes in the poem is that of the verbals themselves and the possibility that readers will be annoyed by the repetitive use of the "-ing" ending. However, he often uses such rhetorical devices as parallelism to create a sense of balance and poise, as in these lines near the middle of the poem: "The ground beneath you neither rising nor falling,/ Neither giving nor taking." Wagoner's ear is attuned to the subtleties of sound, and a careful reading aloud of certain passages will reveal patterns of alliteration and assonance that account for the lyrical or musical impact common to the best unrhymed, free-verse poems: "Whoever stumbles across you in the dark may borrow/ Your hidebound substance for encouragement/ Of mites or angels." The soft *m*'s and *b*'s and the prevailing short vowel sounds become the major key. Later, near the end of the poem, the reader becomes especially conscious of long *e* and *i* sounds: "The chalk-green convolute lichen by your hand like sea fog,/ The fallen tree beside you in half-light/ Dreaming a greener sapling." Wagoner closes his poem with an assonantal triangle featuring the long *a:* "By being here have found the right way out./ Now you may waken."

Themes and Meanings

This poem opens with a dependent clause: "Not having found your way out." The speaker then uses the imperative mode: "begin/ Looking for somewhere to bed down at nightfall." In pointing out that the persona in the poem has "nothing/ But part of yourself to lie on," the speaker implies that the persona must now lie on the bare ground and that the persona has only the self on whom to rely. In the "charmed circle/ Of the night," the persona will discover the way out of the woods, presumably out of confusion and uncertainty. In effect, as the penultimate line declares, the experience of being lost will lead the persona to find "the right way out." One runs into such circumstances frequently in literature and life. Dante Alighieri's persona in *La Divina commedia* (c. 1320; *The Divine Comedy*) is lost "in a dark woods," where he is confronted by wild beasts. A common, paradoxical motif of mysticism holds that light breaks forth out of darkness or that one must become aware of being lost in order to find one's way, and the result is a spiritual awakening or "enlightenment." Essentially, that is what happens in this poem.

The key to the enlightenment of the persona may be found about midway through the poem, where the persona is described as sleeping without ceiling or walls for the first time. In direct contact with the "imponderable" earth, the threshold between the ordinary and the extraordinary, between the conscious and the unconscious, and between sight and insight is depicted as "slackening." The "place where it is always/ Light" is the dream world of the unconscious where the stars that are concealed by leaves and branches in ordinary forests "burn/ At the mattering source/ Forever." Although the playfully sinister speaker teases the persona with the possibility of being reduced to physical food for mites and spiritual sustenance for angels, the persona is assured that "whatever they can't keep is yours for the asking." The persona then promptly "sees" the beauties of the green world and light, and whatever problems led that person into the woods are forgotten. It is at that point, only in the last line of the poem, that the speaker informs the persona, "Now, you may waken." The theme of spiritual awakening, of regeneration and enlightenment through the medium of solitude in nature, is fundamental to this poem.

Ron McFarland

SMALL TOWN WITH ONE ROAD

Author: Gary Soto (1952-   )
Type of poem: Lyric
First published: 1985; collected in *Who Will Know Us*, 1990

The Poem

"Small Town with One Road" is a short poem in free verse, its thirty-three lines forming one stanza. The title suggests a quiet poem, and it is, presenting a reflective commentary on life within the valley as compared with a life beyond. The poem is written in the first person. The speaker is a father, and he and his daughter are contemplating their view of the valley, but the speaker is primarily addressing the reader.

The first section of the poem is primarily descriptive, as Soto depicts the lives of Mexican American farm workers and their families in a hot, dry valley in central California. A road of black asphalt runs through the valley, a road that Soto later uses symbolically as a dividing line between the hard life in the valley and life beyond. "Kids could make it" across, he says, literally meaning that they could "leap barefoot" to the little store where they buy candy and snowcones. Before describing what could be considered the children's bleak future, Soto reminds the reader that these children are like all children, eager to taste the sweetness of candy on their tongues. The lives of the children in the valley include "a dog for each hand,/ Cats, chickens in the yard." At home, the children hear cooking in the kitchen and know they will be having beans for dinner, as they usually do: "Brown soup that's muscle for field work." The universality of the life of manual labor is underscored by the next two lines, "Okie or Mexican, Jew that got lost,/ It's a hard life where the sun looks." The poem is about all migrant workers, no matter what their heritage.

The poem shifts when the view changes from the fields to a life just beyond, one where the "cotton gin stands tall in the money dream." The mill represents a more substantial amount of money, a true "paycheck for the wife." The poem then shifts again; the last section of the poem is contemplative and personal. "We could go back," the poet thinks. The phrase echoes the first words of the poem, "We could be here," the full meaning of which now becomes clear: The poet has lived here before and is speaking of a life he knows personally. He muses, "I could lose my job,/ This easy one that's only words": He could then be working in the fields or performing other manual labor. As he and his daughter eat their snowcones along the roadside, he sees a young boy crossing the road, "'He's like me,'/ I tell my daughter." The poem ends on a hopeful note as the boy leaps "Across the road where riches/ Happen on a red tongue."

Forms and Devices

Soto is a noted author who grew up in California, the son of working-class Mexican American parents; he experienced the rigors of working as a migrant laborer. Knowing two worlds as he does, his sparse language mirrors the world in which he grew up.

The poem's sentence structure is powerful because it is direct. "We could be here," Soto begins. Later, in parallel language, he thinks, "We could go back." In between he explains and describes, using few poetic devices. The poem contains only one simile, an ironic one. Papa's field "wavered like a mirage"—not like the oasis which might be envisioned by a straggler in the desert, but a world so intense that a fieldworker's vision of it shimmers in the heat. The blur of the field becomes the blur of life, a kind of blindness that occurs when sights must be set on little beyond day-by-day existence.

Personification reinforces the connection that Soto feels with those on both sides of the highway. The highway is "big-eyed/ With rabbits that won't get across," an image of anyone trying to escape from the valley without "look[ing] both ways," something the "brown kid" knows how to do at the end of the poem. He knows how to leave the "hard life where the sun looks." The sun is personified; it does not merely shine but "looks" fiercely, the strength of the "look" making work in the field that much more tiresome and difficult. Soto writes of the cotton gin's appeal, a means beyond the field to earn more money to change one's life circumstances. "The cotton gin stands tall," prompting the reader to envision someone with head erect, chin out, shoulders back—an image resonant with being proud of one's industry and accomplishment.

It is noteworthy how this image contrasts with that of the fieldworkers, of the bean pickers as they bend over, day after day, to harvest. Nor is it like the image of the fruit pickers whose heads and shoulders are lost amid the branches of the fruit trees. For the fieldworker, gone is the clarity of figure and accomplishment that one may acquire by working in the mill.

Soto's words are sparse because there is little in the valley that would inspire one to "wax poetic" about. Elaborate, extended metaphors comparing this limiting, physical world to a more complicated one would not work; this poem is about an uncomplicated lifestyle and people who strive to survive. Soto portrays life in the valley as one which is a struggle simply to endure from one day to the next. Yet with a single, one-syllable word Soto provides hope for all those in the valley, and especially for the children, who in their innocence "leap" across the road. The responsibilities and burdens of adulthood are not yet ones which they must shoulder, and Soto knows—from his own experience—that it is possible for children to leave the backbreaking life of their parents and "leap" to another kind of life.

Themes and Meanings

Soto uses children to represent the hope for all people. At the beginning of the poem, the children "leap"—a joyful word, and one that describes well the buoyancy and resiliency of childhood—to the store, just as the "brown kid" leaps across the road at the end. In a larger sense, life beyond the fields is worth leaping for. While money is not the singular criterion for a satisfying life (and while oftentimes in literature money, or the pursuit of it, is equated with corruption), Soto's poem reminds the reader of the effects of poverty. Too much money may corrupt, but sufficient funds are needed to buy the necessities of life: food, shelter, clothing, medical care, and even the ability to send children to school. Once children of migrant workers are seven or eight years old, and sometimes even earlier, they are typically no longer sent to school but are expected to work in the fields. Thus they work to earn their keep.

The speaker has escaped life in the valley, and he and his daughter "suck roadside/ Snowcones" as they "look about." They do not "eat," "nibble," or "lick" the snow-cones, but "suck" them, a much more aggressive word that reflects Soto's statement, "Worry is my daughter's story." Given that he, too, is eagerly consuming his snow-cone, the reader notes that it remains Soto's story as well. The family could conceiv-ably have to go back to that way of life some day; life's twists leave no one immune to situations that might diminish material possessions and force each of us to survive rather than thrive. Thriving in the world beyond the valley means working at careers that not only meet physical needs but also nurture spiritual or intellectual needs. His daughter touches his hand, wanting the reassurance that her father, while acknowl-edging such a possibility, will protect her from it. She is counting on that human connection for comfort and optimism.

While the poem is autobiographical, its appeal is universal. Soto suggests others besides Hispanics who may find themselves "in the valley." He includes the "Okies," a reference to people from Oklahoma who were displaced by the dust storms of the 1930's and came to California to work in the fields in hope of a better life, a plight immortalized by John Steinbeck in *The Grapes of Wrath* (1939). He includes the Jews who "got lost," a reference to the wandering tribes of Israel, perhaps when they were lost in the wilderness for forty years under Moses's leadership, or perhaps the timeless struggle of Jews around the world to find a home.

Soto paints a contemporary picture for all people. In uncertain economic times, anyone—not only Hispanics, Okies, or Jews—"could be here." Yet all people have the possibility to attain the "Riches" that can "Happen on a red tongue," for no matter what heritage, all people have the opportunity to savor "Sweetness," the "red stain of laughter," the essence of life.

Alexa L. Sandmann

THE SNOW MAN

Author: Wallace Stevens (1879-1955)
Type of poem: Lyric
First published: 1923, in *Harmonium*

The Poem

"The Snow Man" is a short fifteen-line poem divided into five tercets. The title conjures up an image of a human artifact. The resemblance between a real human figure and a snowman, however, is hardly exact, for a high degree of conventional stylization goes into the making of a snowman—differently sized balls for head, torso, and limbs, coals for eyes, carrot for nose, and so on. Nevertheless, the snowman is a strategically apt image, for Stevens's poem deals with the attempt of the speaker to resist succumbing to the temptation to anthropomorphize or to personify—that is, to impose human form on nature or to impute human qualities to inanimate things or forces. As the opening line indicates, "One must have a mind of winter" to approach a frigid January landscape on its own terms, to see it as it really is, and thus to keep the snow and the man separate, as Stevens's deliberate separation of the two words in his title suggests.

In spite of this desire for separation, the snow and the man cannot really be kept apart, for any attempt to approach winter on its own inhuman terms is foredoomed to failure insofar as one must use as one's medium the human terms of a shared cultural vocabulary. A scene of winter, verbally rendered, is necessarily an approximation, for word-using animals, by definition, have no nonlinguistic or nonsymbolic access to the structure of the real and thus can only more or less encompass things as they are. The speaker is acutely aware of how difficult it is "not to think/ Of any misery in the sound of the wind,/ In the sound of a few leaves." He concedes that one must "have been cold a long time" to avoid humanizing the scene by personifying it, to avoid seeing it as a reflection of misery or some other negative human feeling. To behold "Nothing that is not there and the nothing that is," one must be nothing oneself. Yet as Stevens reflects in his poem "The Plain Sense of Things" (1952), "the absence of imagination [has]/ Itself to be imagined." The inhuman reality of wordless nature can only be approached through the word-soaked world of human imagination. The poem itself is an enactment of this paradox.

Forms and Devices

To portray the relationship between the mind of winter and the landscape of winter, Stevens uses predominantly visual images: "the boughs/ Of the pine-trees crusted with snow," "the junipers shagged with ice," and "The spruces rough in the distant glitter/ Of the January sun." For Stevens, the seasons are analogues not only for the cycle of human life but also for the cyclical nature of the human imagination. Winter is as close as one comes to an unadulterated reality purged clean of humanizing additions such as personification and anthropomorphism, as close as one comes to an inhuman landscape in which one can find no human meaning. Spring is an analogue for the mind's finding what will suffice by giving reality some measure of human shape. Summer is an analogue for the time of physical paradise, an imagined world wholly bearable and wholly hospitable to human beings. Fall, finally, is an analogue for the overripeness that leads to rottenness and that initiates the slow decay into winter.

It is fitting, therefore, that this poem about the mind of winter visually abounds in wintry images and auditorially attunes itself to "the sound of the wind/ . . . That is blowing in the same bare place/ For the listener." The poem itself for the most part is also a bare place in that the speaker studiously avoids thinking of "any misery in the sound of the wind" by avoiding anthropomorphic figures of speech. The forms and devices that are *not* there make possible the beholding of "Nothing that is not there and the nothing that is." The imagination, Stevens maintains, adds nothing to the world except itself. Save for the paradox inscribed in the final two lines, the poem is virtually devoid of figurative language. Though words such as "crusted," "shagged," and their cognates have connotative value, their evocative function is strictly subservient to their descriptive function.

Themes and Meanings

For Stevens, the imagination is not merely a way of creating but also a way of knowing, and "The Snow Man" is a self-consciously paradoxical attempt to imagine the absence of imagination by trying to capture in words a reality that is in essence wordless and by trying to put into human terms a nature that is in essence inhuman. It is significant that the speaker refers to "a mind of winter," for the one thing he cannot deliver is winter in itself. However much he tries to avoid the pitfalls of personification and anthropomorphism, however much he tries "not to think/ Of any misery in the sound of the wind," he cannot help but posit some connection between the poverty that resides within a mind of winter and the poverty that resides within a landscape of winter. Insofar as "the listener" lives in the prison house of language and is thereby shaped and determined by the preconceptions and values of a given vocabulary, he cannot in reality become nothing himself and cannot behold "Nothing that is not there and the nothing that is." He and his audience are relegated to imagining themselves occupying an absolute vantage point from which they are able to see things as they are and thus to see "Nothing that is not there." Nevertheless, the minute they posit "the nothing that is" and impose philosophical meaning on it (or draw meaning from it), they have entered a realm of imaginative abstraction from which there is no escape. The limits of their language are the limits of their world. Language always adds something that is not there to the nothing that is, and the poem itself is an eloquent demonstration of this insurmountable paradox.

It is no exaggeration to say that the entirety of Wallace Stevens's corpus is about the mutually dependent and perpetually unstable relationship between imagination and reality. As he reflects in *The Necessary Angel* (1965), "[T]he imagination loses vitality when it ceases to adhere to what is real. When it adheres to the unreal and intensifies what is unreal, while its first effect may be extraordinary, that effect is the maximum effect that it will ever have." When language fails to adhere to reality, the result is myth—the deceptive and spurious consolations of religion, romanticism, supernaturalism, and the like. When language adheres too closely to reality, the result is naturalism—the dreary determinism and impoverished reductivism of science, materialism, realism, and so on. For Stevens, imagination and reality are interdependent. By providing ideas of order and explanatory fictions, poetry gives a coherence and meaning to the chaos and poverty of human life, lending to it a sense and savour that "the gaunt world of reason" cannot proffer. Creating fictions, Stevens maintains, is the essential gift of the human mind; believing them is its curse. In a sceptical age, poetry must take the place of empty heaven and its hymns, but the material of poetry must be reality, not myth. Poetry, for Stevens, is life's redemption.

In "Notes Toward a Supreme Fiction" (1942), Stevens maintains that a fiction must have three attributes: It must be abstract, it must change, and it must give pleasure. Humankind makes the world manageable by abstraction, a device of economy that prevents one from being overwhelmed by an excess of sensory data. Such simplifications or even falsifications of intellect have obvious survival value and cannot be permanently discarded. Stevens, however, wants to go beyond intellectual abstractions, beyond the dead formulae and prefabricated notions that the gaunt world of fact and reason enshrines. He wants to fabricate his own imaginative abstractions, fictions that will deautomatize ordinary perception and reveal novel and unexpected configurations of experience, configurations that are obscured by stultifying conventions of common sense. Such fictions must change because the world must be continually defamiliarized and reinvented lest these fresh fictions degenerate into stale myths. Moreover, for the poverty of the human condition to be mitigated, such fictions must give pleasure. What Stevens calls the gaiety of language, with its exaltations of the present and its fortuitous integrations, is the only believable substitute for the obsolete joys of heaven.

Greig Henderson

SNOW WHITE AND THE SEVEN DWARFS

Author: Anne Sexton (1928-1974)
Type of poem: Narrative
First published: 1971, in *Transformations*

The Poem

Like Anne Sexton's other fairy-tale poems collected under the title *Transformations*, "Snow White and the Seven Dwarfs" is a long (164 lines), free-verse narrative based on the version of the Snow White tale collected by Jacob and Wilhelm Grimm in Germany in the nineteenth century. The darkness and violence of this version may surprise readers who are accustomed to fairy tales that have been sanitized to make them suitable for children, but although Sexton has established a very modern voice in this and the other *Transformations* poems, she remains faithful to the action that the Grimm brothers recorded.

In "The Gold Key," the comparatively short poem that introduces the collection, the poet speaks of herself as a "middle-aged witch" with her "mouth wide," ready to tell readers "a story or two." The "witch" then imagines a sixteen-year-old boy who "wants some answers." He is really each of the readers, the witch says, suggesting that the answers are to be found in the tales of transformation recorded by the Grimm brothers. In that introduction, Sexton is explaining why adult readers should pay attention to the sort of story usually considered to be children's entertainment; she implies that these stories have important meanings.

In "Snow White and the Seven Dwarfs," Sexton begins with a verse paragraph that describes the character of the virgin in fairy tales; the virgin is not only pure but also doll-like. Only in the next paragraph does Sexton identify this particular virgin as Snow White. She also introduces the beautiful but vain stepmother queen and the magic mirror that tells her that Snow White is more beautiful than she is. The story progresses through its familiar events: The queen orders her huntsman to kill Snow White and to bring the queen her heart. Instead, he frees her and brings the queen a boar's heart, which she eats. Snow White wanders through dangerous forests for seven weeks and at last comes to the cottage of the seven dwarfs for whom she agrees to keep house. They warn her against opening the door while they are off at their mines, but Snow White is tricked by the disguised queen, who offers her a piece of lacing. The dwarfs rescue Snow White from the deathlike swoon caused by her tightly laced bodice. A second time they rescue her when she is tricked with a poisoned comb. When she succumbs to the queen's offer of a poisoned apple, however, they can do nothing. Sadly they display Snow White's body in a glass coffin. That is how a prince sees her and falls in love with her. When the dwarfs allow him to carry her body to his castle, the poisoned apple is dislodged and Snow White revives and marries her prince. The evil queen is invited to the wedding, where she is given "red-hot iron shoes" in which she dances until she dies. Readers are not told that Snow White and the prince live happily ever after, however; instead, Sexton's final image is of Snow White holding court and looking into her own mirror.

Forms and Devices

As she does with all the *Transformations* poems, Sexton adds her own voice to the plot elements of the story. It is a voice that is sometimes comic and sometimes admonitory. One source of its comedy rises from the introduction of contemporary items into the traditional tale. When the wicked queen eats what she thinks is Snow White's heart, for instance, she chews it "like a cube steak." The queen's gift of lacing binds Snow White "tight as an Ace bandage." When she revives, she is "as full of life as soda pop." When Snow White opens the cottage door to evil a second time, Sexton calls her a "dumb bunny," and the prince lingers at Snow White's coffin so long, Sexton says, that his hair turns green.

Although the cube steak and the Ace bandage show Sexton's gift for the comic simile, her figurative language can also make her story more vivid and underscore the themes that emerge in the tale. During Snow White's trek through the forest, she meets hungry wolves, each with "his tongue lolling out like a worm." The forest's nightmare birds call out "lewdly,/ talking like pink parrots." The poisoned comb is "a curved eight-inch scorpion." Sexton compares the red-hot iron shoes in which the wicked queen dances to her death to a pair of red-hot roller skates, uniting the comic with the darkly grotesque.

In this poem, as in many of Sexton poems, the reader is also aware of another element in the speaker's voice, an admonitory voice that sometimes breaks into the narrative to direct the reader's attention to an important event or to explain how to interpret a motive or theme. Although editorial intrusion seems more characteristic of nineteenth century literature than of work from the latter half of the twentieth century, Sexton's ironic tone makes it seem both modern and appropriate. After introducing the stepmother's beauty, for example, Sexton addresses the reader directly: "Beauty is a simple passion,/ but, oh my friends, in the end/ you will dance the fire dance in iron shoes." The iron shoes foreshadow the end of the poem. Sexton also uses modern details such as the roller skates to unite parts of the story, as she does with references to the mirror.

Themes and Meanings

In the versions of "Snow White and the Seven Dwarfs" that have been sanitized for children, the action of the poem usually seems to concentrate on the possibility of violence aimed at the innocent young. In those stories, although the reader assumes the queen to be motivated by her envy of Snow White's youth and beauty, her motives seem to be subsidiary to the theme of violence itself. In Sexton's version, the queen's pride, which "pumped in her like a poison," is diagnosed directly as motivation. Indeed, Sexton says that before the mirror labels Snow White as the most beautiful woman in the land, the girl has been "no more important" to the queen than "a dust mouse under the bed." The mirror's announcement makes the queen suddenly aware of encroaching age and makes her determined to kill Snow White. At the end, the queen is punished for her pride by dancing to death in the red-hot shoes.

Sexton goes beyond simply making the queen a villain, however. In the poem's second verse paragraph, Sexton uses the second-person "you" to suggest to the reader that everyone is subject to the corrupting effects of pride and may be subject to its rewards: "Oh my friends, in the end/ you will dance the fire dance." At the end, Sexton describes the queen's punishment. After describing the shoes that await the queen, Sexton suddenly returns to the second person as someone warns the queen: "First your toes will smoke/ and then your heels will turn black/ and you will fry upward like a frog,/ she was told." Although the "you" in this second passage refers to the queen, the words "she was told" follow the vivid description and invite the reader to recall the earlier warning. Indeed, at the poem's very end, the last picture is of Snow White consulting her own mirror "as women do." Sexton suggests that even Snow White can be infected by the "simple passion" of beauty and the poison of pride that may accompany it.

Another image at the poem's end suggests a second theme: Snow White's "china-blue doll eyes," which "open and shut" like the eyes of a child's doll. The phrases recall the description of the virgin, that "lovely number" introduced in the poem's first verse paragraph. The virgin is the innocent heroine of this tale and many other fairy tales, but Sexton's imagery suggests that she is as empty and artificial as a toy. The opening paragraph introduces another theme as well. The virgin's eyes "Open to say,/ Good Day Mama,/ and shut for the thrust/ of the unicorn." The reference to the unicorn recalls the ancient folktale that a unicorn can be captured only by a virgin; the animal will willingly give itself up to her. Here, however, the "thrust" of the unicorn underscores its sexual symbolism. The virgin's apparent purity, Sexton suggests, may be a ploy by which she captures and marries the prince. Sexton also hints at Snow White's sexual nature in the description of her wandering through the forests of wolves with phallic tongues and lewdly calling birds until she takes refuge in the dwarfs' "honeymoon cottage." Like the virginal heroines of several of Sexton's Grimm poems, Snow White's purity is mostly appearance, and she carries in her the potential for the same sort of evil as her persecutor, the same evil that may put all readers in the iron shoes.

Ann D. Garbett

THE SOLITARY REAPER

Author: William Wordsworth (1770-1850)
Type of poem: Pastoral
First published: 1807, in *Poems in Two Volumes*

The Poem

"The Solitary Reaper" is a short lyrical ballad, composed of thirty-two lines and divided into four stanzas. As the title suggests, the poem is dominated by one main figure, a Highland girl standing alone in a field harvesting grain. The poem is written in the first person and can be classified as a pastoral, or a literary work describing a scene from country life. The eyewitness narration conveys the immediacy of personal experience, giving the reader the impression that the poet did not merely imagine the scene but actually lived it. However, Wordsworth's sister, Dorothy, writes in her *Recollections of a Tour in Scotland* that the idea for "The Solitary Reaper" was suggested to William by an excerpt from Thomas Wilkinson's *Tour in Scotland*. Since Wordsworth's poem is not autobiographical, one can assume that the poet is adopting a persona, or taking on a fictional identity (usually referred to as the "speaker" of the poem).

"The Solitary Reaper" begins with the speaker asking the reader to "behold" the girl as she works in the field. The first stanza is a straightforward description of the scene. The girl is standing alone in the field, cutting grain, and singing a "melancholy strain." Wordsworth emphasizes the girl's solitude by using words such as "single," "solitary," "by herself," and "alone." Solitaries are common figures in Wordsworth's poetry and are usually surrounded by a natural environment. The act of reaping alone in the field binds the girl intimately to the earth. Also, as the girl sings and the melody fills the lonely valley, she becomes almost completely merged with nature.

The next two stanzas describe the speaker's reaction to the maiden's song. The words of the song are in a language unknown to him, but he remains transfixed by the melody, which seems to stretch the limits of time and space. He associates the sweetness of the reaper's song with the beautiful cries of the nightingale and the cuckoo, both familiar images of transcendence in Romantic poetry. As he allows the song to engulf his consciousness, he envisions far-off places and times of long ago. His imagination transports him from the field in which he stands to the edge of infinity.

In the fourth stanza, the speaker abruptly shifts his attention from his musings to the scene before him. He continues to listen, but the transcendent moment is past. He again calls attention to the reaper, who is unaware of the speaker's presence or the effect her song has had on him. As the speaker walks away from the field, the song fades from his hearing, but its plaintive melody echoes in his heart and his imagination.

Forms and Devices

Wordsworth uses several poetic devices in "The Solitary Reaper." Among them is apostrophe, which is defined as a figure of speech where the speaker of the poem addresses a dead or absent person, an abstraction, or an inanimate object. At the beginning of the poem the speaker invites the reader to "Behold, her single in the field,/ Yon solitary Highland Lass!" He further cautions the reader to "Stop here, or gently pass!" Although the reader is not present, the speaker's imperative to "behold" the girl at her work puts the reader vicariously in the company of the speaker, as if they were walking the Highlands together. After the first four lines, the speaker shifts his attention away from the implied presence of the reader and does not allude to it again.

Metaphor, another common poetic device, is also found in "The Solitary Reaper." The poet uses metaphor to compare two images without explicitly stating the comparison. For example, in the second stanza the speaker compares the song of the reaper to those of the nightingale and cuckoo. Although the three songs are fundamentally different from one another, they become metaphors for transcendence as they suggest to the speaker distant times and places. Because the maiden's song is in a language unknown to the speaker, he is freed from trying to understand the words and is able to give his imagination full reign. The bird-songs and the girl's song are thus intertwined, a further link of the maiden to nature.

Suggestion through imagery is also used in connection with the reaper herself. The poet offers little description of her beyond the bare essentials given in stanzas 1 and 4. All the reader knows is that the reaper is a simple peasant girl singing a rather sad song while harvesting grain in a field. However, the speaker's imaginative associations make her much more. He connects her with shady haunts of Arabian sands, the cuckoo and the nightingale, the seas beyond the Hebrides, epic battles, and the common human experiences of sorrow and pain. From his perspective, she becomes the center of the universe, if only for a moment. Like her song, she dwarfs time and space, to become a metaphor for the eternal.

Music is also a dominant image in the poem. It is reinforced by the ballad form whose tones, rhythms, and rhymes emphasize the lyrical feeling. The musical image is further underscored by the use of alliteration. The repetition of *s* sounds, which are threaded throughout the poem, lend a tonal unity to the piece. For example, in the first four lines of the first stanza, fourteen words contain *s*. This pattern is repeated in the other stanzas but decreases toward the end of the poem as the reaper's song releases its grip on the consciousness of the speaker.

Themes and Meanings

"The Solitary Reaper" is about the power of the imagination to transform common, everyday events into representations of a larger reality. To the Romantic poets, imagination was not a synonym for fantasy. Instead they saw it as closely allied with intuition and emotion. This faculty enabled the poet to see familiar things in a radically different way. Samuel Taylor Coleridge, a Romantic poet himself and a friend of Wordsworth, noted that "the grandest efforts of poetry are when the imagination is called forth, not to produce a distinct form, but a strong working of the mind . . . the result being what the poet wishes to impress, namely, the substitution of a sublime feeling of the unimaginable for a mere image." The aim of the Romantics was to express an abstract idea using concrete images that were usually drawn from nature.

The poem is an example of the commonplace pointing the sensitive observer toward an ideal of unity or completeness of being. Although the reaper is a flesh-and-blood person, she becomes a spiritual gateway for the speaker of the poem. The natural environment that surrounds her only heightens her mystery. Her simple song is an expression of her own heritage and background, yet the speaker imagines it to be an articulation of the eternal, the boundless, the ultimate reality. This intuitive impression of the infinite leaves the speaker a different person than when he first encountered the girl. The wonder of her song permeates his intellect and lingers in his heart long after he hears the last notes.

Wordsworth's conviction that the infinite can be encountered in the finite emerges from his own personal experience. Frequently when he walked alone in nature, he detected a pervading presence, a consciousness that would break into the ordinary moments of his life and turn them into flashes of revelation. In addition to "The Solitary Reaper," Wordsworth's *The Prelude* and "Lines: Composed a Few Miles Above Tinturn Abbey" offer examples of poems that reflect intense instances of mystical insight as well as the sometimes uneasy, sometimes joyous response the poet had toward these visionary experiences. In "The Solitary Reaper" Wordsworth celebrates such illuminating moments. The girl, her song, and her natural surroundings combine in a unified whole and contribute to the speaker's expanded vision of reality.

For modern readers, whose lives overflow with activity, the theme of encountering the transcendent in nature or through everyday events may at first seem strange. Since many people have little chance to walk in the woods or stroll through farmland, readers might be tempted to dismiss Wordsworth's poem because the setting and situation do not reflect their own experiences. Although the values, concerns, and lifestyle of Wordsworth's time were different, the yearning of the human spirit to feel connected to something larger than itself remains as strong today as it was during the nineteenth century. Modern people long for a quiet place to recollect themselves, a place where they can catch a glimpse of the eternal in the details of their lives. Thus the theme of transcendence in "The Solitary Reaper" is timeless, as it speaks to the needs of the human spirit.

Pegge Bochynski

SONG OF NAPALM

Author: Bruce Weigl (1949-   )
Type of poem: Lyric
First published: 1982; collected in *The Monkey Wars*, 1985

The Poem

"Song of Napalm" is a free-verse poem of forty-five lines divided into five stanzas. The title is ironic: "Song" suggests something lovely and lyric, while napalm, on the other hand, is a deadly, incendiary jelly that the United States military dropped on villages during the Vietnam War. When dropped as a bomb, napalm ignites, and the burning jelly sticks to its victims and burns them to death. Because of the title, the reader knows that Bruce Weigl will once again be exploring the Vietnam War, a subject he treats frequently.

The opening stanza presents an idyllic scene of a pasture after a storm told in the past tense. Because the poem is dedicated to the poet's wife, it is easy to assume that the two people watching as horses "walk off lazily across the pasture's hill" are the poet and his wife. However, the image, although pastoral, also contains the germ of foreboding: The narrator stares through a "black screen," he describes the grass as "scarlet," and he associates tree branches with barbed wire. The image of the barbed wire seems to propel the poet into the flux of past and present in the next stanza. The storm has passed, and he asserts that he has "turned [his] back on the old curses." However, his belief is mistaken; in the first line of the third stanza, he shifts to the present tense although he describes a scene from the distant past. The thunder from the storm becomes a "pounding mortar" in his flashback, and, when he closes his eyes, he sees a "girl/ running from her village, napalm/ stuck to her dress like jelly."

In the fourth stanza, the poet tries to imagine that the girl somehow escapes the burning napalm. He does this so that he "can keep on living." Yet he acknowledges the lie and once again returns to the vision of the burning girl. She not only burns to death in the flashback but also is permanently "burned behind" the poet's eyes. This vision from the past continues to haunt the poet. In the last lines of the poem, Weigl connects the pasture and Vietnam by describing the pasture as "jungle-green." This connection between home and Vietnam acknowledges the burning girl's presence in the present, an indication that the experience of the Vietnam War is not something that can remain hidden in the past.

Forms and Devices

Weigl uses a variety of sensory images and metaphors to take the reader on a round trip from a rain-swept pasture to the horrors of the Vietnam War and back again. The poem opens with an image of a storm replete with pounding rain and thunder. Although the storm has passed, its aftereffects can still be seen in the pasture, in the color of the grass, and in the moisture that the retreating horses kick up with their hooves. Likewise, as the poem moves forward, readers realize that the "storm" of

Weigl's Vietnam War experience continues to make its effects felt in the present. Thus, the pounding rain and the thunder become the pounding of a mortar in an auditory image that links the pasture and the Vietnam War.

A second powerful metaphoric image occurs in lines 4 and 5: "We stared through the black screen/ our vision altered by the distance." Literally, the black screen is no more than the screen door of the poet's home. However, readers are reminded of what looking through a screen door is like: People ignore the mesh as they view a scene beyond, yet their vision is subtly shifted by the presence of the screen. Metaphorically, the screen serves two purposes: First, the "black screen" is the canvas on which Weigl's memory plays out its visions of the Vietnam War; second, the black screen serves as a filter or a mesh that screens the memory of the burning girl in a particular way. Thus, Weigl's vision of the horses in the pasture is "altered by the distance" in much the same way that his vision of the past is altered by the distance of time.

In stanza 3, Weigl uses visual, auditory, tactile, and kinesthetic images as the scene from the present melts into the scene from the past. Even with his eyes closed, Weigl sees the burning girl "running from her village, napalm/ stuck to her dress like jelly,/ her hands reaching for the no one/ who waits in waves of heat before her." Readers can feel the heat on their skins as they too watch the girl burn, the mortar pounding in the background. Furthermore, Weigl emphasizes that the past continues into the present by his choice of the present participles "running" and "reaching" to form a kinesthetic image describing the girl's actions. In the final stanza, Weigl presents the ghastly image of the child burning to death:

> and the girl runs only as far
> as the napalm allows
> until her burning tendons and crackling
> muscles draw her up
> into that final position
> burning bodies so perfectly assume. . . .

Again, Weigl has chosen to use the present participles "burning" and "crackling" as kinesthetic images. Used as adjectives, the present participles inject gruesome movement into the poem. Furthermore, the word "crackling" is also an auditory image: Readers not only see the girl burn, but they hear it as well. Ironically, the "final position" the burning body assumes is also the fetal position, the posture of the body in birth as well as death. With his final image, Weigl returns the reader to the opening scene with one important difference: At the very end of the poem he folds home and Vietnam together in the "jungle-green pasture."

Themes and Meanings

Throughout the body of Weigl's work, and most particularly in the poems found in the volume *Song of Napalm* (1988), the poet's experiences in the Vietnam War erupt into the heart of his poetry. Regardless of the intensity of his subject matter, however, Weigl never tries to substitute content for craft. His poetry is lean, spare, and carefully crafted, and he displays an acute awareness of the role art plays in the production of truth. "Song of Napalm," widely anthologized and considered by many critics to be one of the best poems to come out of the Vietnam War experience, is just such a poem, careful in its craft and brutal in its message. Like Yusef Komunyakaa in "You and I Are Disappearing" from the poetry collection *Dien Cai Dao* (1988), Weigl conjures the image of a burning girl to remind readers of the terrible cost of the Vietnam War. At the same time, Weigl questions the possibility of life after the war: How does someone continue to live with the image of a burning girl permanently etched behind the eyes? In "Song of Napalm," as in many of Weigl's Vietnam War poems, home and Vietnam do not exist as separate entities but rather coexist as contiguous realities; that is, even when he is contemplating an American scene, images of Vietnam intrude, changing the scene before him. The two locations, war and home, fuse and become the unit of Weigl's life. Just as in John Balaban's poem "After Our War," collected in *Blue Mountain* (1982), images of the war follow the poet home, raising questions about life after war.

"Song of Napalm" is a poem with three characters: the speaker, his wife, and the burning girl. By opening the poem with a dedication to his wife and returning to the plural pronoun "us" in the final line, Weigl starts and ends in the present, which includes life with his wife. The present, however, encapsulates the memories of the past. Furthermore, the use of the present tense to describe the scenes from Vietnam suggests that the past may exist more immediately for the poet than does his present reality. Yet the past that Weigl remembers is "altered by the distance" of years and miles. Likewise, his vision of the present is altered by the past. A simple meditation on a pasture with horses after the rain turns into a memory of a charred, dead girl.

The central question of the poem, then, is: How can one live with the double vision of home and war? Weigl suggests that his ability to live in the present somehow depends on his ability to either reimagine the past through lies or confront the past's intrusion into the present through art. In "Song of Napalm," Weigl briefly attempts the first: He tries to reconstruct his memory of the burning girl in order to ease her pain, his pain, and the pain of his wife. Yet this attempt fails as "the lie swings back again." Without a solution, he admits that he cannot change the past or deny it. What he does, however, is resurrect the child as art, the image of her charred body serving to remind readers that although their vision is "altered by the distance," the war really happened, and home can never be the same again.

Diane Andrews Henningfeld

THE SONG OF THE INDIAN WARS

Author: John G. Neihardt (1881-1973)
Type of poem: Epic
First published: 1925; collected in *A Cycle of the West*, 1949

The Poem

The Song of the Indian Wars is an epic poem in fourteen sections written in rhymed couplets and iambic pentameter. It is the fourth of a series of poems ("songs") that form a larger epic, *A Cycle of the West*, which deals with a period of discovery, exploration, and settlement in American history (1822 to 1890). It was a period when American Indian cultures were being overcome by the migration of a powerful people (the Europeans) driven by their own needs and their dreams of a waiting paradise. This "song" deals with the period after the Civil War, a period of movement into Indian territory by whites and of resistance by the Plains Indians such as the Sioux, Cheyenne, and Arapahoe. It ends with the death of its main character, Crazy Horse. The events were real events, and the poem's central characters were real historical individuals.

The song opens with "The Sowing of the Dragon," four years after Appomattox, as whites are looking westward to a land "clad with grains and jeweled with orchard." Up along the bottoms of the Kaw, Republican, Platte, and Solomon Rivers come the sounds of wheel and hoof; "ten thousand wagons scar the sandy flat." Ancestral pastures are gutted by the plow, and towns suddenly roar where there had been only space as wide as air. These "takers of the world" are of the "Cadmian brood," sowing the dragon seeds of war. The Indians see the end of their sacred things and dread the dwindling of their holy places, so war sweeps down the rivers. Ox-driven caravans are plundered, and settlers are slaughtered.

In the next section, members of different tribes meet, torn between those who trust the treaties with the whites and those who remember only the broken promises. Spotted Tail, the voice of peace (now and later in the poem), urges conciliation; Red Cloud, the voice of war, urges resistance and carries the day. In the next section, a Cheyenne, Black Horse, comes to the Sioux and urges conciliation but is driven away by an angry mob. Red Cloud speaks again for war, supported by Sitting Bull. In the fourth section warfare begins when Indians attack a log train and soldiers from Fort Kearney scatter the Indians. The Army commander at Fort Kearney hears of a gathering of Sioux on the Powder River. Captain Fetterman boasts that he can easily destroy them, vows to wipe them out, and rides out to find them. He is ambushed, and he and his men are massacred. After the winter lull, Indians attack a wagon train near the fort. The soldiers escorting it crouch behind bales of hay, which the Indians set afire with flaming arrows; they then withdraw.

When summer comes, the Great White Father in Washington intervenes, closing the country to whites between the Missouri River and the Big Horn. Red Cloud is not convinced, however, and the next spring brings news from Kansas of women captured, men slaughtered, and trains burned along the Santa Fe Trail. A contingent of cavalry pursues the Indians, who stop their withdrawal, then turn at Beecher's Island and attack. Beecher is killed, and the soldiers are surrounded for five days until rescued by reinforcements.

In the eighth section, after his victory at the Battle of Washita, the reputation of General George Armstrong Custer, "The Yellow God," spreads throughout the West, and for four years there is peace. Then Custer leads his army into the Black Hills of the Dakotas, an area which they discover is a "paradise of deer and singing streams." Their reports spread back east and bring a stream of whites with dreams of wealth to be exploited. Alarmed, the young Sioux gather and chant their war songs to the drums. Many of them join Sitting Bull at the Tongue and Powder Rivers. The government in Washington orders all Indians to go to reservations or be declared hostile, but Crazy Horse's people stay where they are. The cavalry rides into their camp and sets fire to the lodges where the Indians lie asleep; they leave a trail of blood. The surviving Sioux flee in panic up the slopes of the mountains, later returning to find a destroyed village; the village settles down, now only a "miracle of patches."

When the news of the massacre spreads among the Sioux, the young braves are aroused. The whole white world seems to be sweeping the prairies. The braves set out on a series of raids, but the whites are joined by many from the traditional enemies of the Sioux—the Roos and Crows. The Sioux turn to the Great Spirit for help, raising a pole in the center of their village and performing the Sun Dance. The white army gathering its forces to clear a path for Custer, who then proceeds recklessly, not waiting for the reinforcements. The Indians attack. After the dust settles, there is nothing but bodies "gleaming white the whole way to the summit of the hill." A brooding silence reigns. Reinforcements arrive, but too late. Reno scatters the Sioux, who flee to Big Horn Mountain.

In section 13, despite their victory, the Sioux lose heart. The people are listless. Their only hope is flight, but they are uncertain as to where they should flee. They turn eastward. General Crook follows their diverging trails, which reveal that they are "like quails before the hunter." Crazy Horse and Gall, with their people, have vanished. Crazy Horse turns westward instead and reaches the valley of the Powder River, where he hopes they will find peace. In January, however, news arrives of approaching soldiers. Crazy Horse's people flee to the head of the Little Powder River. Spotted Tail, still the advocate of peace, comes and urges compliance with the whites, and Crazy Horse finally brings his people in. As the last Sioux comes into the reservation, Crazy Horse says, "Now let my people eat."

After a while, news comes how Nez Perce leader Joseph, undaunted, has fought the whites and reappeared down the Yellowstone River. Hearing this, the whites now fear what Crazy Horse might be thinking, since he has left the reservation and gone to the camp of Spotted Tail, his uncle and the advocate of peace, to be with his people there. The white officer asks him to return to Camp Robinson for talks, in all sincerity promising him that no harm will come to him. Crazy Horse believes him and comes to the fort, but when he arrives he is hustled among bayonets to a barred room.

Frightened, he struggles. A soldier, now also frightened, panics and stabs him. Lying on the floor, Crazy Horse sings his death chant, "I had my village and my pony herds/ On Powder where the land was all my own./ I only wanted to be left alone./ I did not want to fight," and dies. Crazy Horse's mother and father come to get the body, and they bear it away on a pony-drag to lie somewhere among the Badlands: "Who knows the crumbling summit where he lies/ Alone among the badlands?"

Forms and Devices

   The Song of the Indian Wars is an epic, one of five in Neihardt's *Cycle of the West.* As an epic it has the traditional epic's battle scenes. Each represents a different facet of warfare: the tense attack on the Wagon Boxes, the battle of Beecher's Island, the massacre of Crazy Horse's village; the ambush of Custer. The sympathy of the epic shifts in each scene between the white troops and the Indians. In each scene the intense battle action is interspersed with human details. At the Wagon Boxes, Old Robertson unlaces a boot and nooses the leather lace to reach between a trigger and a toe; another trooper sits cross-legged calmly picking jammed bullets out of a gun. At Beecher's Island, Condon dashes out from behind a barrel of beans waving his rifle and shouting, "Come on! ye dairty blatherskites. We kin lick yez all," before he falls beneath a shower of arrows.

   The epic hero is Crazy Horse, Neihardt's "ideal epic hero," always portrayed as possessing courage in the face of overwhelming odds, always maintaining a certain dignity, even in death. Of the battle with Custer, Crazy Horse says, "I fought him and I whipped him. Was it wrong/ To drive him back? That country was my own.// I did not want to see my people die.// His soldiers came to kill us and they died." The brother-in-law of Red Cloud, the advocate of warfare in the Sioux council, Crazy Horse was one of the principal chiefs of that tribe and one of the main leaders of those Indians who defied the authority of the United States for several years. Although a relatively young man, he was the most respected man in the tribe. The name "crazy" is a poor translation of the Sioux word *witko*, which means "magic" or "enchanted," referring to his supposed special and sacred vision. Neihardt places him in juxtaposition with the whites' idea of a great general, Custer, who possesses their ideal kind of courage. Crazy Horse is heroic like a lonely man bravely fighting the sea.

   The Song of the Indian Wars, like all true epics, is the mirror of a society—in this case, that of the Plains Indian. It reveals its structure in peace and in war, along with details of daily life and tribal mores. It focuses on the several tribal chiefs, on tribal and intertribal councils for decision making, and on the details of ceremonial procedure. It records the great orations before the councils, most of them accounts garnered from the memories of someone present. The nomadic life is portrayed, as the tribes from time to time fold their tepees and wander up the rivers. As war looms, the young men chant to the drums, and a sacred pole is raised in the center of the village, where the men perform the Sun Dance. Indian strategies in warfare are described: the flaming arrows, the surprise raids, the dissolving of the trails they leave behind, and the fading away after defeats—and sometimes after victories. There is the ceremony in donning the war bonnet and the death-paint. There are the prayers to the Great Spirit, the body-drag for the dead.

Neihardt's method of composition was unique. He believed in a prodding daemon as the motivating force behind his poetry, compelling him to preserve a "great heroic race-mood that might otherwise be lost." As Lucile Aly tells it in her *John G. Neihardt* (a 1976 monograph in Boise State University's Western Writers Series), "To recreate the mood, he began each session by . . . immersing himself in the atmosphere until he reached a near trance state," working and reworking each line. Indian language, for which Neihardt had a well-tuned ear, translates into elevated speech appropriate for an epic—straightforward, dignified, and poetic. The poem often achieves a special, emotionally elevating cadence, especially in the orations before the councils.

Themes and Meanings

The Song of the Indian Wars is an epic of westward expansion and the displacement of Native Americans after the end of the American Civil War—one of the great archetypal movements in the history of the world. White people with their dreams are migrating into the vast expanses of a land that is new to them but ancient and holy to Indians. The poem is a record of a confrontation with tragic overtones for both parties.

The story is told impersonally but with an overriding compassion for both sides. It avoids stereotypes and alternates between the viewpoints of Indians and whites, both involved in a struggle neither fully understands. For the Indians it is the end of sacred things and the dwindling of holy places; for the whites it is the promise of a land "clad with grains,/ Jewelled with orchard." For Indians it involves displacement from their homeland, for whites an unexplored frontier to be conquered and settled. Neihardt saw the Indian Wars as a confrontation between the old and the new, a "watershed of history." It is a struggle fraught with tragedy: the wounded and dead in the massacre of Crazy Horse's village and the vast expanse of white bodies strewn across the valley at the Little Big Horn.

Blair Whitney, in *John G. Neihardt* (1976), sees in this epic the fulfillment of the destiny of a race (whites of European descent) and the triumph—for good or ill—of Western civilization. The struggle brings out the best qualities of the immigrants— intelligence, strength, heroism, and faith. Yet it also involves the demise of a radically different culture of equal value. One, the European, is a logical, rational, acquisitive culture; whites are the masters of technology. The other, the Indian, is a spiritual culture with very simple technology that uses the land for hunting. Praying is an integral part of the Indian faith. Neihardt's theme, Whitney continues, is selfishness versus unselfishness. In the section entitled "The Yellow God," the heading has a double meaning: the debasing greed for gold sought by the invading prospectors, and the blond "yellow god" Custer, who has come to the Black Hills to protect them. The irony shows in Neihardt's lines describing this "errant Galahad" searching for an unworthy grail and mistaking "the color of the gleam." The Indian Wars were more than a fight over territory; they were also contests between two ways of life. The

Indian cannot understand the white drive to conquer the earth, to acquire more and more land. Neihardt symbolically portrays a confrontation between buffalo and train.

This epic is also about a sometimes hostile nature. At times it seems as though the elements had cursed the plains. Burning August gives way to the sudden, chill monotony of rains, and horses must struggle against the suck of gumbo flats and hills of clay. Crows and buzzards hover overhead. In the wagon train, women and children sometimes sicken and even die. The dead must be buried along the trail. *The Song of the Indian Wars*, as Aly observes, is about ordinary men who are transformed into heroes by events, who are struggling against impossible odds to preserve values they cherish. It "represents the universal striving to sustain life, and the pathos of a world where brave and noble men must attack each other in a mistaken attempt to satisfy the same human needs."

Thomas Amherst Perry

SONNET LVI

Author: Fulke Greville (1554-1628)
Type of poem: Satire
First published: 1633, in *Caelica*

The Poem

"Sonnet LVI," reflecting Fulke Greville's peculiarly complex mind, is many things at once. As the title suggests, it is a lyrical "sonnet" (although that term had a much less rigid definition in Greville's day than it does now) on the subject of romantic, erotic love; in this way, it recalls some of the love poems in the sonnet sequence *Astrophil and Stella* (literally, "Star Lover and Star"), written by Sir Philip Sidney, Greville's contemporary and great friend. "Sonnet LVI" is also a satire, however, poking fun at certain key assumptions underlying courtly love poems, including many of Sidney's. Finally, Greville's poem is a kind of waking dream vision, one in which the philosophical, first-person narrator achieves an overblown, grandiose notion of his lover's beauty and of his own importance, only to have his illusions come crashing down around him, frustrating his romantic desires.

Indeed, the narrator is deluded from the very beginning. As the poem opens, he sees himself as a glittering knight, right out of the pages of King Arthur, setting forth on a noble, chivalric quest. This quest, however, turns out to involve sin, vanity, and hypocrisy more than nobility, in that the narrator seeks not for the Holy Grail but for "Cynthia," a married woman with whom the narrator is infatuated and longs to have an adulterous affair. Just at the point of achieving his questionable boon, the narrator is overcome by the lady's beauty and falls into a swooning, ultimately egotistical vision of mythic gods and goddesses, seeing himself as at one in their company, while totally ignoring the real, flesh-and-blood woman beneath him, "Naked on a bed of play." At this point, Cynthia has the good sense to leave him, no doubt in favor of a more sensible, earth-bound lover. Finding himself abruptly alone, the narrator bitterly rues his folly in confusing spiritual love with sexual delight.

As a poet, Greville was notorious for constantly tinkering with his verse, revising his body of work throughout his long, industrious life; accordingly, it is difficult to date any of his poems with precision. Further, the text of "Sonnet LVI" exists in at least two different manuscript versions, one of which, the so-called "Warwick MS," inserts a passage of some twenty-four additional lines (after line 24) into the only version of the poem commonly available today. However, scholar Richard Waswo argues persuasively that these twenty-four "missing" lines are helpful to a proper understanding of Greville's meaning. Therefore, students of "Sonnet LVI" might want to track down a printing of the poem in its longer form—perhaps in Waswo's influential study *The Fatal Mirror: Themes and Techniques in the Poetry of Fulke Greville* (1972).

Forms and Devices

Central to Greville's intentions in the poem is his use of situational irony: The poem is informed from first to last by a sense of the yawning gap between illusion and reality, between expectation and fulfillment. Greville's narrator is a megalomaniac, seeing all the universe as witnessing and applauding his erotic pursuits. Ravished by Cynthia's loveliness, he rashly calls himself "a God," variously identifying himself with Mars (the classical god of war), with Apollo (the patron god of poetry), and with Phaeton (a sun god who once nearly set all the world aflame).

He is none of these exalted figures, of course; he is merely a quite ordinary man intent on conquering an ordinary, if attractive, woman. The narrator, like many people, insists upon elevating both his erotic impulses and his love object into the realm of the spiritual, the heavenly, the mythic. In doing so, he unconsciously reveals that his pursuit of the lady is actually no more than an exercise in exaggerated self-love, and she rightly abandons him. Here, then, lies the central irony of the poem's action: In mistaking earthly delights for spiritual ones and in looking up at the inaccessible heavens instead of down at the available woman, the narrator loses out on the lovemaking he has sought so arduously.

Also notable in the poem is Greville's facility with metaphor, a talent which has led critics to compare him favorably with the better-known John Donne (1572-1631). When the lady flees from him, for instance, the narrator successively compares himself to a riverbed deserted by its river, to the "Articke pole" abandoned by the sun, and finally to a condemned criminal confessing his sins at the site of his execution. These startling, unexpected metaphors have real power and contribute much to the disillusioned tone of the poem's conclusion.

Themes and Meanings

"I know the world, and believe in God," Greville once remarked, thereby revealing the deep fissure that ran through both his public and private lives. As a counselor to three successive English monarchs, the poet assuredly did "know the world," most notably the fractious, artificial world of the royal court. For many decades he was able to survive and even to flourish in this often treacherous environment. Greville was also a staunch Protestant of Calvinist persuasions, quick to pass flinty moral judgments on the same courtly life in which he participated so adroitly.

In the love poetry of the Renaissance English court—all aspiring courtiers sought to become adept at versifying—love is seen as an ennobling passion, the pursued lady as an object of extravagant worship, and the conventions of courtship as semireligious rituals. Furthermore, while the ultimate (and expected) object of the romantic chase is sexual consummation, the lady is nonetheless venerated not simply as an ideal of physical beauty but as an image or reflection of an ideal of spiritual beauty as well.

In some of its important aspects, this courtly love tradition owed much to the fourteenth century Italian poet Petrarch, many of whose sonnets lavishly praise his beloved "Laura" in this fashion. The Petrarchan mode was much imitated by sixteenth century Englishmen; indeed, the *Astrophil and Stella* sonnet sequence of Greville's friend Sidney (himself much imitated) is profoundly indebted to the Italian poet—to the point that Sidney was often referred to as "the English Petrarch" by his own contemporaries.

Greville was well aware of the philosophical underpinnings of such courtly love poetry, and he even toys with Petrarchan norms in the early poems of his *Caelica* collection. Given his Christian convictions, however, he must finally reject and mock these conventions, as he decidedly does in "Sonnet LVI." For the Calvinist Greville, the earth and the men and women who inhabit it are in a condition of steady moral decline, and they have been since humanity's fall from the Garden of Eden. In such a state, even an emotion as potentially noble as love has inevitably devolved into mere carnal lust. Accordingly, the Petrarchan lover, in mistaking his erotic impulse for something fine and spiritual, commits more than a blunder: He commits outright heresy.

The narrator of "Sonnet LVI" is clearly one such benighted courtly lover, intent on deifying both his love object and his own pursuit of her. Thus he likens the lady to the goddess Venus and sees in her earthly beauty a direct analogue to all things heavenly, including the Milky Way constellation. Similarly, he sees himself as godlike ("Surely I Apollo am") and, in a vision, seeks to ascend into the heavenly regions ("I stept forth to touch the skye"). However, at precisely this climactic moment his earthbound mistress, understandably irritated by the narrator's insistent, ego-ridden spiritualizing, deserts him ("Cynthia who did naked lye,/ Runnes away like silver streames"), thereby frustrating his erotic aims.

Deserted now, the narrator can only lament his loss and curse the romantic illusions that have thwarted his conquest. At no little cost, and quite to his surprise, he has learned that human love is a decidedly secular, not spiritual, matter. "Love is onely Natures art," he sorrowfully concludes, "Wonder hinders Love and Hate." In other words—in the words of Greville editor Geoffrey Bullough—human love "is a purely natural business, in which action is all and mute adoration a hindrance." Or as the poet and critic Yvor Winters bluntly puts it, this poem "states that love is physical and no more and that he who is distracted by spiritual concerns [in love's pursuit] is a fool." All that the narrator of "Sonnet LVI" ultimately has to show for his romantic quest is this hard-won, humiliating truth.

William R. Drennan

SONNET XVI

Author: John Milton (1608-1674)
Type of poem: Sonnet
First published: 1694, in *Letters of State* . . .

The Poem

Much of Sonnet XVI (subtitled *To the Lord General Cromwell*) is localized in time and place to England's seventeenth century. The allusions that make up the poem's primary content are to places and events that would have been immediately recognized by John Milton's contemporaries but are understood by a modern audience only if put into historical context. In the spring of 1652, the Parliament appointed a committee to consider the question of how much free religious discussion would be tolerated outside the official Puritan Church and its appointed clergy. This Committee for the Propagation of the Gospel was considering a proposal set before it by a group of fifteen Puritan ministers headed by John Owen, General Oliver Cromwell's personal chaplain. Milton believed that the proposals would place serious restrictions on freedom of conscience and feared that if passed, the new laws would be just the beginning of still greater prohibitions. One of the pamphlets being circulated that detailed the various proposals contained a recommendation that no one should be permitted to speak in public on any religious question without a certificate from two or more "godly and orthodox" ministers. Such a law would have placed unrestricted censorship into the hands of official clergy, who would be the sole arbiters of orthodoxy. Milton's contempt for these behind-the-scenes machinations is stated in no uncertain terms: ". . . new foes arise/ Threat'ning to bind our souls with secular chains."

Cromwell was already well established as a proponent of wide religious freedoms. When the proposals were under discussion in Parliament, Cromwell is reported to have said that he had "rather Mahometanism [Islam] were permitted among us than that one of God's children should be persecuted." Still, Cromwell was a realist and Milton may have feared that the politician might not go as far in the protection of free conscience as the poet's idealism would wish. Sonnet XVI repeats Milton's warnings to the Puritans contained in his prose masterpiece *Areopagitica* (1644) that the purported champions of liberty were soon to be guilty of imposing precisely the same bondage they had previously overthrown or, as Milton stated so succinctly in a previous sonnet, that "new Presbyter is but old Priest writ large."

The poem lends support to a head of state already engaged in a cause for which the poet cared deeply. Although Cromwell may well have been the most powerful person in England when Sonnet XVI was composed, the poem goes far beyond simple hagiography. It does not merely flatter or exalt a powerful man but rather urges his and Milton's agenda in a contentious political struggle—pushing the sonnet, a poetic form utilized primarily for praising some romantic ideal, into the realm of polemic. Furthermore, while Cromwell's achievements are indeed nobly versified in Sonnet

XVI, it is too much to assume that the poem contains Milton's final estimation of the Lord Protector. The relationship between them was not as close, nor was Milton's adherence to the party line as total, as is sometimes assumed. His position as Secretary for Foreign Tongues did not give him any real influence in the government or its councils. He was a secretary whose job was to translate state documents into Latin for publication on the Continent. So, while the poem may appear at first glance to be an attempt to curry favor and exalt the rich and famous, such was not its intention. It functions less as praise for Cromwell than a rallying cry for free-thinking Englishmen.

Forms and Devices

Sonnet XVI is modeled after the heroic sonnets of Torquato Tasso, one of Milton's favorite poets. It is arguably an apostrophe, the form of address that speaks to an absent or dead person, a thing, or an abstract idea as if it were present. While it is possible that Milton, a minor (though celebrated) functionary in Cromwell's Commonwealth government, had the opportunity to deliver the poem directly to the man he is addressing, no record of Cromwell's reception of or reaction to the sonnet is known to exist. Another legitimate way of reading the poem is to let the particulars give way to the general and to see Cromwell as the poetic ideal of people of good conscience who live in all places at all times. Thus the apostrophe's address would be not just to "the chief of men" but also to the best of what is human. The poem's subtitle, "On the proposals of certain ministers at the Committee for Propagation of the Gospel," clearly distances it from the Spenserian and Shakespearean tradition of reserving the sonnet for celebrating love and tender feelings.

Sonnet XVI employs the classic Italian octave-sestet division written in nearly uniform iambic pentameter. Throughout all his sonnets, Milton consistently utilized a rigorous Petrarchan rhyme scheme of *abba abba* for the octave, and Sonnet XVI is no exception. However, its concluding sestet of a *cddcee* scheme is unique for Milton and is his only sonnet to end in a couplet. This couplet is further isolated from Milton's usual pattern by the jarring fourteenth line, which introduces it. Line 14 contains twelve syllables, destroying the pentameter, and its word order is impossible to read with any regular scansion, destroying the iambic. The octave is devoted to praise and the sestet to admonition. Also unique to Sonnet XVI is the joining of the octave and the sestet by enjambment, a sentence or clause that carries its sense of meaning from one line to another: "yet much remains/ To conquer still." In this case, the enjambment not only unites two lines but also serves to bridge what are usually strictly separated poetic units.

Themes and Meanings

Milton has an unmatched ability to weave poetic structure with theme and meaning, making the way the poem is put together part of the meaning of the poem. For new readers, this may mean a frustrating bout of learning poetic terms and traditions. However, once a few of the basics are internalized, one begins to realize how the work of Milton has assumed its place, alone, at the top of the canon. He infused the new and unformed English language with a power and depth that his contemporary readers never dreamed it could possess and that poets of succeeding generations have continually aspired to equal.

In the octave, Milton praises Cromwell for his past achievements. With "matchless Fortitude," Cromwell, "our chief of men," has triumphantly led his country through war and political turmoil. Milton praises Cromwell's military victories at the Battle of Preston on the banks of "Darwen stream" at Dunbar and Worcester. Through every obstacle, Cromwell has plowed his way to "peace and truth." In these seemingly tossed-off lines, Milton alludes to commonly known context. According to Merritt Hughes, the figures of "Peace" and "Truth" were impressed on a commemorative coin issued by Parliament in honor of Cromwell's victories at Preston, Dunbar, and Worcester. Readers of Milton's time, upon first hearing the sonnet, could little anticipate that this lilting, seemingly innocent sonnet filled with happy thoughts could turn into a scathing condemnation of their most cherished institutions.

The enjambment that destroys the separation of the octave and sestet ("yet much remains/ To conquer still") also aborts the homily, cutting short its natural completion with a note of warning. The Puritans have won a kingdom, but will they lose their conscience? Milton urges Cromwell not to rest on his achievements: England has internal enemies of its soul more insidious than any of the external enemies that had threatened its borders. The challenges of wise government call for a valor equal to the battlefield: "peace hath her victories/ No less renown'd than war." Cromwell has an opportunity to rise up to a still greater glory by defending England's freedoms of religious tolerance from its homegrown predators.

The poem's final couplet conflates several well-known biblical references to wolves threatening sheep (for example, John 10:13, Matthew 7:15, and Acts 20:29) that could hardly have been misunderstood by the Puritan ministers targeted by the poet. The portrait of clergy as hireling wolves using the gospel for fangs to tear and rend the very flesh of England is introduced to the reader's ears by the dissonant line 14 that, of necessity, must be read with unnatural stress and emphasis. The final couplet, the only couplet to end any of Milton's sonnets, adds audible bestiality to the scenario with the ugly rhyme of "paw" and "maw." The poet had used the sheep and wolf images before. The ministers under condemnation in Sonnet XVI who were familiar with Milton's poetry might have recognized echoes from "Lycidas" and have been doubly incensed. In this earlier poem, Satan is the "prowling wolf" who leaps over the fence and into the fold. The sheep are successfully defended from external danger but subsequently die of an internal rot while their inattentive shepherds play loud and lively music.

Tony A. Markham

SONNET 35

Author: William Shakespeare (1564-1616)
Type of poem: Sonnet
First published: 1609, in *Sonnets*

The Poem

Sonnet 35, "No more be griev'd at that which thou hast done," is written to a young man, the poet's friend and nominal addressee or auditor of sonnets 1 through 126, by far the largest section of Shakespeare's sonnet sequence. The friend presumably is the "Mr. W. H." of the inscribed dedication of Thomas Thorpe's 1609 printing of the sonnets. This mysterious figure's identity has never been incontrovertibly established, although the scholarly consensus has focused on two candidates: Henry Wriothesley, third earl of Southampton (1573-1624), and William Herbert, third earl of Pembroke (1580-1630), both of whom were patrons of the poet-dramatist.

The true identity of the young man is of relative unimportance critically; in fact, some scholars have suggested that the youth might even be an idealized literary figure rather a real person. However, Sonnet 35 argues, as do some related sonnets, that the friendship is at times strained and certainly less than idyllic, giving it the semblance of an actual relationship. Although the young man's looks bear the stamp of perfection, he is not without character flaws. This poem arises from some unidentified hurt inflicted on the poet by the friend, the source of a momentary estrangement that is dealt with in Sonnets 33 through 42.

In Sonnet 35, the friend is grief-stricken by his trespass, and the poet attempts to assuage his friend's guilt through clever sophistry, reasoning that he himself must bear some of the responsibility for his friend's offense. Because the friend's transgression seems to involve sexual betrayal, a "sensual fault," scholars have traditionally speculated that the friend may have seduced the poet's mistress or been seduced by her, although a few commentators have concluded that the sexual suggestion is homoerotic.

If the wrong done the poet is moot, its effect is not. The friend is "grieved" by it. The poet argues, through parallel examples, that the faults of men have analogues in nature, even in the most beautiful of things: roses and buds, silver fountains, sun and moon. These images of nature's perfection are no less subject to flaws than humans are. The rose stem bears wounding thorns, clouds and eclipses dim the beauty of moon and sun, canker worms devour sweet buds, and the water of the silver fountains may, at times, grow muddy. The poet then argues that he is also blameworthy, since he excuses his friend's fault with his flawed comparisons and his faulty logic, which speciously justify his friend's betrayal. He is thus corrupted by his need to excuse his friend's faults.

Line 8, one of the most difficult of lines in Shakespeare's sonnets, has frequently been emended to read "Excusing thy sins more than thy sins are," with its implication that the friend's transgression was not significant enough to require the poet's reasoned defense, one that turns the wounded party into the wrongdoer's chief advocate. The poet, drawn by the conflicting demands of "love and hate," is put in the untenable position of defending the "sweet theefe" who has stolen his mistress' affections, and he chastises himself as an "accessary" to the friend's crime.

Forms and Devices

Sonnet 35 is in the English or Shakespearean sonnet form, as are all but three of the poems in Shakespeare's sonnet sequence. This form consists of fourteen iambic pentameter lines arranged as three quatrains and a couplet, rhyming *abab cdcd efef gg*. Sonnet 35 is a very regular example. Its phrasing is rigorously maintained by end-of-line punctuation marking full caesuras; Shakespeare employs no enjambment or run-on lines. Each line is a whole syntactical unit, usually a dependent clause. The rhymes, too, are regular, although modern pronunciation turns "compare" and "sins are" of lines 6 and 8 and "Advocate" and "hate" of lines 10 and 12 into apparent sight rhymes rather than true rhyme. There is also some metrical inversion, beginning in line 2, with "Roses," a trochee. Similar variations in meter occur in lines 3, 6, 8, 10, 13, and 14. Metrical inversion is common throughout Shakespeare's sonnet sequence. It is often used to counterpoint the basic iambic scheme, which might otherwise become too monotonous.

The sonnet's regularity complements its basic idea. The poem takes the form of logical discourse, of a legal argument, ostensibly rational rather than emotional. Although the poet admits to using what elsewhere he calls "false compare" (Sonnet 130), he starts out to justify his friend's betrayal by arguing that nothing is perfect. In the manner of much Elizabethan verse, the lyric uses multiple examples from nature, although as either analogies or analogues they are clearly strained if not completely inappropriate. The fault of the young man lies in his own character, whereas the analogies in nature involve such phenomena as an eclipse of the sun or moon and the destruction of a flower bud by a canker worm. Such "flaws," except for the rose's thorns, are not intrinsic in the object but are introduced by some external or invasive presence. However, at a metaphorical level, that presence—the shadow on the sun or the mud in the water of the silver fountain—might be interpreted as the "Dark Lady," the poet's mistress and the corrupting influence on the young man. Elsewhere in the sequence, including Sonnet 34, Shakespeare uses the sun as metaphor for his friend—thus, when read in sequence, Sonnet 35 takes advantage of resonant associations established in the lyrics preceding it.

In the reasoning that follows the examples of lines 2 through 4, the poet turns the argument against himself, claiming that he is flawed for "authorizing" his friend's wrongdoing through an involuted reasoning that uses "sence" or logic to justify his friend's "sensuall fault." He thereby becomes both plaintiff and the offender's advocate, a paradoxical situation arising from the "civill war" that pits his feelings of "love and hate" against each other. These ambivalent feelings are very succinctly expressed in the vivid "sweet theefe" oxymoron of the last line. There is perhaps a hint of self-contempt in the alliterative use of sibilants in lines 7 through 9, the hissing sound of words in phrases like "salving thy amissse" and "excusing their sins," tingeing the poem with some self disgust. Ironically, although the poet is clearly the wounded party, he seems more willing to forgive his friend than he is himself for doing so. Such convoluted sophistry was part of the rhetorical tradition so much admired by Shakespeare's contemporaries. It provided evidence of a poet's invention and wit, though to a modern ear it may seem somewhat contrived and insincere.

Themes and Meanings

Sonnet 35 investigates the conflicting demands of erotic love (*eros*) and spiritual love (*agape*), a familiar Elizabethan theme. Friendship, because it is based on reason, was perceived as a higher order of love than that based on physical attraction, and although it might exist between members of the opposite sex, it was generally restricted to relationships within the same sex, since, for heterosexual men and women, that exclusiveness would preclude carnal attraction and preserve the love's purity. One test of such a friendship, exploited by Shakespeare in both lyrics and plays, is the threat posed by sexual jealousy. Since a man's will can be corrupted by desire, he could betray a friendship by engaging in a sexual liaison with his friend's mistress, as seems to be the situation behind Sonnet 35 and related sonnets dealing with the temporary estrangement of the poet and the young man. That the friendship can survive the conflicting demands of *eros* and *agape* is evidence of its enduring strength.

The poem also reflects an idea prevalent in much of Shakespeare's work, one that suggests a great generosity of spirit and ensures the poet's lasting place among the world's most humane and forgiving writers. Humankind is susceptible to sin, having, as Friar Laurence in *Romeo and Juliet* discloses, both "grace and rude will," two opposing factions that correspond to reason and appetite. Susceptible to sin, humans will err and therefore must be forgiven. Capable of sin themselves, those victimized by it must be merciful, since, as Portia explains to Shylock in *The Merchant of Venice*, mercy is an attribute of God himself and is a quality that transcends retributive justice. Humankind is thus enjoined to forgive the sinner while condemning the sin. As Hamlet tells Polonius in *Hamlet*, if people were given only their just desserts, none would "'scape whipping." It is this belief that is the ethical lodestone of the New Testament.

Sonnet 35 seems to reflect a testing of the poet's belief in the necessary charity of the human spirit at a very personal level. The act of forgiving exacts its toll, primarily because the poet's pride resists the humiliation attendant upon manufacturing such a tenuous excuse for his friend's behavior. Shakespeare's sonnet vividly captures a sense of the struggle between the poet's wounded ego and his need, from love, to forgive his friend.

John W. Fiero

SONNET 55

Author: William Shakespeare (1564-1616)
Type of poem: Sonnet
First published: 1609, in *Sonnets*

The Poem

Sonnet 55 is one of a collection of 154 sonnets written by William Shakespeare and expresses one of the major themes of these sonnets: Poetry is eternal and will immortalize the subject of the poem. The tone of the first quatrain, or first four lines, reflects the extreme confidence of the poet: His "powerful rhyme" is compared to durable marble and solid, gilded memorials that mark the graves of princes. The monuments for the Elizabethan royals and aristocracy often consisted of a full-length portrait of the deceased carved in high relief on the stone cover of a coffin. The sonnet is compared not only to the lastingness of stone but also to an enduring image of the deceased. The poet asserts that his portrait of the young man, written in verse on fragile paper, will outlive even the marble memorials of princes, which will inevitably become neglected, "unswept stone" with the inexorable passage of time. In this sonnet, Shakespeare gives time a character. In this case, time is "sluttish," suggesting that it is dirty and careless. "Sluttish" can also mean whorish. Time, then, cares for no individual; it is immoral and will, in its slovenly and whorish manner, pass. The grand memorials will become eroded, and the people memorialized will eventually be forgotten. However, the subject of the poem will "shine more bright" than the time-smeared monuments and live not in effigy but in essence in Shakespeare's verse.

The second quatrain intensifies the poet's declaration. The imagery of long-forgotten, cold stone monuments gives way to active, deliberate devastation. The young man will be remembered despite the wrack and ruin of "wasteful war." When marble statues topple and stone buildings and other "works of masonry" are destroyed, the poetry will live on. Not even the flaming sword of mighty Mars, the god of war himself, is able to "burn/ The living record" of the young man's memory. The final quatrain contains the powerful image of the young man striding like a Titan through time "'Gainst death and all oblivious enmity." He will "pace forth" and be not only remembered but also praised in the eyes of "all posterity" even to posterity's end. His memory will outwear the world and survive "the ending doom," the Apocalypse itself.

The couplet—the final two lines of the poem—draws a conclusion and sums up the ideas that have accumulated with each successive quatrain. The young man will live in "this," the poet's verse, until Judgment Day. On that day, the bodies of all humanity are to be resurrected and reunited with the soul, and judgment will be passed as to which souls will suffer in hell and which will rise to heaven. He, too, will face his individual judgment and will "arise" to heaven rather than be damned to hell.

Forms and Devices

Sonnet 55 is one of a series of 154 sonnets written in the first person—the first 126 are addressed to a young man, and the remaining sonnets (127-154) are addressed to or refer to a dark lady. A rival poet is a third character in the drama of the sonnets. Some scholars believe that the sonnets tell a story that is a reflection of Shakespeare's private life, while others claim that the sonnets are a literary exercise. In either event, the accumulated sonnets tell a story of love, lust, separation from the beloved, betrayal, repentance, and self-loathing.

Sonnet 55 is typical of the form that has become known as the Shakespearean sonnet. Its fourteen lines generally consist of three quatrains (three sets of four lines each), the first of which puts forth a poetic idea that the two following quatrains explore and develop. The quatrains are followed by two final lines (a couplet) that punctuate, draw a conclusion to, or make an ironic comment on the ideas the poet has been exploring in the quatrains. The lines are written in iambic pentameter, and the rhyme scheme of the Shakespearean sonnet is *abab cdcd efef gg*.

Although the sonnets, as a rule, can stand on their own as individual poems, it is a good idea to look at the sonnets that surround it. Sonnet 54 sets up Sonnet 55 by bringing up the idea that the essence of a person may be distilled by poetry in the same manner that the essence of a rose may be distilled. After death, the substance of the rose or of the person may perish, but it lives on by virtue of its remaining essence. The first quatrain of Sonnet 55 elaborates the idea that the young man will live perpetually in the poet's verse. The imagery of fragile flowers gives way to grand marble and elaborate, gilded stone monuments. The final line of the quatrain is thick with alliteration and vivid imagery that tells of "unswept stone, besmeared with sluttish time." The contrast implies the passage of a very long time—centuries, perhaps—and reinforces the power of the verse that will eternalize the essence of the young man's brightly shining self.

The second quatrain elaborates the idea of the durability of poetry through the use of images of war and destruction. Overturned statues and "broils" (battles) that "root out the work of masonry" summon up the image of a city left in ruins. The introduction of Mars, the ancient god of war, suggests once again the passage of ages. Shakespeare's use of the word "record" evokes the image of record books and reminds the reader that a poem is written on paper that is easily destroyed by the fires of war. Yet the essence of a poem lies not in the paper upon which it is written but in the ideas and emotions expressed by the poet, who contends that his rhyme is so powerful that it will outlive even this dire threat of destruction.

The third quatrain puts the idea of eternity in the foreground. The lines speak of death, oblivion, and the "ending doom." Most people's memories fade into the oblivious mists of time. However, the young man of the sonnets will keep pace with the time. As time progresses, this praise, this poetry, this essence of the young man will keep pace with its passage. Even to the end of days, when posterity's posterity has outworn the world, men will remember and praise the young subject of the verse—he will live in their eyes, the window to their souls. The "So" of the final couplet announces the summing up of the ideas and the themes of the sonnet. The phrases "ending doom" and "the judgment" are references to the Christian belief in the Last Judgment. On this day, after the Second Coming of Christ, the world and time will come to a violent end. This suggests that the essence or the life force of the young man, distilled in the poet's words, will outlive life itself.

Themes and Meanings

The idea that verse would ensure the poet's immortality is a common Renaissance theme that came to the Elizabethans via Latin poets such as Ovid in his *Metamorphoses* (c. A.D. 8; English translation, 1567) and Horace in his odes. Shakespeare puts a twist on this idea by claiming that his poetry will guarantee the undying fame of the subject of the poems rather than the author himself. The motif of immortality in the sonnets is expressed differently in the first seventeen poems, in which the poet urges the young man to marry and procreate so that he will continue to live through his children after his death. Beginning with Sonnet 18, and in several sonnets thereafter, the notion that the ineluctable power of poetry will ensure perpetual remembrance is expressed. The relentless passage of time is a major theme of the collected sonnets, and time plays an active role. Time will age the beautiful young man to whom the sonnets are addressed. With the passage of time, summer roses will wilt and die. However, just as the perfume, or "essence," of the rose can be distilled and kept long after the rose is gone, so too can the essence of the young man, his physical and spiritual beauty, be distilled in poetry and remain long after his death. Poetry is time's most effective enemy.

Scholars have gone to great lengths to discover the identity of the young man who was to be immortalized in the sonnets. The dedication of the 1609 printing of the collected sonnets to a "Mr. W. H." as "the onlie begetter of these insuing sonnets" has been cited as evidence that the young man was, in fact, a living person and perhaps a patron of Shakespeare. Henry Wriothesley, earl of Southampton, and William Herbert, earl of Pembroke, are persons most often considered as the potential "Mr. W. H." There has also been great speculation as to the identity of the "dark lady" and the "rival poet" of the sonnets. The great irony is that it is Shakespeare himself who is immortalized in sonnets and none of the collection's major players. The "beautiful young man" who was to live until doomsday in the verse of the poet has long been forgotten, while Shakespeare lives on.

Diane M. Almeida

SONNET 87

Author: William Shakespeare (1564-1616)
Type of poem: Sonnet
First published: 1609, in *Sonnets*

The Poem

In his cycle of 154 sonnets, Shakespeare directs the first 127 to a handsome young man usually identified as his patron, Henry Wriothesley, the earl of Southampton (1573-1624). Sonnet 87 concludes a series of ten known as the Rival Poet group. It s unknown who the rival poet was, and in fact it is possible that he never really existed. Among Shakespeare's contemporaries who have been suggested are Edmund Spenser, Christopher Marlowe, Samuel Daniel, and others, although because certain lines in Sonnet 86 seem to allude to George Chapman, he is the most favored candidate. On the other hand, some of the sonnets in the series, for example, Sonnet 85, suggest that more than one poet may rival Shakespeare for the young man's attentions.

Throughout the Rival Poet group, the writer reveals an increasing amount of self-deprecation as he realizes that he is losing out to his rival. Sonnet 87 thus brings the competition to an end by renouncing the speaker's claims to the young man. It is a moving farewell but not an unambiguous one: Shakespeare's sonnet operates at several levels simultaneously. Although the speaker recognizes that the young man has grown quite beyond his ability to hold, and that he no longer deserves his favor, his sense of regret and loss is sharp. If the relationship was once based upon an acknowledgment of reciprocal worth, or deserving, that no longer appears to be true. The young man apparently overvalued the writer's qualities and, since he now can more clearly see their true worth, has withdrawn his love.

The final two lines of the sonnet express the speaker's regret most poignantly. For him, the relationship with the young man has been like a dream, in which he ruled like a kind of sovereign or prince. Now that the young man has withdrawn his love, the speaker has awakened to reality. It is a brutal awakening, at once destroying the "flattery" with which his "dream" deluded him.

Forms and Devices

Shakespeare's sonnets differ from the Italian (or Petrarchan) form of the sonnet. Unlike Italian sonnets, his have three quatrains followed by a single couplet—instead of an octave (eight lines, rhyming *abba abba*) followed by a sestet (six lines, usually rhyming *cdcdee*). In some of Shakespeare's sonnets the octave-sestet form may still be discerned, but Sonnet 87 is not among them. Sonnet 87, moreover, is unusual not so much in having all its lines end-stopped, but in the number of weak, or feminine, endings—twelve of a possible fourteen. These weak endings are generally held to be more appropriate to a comic poem (such as George Gordon, Lord Byron's poem *Don Juan*) than to the solemn occasion that this sonnet ostensibly describes.

The poem begins with a firm "Farewell" and proceeds through the next twelve lines to explain, if not to justify, the parting of the two friends. The weak line endings signal and tend to underscore the ironies and ambiguities that pervade the sonnet. These devices bespeak the speaker's underlying reluctance to let go as well as his sense of undeserved dismissal. The words "too dear" in the first line state that the young man is too precious or of too high a rank for the speaker, but they may also imply that his friendship costs too much. The last word in the line, "possessing," introduces further ambiguities involved in the legal and commercial language of the next eleven lines. The second line is fraught with ambiguity; it may be interpreted to signify (among other possible meanings) "Very likely you know how highly I regard you," "You probably know your own worth very well," and "You know how much you deserve to be loved." The "charter" in line 3 is a legal metaphor for privilege that his noble rank or intrinsic value bestows on the young man, a privilege that allows him to sever with impunity their relationship. Hence, the speaker's "bonds" (ties plus legal covenant) are all "determinate"—that is, ended and outdated, as applied to legal bonds, but also circumscribed.

In the second quatrain, the speaker explains how all this has come to pass. His "possession" of the young man was in the first place made possible only by the latter's voluntary granting, which the speaker's merits perhaps did not justify. Since those "riches," or the "fair gift" of the young man's favor, were insufficiently deserved, they revert, as in any legal or commercial arrangement, to the owner. "Fair" conveys a multiple ambiguity: "handsome," "legally equitable," "desirable," and perhaps "flattering." The "patent" in line 8 refers to a license or exclusive privilege that the young man had granted the speaker, which now returns intact to the grantor.

By the third quatrain the underlying resentment bordering on hostility becomes more acute. The young man had freely given himself, possibly without knowing how much either he or the receiver of his love was "worth." The misjudgment thus has led to a withdrawal of his "great gift," his love, once he has evaluated the relationship more precisely. By framing the situation in terms that carry suggestions of commercial trading, the speaker reveals his bitterness that their relationship—or any such relationship—should be measured in this way. The resentment deepens further, since "misprision" in line 11 signifies "contempt" as well as "error": What once was mutual affection has now turned into near despising, mutual or otherwise.

The final couplet summarizes the speaker's attitude in succinct terms, using a quite different but nonetheless appropriate metaphor. It has all been like a dream, and on awakening, the poet sees the reality of the situation. If in dreaming he felt like a king, possessing the "fair gift" of the young man (with a possible pun on the sexual significance of "had"), upon awakening he sees himself and the situation for what they are: He is not at all like royalty, and their friendship was merely illusory. Since "king" may also refer to the young man, the further implication is that the young man is something less than the speaker believed while he was dreaming. The emphasis on "matter," with which the poem ends, conveys disgust both in its ambiguity and in its enunciation, for "no such matter" means "nothing of the sort" but also "real substance" (as opposed to illusion), with a further allusion to the sexual sense of "matter" (as in Hamlet's reference to "country matters" in *Hamlet* 3.3.111).

Themes and Meanings

As the valediction to an affair or to a deeper personal relationship, Sonnet 87 conveys the mixed feelings, thoughts, and emotions that often accompany such moments. Although it is grouped among sonnets that have as their object, or auditor, a young man, the sonnet itself does not specify a particular person or sex. Removed from its immediate context, then, it has a more universal application and resonance. By the kinds of diction and metaphors it uses, it reveals a subtlety and sophistication worthy of any profoundly affected friend or lover faced with the ending of something once—and perhaps still—highly esteemed and cherished.

The ambiguities noted in the previous section reflect the kind of ambivalence typically found at the breakup of an affair. Examining the sonnet closely, one sees that the renunciation may be occurring on either side. In *Shakespeare's Wordplay* (1957), M. M. Mahood remarks: "Either Shakespeare is saying: 'You are so good and great that you may well end our friendship on the ground that there is no corresponding worth in me,' or he means: 'Because of your social advantage over me, you exact too high a price for our friendship, so I have decided to break free.' In addition, there is a strong hint of the meaning: 'I have lavished affection on a creature who is just not worth it." On the other hand, as Mahood recognizes, Shakespeare may be saying all three things at once. Contradictory feelings at such times are perfectly natural, and Shakespeare accordingly may be expressing them in this sonnet.

As in many of his poems and plays, Shakespeare shows himself to be aware of the ironies in human experience. That one can love a person who is undeserving of that love is one such irony; that one can praise a person while at the time being aware that the praise may not be fully—or at all—deserved is another. Both are found in Sonnet 87. The young man, handsome and attractive in many ways, may be too full of himself, too aware of his own "worth," to merit the kind of devotion the speaker in the sonnet is foolishly willing to give him. The situation, however, cannot continue. In the context of the Rival Poet sonnets, Shakespeare as the speaker of the sonnets cannot compete with the other poet to whom the young man has turned. Nevertheless, the speaker knows his own worth, or rather the value of his love, which unlike the young man's is neither shallow nor fickle. On this count alone he may deserve more, though the young man fails to recognize it, and their relationship therefore seems doomed.

Jay L. Halio

SONNET—TO SCIENCE

Author: Edgar Allan Poe (1809-1849)
Type of poem: Sonnet
First published: 1829, in *Al Aaraaf, Tamerlane, and Minor Poems*; collected in *The Complete Works of Edgar Allan Poe*, 1902

The Poem

In Edgar Allan Poe's later collections, "Sonnet—to Science" appears with a foot-note describing it as one of "the crude compositions of my earliest boyhood." The same footnote excuses its re-publication with reference to "private reasons—some of which have reference to the sin of plagiarism, and others to the date of Tennyson's first poems." Alfred, Lord Tennyson had been born in the same year as Poe and had published his first volume of poetry, *Poems by Two Brothers* (in association with his brother Charles), in 1827, the same year in which Poe's earliest publications appeared.

The sonnet's rhyme scheme follows the English, or Shakespearean, form rather than the Italian, or Petrarchan, sonnet form. Its substance, by contrast, has more in common with the Italian tradition, which characteristically involves the posing of a question, than with the English tradition, which tends to be more meditative. Where the Petrarchan sonnet would usually supplement an interrogatory octave with a responsive sestet, however, "Sonnet—to Science" maintains its inquiring tone throughout the three quatrains and the concluding couplet.

"Sonnet—to Science" addresses its object from a point of view solidly anchored within the Romantic movement, likening science's keen-eyed inquiry to a vulture whose wings cast a shadow of "dull reality" upon the landscape of the imagination. It asks how the poet, having discovered such a predator "upon [his] heart," can possibly love the scientific revelation or concede its wisdom. It is only natural, the sonnet suggests, that poets should flee the shadow of dull reality in search of better and brighter pastures, lit by "jewelled skies."

The last six lines of the sonnet add detail to the charges presented in more general terms in the first eight. Like a prosecutor engaged in cross-examination, the sonnet demands an accounting of specific sins. Has science not dragged Diana (a Roman goddess associated with nature and birth) from her "car"? (Diana was associated in Rome itself with moonlight, so the car in question is the moon.) Has not the Hamadryad (a type of nymph associated with oak trees) been "driven . . . from the wood" and the Naiad (a species of water nymph) from her "blood"—the blood in question being the stream or spring embodying her spirit? Has science not banished the Elfin—the Anglo-Saxon fairy race—from their pastoral haunts? And has it not, in consequence, robbed the poet of the "summer dream" which might otherwise have visited him in the shade of the tamarind tree?

The accusative tone of these questions implies that they are rhetorical—that they do not actually require an answer because it is obvious that each charge is correct. The fact remains, however, that no answer is given and that the questions are questions rather than statements. The poem preserves a margin of uncertainty, which the poet's voice invites the reader to share. "Sonnet—to Science" is a poem that seeks to address a problem and thus to define the problem's nature. As might be expected of a poem composed at the outset of an adventurous career, it is essentially open-ended. It is setting out an agenda rather than delivering a verdict.

Forms and Devices

Although Poe was well aware in his later years that he had been born in the same year as Tennyson, he probably was not conscious of the fact that he had also been born in the same year as Charles Darwin, whose theory of evolution was not published until ten years after Poe's death. It was Darwin's science which finally picked the bones of mythology clean, extrapolating in the process Tennyson's key image of "nature red in tooth and claw" ("In Memoriam," 1850).

Whether or not he was aware of Charles Darwin, however, Poe would certainly have been aware of Charles's grandfather, Erasmus Darwin (1731-1802), who was renowned in his own day as a poet as well as a naturalist. Erasmus Darwin frequently reported his scientific discoveries in poetic form, and his earlier publications—including *The Loves of the Plants* (1789)—are not ashamed to formulate his discoveries as news conveyed by nymphs and elemental spirits. The imagery of "Sonnet—to Science" implies a stark contrast between myth and science—a frank enmity expressed in the violence with which it treats Diana and the dispossessed nymphs—but the implication is more tentative than it may seem.

By choosing the metaphor of a shadow-casting wing to represent science Poe admits—and then re-emphasizes in the vital eighth line—that science has its own soaring imagination and its own admirable courage. The first line, too, concedes that science is a "true daughter of Old Time," the time in question being that which brings self-knowledge and reveals previously hidden truths—and perhaps also the time that heals wounds.

The concessions of the first and eighth lines would be more generous, of course, were it not for the fact that the shadow-casting wing of science is attached to a vulture: a bird of ill-omen more disreputable even than a raven. The third line makes it explicit, however, that Poe conceives science as a predator, not as a scavenger, and this is re-emphasized in the second part of the poem. Science drags, drives, and tears; it does not sit around waiting for myth to die of natural causes. It is, in fact, more like an eagle than a vulture. There is a hesitation here, if not an outright ambiguity.

Themes and Meanings

Even in this early work, Poe seems to have been considering—albeit a bit reluctantly—the possibility that he might align himself with those Romantics who celebrated the awesome revelations of the scientific imagination (among whom Percy Bysshe Shelley was the most outstanding) rather than those who viewed the intellectual and industrial revolutions with mournful regret. He never did resolve that dilemma, and that was greatly to the advantage of his work. No other nineteenth century

American writer fled as far as he "to seek for treasure in the jewelled skies," and the flight in question began in the poem which follows "Sonnet—to Science" in his collected works: the brilliantly bizarre "Al Aaraaf."

The first footnote to "Al Aaraaf" links it to Tycho Brahe's "new star," which revealed once and for all that the heavens are not fixed and finished, but the imagery of the long poem is as rich and exotic as anything Poe was later to produce. Other footnotes set Classical references and scientific references side by side, but not as Erasmus Darwin might have done. Poe never lost the sense of a vital and violent struggle between the hallowed glories of mythology and the new revelations of science; he never could combine the two without a keen awareness that he was doing something paradoxical. But Poe was a very paradoxical man, and he took pride in that fact. He conceived of his own self as something deeply divided, echoed that division in many of the characters with whom he populated his phantasmagoric tales, and saw it reflected in the war between science and romance for possession of the modern imagination.

"Sonnet—to Science" is a very modest poem by comparison with the works for which Poe is best remembered. It lacks all trace of the greatness of his best work, yet it is an interesting poem, both in the context of its time and in the context of the career that grew from it. Even as an adolescent Poe was aware of the overarching importance of the march of science and was concerned with calculating its costs and rewards. "Sonnet—to Science" emphasizes the costs, but it does not do so blindly or blandly; it has intelligence enough to acknowledge that the imaginative predations of science are not without a certain grandeur as well as an ominous inevitability.

Toward the end of his life, Poe was to expand greatly on his perception of the problem posed in "Sonnet—to Science" in the long poetic essay *Eureka* (1848). *Eureka* protests against the reductionist method of science while celebrating the magnificence of its revelations. Like "Sonnet—to Science," *Eureka*'s first concern is the astronomers who dethroned Diana and the other deities embodied in the heavens. In a sense, "Sonnet—to Science" is the more prophetic work in that it proceeds to pay more attention to the disenchanting effects of biological science.

In answer to his own not-quite-rhetorical questions, Poe decided that if science was neither lovable nor entirely wise, then the duty of the poet was to take arms against it and fight for the conservation of the Elfin and their classical analogues. The heroic quality of that mission was never properly appreciated in his native land, where nonbelievers in science and technology preferred to sequester themselves within the walls of religious fundamentalism. In the lands where the fugitive Elfin and the Dianic mysteries were still remembered, however, and their force still felt, Poe's progress from sonnet, "Sonnet—to Science," to epic, *Eureka*, via the most scenic route imaginable, has been celebrated with all appropriate reverence.

Brian Stableford

SOURDOUGH MOUNTAIN LOOKOUT

Author: Philip Whalen (1923-   )
Type of poem: Meditation
First published: 1960, in *Like I Say*

The Poem

"Sourdough Mountain Lookout" reflects on Philip Whalen's experience as a fire lookout in the Cascade Mountains in the western United States. The poem does not develop ideas or narrative in a linear fashion; instead, it wanders and loops in a manner that suggests the natural course of the thoughts of someone ruminating on experience. In his notes on poetics in *The New American Poetry 1945-1960* (1960), Whalen describes his poetry as "a picture or a graph of a mind moving, which is a world body being here and now which is history . . . and you." The title names the mountain where Whalen was a lookout in the summer of 1955. The poem is dedicated to Kenneth Rexroth, a poet of the generation before Whalen's. Rexroth influenced and encouraged the poets of the San Francisco Renaissance, including Whalen. Rexroth also helped make Chinese and Japanese poetry known in the West through his translations and essays. Since "Sourdough Mountain Lookout" makes a number of references to Buddhist and Asian topics and since Rexroth shared an interest in mountaineering, the dedication is quite appropriate.

"Sourdough Mountain Lookout" has a loose, associational form. It is a series of more or less developed notations reflecting on Whalen's experience as a lookout. It divides into roughly forty verse paragraphs, including several that are only one line long. On a larger scale, the poem may be seen as divided into four sections of unequal length. These divisions are marked by quotations that set a tone for that section. The quotations are introduced by the source's name in capital letters. There are section quotations from the Greek philosophers Heraclitus and Empedocles and from the Buddha. Whalen quotes other figures as well, including his grandmother, eighteenth century English writer Samuel Johnson, and another Forest Service employee.

The poem differs slightly in its published versions. In *On Bear's Head*, it has an epigraph from the ancient Chinese writer Tsung Ping that anticipates the tone of Whalen's poem as a meditative reflection on mountains. The epigraph does not appear in *Like I Say*. In *The New American Poetry 1945-1960*, the poem includes a transliteration of a Sanskrit mantra as well as Whalen's colloquial translation. The epigraph from Tsung Ping not only establishes a tone for the whole poem but also governs the first section. Whalen begins by stating that he always says he will not return to the mountains. This opening makes it clear that he is reflecting on his experiences as a lookout but that his perspective includes more than just that experience. In seven paragraphs, this first section establishes the feeling of being on the mountaintop. The details of fog, lakes, and animals establish the setting, with Whalen placed firmly within it: His "bootprints mingle with deer-foot" in "the dusty path to the privy." Whalen assumes a very human and ordinary persona throughout the poem so that despite its concern with elevated topics, it never becomes ponderous or self-serious. Consistent with Whalen's general attitude in his poetry, "Sourdough Mountain Lookout" is playful and relaxed.

Forms and Devices

The language of "Sourdough Mountain Lookout" is colloquial and casual without being slack or unclear. Whalen uses colloquial American language much like a music composer such as Aaron Copland may use folk tunes for formal compositions; the spoken language becomes the medium for thought and perception that rise beyond the rather cloudy level of ordinary awareness. The first three lines set the tone and attitude for the remainder of the poem: "I always say I won't go back to the mountains/ I am too old and fat there are bugs mean mules/ And pancakes every morning of the world."

Whalen varies line length and paragraph length expressively. The longer lines include more poetic language:

> Morning fog in the southern gorge
> Gleaming foam restoring the old sea-level
> The lakes in two lights green soap and indigo
> The high cirque-lake black half-open eye

These lines describe the fog in the gorge with respect for what it is while still keeping in mind the process of change that is a major theme of the poem. The language is careful and exact without fancy effects. The only unusual term, "cirque," is chosen not for poetic effect but for geological accuracy. The poem's shorter lines are terse and tightly focused. A later passage of seven lines falls into a syllabic pattern. The first two and the last three lines have four syllables each, and the third and fourth lines have eight syllables, accommodating polysyllabic words: "There was a bird/ Lived in an egg/ And by ingenious chemistry/ Wrought molecules of albumen/ To beak and eye." This paragraph draws the reader's attention to the specifics of avian reproduction to express the theme of change. These two passages illustrate Whalen's skill in combining different types of diction in the same poem as well as his skill in writing in different modes. The quotations he includes extend the dictional range of the poem from the colloquialism of his father and grandmother to the aphorisms of the philosophers.

Whalen makes little use of metaphor or simile in the poem. The figurative language that he does use does not call attention to itself. An example is his description of the fossil of a palm frond as a "centipede shadow" and a "limestone lithograph." Generally, Whalen uses literal language but loads it with meaning. Toward the end of the poem, however, he uses an emphatic metaphor that extends into symbolism. The mountains surrounding him are a "circle of 108 beads." The description of the circle of beads is developed in detail. Whalen is referring to a string of *mala* beads used by both Hindus and Buddhists in meditation. As a string of prayer beads, the mountains acquire a specific meaning for Whalen as they become the means by which he meditates.

The next-to-last paragraph of the poem gives a colloquial American translation of the mantra of the Heart Sutra. A very brief Buddhist scripture, the Heart Sutra is an important text in Zen as well as other Mahayana Buddhist schools. A translation more literal than Whalen's would read "gone, gone, gone beyond, gone all the way beyond, awareness, bliss." Its position at the very end of the poem suggests the mantra's importance to the poem's meaning.

Themes and Meanings

The style and structure of "Sourdough Mountain Lookout" not only reflect and express Whalen's Buddhist views but also express his way of thinking. Whalen speaks for himself in the poem as a witness to his experience. He clearly does not take himself seriously, a stance appropriate to any spiritually oriented poem and especially to a Buddhist poem. In the Buddhist view, the "self" is unreal, an aggregation of various elements. The quotation from the Buddha expresses this view: "All the constituents of being are/ Transitory." That being the case, the constituents of this poem are also transitory as Whalen's loose, notational style suggests. He does not try to create a poem as an eternal monument to his experience; instead, his poem is a loose, tentative testimony to what is passing and ephemeral. About halfway through, Whalen suggests that like Buddha and Jesus, he is preaching on a mountain: "Flies & other insects come from miles around/ To listen" to Whalen tell them and the reader that all things are transitory. Whalen's awareness ranges from the very rocks of the mountains to the sun, from the flies that come to listen to him to the brontosaurus that has left fossils in the rocks. The sun flames in the background of the poem as the unavoidable fire that burns and transforms all things. In referring to Heraclitus, Whalen introduces a Western philosopher of change to match the Buddha's sense that all things are in flux. The second quotation from Heraclitus presents the world as a system of transformations that flow without ceasing.

In the first lines, Whalen says he is too "old and fat" to go up the mountain again. In the last two lines, he says that he has never left: "'Four times up,/ Three times down.' I'm still on the mountain." He is still on the mountain because his experience of transcending the world of flux remains with him. The mantra that just precedes these lines expresses and engenders that experience. The Heart Sutra teaches that "form is emptiness, emptiness is form." Whalen implies that he has somehow incorporated that teaching and that it stays with him. Written about fifteen years before Whalen formally became a Zen Buddhist monk, "Sourdough Mountain Lookout" clearly expresses the Zen teaching that samsara, this world of change, is nirvana, the world of freedom.

Gene Doty

THE SPANISH TRILOGY

Author: Rainer Maria Rilke (1875-1926)
Type of poem: Lyric
First published: 1927, as "Die Spanische Trilogie," in *Gesammelte Werke*; English
translation collected in *Poems 1906 to 1926*, 1957

The Poem

Rainer Maria Rilke wrote "The Spanish Trilogy" in Ronda, Spain, between January 6 and 14, 1913. He had seen El Greco's dramatic painting of Toledo in 1911 and made the trip to Spain to see the landscape. The opening lines of the poem capture his great enthusiasm for the rugged countryside, which is full of movement and charged with portent on a windy night. Rilke's engrossment in the landscape is reflected structurally in the complex, long first sentence of the poem, which spans all twenty-four lines of part 1. Its repeated prepositional phrases beginning with "from" convey a sense of involvement in an active, synthetic process, the purpose of which is revealed in an infinitive clause without subject: "to make one Thing." Something is happening to the poet. In a moment of heightened awareness, he becomes one with his surroundings. His impassioned language, "Lord Lord Lord," reveals his rush of ecstasy. His clever closing simile, comparing the "Thing" with a meteor, emphasizes the speed and significance of the occurrence.

Part 1 is written in a rhythmic iambic pentameter without rhyme. In the original German, all lines have a masculine ending except for the last line, whose extra, unaccented syllable gives a sense of graceful completion to the last word: "arrival." Part 2 is, by comparison, more introspective, more involved in the human condition. Its twenty-two lines are divided into three stanzas. The poet has been in the presence of the extraordinary, which he must accept with imperfect understanding. Rilke managed to write all of part 1 without naming a subject. Now, in part 2, he humorously likens himself to a servant who does not dare to ask "Master, why this banquet?" He makes the same point more seriously in the second and third stanzas, choosing the likeness of a shepherd. The man is necessarily so alert and so observant that he is bombarded with "world": He has "world each time he lifts his head;/ each time he looks down—world." Again the repetition of a word, in this case "world," lends an emotional element to the description.

Part 3 returns to the first-person point of view and relaxes the metric scheme. Its twenty-one lines of free verse sound more like conversational commentary. The poet is resolving to use his memory of the shepherd to his advantage when he returns to the city of Paris, France. At the end of the poem, Rilke resorts to a more pastoral, idealized picture of the shepherd, even describing him as majestic and godlike. The four-line coda at the end of the poem explains that the image Rilke retains of the shepherd is, for him, a means of accessing inner peace, of returning to a most meaningful experience, a moment of oneness with the universe that was so intense he would happily have died afterward.

Forms and Devices

Since the three parts of "The Spanish Trilogy" are different in tone and content, Rilke relies on structural similarities to unify the poem. Each of the three parts begins with anaphora. In part 1, lines 1, 3, and 5 proceed from the same preposition: "From this cloud," "from these dark clustered hills," and "from this stream in the valley." Lines 2, 4, and 6 complement that with epistrophe, all ending with "(and from me)." Rilke has introduced the two main components, the landscape and the poet, from the left and the right and uses the rest of the stanza to combine them. In part 2, the first two stanzas begin with the identical rhetorical question "Why must a man." In part 3, Rilke uses the repetition of "Let me" at the beginning of lines 1 and 4 to lead in the poet's resolution. The anaphora at the beginning of each part of the trilogy helps underline the sequence of the parts. First the poet has an extraordinary experience, then he has a period of questioning, and finally he decides his further course of action.

Rilke provides the reader with a wealth of images in the course of the poem. The image of the shepherd is given extended treatment in parts 2 and 3 and can also be inferred in part 1 from the mention of the flock. Yet Rilke cautions, in the coda, against seeking hidden meaning in the figure of the shepherd: "Let him be whomever you wish." He is interchangeable, simply a means to an end. The poet is not so much interested in the shepherd as in the elements and forces in the midst of which he appears: night and day, the earth and sky, old age and youth, this world and the next; in short, the universe in its totality. The "Thing" of part 1 is both "earthly and cosmic." In part 2, the shepherd takes "all the galaxies/ into his face." In part 3, he is "like the day itself" with space thinking for him. These are grandiose, mind-expanding images.

In "The Spanish Trilogy," Rilke is dealing with something very real but at the same time elusive. It can only be indicated as an abstract "Thing" or approximated through analogous descriptions. Rilke ends each stanza with a striking simile. The position of the similes provides structural unity, and each of them makes the meaning more precise. For example, the simile at the end of part 1 that compares the "Thing" to a meteor shows the substantial becoming insubstantial. It emphasizes the transitory nature of the experience and its subsequent inaccessibility while leaving no doubt in the reader's mind about the actual event. The image used in the final simile of the poem is scaled down considerably from that of the first. For the poet, evoking the memory of his Spanish experience has the same stabilizing effect as placing a stormlamp around a fluttering candle. This is the fire of the meteor in more manageable form. Implicit in the simile are elements of volition and control, of quiet domesticity, duration, and fulfilment. The poet has come a long way in the course of the poem.

Themes and Meanings

Rilke was in his late thirties when he wrote "The Spanish Trilogy." In 1910, he completed his novel *Die Aufzeichnungen des Malte Laurids Brigge* (*The Notebooks of Malte Laurids Brigge*, 1930), felt exhausted, and wondered whether he could continue writing. Another major project, *Duineser Elegien* (1923; *The Duino Elegies*,

1930), was also proving more difficult than expected, and, at the time of his trip to Spain, Rilke was entertaining alternative career plans. For this reason, some critics have interpreted "The Spanish Trilogy" as dealing specifically with the "processes of poetry, as Rilke experienced them," as a three-stage description of the creative process: First, poets have an intense experience; second, they struggle with the materials of that experience; and third, they feel the satisfaction of successfully converting the essence of the experience into a permanent form, a poem that effectively communicates their sensations and perceptions to others. While this approach is too narrow to do justice to the entire poem, it does have merit. Rilke had written a short prose piece a year earlier titled "Über den Dichter" (about the poet), in which he describes a situation that presented itself as an allegory for the role of the poet. Sailors rowing a becalmed boat upstream are energized when a man standing at the bow bursts into song. His voice connects them with the distant goal that only he can see. The poet, for Rilke, is the person who can make that connection and convey that vision to others. If this insight is applied to "The Spanish Trilogy," the poet is the person who, in the turmoil of the big city, can recall the calm of a pastoral scene. Of course, people who are not poets also calm themselves through recourse to special memories, and this is what Rilke is recommending. He does not expect that his experience of the shepherd will have a similar effect on others, but he does suppose that others have their own significant sources of peace and harmony: "Let him be whomever you wish."

The last lines of the poem, which must be included in any comprehensive interpretation, go far beyond any comment on writing. They place Rilke's Spanish experience in the order of the ultimate considerations of life and death: "May death/ more easily find its way." In Ronda, Rilke felt extraordinarily at one with the world. A few weeks after writing "The Spanish Trilogy," he wrote "Erlebnis" (experience) 1 and 2, prose pieces that also describe states of unusually heightened awareness. He remembers how, in a garden by the sea, he felt the subtle vibrations of the life force itself in a tree trunk and how the blue of a periwinkle was of inexhaustible significance. A bird call was simultaneously outside and within him. Once privy to this transcendent state, he had a new perspective on everyday life since he had, in a sense, overcome its restrictions. "The Spanish Trilogy" is written with the knowledge of universal harmony. Having glimpsed the massive forces that contain life and death, the poet quietly accepts their sovereignty.

Jean M. Snook

SPEAK, PARROT

Author: John Skelton (c.1460-1529)
Type of poem: Satire
First published: 1545, as "Speke, Parrot," in *Here after foloweth certayne bokes cöpyled*; collected in *John Skelton: The Complete English Poems*, 1983

The Poem

"Speak, Parrot" has been regarded as John Skelton's masterpiece, a brilliant tour de force which links his strong sense of moralism, keen observations of contemporary court and political events, and his extraordinary poetic talents. It is a long poem, over 520 full or partial lines in its definitive modern edition. While it is written largely in blocks of seven-line stanzas with a consistent *ababbee* rhyme pattern, it is also interspersed with various other line lengths and rhyme patterns, and it includes snatches of dialogue, much of it in languages other than English.

"Speak, Parrot" is typical of much of Skelton's work. It is a commentary on public events that would have primarily interested the court of Henry VIII but also would have had wider political implications. As court poet (essentially the same as the modern poet laureate) Skelton would have been expected to produce such works. In addition, the poem carries a strongly moralizing element, which again is characteristic of Skelton's verses. The combination of the two threads produced a rich, densely compact poem presented in a brilliant but sometimes enigmatic style.

The poem is one of Skelton's most difficult to understand, not only because of its vocabulary and organization but also because it is an extended allegory, many of whose meanings and references are presented in veiled imagery that would have been familiar to a limited number of persons at the time the poem was written and that has become fainter over the years. Still, the work retains a vigorous sense of form and meaning that makes it accessible to the modern reader.

In large part a political satire on life and affairs in the court of the English king Henry VIII, the poem's central target is Cardinal Thomas Wolsey, Henry VIII's most important minister. However, a number of other topics, including new ways of teaching Latin in English universities and the moral decay of the times, are included. Because of this range of subjects, and because "Speak, Parrot" has a structural pattern that, like its language, is rather freely and loosely assembled, the work has been termed a "gallimaufry," or confused medley. With "Speak, Parrot," this is literally true, since the poem presents several different rhyming and rhythmic patterns as well as shifting from English to Latin with sometimes bewildering frequency.

However, this seeming confusion is deliberately manipulated by Skelton to suit his satirical purpose. Because of the open nature of the poem, it can address any subject freely and move from one to another without bothering with strictly logical consistency. Because of its hidden and allegorical nature, it can suggest and imply more than it openly states.

The "Parrot" of the title is the narrator of the poem and may be identified with

Skelton. Within the poem, as a "byrde of Paradyse," Parrot is a special pet of the ladies at the court, who beg him to speak to them: "'Speke, Parott, I pray yow,' full curteslye they sey,/ 'Parott ys a goodlye byrde and a pratye popagay'" [prattling popinjay]. As a prattling popinjay, or chatterbox, Parrot is given leave to speak freely, much in the tradition of court jesters or royal fools, and he takes full advantage of this, especially in his attacks on Cardinal Wolsey.

The poem moves from the general to the particular. Its early stanzas set the context, placing Parrot in the court of Henry VIII and Katherine of Aragon, then still Henry's wife. Parrot is established not only as witty but also as learned: He knows a number of languages, including Latin, Hebrew, and Chaldean (the languages of the "New Learning," or Renaissance) as well as Dutch, French, and Spanish (the languages of contemporary diplomacy). In addition, in the poem Skelton has Parrot imitate Scots and Irish accents. As Parrot modestly remarks, his mistress Dame Philology gave him the gift "to lerne all langage and hyt to speke aptlye."

Having confirmed his linguistic abilities, Parrot uses them to paint a picture of contemporary abuses—the most important of the traditional roles of satire. He attacks the new method of teaching in English schools, especially Oxford and Cambridge Universities, where Greek is displacing the traditional Latin, and Latin itself is taught in a fashion that makes it less useful than before. On the one hand, Skelton is defending the old order, while on the other he is covertly attacking Cardinal Wolsey, who openly supported the New Learning, especially the teaching of Greek. Having finished with this pedagogic matter, Skeleton has Parrot signify a change in subject by presenting his version of "My proper Besse," a popular song of the period which had both an amorous and a moralistic meaning: It could be interpreted either as a lover's carnal desire for his beloved or the soul's longing for God.

Skelton then shifts the poem again, giving Parrot a series of envois in which he comments again on contemporary events, especially Wolsey's diplomatic mission to France and Belgium during 1521. These attacks finished, the poem concludes with Parrot, in highly rhetorical and mannered language, railing against the abuses and excesses of the times, including those in the royal court, the church, and contemporary English life.

Forms and Devices

Like so many Tudor and early Elizabethan poets, John Skelton made highly conscious and conspicuous use of rhetorical techniques and devices. These are central points of "Speak, Parrot," as are the frequent Latin phrases and quotations which would have been easily read and quite familiar to his courtly readers.

The basic structure for most of the poem is a seven-line stanza, with a steady but varying meter that is not quite iambic pentameter but which provides a sense of order and regularity. It is against this sense of order that Skelton places what he, as a moralist and satirist, sees as the disorder of the world: the decline of learning in the universities, abuses of the clergy in the church, and, above all, the inordinate power and malign influence of Cardinal Wolsey over the court and the entire kingdom.

The three most noticeable rhetorical devices throughout "Speak, Parrot" are alliteration, anaphora, and antithesis. They bring both artistic variety to the poem and help underscore its themes and meanings. The first, alliteration, appears early, in line 3 of the poem, when Parrot describes himself as "Deyntely dyetyd with dyvers delycate spyce." It is found throughout the work, as in line 60, where Parrot notes that "Melchisedeck mercyfull made Moloc mercyles," as well as near the end of the poem, in line 357, when one reads, "Go, propyr Parotte, my popagay."

Anaphora is similar to alliteration. The latter is the repetition of a sound within a line, while the former is the repetition of a word or words at the beginning of successive lines or phrases. This device is used throughout the poem but is generally limited, as in lines 205 through 207, which follow the same format: "Parrot is no pendugum," "Parrot is no woodecocke," "Parrot is no stamerying stare." However, as the poem approaches its climax and Skelton wishes to underscore the work's satiric content, he uses a highly anaphoric pattern to present and emphasize his message:

> So many morall maters, and so lytell usyed;
> So myche newe makyng, and so madd tyme spente;
> So myche translacion into Englyshe confused;
> So myche nobyll prechying, and so lytell amendment.

This is the pattern—constantly recycling the same limited set of words to introduce lines and phrases—for the final ten full stanzas of "Speak, Parrot." It presents the culmination of Skelton's argument to the reader in a fashion that is both powerful and memorable.

The impact is increased because the anaphora is frequently found with another rhetorical device, that of antithesis, in which two contrasting ideas are linked by being presented in similar grammatical and syntactic form. Thus, in the example above, "So many morall maters" is both joined to and contrasted with "so lytell usyed," as "So myche newe makyng" parallels "so madd tyme spente." Antithesis allows Skelton to set the positive and negative aspects of contemporary life side by side, emphasizing how people should behave as opposed to how they actually act. The rhetorical pattern reinforces the moral meaning and the use of anaphora, with its insistent repetition, further strengthens the lesson that Skelton, through Parrot, is teaching his reader.

Finally, Skelton makes skillful use of languages other than English, but none more so than Latin. The second—sometimes first—language of any educated person during this period, Latin was regarded as the tongue for knowledge and artistry—although, as "Speak, Parrot" itself notes (and to some extent laments), Greek was quickly becoming a respectable rival.

Because of this universal knowledge of Latin among his readers, Skelton could lace his poem with Latin throughout, beginning with the opening epigraph, which can be translated, "The present book will grow greatly while I am alive; thence will the golden reputation of Skelton be proclaimed." In other words, Skelton is staking out a bold claim for himself and his work: It will last, and the poet will long be remembered. This is a familiar conceit in European poetry, its most memorable statement was by the Roman poet Horace, echoed in William Shakespeare's Sonnet 55: "Not marble, nor the gilded monuments/ Of prices, shall outlive this powerful rhyme."

Skelton closes his poem with another Latin epigraph, which is a slight variant of his opening lines. Now it is Parrot himself, rather than the book, which will live and preserve Skelton's memory and message. Parrot, the created character who points out abuses and condemns them, will ensure the fame of "Skelton Lawryat/ Orator Regius" (Skelton the poet laureate, orator of the king).

Themes and Meanings

Although "Speak, Parrot" is one of Skelton's greatest poems (perhaps his masterpiece, according to a number of scholars) it is a difficult poem to read and understand. Its themes are masked by its allegorical method, which hints at but does not always openly disclose its references. In addition, Skelton's languages (since he includes a goodly portion of Latin, French, and other tongues) can be difficult, even obscure.

There are valid reasons for this difficulty, chief among them the fact that "Speak, Parrot" is a poetic satire—an attack on what Skelton felt to be the follies and abuses of the times. Specifically, he is concerned with the state of education in English universities, the conduct of the court of Henry VIII, and the position and activities of Thomas Wolsey, cardinal of the Catholic Church and Lord Chancellor of England, about whom he is particularly vehement.

Skelton was closely connected with the higher education of his day. A graduate of Oxford, he had served as both court poet and as tutor to Prince Henry, who later became king, and in 1512 he was appointed *orator regius* (orator of the king). He was recognized with a number of honorary academic degrees, or "laureated," by colleges and universities in England and in Europe. In all these areas he was greatly concerned with the education of the rising generation, especially in Latin, which was still the universal language of any educated person. In "Speak, Parrot" Skelton attacks the new fashion of favoring Greek over Latin:

> In Achademia Parrot dare no probleme kepe,
> For *Greci fari* [Greek] so occupyeth the chayre,
> That *Latinum fari* [Latin] may fall to rest and slepe.

Parrot goes on to state his fear that in addition to supplanting Latin, Greek studies will replace the "Tryvyals and quatryvyals" (the Trivium and Quadrivium, the traditional "seven liberal arts"), which had been the basis of European learning since the early Middle Ages. Skelton, through Parrot, takes an essential conservative position, accepting the place of Greek in the New Learning but insisting that the older ways are better than the new.

The poem's second major theme concerns abuses in contemporary England, especially in the court of Henry VIII. Skelton, who was an ordained priest, had a strongly moralistic streak and deplored the excesses of his day. He attacks these same abuses in other of his works, such as his earlier poem "The Maner of the World Now a Dayes" and the later "Colin Clout." In "Speak, Parrot" he reaches a sustained pitch of feeling, especially in the long set of closing stanzas that speak of "So manye bolde barons, there heartes as dull as lede" and "So hote hatered agaynste the Chyrche, and cheryte [charity] so colde." Clearly, in many ways the times are out of joint in Henrican England.

One great reason this is so is Thomas Wolsey, cardinal and Lord Chancellor. To Skelton, Wolsey seemed to embody all the abuses and excesses of the times. Wolsey's accumulation of wealth, titles, and power must have made him seem the very personification of the seven deadly sins, especially those of avarice, gluttony, and, above all, pride. Having risen from humble beginnings (his father was a butcher), Wolsey had, through his brilliance and ability, made himself indispensable to the young king. In 1521, when "Speak, Parrot" was most likely composed, Wolsey was in Europe on a delicate diplomatic mission to France and the low countries, seemingly to mediate a peace between France and the Holy Roman Empire, but more likely to support Emperor Charles V, who had promised Wolsey help in his quest for the papacy. Skelton was greatly offended by such blatant political maneuverings, which subordinated England's welfare to Wolsey's personal ambition. His distaste for Wolsey is clear throughout the poem, especially when he declares that Wolsey "caryeth a kyng in hys sleve." The reference to Henry VIII, whose dependence on his chief counselor was well known, is clear. When Skelton describes Wolsey himself, his invective is scathing:

> So rygorous revelyng, in a prelate specially;
> So bold and so braggyng, and was so baselye borne;
> So lordlye of hys lokes, and so dysdayneslye [disdainfully];
> So fatte a magott, bred of a flesshe-flye.

The image is clear and highly unflattering. Skelton, himself a clergyman and a social conservative, is highly offended by Wolsey's inappropriate, even scandalous behavior. Perhaps the worst aspect of that behavior, and the major offense against which Parrot speaks, was his meteoric rise from his humble beginnings.

Michael Witkoski

SPRING AND ALL

Author: William Carlos Williams (1883-1963)
Type of poem: Lyric
First published: 1923, in *Spring and All*

The Poem

"Spring and All" is a short descriptive poem in free verse. The scene described is not what the title would lead one to expect: It is a muddy field populated by a few trees and bushes beside "the contagious hospital," Williams's phrase for a sanitorium that isolates people with contagious diseases. This unlikely setting becomes the occasion for one of poetry's oldest tasks—the description of springtime.

The poem begins with a series of prepositional phrases, followed by some noun phrases. The uninviting landscape is wet and cold; the leaves are "dead" and the vines "leafless." At line 14, however, something changes. Spring is personified as a drowsy slumberer awakening. The next verse paragraph introduces an ambiguous "they," which "enter[s] the new world naked." Though that phrasing understandably may remind one of newborn babies, the context suggests that the speaker is referring to emerging spring growth, the puny stems of grass and weeds that arise from the mud into the "cold, familiar wind." The reader realizes that this unlikely landscape represents the very beginning of spring. The ground is wet from rains or melting snows, and the first harbingers of the more conventionally celebrated spring are making their appearance.

The speaker then enumerates some of the new growth and anticipates the appearance of "the stiff curl of wildcarrot leaf." The coming of new growth is described as a kind of definition whereby individual plants take on clarity and individuality from the undifferentiated muck from which they sprout. The final lines celebrate this process as possessing "stark dignity" and representing a "profound change," presumably from nonexistence to life. The new growth is described as downward as well as upward: the roots "grip down," and the plants "begin to awaken." Though the scene has not changed much from the initial, uninviting landscape, the final word "awaken," echoing the life-giving associations of the earlier "quickens," seems appropriate for a poem of spring.

Forms and Devices

"Spring and All" is primarily descriptive. As such, it abounds in imagery. Though the imagery is rich and detailed, it is not lush in the traditional manner of poems to spring. No blossoms, buzzing bees, or sweet perfumes animate the poem. Instead, the imagery focuses on precision, on a realistic rather than romantic evocation of natural detail. The clouds are "mottled" and driven by a wind that the poet notes comes from the northeast. Brown is the most common color; the word appears twice and is relieved only by "reddish" and "purplish." The items delineated early in the poem seem distributed randomly: "patches of standing water," "the scattering of tall trees," "twiggy/ stuff of bushes." After the appearance of spring in line 15, objects take on definition and are enumerated "one by one," as individual living things. Though the clarity of outline characteristic of the latter part of the poem contrasts with the "broad" indiscriminate waste of the first half, the description is still unreservedly spartan. No romantic effusion is permitted.

The stark visual imagery is complemented by the tactile imagery of coldness. The wind is twice described as "cold," and the word "cold" modifies "they"—presumably new spring plants—of line 16. This repetition is significant: The warmth of spring is only anticipated in the poem. The birth of spring is a harsher process, but it is also a familiar one, repeated every year and undergone by all living things. This quality is expressed by the unusual word choice of "familiar" to describe the cold wind of line 19. The pain of passing into existence is shared by all of the animate, natural world; it is a familiar coldness. The bleak landscape into which the blades of grass emerge is the world's stage on which all creatures have their day. The presence of a hospital nearby connects the images of birth with those of death: The cold wind that welcomes the new plants casts a chill over the suffering souls in the hospital, who may not live to see another spring. The setting unites birth and death.

The adjective "naked" suggests human birth, and, indeed, one can read this poem (written by a pediatrician who assisted at hundreds of deliveries) as a poem about the birthing process. Perhaps the ambiguous words "and all" of the title connect the traditional images of spring to the conditions that precede it and connect the burgeoning of the natural world with the human life cycle. The title "Spring and All" thus unites the typical Williams understatement—a sort of a shrug—with a celebration of universality.

In a poem dominated by natural imagery, abstract terms such as "dignity" and "profound" in the concluding lines stand out. These more abstract words, with their connotations of importance, contrast with the realist assembling of drab natural details that characterizes the poem. "No ideas but in things" is Williams's famous dictum, and here it implies that the assertions of the final lines must be earned by the painstaking description earlier in the poem. The poet is a clear-eyed observer, who, by paying attention to the early signs of spring growth in a muddy field, is allowed a glimpse of "the profound change" represented by coming alive. The concreteness of the bulk of the poem supports the abstraction of its conclusion.

Consistent with the refusal of the poem to engage in poetic effusiveness about spring is the virtual absence of figurative language. There is no metaphor in the poem, unless one takes "naked" figuratively. Spring is personified, but even that figure of speech undermines traditional associations by stressing the "sluggish/ dazed" quality of the season. More subtly, the new growths are personified by being granted uncertainty and the ability to feel the cold.

Williams plays with the sounds of words throughout the poem. The consonance of *r*, *s*, *t*, and *f* works effectively in the following lines to suggest the roughness of the scrubby landscape: "All along the road the reddish/ purplish, forked, upstanding, twiggy/ stuff of bushes and small trees." The most meaningful wordplay is the sound echo that transforms "leafless" to "lifeless" between the third and fourth stanzas.

These similar sounding words have similar meanings, but the latter is qualified by the phrase "in appearance," which marks the turning point of the poem and the introduction of spring. The leafless landscape appears lifeless but, on closer examination, reveals itself to be full of the early growth.

Line endings significantly add slight (and unexpected) pauses. The line and stanza break after "fallen" (lines 6-7) illustrates a typical characteristic of Williams's verse. The break makes the phrase "standing and fallen" ambiguous: Does it modify the "dried weeds" or the "patches of standing water"? Williams uses unusual line breaks to create an expectant pause after "tomorrow" (line 20) and to break the phrase "dignity of/ entrance" over two lines (24-25). These may seem minor points, but they are important in free verse. Since meter does not determine where lines end, the poet must have a different and distinct rationale—or he or she might as well be writing prose. Williams often breaks lines in mid-phrase (or, as he does famously in "The Red Wheelbarrow," in mid-word). The effect is to slow the reading, to force the reader's attention to detail, and to call attention to the poem as a made object.

Themes and Meanings

The most important theme of "Spring and All" has already become apparent: The poem demonstrates that the awe-inspiring process of coming to life is a springtime miracle visible in the details of the thawing landscape. They come alive through close observation by the poet, who commits them realistically to language. The poem should be read in the context of a whole history of poetry heralding springtime. Writing in the early twentieth century, Williams looks for a way to treat a virtually hackneyed topic with freshness. For Williams that freshness comes from unadorned simple language and closely observed detail.

The time of the poem's publication suggests another useful context for interpreting it. The poem appeared in 1923, the year after T. S. Eliot's famous poem, *The Waste Land* (1922). Williams felt that Eliot's *The Waste Land* took poetry in the wrong directions: away from American traditions and language and toward the European, and away from direct language and imagery and toward highly allusive quotations from literature and mythology. Williams's evocation of a wasteland landscape in the opening lines (including the word "waste," opening line 5) hints that this poem may be a response to Eliot's work. In particular, the poem echoes the imagery of a depleted natural landscape with roots struggling to survive—images from the beginning of Eliot's poem. Where Eliot's use of roots becomes a metaphor for cultural traditions, however, Williams's use of roots is organic, suggesting rootedness in the natural world. In this light, it makes sense to read the penultimate paragraph as Williams's statement of a poetic credo. Then the concepts of "definition," "clarity," and "outline" make sense: The natural world offers to Williams a model for poetic expression. Poetry will quicken or come to life—freeing itself from the morbid excesses of late nineteenth century ornamentation and avoiding the arid excesses of Eliot's appeal to scholarship—by faithfully outlining and defining the stuff of the world.

Christopher Ames

STANZAS FOR MUSIC

Author: George Gordon, Lord Byron (1788-1824)
Type of poem: Lyric
First published: 1816, in *Poems*

The Poem

"Stanzas for Music" is a brief lyric poem of sixteen lines, one of five that Byron wrote with the same title. As its title suggests, it was written to be set to music, and its musical qualities have bearing upon its theme and structure.

The poem is written as an address by the poet to a person with whom he is infatuated. It is couched in feminine references and is most conveniently discussed as a love lyric to a woman, but it is important to note that the gender of the addressee is never specified. For that matter, the word love is never mentioned. The tone of the poem is one of adoration, and the poet carefully chooses words and images to evoke emotions that transcend feelings of simple affection. In the first two lines, for example, he creates a persona for his addressee by comparing her favorably to "Beauty's daughters." By alluding that she is more enchanting than the children of a personified ideal, he endows her with a godlike presence. He reinforces this apotheosis through the application of synecdoche, the use of a part or element to suggest a whole. The only aspect of the addressee that the poet describes is her voice, and just as readers are able to infer the totality of the Old Testament God from his manifestation as a disembodied voice, so can they envision a being of divine nature from the phenomena for which the woman's voice alone is responsible.

The poet conveys the majesty of his subject by comparing her effect upon him to the effect of a supernatural influence upon the ocean. He attributes "magic" to her and imagines that she has the power to leave the ocean "charmed" to stillness. Throughout the poem, the poet treats these powerful subjective impressions as objective reality: The woman has "magic" because her effect upon him can be understood in terms of natural phenomena that are beyond ordinary human control.

The poem is rich with sensory images. The poet begins by comparing the woman's "sweet voice" to "music on the waters" whose sound causes the waves to pause. In the absence of their sound and movement, a striking visual tableau presents itself: an ocean whose waves "lie still and gleaming" as "the midnight moon is weaving/ Her bright chain o'er the deep." The sensuality of these images notwithstanding, their impact on the poet transcends the physical and achieves a spiritual quality. As he tells the woman, "the spirit bows before thee,/ To listen and adore thee." Ultimately, the poem is a paean to a person who inspires near-religious veneration in the poet.

Forms and Devices

In "Stanzas for Music," there is a fundamental tension between form and content that contributes to the poem's effect. The poem was written to be set to music; this fact is evident from its songlike structure. Its sixteen lines are broken into two stanzas of eight lines apiece. Each stanza is thus composed of a quatrain followed by two rhyming couplets, not unlike a song in which each verse is followed by a chorus. The poem is composed with musical precision and balance: It begins with a subjective observation, supports this observation with objective description, and concludes with an image that synthesizes its subjective and objective elements. The theme of the poem, however, refuses to be contained within such a tidy structure.

The poet hopes to elaborate the overwhelming emotion his subject excites in him through a series of similes that evoke the awe and splendor of the natural world: "like music on the waters/ Is thy sweet voice to me:/ When, as if its sound were causing/ The charmed ocean's pausing." Similes, though, are at best only approximations. They suggest equivalence through powerful comparisons, but they do not fully capture the uniqueness of what is being compared. There is an ineffable quality to the woman that resists definition, and it is this quality which earns the poet's adoration.

The tension between the poem's form and content is mirrored in Byron's use of nature imagery. Like other poets of the Romantic era, Byron often described his characters and their endeavors in terms of the natural world in order to elevate and exalt them. The Romantics saw the natural world as a secular manifestation of the divine that superseded theological interpretations of godliness. A good example can be found in the third canto of *Childe Harold's Pilgrimage,* in which Byron uses the inexorable and immutable ocean to symbolize the tide of time upon which human destiny is borne. When Byron uses natural phenomena to describe the influence of the woman addressed in "Stanzas for Music," he transfers their divinity to her. Indeed, he suggests that she transcends their divinity because she can arrest them in their course. By implying that her voice can quell the winds and still the waves, he attributes awesome power to her. Nevertheless, her command over nature is depicted as gentle, rather than violent. In response to her voice, "the lull'd winds seem dreaming" and the swelling ocean's "breast is gently heaving,/ As an infant's asleep." Her effect upon nature at its most volatile is that of a mother to a sleeping newborn child. Hence the poet's adoration of her, through "a full but soft emotion" that differs from simple worship or respect for nature's majesty. Although powerful forces underlie the poem's imagery, its mood is one of tranquility and serenity.

Themes and Meanings

"Stanzas for Music" is a poem concerned with idealized love. In his definitive *Byron: A Biography* (1957), Leslie Marchand proposes that Byron's inspiration for the poem was John Edleston, a choirboy to whom Byron formed a romantic attachment while at Cambridge and whose death in 1811 inspired the five elegiac "Thyrza" poems. Byron created the female persona Thyrza to express, as he said in his diary, "the violent, though *pure,* love and passion" he felt for Edleston. His description of Thyrza in "'If Sometimes in the Haunts of Men'" as "too like a dream of Heaven,/ For earthly Love to merit thee" corresponds to the platonic ideal of a love that transcends sexuality at the core of "Stanzas for Music." There is no physical dimension to the love articulated in the poem. Despite Byron's use of vigorous natural imagery, the intense feelings the poem conveys occur on a purely emotional level and almost entirely within the poet's imagination.

Love is the theme of many lyrical poems, but it has a special significance for Byron and the Romantic poets. "In the broad Romantic application of the term 'love,'" Meyer H. Abrams writes in *Natural Supernaturalism: Tradition and Revolution in Romantic Literature* (1971), "all modes of human attraction are conceived as one in kind, different only in object and degree, in a range which includes the relations of lover to beloved, children to parents, brother to sister, friend to friend, and individual to humanity. The orbit of love was often enlarged to include the relationship of man to nature as well." In "Stanzas for Music," Byron describes the ideal love of the poet for his beloved in terms of several of these relationships. In a different context, the amorous feelings of lovers, the affection of mother for child, and humankind's awe at the mystery of nature might seem very different emotions that bear little relationship to one another. In the poem, however, Byron presents them as flowing from a single pure source. In keeping with the poem's musical format, one could say that the various manifestations of love Byron addresses in the poem are harmonic expressions of the same theme.

"Stanzas for Music" is an example of what Abrams refers to as "natural supernaturalism," the Romantic poets' tendency "to naturalize the supernatural and to humanize the divine." The poem ennobles the person to whom it is addressed by endowing him or her with uncommon powers that are all the more extraordinary for their unconscious expression. It frames supernatural experience in terms of natural phenomena that are universally recognized and understood. In essence, the poem suggests that a love relationship as strong as that known to the poet offers the same emotional fulfillment as an encounter with the divine. It is worth noting that Byron wrote this poem shortly after another love lyric entitled "Stanzas for Music" was published in *Hebrew Melodies*, a collection of verse written to be set to traditional synagogue music. Byron clearly perceived an association between love and religious experience. Although steeped in the ideology of Byron and his time, the reverent tone and emotional intensity of "Stanzas for Music" make it seem as timeless as a devotional prayer.

Stefan Dziemianowicz

STELLA'S BIRTHDAY, 1727

Author: Jonathan Swift (1667-1745)
Type of poem: Epistle/letter in verse
First published: 1727, as "Stella's Birth-day. March 13. 1726/7," in *Miscellanies in Prose and Verse*; collected in *The Poems of Jonathan Swift*, 1958

The Poem

"Stella's Birthday, 1727" is a verse epistle, or letter written in verse. It is the last in a series of birthday poems written by Irish satirist Jonathan Swift for his beloved friend Esther Johnson. Swift met Johnson ("Stella") when she was a child of eight. The daughter of a retainer to Swift's friend and patron Sir William Temple, Johnson served not only as one of Swift's most important correspondents but also as his literary muse. Swift's charming custom of presenting Johnson with the gift of a verse epistle commemorating her March 13 birthday began in 1719 and resulted in a series of "Stella's Birthday" poems culminating in the final poem of 1727.

Johnson died on January 28, 1728, at the age of forty-seven, after years of intermittent poor health. Swift's touching birthday poem of 1727 is both a moving testament to a woman who exemplified for him the feminine ideal of decency, modesty, and prudence, and a tender valedictory to a dear friend. On learning from a servant on January 28 that Johnson had died "about six in the evening of this day," a heartbroken Swift recorded in his journal that he had lost "the truest, most virtuous, and valuable friend, that I, or perhaps any other person ever was blessed with." The following day, still grief stricken, he notes sadly in his journal, "My head aches, and I can write no more" (*On the Death of Mrs. Johnson*, 1765).

Swift begins the poem by assuring Stella that despite her failing health and his own advancing age and increasing infirmities, he intends, as always, to celebrate her birthday with optimism and joy: "This day, whate'er the Fates decree/ Shall still be kept with joy by me:/ This day then, let us not be told,/ That you are sick, and I grown old." Although Swift seeks throughout the poem to cheer his ailing friend by recalling her past acts of generosity and compassion, he also attempts to assuage his own pain at the possibility that she is dying. Unlike the earlier "Stella's Birthday" poems of 1719 and 1721, which are informed by a mood of playful optimism and satirical whimsy, the final 1727 poem contains an air of unrelieved morbidity expressed in a series of pointed questions implying that the person most in need of cheering is not Stella but Swift. In reminding Stella of the lasting value of her past acts, he asks,

> Does not the body thrive and grow
> By food of twenty years ago?
> And, had it not been still supplied,
> It must a thousand times have died.
> Then, who with reason can maintain
> That no effects of food remain?

Swift suggests that true virtue has permanence, nourishing both the virtuous individual and the lives of those who have been touched. These lines reflect the poet's pained awareness not only that he is losing his dearest friend but also that the world is losing an exemplary human being, and it is this sobering realization that haunts the moving central sections of the poem.

Beginning with line 15, the poet beseeches Stella not to dwell on present miseries but rather to take comfort from having lived an unblemished life. In line 18, he urges Stella to "look with joy on what is past." Later, still intent on raising her spirits, he gently challenges her not to dwell on the bleakness of the future but rather to derive satisfaction from a lifetime of virtuous achievement: "Say, Stella, feel you no content,/ Reflecting on a life well spent?" "Virtue," as Swift is at pains to remind Stella, himself, and the reader, can, if properly recalled, "assuage/ Grief, sickness, poverty, and age."

As proof of Stella's exemplary conduct and as a means of paying tribute to her integrity and decency, Swift provides a brief but eloquent catalog of her virtues. He extols her selflessness in ministering to the needy and sick, reminding her that had it not been for her compassion, others less fortunate would surely have died of disease or want: "Your skilful hand employ'd to save/ Despairing wretches from the grave;/ And then supporting with your store/ Those whom you dragg'd from death before." He praises her "gen'rous boldness" in staunchly defending the reputation of "an innocent and absent friend" against the idle gossip and malicious slurs of others. He commends her "detestation" of "vice in all its glitt'ring dress" and, finally, notes with awe her remarkable "patience under torturing pain/ Where stubborn stoics would complain." In thus enumerating Stella's many virtues, the poet establishes for both his subject and the reader that here is an individual of extraordinary merit worthy of everyone's esteem.

Although Swift seeks throughout the poem to repel darker thoughts of Stella's death, he confronts, at the conclusion, the likelihood that she is dying. In the final section, Swift implores Stella to pity those who, like himself, will suffer most from losing her: "O then, whatever Heav'n intends,/ Take pity on your pitying friends!/ Nor let your ills affect your mind,/ To fancy they can be unkind." The poem ends with a deeply moving tribute in which the poet expresses both his desire to change places with the dying Stella and his gratitude that he is at least able to tell her so:

> Me, surely me, you ought to spare,
> Who gladly would your suff'rings share;
> Or give my scrap of life to you,
> And think it far beneath your due:
> You, to whose care so oft I owe
> That I'm alive to tell you so.

Forms and Devices

A standard eighteenth century verse epistle, "Stella's Birthday, 1727" is written entirely in couplets: forty-four pairs of rhymed eight-syllable lines. This poetic form helps convey the intimate, almost conversational tone of the poem while providing a tightly controlled frame for the poet to express his innermost thoughts. Despite the regularity of the meter and the rigidity of the rhyme scheme, the form is not as confining as it may appear. Swift takes advantage of the epistle form to speak directly and concisely to Stella. The poem's lines are short, to the point, and virtually devoid of imagistic language or extended metaphor. Rather than masking his message in rhetorical flourishes or highly elevated language, Swift employs the more direct and humble address of the letter writer and friend. For example, late in the poem he urges Stella not to abandon herself to despair but rather to gain strength from the visible effects of her past virtuous actions:

> Believe me, Stella, when you show
> That true contempt for things below,
> Nor prize your life for other ends,
> Than merely to oblige your friends;
> Your former actions claim their part;
> And join to fortify your heart.

This is not to suggest, however, that Swift wholly abandons the use of poetic device or diction. At various points in the poem he uses metaphor and personification to convey the active importance of "Virtue" in Stella's life. In line 62, for example, he likens virtue to a "nutriment that feeds the mind," and later, in lines 73 and 74, he equates the personified Virtue to Janus, the mythological god possessing two faces, one looking forward and one backward. Such comparisons are important devices for conveying the poem's larger purpose and message.

Themes and Meanings

On one important level, "Stella's Birthday, 1727" is Swift's heartfelt tribute to a much-loved and dying friend. Yet, like virtually all of Swift's works, "Stella's Birthday, 1727" contains satiric elements that allow the central message of the poem to operate on a more universal level. The speaker's voice is both intensely personal and broadly didactic. One of the central issues raised in the poem is the importance of virtue, "by all sages understood/ To be the chief of human good." The poet thus paradoxically uses the twin occasions of Stella's forty-seventh birthday and her impending death to reflect broadly on the importance of a virtuous life well lived.

The Stella of Swift's poem is a model of rectitude, courage, and moral decency, and, as such, she stands as a shining example to all human beings. Stella's willingness to place the needs of others before her own, her devotion to truth and honor, her many charitable deeds, and, above all, her keen understanding of what it means to be a friend all mark her as an individual of the highest moral character and thus worthy of emulation. Swift's personal anguish at the thought of losing so beloved a friend ultimately contains a larger message: that true virtue is an irreplaceable commodity and that those who possess it, such as Stella, need always to be reminded of their value to others. In the concluding lines of the poem, Swift pays lasting tribute to a woman he regarded as the embodiment of virtue, decency, and moral rectitude, a woman he once described, in *On the Death of Mrs. Johnson*, as having "all the softness of temper that became a lady, [and] the personal courage of a hero."

Jacqueline Lawson

STEPCHILD

Author: Garrett Kaoru Hongo (1951-   )
Type of poem: Dramatic monologue
First published: 1982, in *Yellow Light*

The Poem

"Stepchild" is a dramatic monologue in free verse divided into seven sections. Section 1 was first published in *The Nation* under the title "Evacuation." The complete poem under the current title was published in Garrett Kaoru Hongo's poetry collection *Yellow Light*. The title thematically suggests how Japanese Americans feel they are treated in the United States. It also calls the reader's attention to the narrator's relationship with his parents, which, according to the narrator, is built on "lies" and "fairy tales."

In part 1 of the poem, the narrator urges the reader to revisit the experiences of 120,000 Japanese Americans during World War II. Under President Franklin Delano Roosevelt's Executive Order 9066, they were evacuated from the West Coast and put in relocation camps. The narrator then places the Japanese American internment in a larger picture. He lists the discriminatory laws against Asian Americans in the history of the United States: the Chinese Exclusion Act of 1882, a bill passed by the United States Congress that made it illegal for Chinese laborers to come to or stay in the United States; California's Alien Land Law of 1913, which prevented the Issei (first-generation Japanese immigrants) from purchasing land and obtaining leases for more than three years on the basis that they were aliens ineligible for citizenship; and the 1922 United States Supreme Court ruling that stipulated that Japanese immigrants were not eligible for citizenship in the United States (referred to as "the Exclusion Act of 1921" in the poem). Unmentioned by Hongo is the Immigration Act of 1924, also known as the Asian Exclusion Act, which was directed against Japanese and Asian Indian immigration.

Parts 3, 4, and 5 describe the narrator's eagerness to find out what happened to thousands of Japanese immigrants after they arrived in the United States. In part 3, the narrator talks to his parents. He is very upset that he has been fed "fairy tales" about the Nisei (second-generation Japanese Americans) "emerging full-grown/ Americans at birth." Since the narrator cannot find truth from his parents, he decides, in part 4, to do some investigation on his own. He examines stories, brief chronologies, photocopies of documents, records, newspapers, and documented newsprint with "genealogies,/ obituaries, births, driver's licenses,/ land sales, moving sales, leases,/ and 'Evacuation! Must Sell!' sales." The narrator is shocked by the fact that he is able to find only "ten or twelve books/ a handful" that accurately portray the Asian American experience.

As a result of his research, the narrator becomes very angry. "The Dragon" wants him to scream; the "Shark" wants him to kill, "to tear at the throats of white children." He then remembers, however, that his wife is also white, "a descendant of Mennonites/ and Quakers/ who nursed the sick" at the Manzanar and Gila River Japanese American internment camps and who "rowed the long boats/ of their outrage, their protest,/ into the shoals of storms/ gathering on the peaks/ of Heart Mountain." In the last section of the poem, the narrator reconciles with the past, with his feelings, and with the environment. He is at peace with himself and the world.

Forms and Devices

Dramatic monologue consists of words spoken by a fictional character to a silent audience at a critical moment of his or her life. Sometimes these speakers reveal aspects of their own personalities of which they are unaware. "Stepchild" uses the form of dramatic monologue effectively. In the poem, Hongo creates a persona who feels frustrated about being cut off from history. Sometimes the narrator appears to be talking to the reader; other times he is talking to his parents or himself. The form concretely objectifies a person's loneliness and frustration in his search for truth. The narrator's attempt to learn about his family history has been obliterated by "lies" and "fairy tales." He feels alienated from a society that has denied him the opportunity to connect to history and to his ethnicity. He is trapped in a situation in which a false sense of security has secluded him from knowing who he really is.

In "Stepchild," the metrical device of free verse is used to celebrate the human aspiration for freedom and dignity. The narrator's determination to reclaim his sense of history and identity leads him to writings by people who have the courage to speak the truth. In parts 4 and 5, the narrator quotes directly from Japanese American writer Tokio Akagi, Japanese American artist Paul Chikamasa Horiuchi, and Filipino American writer and activist Carlos Bulosan, turning prose into poetry and form into message. Bulosan's autobiography, *America Is in the Heart* (1973), has been hailed by many as a book that has stripped the recording of Asian American history of its euphemism and verbiage. The quotations serve as a bridge between the narrator and the part of history he has never been told, filling a gap left in his heart by the lies people have been telling about themselves, about their families, and about the past. They also situate the narrator firmly among other writers with whose experience he can empathize.

"Stepchild" abounds with images of violence. The mother who takes part in the evacuation has a mouth "like crushed rose petals/ fresh with the shock of lipstick." After "all the veins had collapsed/ from the needles of a thousand mine shafts,/ after all the rail was laid/ and the last spike driven through," the Chinese laborers were "chased back home to Frisco/ or shipped to Kwantung"; if "they refused to be herded,/ they were buried where they stood." The narrator has learned that Japanese American "history is bitter;/ a farmer's thick arm/ slashed on the spiked teeth/ of barbed-wire fences." However, something "stopped the telling./ Someone pulled out the tongues/ of every Nisei/ raped by the felons/ of Relocation." The narrator's anger makes him want to kill, "to tear at the throats/ of white children,/ exterminate them/ like the Angels of Auschwitz." The poem ends, however, with the narrator's realization that "There is always a need/ to hate, a need to find/ victims for that hatred." In part 7, he makes peace with himself, with the past, and with the environment. He thinks about nothing for a change except "what it is that flowers from itself and shakes the yellow dust of thought/ onto the red cloisters" of his heart and his passions.

Themes and Meanings

Asian Americans have stereotypically been labeled the "model minority." Many Japanese Americans who were interned during World War II feel too ashamed and embarrassed to talk about that part of history. Except for books such John Okada's *No-No Boy* (1957) and Jeanne Wakatsuki Houston and James D. Houston's *Farewell to Manzanar* (1973), there are not many history or literary books providing honest portrayals of Japanese Americans' experiences in the relocation camps. Hongo is a Yonsei (fourth-generation Japanese American), and "Stepchild" is apparently based on his personal experience. It portrays a person's anger at finding out about the discrimination and mistreatment his parents and grandparents have experienced.

The title of the poem has a strong bearing on Hongo's thematic preoccupations. Following along the same line as Okada's *No-No Boy*, it reveals the confusion many Japanese Americans experienced during and after the relocation camps. According to Chinese American scholar and writer Frank Chin, the experience of the narrator in *No-No Boy*, Ichiro, is based on that of Hajiime Akutsu, a Nisei who participated in the resistance movement in the relocation camps and who demanded constitutional and legal rights for Japanese American internees during World War II. In Japanese, both Ichiro and Hajiime mean "firstborn." The name is appropriate for a whole generation of people who struggle with the confusion about their relationship with both the mainstream culture and their ethnic culture.

What is also interesting about the title "Stepchild" is that it reveals the narrator's ambivalent relationship with his parents. The narrator grows up in a house where people believe that Japanese American internment is "to laugh at,/ its lesson best told/ in a fairy tale/ about the Nisei/ emerging full-grown/ Americans at birth." Eventually, however, the narrator learns of the bitterness of Japanese American history, and no one knows that part of history better than the grandfather "who spent the years/ of his internment/ sealed in the adobes/ at Leuppe in Arizona,/ sleeping on packed earth floors/ under sheepskin blankets,/ and twisting the iron bars/ of his cell."

"Stepchild" represents an effort to search for a connection with history and to reclaim a person's sense of identity. The narrator's discovery in his search for truth can very easily lead him into outrage and hatred. Revenge, however, "blisters" the narrator's tongue and "works in these words, says,/ 'Teach a Blessingway.'" By reclaiming the past, the narrator has reached peace with himself and with the world. He revels in a scenery where "the sun blonds nothing/ but the sands outside [his] window/ and melons ripening on the sill,/ the yellow ones [they] call bitter."

Qun Wang

STILL FALLS THE RAIN

Author: Edith Sitwell (1887-1964)
Type of poem: Meditation
First published: 1941; collected in *Street Songs*, 1942

The Poem

"Still Falls the Rain" is a meditation on suffering in the world. This poem begins with a reference to the bombing of England by the Germans during World War II, then spins a tapestry of references to suffering throughout the history of the world. The thirty-four lines of the poem are divided into seven stanzas, perhaps to symbolize the seven days of the week and thereby emphasize the comprehensiveness of the suffering Christ still endures. The title of the poem is repeated six times throughout the poem, the number six traditionally being associated with humankind, which was, according to Genesis 1, created on the sixth day of creation.

The poem begins with a somewhat ambiguous and somber allusion to the rain that could refer to a typical rain of water or to a rain of bombs during the air raids. Whichever rain is intended, the allusion is related to the sacrifice of the "Starved Man" or Christ upon the cross so that the rain is finally seen as a flow of blood from Christ's side. The years since the birth of Christ (1,940 at the time the poem takes place) are represented by nails in the cross, thus indicating that Christ suffered for all the sins of the world committed after his death as well as before it.

The poem makes several allusions to biblical accounts related to Christ's betrayal, Crucifixion, and ministry on earth. "The Potter's Field" or "Field of Blood" is the plot of land purchased with the thirty pieces of silver that Judas Iscariot received for betraying Christ and later returned to the Jewish leaders before he hanged himself in despair, as detailed in Matthew 27:3-10. The "worm with the brow of Cain" alludes to the mark placed on Cain after he murdered his brother Abel, as described in Genesis 4. The plea for mercy on "Dives and on Lazarus" refers to the parable of Jesus, given in Luke 16:19-31, about a rich man (traditionally called Dives) and a beggar named Lazarus. In this parable, the rich man lives for himself and ends in Hades where he is tormented with flames, while the poor man ends in the bosom of Abraham, or in heaven. The poet's plea is for both the innocent and the guilty, since the two are often hard to distinguish this side of eternity.

By stanza 5, the rain and the blood of Christ on the cross are presented in parallel lines, emphasizing how he suffers for all creation. The number five is traditionally associated with the five wounds of Christ (two in his hands, two in his feet, and one in his side), making the fifth stanza an appropriate one for this reference to how Christ "bears in His Heart all wounds." The second line of the sixth stanza refers to some of the final words of the self-condemned Faustus in Christopher Marlowe's play *Doctor Faustus* (1588) in which Faustus made a pact with the devil in exchange for twenty-four years of power and fame much as some leaders during World War II bargained with their lives for the sake of worldly gain. In contrast to all these human failings, in stanza 7, the final words of Christ in this poem are those of benediction or blessing as he offers forgiveness at the price of his own life.

Forms and Devices

Edith Sitwell uses a free-verse form for this poem, but she still includes a wide variety of rhymes, including scattered end rhymes. For example, the four lines in stanza 1 end with the words "Rain," "loss," "nails," and "Cross," the first and second forming a half-rhyme and the third and fourth forming a perfect rhyme. In stanza 4, in contrast, the five lines end with the words "Rain," "Cross," "us," "Lazarus," and "one," the middle three words rhyming while the outside two are again a half-rhyme, this time in a form sometimes called consonance. Because the pattern of rhyming is varied throughout the poem, the music of the poem underscores the unpredictable nature of life in the twentieth century.

As noted in the previous section, this poem makes careful use of biblical allusions. No fewer than fifteen of the thirty-four lines contain direct allusions to biblical accounts or concepts, and many of the other lines contain statements consistent with the Christian perspective. These allusions, combined with carefully modulated rhymes and the repeated refrain "Still falls the Rain," give this poem a liturgical quality as it moves from contrition to confession to benediction. In the preface to her book *The Canticle of the Rose* (1949), Sitwell notes that she thought of her poems as "hymns of praise to the glory of life." "Still Falls the Rain" is part of this hymn tradition. The title and refrain also contain a pun on the word "still," which can mean "yet" or "without motion," as if to say the observations in this poem are about a timeless moment that is at once perpetual and complete. This pun emphasizes the eternal nature of Christ's sacrifice even though it took place about two thousand years ago.

One can also see in this poem evidence of the influence of the Symbolist movement from France. T. S. Eliot helped Sitwell discover the genius of this movement in poetry. The Symbolist movement, as interpreted by Eliot, sought to create "objective correlatives" that would use images, either verbal or visual, to indirectly evoke a certain emotional state or response. Because of the subtlety of this approach, the emotional impact is all the greater for its subterranean arrival. In this poem, the collection of images such as "hammer beat," "Tomb," "worm," "Starved Man," and "Baited bear" evoke a feeling of suffering and near despair. In contrast, the music of the poem propels it forward to the concluding benediction so that the final note is one of hope above despair. These two contrary emotions are conveyed or evoked indirectly.

Themes and Meanings

"Still Falls the Rain" represents one of the first serious poems Sitwell wrote after she completed *Gold Coast Customs* (1929). Her decade of relative silence was broken by the encouragement of her brother Sacheverell Sitwell and by the arrival of World War II. Rather than rail at Germany and the other wartime enemies of Great Britain, Sitwell focuses on the larger issues of suffering and absolution as related to all humanity. She prays for Dives and Lazarus, the undeserving as well as the deserving. She acknowledges that Christ suffered for all people and that each year of life (rather than just the war years) is in some sense a cause for his death on the cross. The scene she paints of wartime England becomes a portrait of all history in which humanity is in continual need of redemption. The portrait of Christ at the end of the poem is one of unceasing love and sacrifice. The crimes and griefs of the world seem innumerable, yet the love of God exceeds them all. Thus, in spite of the war era being treated in this work, this poem is very positive in its confidence in God's ability and willingness to act in a chaotic world.

Beginning with this poem and others of the World War II era, the reading public in England began to recognize that Sitwell was a poet of considerable depth and spiritual insight. This poem is dense with historical allusions and profound in its theological statements. Her readings also gained notoriety, especially one given in the fall of 1944. She and her two brothers, Osbert and Sacheverell, were giving a poetry reading at the Allied Forces' Churchill Club in London that was heavily attended by numerous notable literary figures. Just as Sitwell began to read "Still Falls the Rain," a warning sounded that a "doodle bug" or "buzz bomb" was heading toward London. Edith refused to halt her reading, even when many thought of heading for shelter. Her voice and demeanor kept them spellbound as she spoke against the impending doom. She finished her reading as the bomb exploded in the distance, and the audience burst into deafening applause.

Sitwell's poetry reflects her heroic posture of facing the terrors of life with an unflinching conviction that faith and poetry will triumph in the end. In recognition of her valiant spirit and fine poetry, Sitwell was named Dame Commander of the British Empire in 1954. The endurance of "Still Falls the Rain" is proof that such honor was well deserved. Between 1940 and 1949, she wrote an impressive array of poems of striking intensity and beauty, including "Invocation," "An Old Woman," "Eurydice," and "The Song of the Cold." Among these poems, "Still Falls the Rain" stands as one of her finest works.

Daven M. Kari

THE STONE HARP

Author: John Meade Haines (1924-   )
Type of poem: Lyric
First published: 1971, in *The Stone Harp*

The Poem

"The Stone Harp" is a free-verse poem of twenty-five lines divided into six stanzas. The title, evocative of a mysterious sound, illustrates John Haines's tendency toward surrealism, a quality noted in many of his poems from the 1971 collection *The Stone Harp*. Haines homesteaded in Alaska (1947, 1954-1969) and established himself as a nature writer. He published this volume, an assortment of mystical and loosely political poems, to mixed reviews. Although he was caught up in the political atmosphere of the late 1960's, he has noted that he was probably too far removed from the events to communicate effectively about them. Perhaps this situation accounts for the somewhat ethereal quality of his work at the time.

"The Stone Harp," Haines says, "was inspired . . . by the sound made by a sudden drop in winter temperatures at my old homestead outside Fairbanks: a very loud humming in the telephone wires, pronounced enough to vibrate in the pole itself." To him, this suggested the earth as a harp with telephone wires as strings. The first stanza describes it thus:

> A road deepening in the north,
> strung with steel,
> resonant in the winter evening,
> as though the earth were a harp
> soon to be struck.

From this simple image, Haines weaves a metaphor that works on several levels, but its essence reflects nature's basic indifference to the struggles of humankind. Stanzas 2 and 3 use a dreamlike sequence to intensify the original image and further evoke the cryptic sound.

In the fourth stanza, the poem shifts to a more specific subject, although indirectly enough to have received varying interpretations from different scholars. "Now there is all this blood/ flowing into the west" seemed to some to refer to the construction of the Alaskan oil pipeline. (In this interpretation, the stanza's final line, "that ship is sinking," could be read as an eerie prediction of the *Exxon Valdez* disaster.) However, Haines himself has asserted that the stanza's flowing blood and sinking ship refer to the Vietnam War.

The final two stanzas shift from universal to more personal reflection. Haines likens himself to the wind, "a drifter/ who walked in from the coast/ with empty pockets." Use of the words "empty pockets" imparts both hope and hopelessness. The five lines of the last verse circle back to the title image of the harp. Left standing on a road at twilight, the poet creates a sound similar to the wind strumming "a stone harp" with "a handful of leaves."

Forms and Devices

The best nature writers, of which this poet is arguably one, possess a gifted sense of "negative capability." The phrase, originating with John Keats, does not imply fatalism (although most nature writers, including Haines, find their work inevitably linked with death), but rather an emptiness, a waiting-to-be-filled quality. One sees this quality developing in Haines's memoir of his Alaskan homesteading years, *The Stars, The Snow, The Fire* (1989). The book is filled with the observations of a careful man surviving alone in the last great American wilderness, and there is much of the watcher, the thinker, and the patient hunter portrayed there. Wendell Berry writes that Haines's poems seem "to have been made with a patience like that with which rivers freeze or lichens cover stones" (*The Wilderness of Vision: On the Poetry of John Haines*, ed. Kevin Bezner and Kevin Walzer, 1996). Indeed, "The Stone Harp," a relatively short poem, took more than two years to assume its final shape.

The beginning stanza uses the metaphor of the earth as a harp about to be struck. Haines then engages the reader's senses with simile. After setting a scene of waiting silence, he introduces sound, emphasizing it with a two-line second stanza that reads, "As if a spade/ rang in a rock chamber:" The colon establishes a bridge to the next stanza, and the resulting momentum carries the reader more easily through the most obscure imagery of the poem. Stanza 3 ends with another reference to sound, as a figure "tries to sing." The reference allusion to singing subtly underscores the poem's readable, almost songlike quality, produced through an unobtrusive use of alliteration and consonance.

The fourth stanza portrays the anguish of the Vietnam War: "It was not in my nature to speak directly of such things, but to find a way to suggest them . . . a ship going down, and blood draining across the sea" (Haines, in *Living Off the Country*). The third line, "ragged holes in the waterline of the sun," describes Haines's observation of dark clouds appearing like holes in the sky and provides an exceptionally threatening image.

Much effective free verse ends with a striking metaphor that provides a flash of deeper knowledge, and this poem is no exception. Haines reinforces the figurative image in stanzas 5 and 6 with simile in the last verse. The final few lines describe a poet's words as no more than the scratching of wind-blown leaves against stone, easily ignored by the natural world and humankind alike.

Themes and Meanings

Kevin Bezner (*The Wilderness of Vision*) asserts that "Haines has continued to write a variation of the same poem, making it finer and finer." Though this is perhaps an oversimplification, it echoes the belief of many that Haines's poetry reflects a deeply personal attempt to define and refine a fresh archetype of humankind's place in the world. Many nature writers bemoan the effect of civilization upon the natural world, and their writing consistently and pessimistically argues that the earth would be better off without its human "parasite." Haines, having lived in the wilds, writes from a different perspective. His critical writings refer repeatedly to the need for authenticity and sincerity, and indeed he seems tenacious in his honesty. He refers to art as "a version of the truth." As a poet, Haines served an internship in the pre-language world of the wilds, and his voice is the voice of experience—of a man who has run trap lines throughout a brutal Alaskan winter. His work exhibits a solid sense of time passing, the slow wheeling of the seasons, and the inevitability of both winter and spring, of death and life.

Noteworthy too are the repeated references to stone, root, and leaf in much of Haines's work, including this poem. To a poet coming of age in an unforgiving wilderness, the images evoked by these three parts of the natural world are plain yet unending in their possibilities. Stone is hard, cold, unyielding, but it can be broken by a living root. Roots are necessary before leaves can exist. Leaves enable a plant to thrive, yet when leaves die and blow away, the root still lives, guarding its life-blood unseen below the cold frozen earth. Haines continually plumbs this endless cycle in graceful and revealing ways.

Close inspection of the ending of "The Stone Harp" reveals a double meaning that nicely illuminates the mind of the writer. The wind is both poet and wind. As wind, it ignores the efforts of civilization, continuing to blow the leaves across the landscape as it has always done. As poet, it almost abdicates the work of the writer, for the poet's words make only a sound as faint as a rustle. Such implicit simplicity and self-deprecation stand at the heart of Haines's poetry and to a large extent constitute its power.

Sue Storm

THE STONE OF HEAVEN

Author: Jane Hirshfield (1953-   )
Type of poem: Ode
First published: 1988; collected in *The October Palace*, 1994

The Poem

"The Stone of Heaven" is a free-verse ode of thirty-two lines arranged in five stanzas. The stanzas range from two to sixteen lines of irregular length. The last stanza, a sixteen-line hymn to the earth, includes human beings in its praising and naming and is marked by many repetitions of initial words in succeeding lines (anaphora). The voice of the poet serves as a guide in the first two stanzas of the poem, signifying a place ("here") where the earth is the many greens of jade (known as the stone of heaven in Chinese religion). She further specifies the place in the next stanza, identifying it as the home of the "Flemish Masters," painters of the fifteenth century known for the brilliance and depth of their colors; the poet's voice takes on the tones of an enamored tourist as she describes the town, the houses, and the wine.

In the closing line of the second stanza, she compares the detail in the paintings to brightly colored, leaping fish. A reader familiar with Jane Hirshfield's Buddhist imagery will recognize the appearance of fish in the poem as a kind of shorthand for the abundance of life. This is reinforced in the following image of the woodthrush who sings not in order to fill the world with his song but because he is overflowing with the world's abundance. From here the poem moves to instruct the reader in the many forms of this abundance, striking another of Hirshfield's Buddhist keynotes: Human beings are not the center of the universe ("But the world does not fill with us"). On the contrary, the world generates its own continuous spectacle of sights and sounds. It is "a carnival tent, a fluttering of banners."

The last long stanza is a celebration of the whole world in its abundance and variety, beginning with human beings as multitalented creators. The poet refers to humans as bakers, sword dancers, seamstresses, and glassblowers. Then she apostrophizes the forces in the universe ("whirler of winds"), the mighty sea ("boat-swallower"), and the earth's powers of renewal ("germinant seed"). Returning to the colors of jade with which she began, Hirshfield extends the palette to include the plain colors of earth seen in other minerals, animals, plants, and rippling water. She names the brilliant and the nearly colorless: "roof flashing copper, frost-scent at morning, smoke-singe of pearl." Her catalog embraces the visible signs of creation and those invisible to the naked eye ("flickering helix," "barest conception"). From "the almost not thought of, to heaviest matter," from north to south ("glacier-lit blue to the gold of iguana"), her naming encompasses all of creation. In naming and in seeing the things of this world, she concludes that humans "begin to assemble the plain stones of earth."

Forms and Devices

Its form and structure and the treatment of its subject mark "The Stone of Heaven" as a free-verse ode in the Pindaric mode of encomium, or a poem in praise of something. The classical Pindaric ode includes a paean (a hymn of praise) as Hirshfield does in the final stanza of "The Stone of Heaven." Like the classical ode, it is characterized by apostrophe and anaphora. The poet has set herself the task of praising the whole world (animal—especially human—vegetable, and mineral), including the four elements: earth, fire, air, and water. Throughout the poem, she juxtaposes nonhuman with human creativity in imagery that is predominantly visual and emphasizes color; its palette ranges from brilliant, intense colors to the near colorlessness of smoke and water.

Hirshfield begins by juxtaposing certain colors of jade with human creations (paintings). She refers to jade as the Chinese do: It is a religious symbol, "the very stone of Heaven." The effect of the implicit metaphor that follows ("And here, in the glittering/ hues of the Flemish Masters") is to place the viewers of the scene and the reader in both the paintings and the town: "we sample their wine;/ rest in their windows' sun-warmth,/ cross with pleasure their scrubbed tile floors." Thus the following simile of the leaping and darting fish depicts the colors of both the paintings and the town: "Everywhere the details leap like fish—bright shards/ of water out of water, facet-cut, swift-moving/ on the myriad bones." Fish also symbolize plenty in Buddhist iconography, and thus they, together with the stone of Heaven, perform a dual function: poetic device and religious symbol.

The singing woodthrush is the poet's counterpart in the animal world and the embodiment of the world's abundance. His importance is emphasized in the two-line stanza devoted to him: "Any woodthrush shows it—he sings,/ not to fill the world, but because he is filled." This and the following stanza are transitional, leading into the hymn, a version of a classical paean, with which the poem ends. In encompassing the whole universe in a carnival metaphor, Hirshfield personifies it, emphasizing its spectacle and its amazing feats: "It spills and spills, whirs with owl-wings,/ rises, sets, stuns us with planet-rings, stars." In the long final stanza of the poem, she praises human beings as well as the forces in the universe:

> O baker of yeast-scented loaves,
> sword dancer,
> seamstress, weaver of shattering glass,
> O whirler of winds, boat-swallower,
> germinant seed,
> O seasons that sing in our ears in the shape of O—

Together with the woodthrush's song, this depiction of the wind and the "arpeggio" of ripples it creates in a pond ("we name them arpeggio, pond") provide the few but vivid sound images of the poem; the wind's "O" and the pond's arpeggio are synthetic images, fusing sight and sound. The repetitions characteristic of the classical paean form the very scaffolding of this final stanza as the poet shifts to naming, beginning each of the next five lines with "we name." The poet then shifts the initial repetitions to "from" for three lines, then to "naming," and finally to "seeing." This is the only place in the poem where she actually uses the word "see," though the poem attempts to dazzle the reader with its visual imagery from the outset.

Themes and Meanings

The linked themes of "The Stone of Heaven" are the overflowing abundance and creativity of the universe and the unity of all life. Hirshfield sees the former in every object from the most microscopic to the grandest. In keeping with her Buddhist ideas, the poet celebrates all forms of life from the minute salt crystal and the microscopic helix within the cell to the mighty forces of the earth and the heavens. She uses jade, a stone of widely varying colors, to symbolize the unity of all creation. The colors named in the poem range from yellow to shadings of green to azure blue. Though many traditions other than the Chinese have attached religious significance to jade, the Chinese call it the stone of heaven, and it has been used extensively to symbolize both heaven and earth in religious rites. As the embodiment of the power of heaven, jade plays a large part in funeral practices as well. Taoist belief is even more specific, ascribing cosmic power to jade. The history of jade's religious importance in Buddhist thought can be seen in the theme of Hirshfield's poem in several ways. Her very first naming of the stone in the poem's opening lines connects it to both heaven and earth. She calls it "the stone of heaven," but the jade she names is the common type dredged up on the riverbank and named after the colors of familiar earthly products—muttonfat, kingfisher, and appleskin.

The moral of this celebration is implied in the two-line stanza devoted to the woodthrush who sings because he is overflowing with the world's abundance. Similarly, the job of human beings is not to fill up an otherwise empty universe but to express its plenty. This lesson in perspective and—one could say—in ecology culminates in the naming and praising of the poem's last stanza. Humans may not be the center of the universe, but they are privileged. They are the painters and the poets (the namers), and they make crude matter into objects of beauty and utility. Humans have also been given the power of scientific discovery and the secrets of the cell. As namers and makers, it is "our" (this explains Hirshfield's use of the inclusive pronoun "we" throughout the poem) job to fully apprehend the multifaceted world in all its beauty. To "begin to assemble the plain stones of earth" may be read as instructions for building a heaven on earth now that humans have named it and begun to truly "see" it. Finally, the power Hirshfield accords language and the artist (the namer or the poet) should be mentioned, for it is great and is announced in the reference to the Flemish painters early in the poem.

Sandra Cookson

THE STORY OF OUR LIVES

Author: Mark Strand (1934-   )
Type of poem: Narrative
First published: 1972; collected in *The Story of Our Lives*, 1973

The Poem

"The Story of Our Lives" is a 201-line narration divided into seven numbered sections. Although the title suggests a history, the poem plays with the discrepancy between what one would expect in a story and the speaker's reluctance or inability to share substantial narrative details. To be sure, traditional narrative elements exist: The speaker reveals that the poem takes place in a room that looks out onto a street, and there are characters. The plural pronouns "we" and "our" in the poem hint at a married couple whose life is not so much told as lived, a life upon which the speaker meditates. Another important "character" exists and speaks in the poem: the book that contains the story of their lives from which the poet quotes; fifty-six lines (28 percent of the total) are italicized as coming from this book. In other words, another important tension in the poem lies between the story in the book that the speaker quotes and the story that arises from his own meditations.

The poem's seven sections suggest an ironic, archetypal period of creation. Although stories usually record past events, this poem, written mostly in the present tense, presents an unfolding of events. Sections 1 and 2 both begin with the line "We are reading the story of our lives." In the first section, the couple is sitting on the couch reading, "hoping for something/ something like mercy or change." The first notes of barrenness are sounded: "it would seem/ the book of our lives is empty." In the second and longest section (forty-six lines), the speaker and the woman continue to read and write (live) the story of their lives as the theme of separation is introduced: "when I lean back I imagine/ my life without you, imagine moving/ into another life, another book."

A dreamlike mood pervades the third and fourth sections, while a tone of yearning pervades the fifth section in which the speaker says, "If only there were a perfect moment in the book." Simultaneous with this yearning, however, is a desire to retreat: "Each moment is like a hopeless cause./ If only we could stop reading." In the sixth and shortest section (sixteen lines), the book chronicles the contradiction between intent and inaction: *"They would patch up their lives in secret:// They did nothing."* The final section ends by pointing toward hope as the speaker says "yes to everything" and the book records that *"They were determined to accept the truth./ Whatever it was they would accept it./ The book would have to be written/ and would have to be read."*

Forms and Devices

Mark Strand's "The Story of Our Lives" plays at pushing language to its limits. One device with which the poet attempts to accomplish this is the use of patterns of assertion and contradiction. Many lines blatantly run against each other: "so much seemed to vanish,/ so much seemed to come to life again." In another instance, the characters vow to patch up their lives and then do nothing. When the speaker says, "I say yes to everything./ You cannot hear me," one wonders what good a universal affirmation is if the person to whom he is speaking does not hear it. Toward the end of the poem, the couple is "horrified by their innocence," and, two lines later, they are "determined to accept the truth"; the juxtaposition of active and passive reactions pushes language against itself.

A variation of this strategy is the use of sentences that contradict each other only if read in a certain way: "If only we could stop reading./ *He never wanted to read another book.*" If the second clause is interpreted as meaning "he wanted to read *only* this book," it contradicts the meaning "he was tired of reading all books." Another instance of contradictory language based on interpretation is the assertion that "The book will not survive./ We are living proof of that." Since the poem postulates that "they *are* the book," how can they be living proof of the book not surviving? Yet another variation of this device of pressing language to its limits is seen in the tendency toward solipsism, the idea that the self is the only thing that can be known and verified: "We say it is ideal./ It is ideal." What "we say" is truth. Another instance is the line "We study what we remember." Memory and analysis seem to be contrasting rational functions.

These examples of language confronting itself in "The Story of Our Lives" show the surreal leanings of the poem. Strand suggests the play between the real and the imaginary: "The rugs, the furniture,/ seem almost imaginary now."; the room looks onto a street but "There is no one there,/ no sound of anything"; and "The furniture in the room is never shifted." The woman in the poem falls in love with the man across the street because she knows "that he would never visit." The use of the absolute negatives "no" and "never" applied in these circumstances throw readers into a fantasy world where the language of their experiences is being applied to physical and social phenomenon that do not follow. Everywhere in the poem, images of waking are set up against images of sleep and dreaming.

Strand's minimalist style strips events and language to essentials. However, there is a troubling quality to these essentials. Taken alone, the assertions seem simple and reasonable enough, but Strand combines them in such a way as to create a distressing, alienated world. The cadence of simple sentences builds a surface rhythm of reasonableness. The author, however, couples images and assertions in such a way that readers feel the world undermining itself, shifting beneath them as if a constant, though subtle, earthquake was making their most basic assumptions unstable.

Themes and Meanings

Strand's chief theme is the exploration of the mind working through language to define the nature of the self. The attempt to reconcile two opposing selves is perhaps best seen in the relationship between the book and the speaker's supplement to and commentary on the book. The closing two lines of the poem read "*They are the book and they are/ nothing else.*" Yet the previous two hundred lines have attempted to explore the reality that their life must be, or at least wants to be, more than the book. For example, at one point the speaker awakens and believes that there is no more to their lives than the book, but the woman disagrees and then goes back to sleep, attempting to elude the control of the linguistically constructed self.

The key tool in this exploration is language. Because language is such a problematic tool, however, writing provides hopeless hope. Language can construct the self, but anything constructed by language is suspect. At a key moment, the speaker says of the book, "It describes your dependence on desire,/ how the momentary disclosures/ of purpose make you afraid." The pronouns "you" and "your" have three possible antecedents. In the structure of the poem, they most literally refer to the woman. They could also be used as a universalizing substitute for "I" and "my." Finally, they could refer to the reader being directly addressed. At any rate, language exists, the passage tells readers, essentially to express desire ("momentary disclosures of purpose"). Those descriptions and disclosures make readers afraid for two reasons: First, language expresses the self's wishes, making them public and permanent; second, another self or part of the self realizes the discrepancy between what is meant or felt and what is said. The speaker says that they keep "hoping for something,/ something like mercy or change,/ a black line that would bind us/ or keep us apart." Language is the black line that both unifies and severs.

For Strand, language is the source not only of hope but also of hopelessness— hopelessness because it will not stay pure and straight; it is, by its nature, contaminated, inadequate. When the speaker says "I write that I wish to move beyond the book,/ beyond my life into another life," he embodies this paradox. Both the world of the book and the world of "the life" are the world of language, of writing. There is a strong undercurrent in the poem flowing toward the idea that hope comes in love or feeling: "what I feel is often the crude/ and unsuccessful form of a story/ that may never be told." It may never be told because, for Strand, there is only crude language and unsuccessful forms of telling stories. Yet the desire to get beyond language and story always exists. The poet is finally a problematized king: "*A bleak crown rested uneasily on his head./ He was the brief ruler of inner and outer discord,/ anxious in his own kingdom.*"

Scott Samuelson

SUNDAY AFTERNOONS

Author: Yusef Komunyakaa (1947-   )
Type of poem: Lyric
First published: 1991; collected in *Magic City*, 1992

The Poem

Written in free verse, "Sunday Afternoons" is a relatively short poem of thirty-five lines divided into seven stanzas. The title refers to the day and time of the week when the poet's parents excluded their children from the family house and locked the doors to ensure their privacy while they had sex. This poem is just one of a number of verse compositions, most of them collected in the volume *Magic City*, wherein Yusef Komunyakaa explores his and, by extension, the readers' shared childhood. In this regard, most children have memories of coping with the mystery of forbidden access, of engaging in the frustrated attempt to decode the parental sounds heard on the other side of closed doors.

Using the first-person plural pronoun "we," the poem is told from the perspective of the poet and his siblings when they are excluded from the monitoring parental presence and left to their own devices. Even in the confines of the family yard, however, the children discover their own innate animal nature by identifying, in the second and third stanzas, with the sometimes wild creatures that cross their field of experience. They become "drunk" on mayhaw juice and terrorize nesting birds. After this exercise of animal spirits and animal cruelty, the children, in the fourth stanza, refocus their attention on the house and their shared realization that there is something going on inside, something to be interpreted solely by auditory evidence. What they hear are the parental cries of passion and anger. With the words "We were born between Oh Yeah/ and Goddammit," the poet summarizes the trajectory of his parents' marriage.

It is at this point that the first-person perspective shifts from the plural to the singular, "we" becoming "I." For the last three stanzas, the collective experience is replaced by the personal vision of the dreamer-child who will one day become the poet-adult. While his brothers heed the parental stricture to stay away from the house, Komunyakaa remains at the screen door, persisting in his attempts to discover the truths of the bedroom and of the adult world. Yet despite his stubborn and ultimately transfiguring refusal to abandon his need to find answers, his quest is marked by a quiet sadness. This is in keeping with the general climate of all the poems contained in *Magic City*. Magic is a two-sided coin, and the poet reinforces that contention by presenting the reader with enchanted childhood memories that combine the elements of delight and horror.

Forms and Devices

In both the poems about his childhood in rural Louisiana and his celebrated compositions on his Vietnam War experience (*Dien Cai Dau*, 1988), Komunyakaa displays the Romantic trait of finding correspondences between humanity and the natural world. Set free in the yard, for example, the children mimic, in their engagement with the landscape, the pattern of many adult relationships. First, they are intoxicated by the juice of the mayhaw and the crabapple. The ripe fruit embodies that period of sexual fertility that adolescence will bring. Then, the children feel "brave/ As birds diving through saw vines." Similarly, future hormonal urges may lead to the potentially painful risk-taking that is also a component of adolescent experimentation. Finally, they observe dogs in heat, and this image of feverish intensity is followed by the children holding speckled eggs in their hands as a hawk circles overhead. Thus, natural images of puberty and fecundity foretell the end of the state of sexual latency the children now experience. Most of the poems in *Magic City* explore this engagement with the natural world. In a 1994 *New York Times* interview, Komunyakaa recalled his hometown of Bogalusa, Louisiana, as a "place where there was vegetation all over. There was a chemistry going on in the landscape and I identified with it, so I kind of look for that wherever I go."

In the second half of the poem, when the poet refocuses on what may be taking place inside the house, there is an acknowledgment of the consequences of sexual union, the recrimination that sometimes follows procreation and the enforced union of the partners. Gospel music can be heard playing on the radio, as "Loud as shattered glass/ in a Saturday-night argument/ About trust and money." In this instance, the music is intended to camouflage the sounds of passion, but, to the children, the music recalls parental arguments about infidelity and finances that have sometimes turned violent. Komunyakaa has written elsewhere about his parents' troubled marriage and his father's anger and abusive propensity. The poem "My Father's Love Letter," also collected in *Magic City*, recounts the poet's memory of writing a letter for his father to his estranged wife, promising that he would never beat her again. The boys, in their yard gambols, prefigure their father's inability to understand the full ramifications of his nature as a sexual being, the fact that the consequence of just one episode of sexual congress may be the often-unanticipated responsibilities of being a husband and a father.

To enhance the realism of his message, Komunyakaa is also noted for his use of the vernacular. This poem, for example, uses the Southern names for various flora: The poet writes "mayhaw" instead of "hawthorne" and "saw vines" instead of "green briars." The use of these regionalisms enforces the sense of a localized landscape rendered through the filter of the poet's memory. Also characteristic of Komunyakaa's work is the layering of simile upon simile. Some critics have accused the poet of overusing this device while others have praised him for his inventiveness in this regard. In the last poetic sentence of "Sunday Afternoons," for example, there are two similes. The first one is rather hackneyed: "Like a gambler's visor"; the second is nothing short of inspired: "like a moon/ Held prisoner in the house." Komunyakaa is also fond of enjambment or the use of run-on lines. Sometimes, in fact, the lines in this particular poem run on not only within stanzas but also between stanzas. The poet is quoted as saying that for him enjambment represents "extended possibilities." For this reason, the device is most appropriate when used in poems without narrative closure such as "Sunday Afternoons," wherein the identity of the child protagonist is not fixed but is in the open-ended process of becoming.

Themes and Meanings

The theme of the outsider pervades the poem. As an African American raised in the segregated South, Komunyakaa would naturally be drawn to this concept of exclusion, and the reader finds evidence of this theme in the poet's other works. "Between Angels and Monsters," another poem collected in *Magic City*, tells of how Komunyakaa and his boyhood friends helped set up the big tent for a traveling circus; they stood "like obsidian panthers in a corner of the white world." Even as a soldier in Vietnam, as evidenced by the poem "Tu Do Street" from the volume *Dien Cai Dau*, the poet confronts exclusion in the informally segregated bars and brothels of Saigon. When he enters a bar patronized by white soldiers, Komunyakaa writes, "I'm a small boy again in Bogalusa. 'White Only' signs and Hank Snow."

Banished from the house and prohibited from viewing the bedroom behavior of their parents, the poet's brothers retreat from the screen door. The child-poet, however, stands his ground to gaze into the light from his dark vantage point. The speaker yearns for the knowledge he will need to interpret the adult mysteries, so he bends toward the light like a phototropic plant. In this case, however, it is not the sun that he glimpses but the dresser mirror cut in half "like a moon/ Held prisoner in the house." The moon is not a source of light but a reflective surface, and it may be that the poet wants the reader to comprehend that the knowledge sought by the child is already within.

Regardless of the parental efforts to "latch the screendoors/ and pull Venetian blinds," the children unconsciously carry within themselves, as reflected in their behavior in the yard, the seeds of adult sexuality and the latent awareness of its sometimes troubled consequences. One can also argue that, like the poem "Out of the Cradle Endlessly Rocking" by nineteenth century American poet Walt Whitman, this work chronicles that single moment when the child-poet recognizes his difference from others, even from his own family. His brothers shy away from the house, but the poet who was then a child struggles stubbornly for a view of what has been denied. Unlike the others, the poet seeks vision. From this childhood experience, one can trace Komunyakaa's career as a seer and an interpreter.

S. Thomas Mack

SUPERNATURAL LOVE

Author: Gjertrud Schnackenberg (1953-   )
Type of poem: Lyric
First published: 1982; collected in *The Lamplit Answer*, 1985

The Poem

Like many lyric poems, Gjertrud Schnackenberg's "Supernatural Love" contains a narrative element, a sort of dramatic situation that provides the framework for this meditation on the nature of supernatural love. At the end of this brief story of a young child and her father, the reader is invited to see the similarities between divine love and human love, similarities which the poem's ambiguous title suggests from the beginning.

The poem opens as the narrator visualizes herself as a four-year-old child as she and her father work in his study. She is cross-stitching a sampler text while her father looks up word origins in the dictionary. The intertwining of the needlework, the etymologies, and the text of the sampler create the thematic web of the poem. The poem hints that carnations are present in the room. In any event, the narrator has apparently said that she calls carnations "Christ's flowers," although she can give no reason why. Curiosity has led her father to look up "carnation" in the dictionary. As he does so, the child notes how his eyes look through the magnifying glass he holds. In return, she peers at him through the eye of the needle and then returns to work on the word "beloved." Later it becomes clear that her sampler has a religious motto and that "beloved" is one part of it.

From the dictionary, the father learns that the root of "carnation" is the Latin word *carn*, meaning "flesh," perhaps because the flowers are commonly pink or red. Since the child cannot explain the source of her version of the name, the father goes on, noting the dictionary's information that carnations are a variety of clove. When he looks up "clove," he learns that the word has its roots in the French word *clou*, meaning "nail." At about that moment, the child accidently stabs herself with her needle, running it into her finger clear to the bone. When she cries out in pain, her father gently touches the wound, just as earlier he had gently touched the words on the page.

In addition to these actions, Schnackenberg records the words of the sampler's motto, "Thy blood so dearly bought," and two other sentences, the origins of which are not entirely clear. One is *"Child, it's me,"* which the child hears in the squeak of her scissors; the other is punctuated as an isolated sentence in quotation marks in the poem: "'The obligation due to every thing/ That's smaller than the universe.'" In the context of the rest of the poem's references, the first of these sentences may come as Christ addresses the little girl. The second is treated as if it is part of the dictionary's entry and must be read as a commentary on the word "carnation."

Forms and Devices

"Supernatural Love" is written in nineteen three-line stanzas of iambic pentameter. The three rhyming words of each stanza share a single rhyme sound. The three-line stanza (called terza rima when it rhymes *aba*, *bcb*, and so on) was most notably used by the medieval poet Dante Alighieri (1265-1321) in his long narrative poem *The Divine Comedy*, in which he used it to honor the doctrine of the Trinity—the Christian doctrine of the essential unity of God as Father, Son, and Holy Spirit. Schnackenberg, as a poet who frequently uses formal structures, would be well aware of the traditions of this verse form. In this poem, the triplets harmonize with the poem's theme of supernatural love, love which in Christian doctrine was expressed by God's appearing in human flesh on earth in the person of Jesus.

In the poem, this theme emerges from a network of images concerning the carnations, their roots (both real roots and etymologies), flesh, blood, and nails. The "iron-fresh" scent of the flowers floats up to the child narrator, a scent she calls "drifted, bitter, secret ecstasy." In a context which has already united the flowers with the idea of Christ, this reference to iron and bitterness inevitably suggests the crucifixion, a reference which is reinforced when the father's dictionary identifies cloves with a word for "nail." Significantly, the father reads the definition twice, "as if he hasn't understood," just as the child, who cannot yet read, does not understand the text she is cross-stitching. Moreover, the dictionary's reference to cloves as a spice also suggests the spices with which Jesus's body was prepared for burial. The very *X* 's of the child's cross-stitching use the Greek letter *chi,* the first letter of the Greek word for *Christ* and a traditional abbreviation of Christ's name. This union of images is what makes the narrator say, "The incarnation blossoms, flesh and nail." The pun on "blossom" is one of several puns in the poem, including the "cross" stitching of the child's needle work and the "roots" of both words and flowers.

As the child twists the threads of her work "like stems," she accidently jabs herself. She has been working the phrase *"Thy blood so dearly bought,"* an explanation of Christian understanding of the meaning of the crucifixion—Christ's blood was the high price paid for human salvation. Now the blood being shed is the child's; it reminds her of the threads she has been working with, and she calls for her father using the intimate "Daddy daddy," which is undoubtedly intended to recall for the reader Jesus's use of a similar word (*Abba*) in addressing his heavenly father. In response, her father gently touches her injury, just as before he gently touched the dictionary's page. Now the italicized *"Child, it's me,"* which earlier seemed to emerge from the flowers and the child's scissors, sounds like a reassurance both from her father and from Christ himself; it is the sort of thing a loving parent might say to an injured child.

Themes and Meanings

This poem is the last in a series of three poems on religious themes that conclude Schnackenberg's volume *The Lamplit Answer*. Their theme makes them rather uncommon in the corpus of twentieth century American poetry. Religious poets such as John Donne and George Herbert flourished in seventeenth century England, but twentieth century America has been a basically secular place for poems. Perhaps that is why Schnackenberg has chosen to explicate a very basic concept of Christian theology in this poem—the concept of supernatural love. The poem's title suggests the mystery of divine love, God's love for human beings. It also suggests other remarkable loves, such as the love parents feel for their children. In the New Testament, Jesus used parent-child love to illustrate the nature of divine love, thus establishing a tradition of imagery.

Implicit in this image is the idea that the loved creature cannot understand such love. Children cannot grasp the depth of their parents' love for them any more than human beings can grasp the depth of God's love. Thus the child in the poem cannot read the text she is cross-stitching, and even the father seems not to understand what he reads in the dictionary.

At this point it seems useful to look again at the images of the poem's opening. The father gazes at the room through the magnifying glass almost like God looking at the world as he touches a word which seems to ring like a "distant, plucked, infinitesimal string." The message of that string seems to refer to "The obligation due to every thing/ That's smaller than the universe." Although that sentence can scarcely be part of the definition for "carnation," it is relevant to the concept of "incarnation," which Christians have understood to be the result of God's love for creation—the decision to take on human flesh and eventually to undergo the agonies of crucifixion. At the same time the father looks through the magnifying glass, the child peers at her father through her needle's eye and receives a sort of miniaturized vision—the sort a butterfly might have, she muses—thus reinforcing the suggestion of her smallness in comparison to her father.

When the child wounds herself while stitching the "perfect text" and calls for her father, he touches her wound with the same hand which earlier had touched the "obligation due" text, and the themes of the poem are drawn together. The father is moved by love for his child and concern for her pain. Such concern is the nature of supernatural love. The child has perceived this dimly, perhaps, in her naming carnations "Christ's flowers," and the idea is reinforced by the etymologies that the father has uncovered. Supernatural love is the mystery at the root of everything; it is the "lamplit answer" that this poem names.

Ann D. Garbett

SURPRISED BY JOY

Author: William Wordsworth (1770-1850)
Type of poem: Sonnet
First published: 1815, in *Poems*

The Poem

"Surprised by Joy" is a short lyric written in the form of a sonnet about a person who continues to grieve over the death of a loved one. Late in life, William Wordsworth told a friend that the "Thee" to which he refers in line 3 was his daughter Catherine, who died in June of 1812. He also may have been thinking of his son Thomas, who died later that year. Wordsworth meditates on this dramatic and highly emotional experience in such a way that his meditation also becomes a dramatic and significant experience in itself. (Most readers find it necessary to read this poem several times before its time scheme and its implications become clear.) The poem opens with the poet describing a vivid, past experience: He had a joyful thought. "Joy" is an important word to Wordsworth and can suggest not only a happy feeling but also a life-giving, mind-altering, deeply emotional, and profound sense of harmony and well-being. A moment of such joy "surprised" the poet, implying that it came suddenly and without warning. It surprised him (as the reader understands from the rest of the poem) because, previously, he had not been joyful.

After being surprised by joy, the poet turned with impatience to share his new and highly emotional state of mind (his "transport"). As illustrated elsewhere in his work, when Wordsworth feels a joy, he often wishes to communicate with someone else. The phrase "impatient as the Wind" implies that he turned quickly, forcefully, and thoughtlessly to someone he assumed was standing beside him, a person who had often stood beside him in the past as his daughter must have done. However, when he turned joyfully to his daughter, he realized she was not there to share his emotion because she was dead. The poem breaks into an exclamation ("Oh!") to communicate the excruciating pang of sorrow Wordsworth felt at that time in the past and also the emotion he feels when he thinks about it later as he writes this poem. He had turned to share his joy with "Thee" in vain because, as he knew and still knows, she is buried in a tomb that is both "silent" (she cannot hear her father) and beyond "vicissitude" (she has been removed from the change or mutability of mortal life).

Lines 5-9 can be read either as a report of the poet's original experience or as his later thoughts about that experience. Either way, Wordsworth tells the reader that his "faithful love" (not just a momentary feeling) is what made him think of his daughter. Why the poet should insist on his faithfulness becomes clear in the next three lines: He feels guilty. He asks how he could have been so unfaithful as to have forgotten the "most grievous loss" of his dear daughter even for a moment, for "the least division of an hour," for a unit of time long enough for him to have had a joyful thought. Although his daughter is now beyond vicissitude, the poet laments his own changeable nature. He does not answer his question, but he seems to hope that his unfaithfulness will somehow be excused. Remembering his daughter proves his "faithful love." Beginning with the middle of line 9, the later, more meditative Wordsworth reflects on his earlier experience. "That thought's return" (that is, suddenly recalling that his daughter was dead) once caused a pang second only to the one he felt when he first learned she had died. In all cases, he is affected not only because a loved one is dead but also because he has lost the thing he loved more than anything else ("my heart's best treasure").

Forms and Devices

"Surprised by Joy" is a fourteen-line Italian sonnet, though Wordsworth somewhat modifies its traditional form. The usual break in sense between lines 8 and 9 actually occurs in the middle of line 9. Wordsworth's rhyme scheme is not as rigid as usual: In a strict Italian sonnet, lines 3 and 4 would rhyme with lines 6 and 7, and in this poem they do not. In line 11, "return" may have been pronounced by Wordsworth to rhyme perfectly with "forlorn." Wordsworth's modifications are appropriate to the dramatic progress of the poem, for it is both a dramatic utterance full of the fits and starts that proceed from a disturbed yet thoughtful mind and a controlled reflection on what that utterance means to the poet.

The dramatic complexities are communicated by the poem's jumbled syntax. Line 1 begins calmly enough with a participial phrase, but, halfway through, the poet provides a dash to show that his mind interjects a clause to describe what he did after joy came over him. This account is, in turn, interrupted partway through line 2 with a dramatic interjection ("Oh!"), followed by a string of phrases and appositions that modify "turned." What technically may be a sentence in lines 1-4 may strike readers as less than grammatically stable because of its two dashes. Such patterns persist. The statement in line 5 contains an interruption ("faithful love"), and a dash at the end of the same line implies that the question in line 6 is an interruption, a shift in the poet's thinking. The poet's thought and mood shifts again in the middle of line 9. His statement about his "worst pang" is no sooner uttered than qualified by a string of dependent elements that extend to the end of the poem. In short, the poem's somewhat chaotic grammar helps express the poet's mental anguish and communicates the freshness of his experiences when he was surprised by joy, when he reflects on that experience, and when he first knew of his daughter's death. Despite its informality of structure, the poem is moderately formal in diction ("transport," "vicissitude," "beguiled," "grievous"). It uses tropes only to reflect simple emotional experiences. A simile ("impatient as the Wind") describes the poet's reaction to joy, and a metaphor ("heart's best treasure") suggests his first reaction to his daughter's death.

The intensity of Wordsworth's complex experience is communicated by the emphatic nature of the verse. Readers can hear the poet's voice stress such words a "Wind," "Oh!" "tomb," "love," "power," "hour," and "blind." Some of these stresses are caused by words themselves; they often have long vowels, deep or strident, that are seldom clipped off. The rhythm of the lines themselves work up to stresses, as in the haste with which line 7 ("Even for the least division of an hour") speeds to its conclusion. Readers sense a relaxation of tension toward the end of the poem. Its more pensive tone is caused by its verse, which is less emphatic and more regularly paced.

The tone of this poem is complex, a mixture of emotion and restraint. The poem communicates the anguish Wordsworth felt in the past and feels in the present. At the same time, the poet shows the psychic control of a mature adult. Perhaps one way he expresses this mixture of emotion and control is by filling a strict form such as the sonnet with irregularities of syntax and heavy emphasis. The poem's juxtaposition of anguish and control suggests how much the poet's maturity has cost him.

Themes and Meanings

This poem is not simply one that remembers the death of a loved one. It is both about death and about remembering that death. Even though Wordsworth the poet often wrote about transcendental influences and Wordsworth the mature man entertained thoughts of Christian immortality, such matters are not part of this poem. The poet thinks of his daughter in two ways: in her grave and in his memory. Her body is buried in a tomb, a physical spot where all is silent. The Wordsworths once lived across the road from the church where Catherine was buried, but Mary Wordsworth was so affected by seeing her daughter's grave so close to her home that the family had to move. In this poem, however, memories are more potent reminders than graves. The impact of "Surprised by Joy" comes first from its vivid rendering of a moment of joy, immediately followed by the realization that the loved one with whom the poet needed to share that joy to make it complete was not present. Most readers will remember similar moments. The full meaning of the poem embraces not only that moment but also subsequent reflections on that moment as well as other memories it calls forth. The poem is about the way a human being's emotional life is an interactive mixture of immediate and remembered (but no less vivid) emotional experiences.

George Soule

A TALE OF TWO GARDENS

Author: Octavio Paz (1914-1998)
Type of poem: Lyric
First published: 1969, as "Cuento de dos jardines," in *Ladera este*; English translation
  collected in *The Collected Poems of Octavio Paz: 1957-1987*, 1987

The Poem

"A Tale of Two Gardens" is a long poem in free verse that evokes the concept of
rebirth and renewal found in the return to a timeless beginning symbolized by images
of gardens. The poem uses garden imagery to represent key and dynamic moments in
Octavio Paz's life in Mexico and India. As the title of the poem indicates, there are
two gardens in the work. The first is associated with Paz's childhood in Mixcoac,
which is now a part of Mexico City. The second garden is located in India where the
poet served as an ambassador from Mexico for a number of years. This garden also
provides the setting for the author's second marriage. The poem is written in the first
person and genuinely reflects an intense personal experience with universal implications. The beginning of the piece immediately establishes the garden not so much as
a place but as a moment outside of normal time and space. It is depicted as a void, an
archetypal center through which the rivers of cosmic life flow.

The first experience in the garden occurs during the poet's childhood. It is a time
of idyllic vision that only the innocence of youth can create. As the protagonist leaves
his youth, he also symbolically abandons the garden and its transpersonal nature. The
garden of childhood becomes a ruin for ants to harvest. The protagonist's return to the
garden during adulthood represents a return to that magical center abandoned after
childhood. This time it is in a garden in India under a neem tree that awareness is again
expanded and a universal experience is achieved through passionate and erotic love
with the woman he married; the poet depicts her as Almendrita, the "Little Blond
Almond" of fairy tale in the children's book by the same name. This passion turns
everything into rivers that cover the world, destroying the old and creating the new.
Contradictions that come from opposites are symbolically resolved. Even the contradictions of life and death find common ground in the realm of the Great Mother as
expressed by a variety of feminine deities in Indian lore. The two gardens of the poem
are active places of wonder that carry the protagonist away from his human condition
to partake of the universal source. When the protagonist leaves India at the end of the
poem, he does not leave the garden behind because "there are no more gardens than
those we carry within."

Forms and Devices

The poem develops around the garden as a central image. The garden is part of the
life and everyday history of the protagonist. The memory of the garden in Mixcoac
includes the grandfather with whom he spent much time as a boy and the fig tree that
was the center of life there. The garden in India includes the memory of his marriage

to his new wife and a neem tree that plays the same role in India as the fig tree did in Mixcoac. However, this image is also presented as both symbol and metaphor. As a symbol, the garden manifests the archetypal center of authentic being. As a metaphor, the garden provides the method by which the protagonist is able to achieve a transformative experience and renew his spiritual condition.

It is the image of the garden as a symbol that provides the mythical setting for the magical moments in the protagonist's life. In it, the fig tree is depicted as the mother goddess whose opened trunk reveals "the other face of being,/ the feminine void," and the neem tree resolves all contradictions: "The other is contained in the one,/ the one is the other." The garden as the setting for the other side of being teaches the protagonist "to wave . . . goodbye" to himself. To return to the garden is to return "to the beginning of the beginning." The garden represents both Prajnaparamita, "Our Lady of the Other Bank," the Indian goddess of perfect wisdom, and Yakshi, the goddess of trees and plants.

The garden as a metaphor begins with the notion that "A house, a garden,/ are not places:/ they spin, they come and go./ Their apparitions open/ another space/ in space,/ another time in time." In another passage, the speaker states that "a garden is not a place:/ it is a passage,/ a passion." The garden is a "Mumbling river" that "flows through the night." The image of the garden acts as a bridge that brings together the concrete and the universal, a manifestation of the dynamic process that leads to magical transformation. The story of the protagonist's union with Almendrita is a story of universal fulfillment. It takes the form of a water-filled journey that destroys the old reality and creates a new world. The journey symbolically resolves all human contradictions. "We don't know where we're going," says the speaker, "to pass through is enough,/ to pass through is to remain." That is, the paradox associated with passing through and remaining is resolved. The garden as a transformative metaphor is confirmed when the speaker states that "there are no more gardens than those we carry within." The garden as passion and as passage is the way by which one reaches self-realization. This self-realization is described in the poem as "the other bank." Once the garden completes its work and allows the protagonist to reach a new level of existence, it disappears only to appear again when the next renewal experience is sought. "The garden sinks," states the speaker in conclusion, "The signs are erased:/ I watch clarity." The garden has transported the protagonist to his ultimate destination. Clarity and wisdom are achieved at the conclusion of the journey.

Themes and Meanings

"A Tale of Two Gardens" is about an archetypal journey to achieve spiritual renewal and a vision that transcends the contradictions caused by the rules of human existence. Adam and Eve's biblical Garden of Eden is an example of that undifferentiated original state of innocence sought by the poetic experience. The journey motif provides both the theme and structure for the work. The concept of the archetypal journey is very much a variation of anthropologist Joseph Campbell's "adventure of the hero" as well as the process of individuation outlined by psychoanalyst Carl Jung.

In it, the hero travels to the center of a magical reality to obtain the secrets that symbolically resolve human contradictions. The garden represents such a place.

The garden in Mixcoac manifests the realm of the protagonist's original state of innocence. In that environment, the boy is nurtured. "The garden for me," says the speaker, "was like a grandfather./ I clambered up its leafy knees." The fig tree is then depicted as the mother and the feminine void that dominates the center of that magical world. The protagonist then grows up. Natural innocence is left behind and the garden of his youth no longer exists. The garden as a universal center becomes available again when, as an adult, the protagonist comes in search of its magical gift. What the protagonist achieves in the garden this time is expressed both intellectually and through erotic passion. Intellectually, the protagonist comes to understand the garden as a transformative experience that resolves the paradox of the "one" and the "other" to make both the same. The paradox of life and death is resolved in the notion that views "death is expansion." Finally, the denial of self and the expansion of self are brought together by the concept that sees that "self-negation is growth."

Erotically, the adventure with Almendrita, the symbol of feminine principle and the protagonist's opposite, results in the poetic inundation and destruction of the old reality and the creation of a new world by their love and their archetypal union as representatives of the masculine and the feminine principles. The poem is populated by Indian deities of love, passion, and wisdom. They serve to communicate to the reader that the work is not only a love poem but also a powerful instrument of change and renewal with archetypal implications. In "A Tale of Two Gardens," intellect and passion combine to construct a superior work of art. Symbol, structure, metaphor, and theme come together to provide a way of transcending the human condition.

David Conde

THE TASK

Author: Denise Levertov (1923-1997)
Type of poem: Lyric
First published: 1982; collected in *Oblique Prayers: New Poems with Fourteen Translations from Jean Joubert,* 1984

The Poem

"The Task" is a twenty-five-line poem composed of two stanzas written in free verse, which Denise Levertov herself would describe as "organic poetry." The poem discusses the character and—as the title implies—the work of God. The opening six-line stanza presents a false image of God as an uncouth and somewhat threatening old man "always upstairs, sitting about/ in sleeveless undershirt," his arms folded over his rumbling stomach. He is asleep and probably snoring since she concludes the stanza with the lines "his breath from open mouth/ strident, presaging death" (an image suggestive of the "death rattle"). The stanza ends with an ellipsis, as if the description was unfinished, and the second stanza interrupts and proceeds to correct this image of God.

In the corrected image, God is depicted as a weaver working at his loom "in the wilderness," described as a "huge tundra room" with no walls and a "sky roof." However, he is not far away; he is just next door. His work is absorbing and loud, and he seems to be in some hurry to finish it. The sounds of human screams and prayers come through the clamor of his task, but the poem is somewhat ambiguous about the kind of attention God pays to them. He "hears far-off" humanity's screams and "perhaps listens for prayers in that wild solitude." Ultimately, humans "can't stop their/ terrible beseeching," but "God/ imagines it sifting through, at last, to music." The poem concludes with the task complete, the loom quiet, and "the weaver at rest."

Forms and Devices

Concerning the forms of her poems, Levertov, in *The Poet in the World* (1973), distinguishes between free verse, which rejects precast or reusable forms in favor of freedom from all bonds, and her "organic poetry," which, having freed itself from imposed forms, voluntarily submits to the forms that content reveals and imposes on it. The form of "The Task" is an outgrowth and expression of its contents. The poem's two-stanza structure permits the contrast of the false image of God with the corrected image. The first stanza begins conversationally with the words "As if," implying the conditional character of the description and establishing a skeptical tone. The reader understands immediately that this is not the true image of God. The second stanza begins with a resounding "No," specifying—in no uncertain terms—a contradiction to the first stanza.

The controlling metaphor of the second stanza is God as a weaver whose work is weaving a great garment. The structure of the stanza is loomlike: Elements of both sense and sound are threaded into the poem, not in prose sentence order but in alternating and somewhat irregular arrangements that only present a finished pattern in the fully woven poem. For example, visual images of the wilderness in the first two lines of the stanza are followed by a line combining the introduction of the loom with a picture of berry bushes, which in turn is followed by a line in which "rain" and "shine" are juxtaposed to the aural image of the "clacking and whirring" loom. Human screams, introduced in lines 14 and 15, are commented on in lines 21 and 22; likewise, God's listening, introduced in lines 15 and 16, is related to human voices in line 19. The "hum of bees, not the din" that he hears in line 13 is echoed by his imagining human "beseeching" as "music" in line 23. Similarly, line length at the center of the second stanza is patterned, with pairs of longer lines alternating with shorter lines. Line breaks seem to be determined by emphasis, with key words such as "solitude," "woven," "task," "God," and "music" occurring at the ends of lines.

These devices illustrate Levertov's ideal of the elements of a poem working together to create "a kind of extended onomatopoeia" that imitates "not the sounds of an experience . . . but the feeling of an experience" (*The Poet in the World*). However, the poet also uses onomatopoeia in the traditional sense of using words that sound like their referents: a stomach rumbling, the loom clacking and whirring, and the bees humming. In her description of the false image of God, repeated sibilants (as in "sleeveless undershirt, asleep") sound like breath passing through dentures, and the assonant sounds of the dull, open vowels intensify the image of the open-mouthed sleeper.

Themes and Meanings

Levertov begins her poetry collection *Oblique Prayers* with a note explaining that the book and the sections within it represent a thematic rather than a chronological order. The order of the fourth and final section, "Of God and Of the Gods," seems to represent the Judeo-Christian Creation story: not just the initial Creation of the biblical account but also an active and continuous creation that finds completion in the individual believer's life. "The Task" stands exactly at the center of the fifteen poems that comprise this final section and can be fully understood only in its relationship to the others. The first seven poems account for the creation of the natural world: of rivers, of "earth-gods," of trees and flowers. In most of these poems, God is designated as unknowable, at least to "the gods." In "The Avowal," God is named "Creator Spirit" and man is placed in the natural context. In the next poem, "The God of Flowers" (which precedes "The Task"), though the god of flowers cannot know God, her work pleases him and he "watches and smiles."

Levertov has referred to God and the gods in poems written before this collection, notably in *Candles in Babylon* (1982), and has written much overtly Christian poetry since; however, "The Task" was her most explicit and most nearly orthodox poem about God at the time of its publication. The poem implies much about the character and work of God. That God is "in the wilderness next door/ —that huge tundra room, no walls and a sky roof—" implies that while God may be unbounded, neither he nor his whereabouts are unknowable. He seems near and exists not apart from but within the created world.

Since the poem follows a catalog of Creation in the first seven poems, the task of the title seems to be the work of Creation itself. Elsewhere in *Oblique Prayers*, Levertov uses images of knitting to represent re-creative acts, as when she describes an old grey sweater being conjured into a poem: "it and your need for it," she writes, "are/ the knit and purl of the poem's rows/ re-raveled" ("Grey Sweaters"). The reader is prepared then to regard the task in which God, without raw materials, "hurries on with the weaving:/ till it's done, the great garment woven" as Creation. However, God is involved in this poem with more than the creation of the natural world. The poem affirms that while God is "absorbed in his work," he "hears far-off" human screams and "listens for prayers." Though he "hurries on with the weaving," the human voices are "clear under the familiar/ blocked-out clamor of the task." The human cries are not annoying or irrelevant. Though they leave the lips or hearts as "terrible beseeching," they become, like the spacious hum of bees, the music that accompanies God's work.

At the end of "The Task," the loom is idle, suggesting the completion of God's task, but the implication of the last seven poems is that God's creative work is not finished. These final poems outline a kind of apostolic succession from Saint Peter to the poet and a sequence of belief from spiritual dryness to transcendent joy. In the final poem, "Passage," God's spirit, walking "upon the face of the water" and moving the meadow grass, provides new life not only to believers but also to their world.

Gaymon Bennett

TELLING THE BEES

Author: John Greenleaf Whittier (1807-1892)
Type of poem: Ballad
First published: 1858; collected in *Home Ballads and Poems*, 1860

The Poem

Originally published as "The Bees of Fernside," "Telling the Bees" is a poem of fourteen quatrains, or stanzas of four lines each. Each stanza displays *abab* rhyming, which means that the first line rhymes with the third and the second line with the fourth, a typical pattern for a ballad. A note written by John Greenleaf Whittier precedes the poem, informing readers that on farms in Essex County, Massachusetts (Whittier's home), a custom dating from colonial times was long observed: When a death occurred in the family, someone would "tell the bees" kept on the farm about the death and drape the hive with black crepe to allow the insects to mourn for the deceased. At one time people believed that not doing so would cause the bees to leave, frightened by a death they did not understand.

This poem uses a first-person narrator, a young man who is distinct from Whittier. He is reminiscing a year after the events he describes, walking down the same path he took the previous June. Twelve months earlier, he was going to see his sweetheart, Mary, after being away a month, which, he adds, seemed to be a year without her. The young man's remark ironically suggests the year of grief which began on the day he recalls. As he walks, he describes the earlier trip. He steps through an opening in a tumbled wall and crosses a brook. He comes within sight of Fernside, Mary's farm, and notices the red gate, tall poplar trees, brown barn, and white horns of the family's cattle showing above a stone wall. He sees the beehives kept near the barn, the spring flowers by the brook, and describes the "sweet clover-smell in the breeze" from the meadows nearby. It is a beautiful spring day, much like the one he recalls from the previous year.

The speaker reminisces that a year before, he took a drink from the stream, admired the blossoms, and brushed off his coat, preparing to see Mary. However, as he drew near, he saw a servant girl draping the beehives in black and singing to the bees. Despite the sun's warmth, he felt chilled, knowing that the crepe meant a death had occurred. He assumed that Mary's frail grandfather had died, and he felt pity for the sadness she must feel. However, as the young man came closer to the house, he heard Mary's dog whining from the house and saw her grandfather sitting on the porch, resting his chin on the end of his cane. At the same moment he finally made out the words the servant sang, and he realized that it was Mary who had died. The poem ends with this realization.

Forms and Devices

Ballads, in general, are narrative poems modeled on English and Scottish folk songs. Such poems are generally more effective at depicting action than thought or feeling; emotions are typically shown through the depiction of situations and deeds rather than through a discussion of mental states. Accordingly, despite the first-person narration, Whittier relies on sensory details and setting to develop the emotion of "Telling the Bees." The young man, going to see his beloved, mused happily on the scenery along the path. Everything was familiar, friendly, and warm; these details allow the reader to sense the speaker's past joy, equating the bright day and fragrant vegetation with young love.

Similarly, the subsequent shock and grief are neither described nor portrayed. Instead, the reader is presented with the contrast of the living, pleasant colors (the hues of the flowers along the brook as well as the red, green, brown, and white of the farm) with the somber black being draped about the beehives. The birds' songs contrast with the sad voice of the hired girl. At that point, the narrator says, he felt cold, as if he were walking on a snowy day in winter (itself a contrast with the sunny June weather). Even here the narration dwells not upon the emotion but its physical manifestation, the chill and shiver that people feel as they anticipate bad news. The narrator regarded the loss of life as sad but not unexpected, for Mary's grandfather was obviously unwell. Observed detail, rather than description, then communicates the final destruction of the speaker's comfort, as if the reader can see through his eyes and hear through his ears the events leading to the realization. First, Mary's dog cried for its owner, and then the grandfather appeared on the porch, staring into space as if heartbroken. Finally, the words of the dirge sung by the "chore-girl," "Mistress Mary is dead and gone," became audible. The young man's emotions at the loss of his sweetheart, whom he expected to see after a month's absence, strike the reader even though the feelings are never described.

Also effective in engaging the imagination is the use of detail. As with the colors, a few traits of the day are suggested, but most are omitted, allowing the mind's eye to create the scenes more easily from individual experience. The pasture smells of clover, as do most meadows in the late spring; in this, and similar details, Whittier allows the reader to fill in the larger picture from memory. Such personalized scenes help the reader to experience vicariously the sadness of the young man. Everything else the speaker notices is unchanged—even the tumbled wall through which he walked many times before is still in the same state of disrepair, and the flowers near the brook are still overgrown with weeds; only Mary is missing. The sun is the same, the fields and cattle are the same, but the person who gave everything meaning for him is gone.

Themes and Meanings

Scholars have pointed out that Whittier combines the custom of telling the bees about a death in the family with a description of his own family farm. He wrote the poem as a memorial tribute to his mother, Abigail Hussey Whittier, who died in December, 1857, three months before its publication. She had lived on the family farm most of her adult life. Whittier, who sometimes has been viewed by critics as artificially sentimental, here weaves details from his own life into a masterful evocation of grief and loss. His almost conversational tone, which contains very little "poetic" diction, helps the reader imagine the scene through which the narrator walks. He does not depict emotion, but rather draws the reader into the situation so skillfully that one feels something of the young man's loss.

Whittier's self-discipline, which allowed him to express his profound sorrow in a brief poem, also helped him make that poem powerful. Instead of pouring out the lamentation that might seem natural to a grieving person, Whittier kept direct expressions of emotion out of the poem, focusing instead on details of the physical world to suggest the emptiness which the bereaved feel. Further, by having the speaker reminisce a year later, Whittier was able to show someone who still mourned Mary but who could ponder his situation without the despair and confusion which would be associated with a more recent death.

Even though the poem was a tribute to his mother, Whittier chose not to make the lost loved one a mother, but rather a sweetheart (named for his elder sister, Mary Whittier Caldwell). By fictionalizing the loss in this way, the poet both kept his personal sadness private and made his perceptions more accessible for a wide range of readers. As innumerable songs, legends, and literary works attest, the fear of losing a lover is common. It is easy to imagine such a loss, which makes the shock accessible for a wide range of readers, young and old. In the ensuing years, as he continued to contemplate the death of his mother and later of his sister Mary, Whittier wrote many religious or inspirational verses. In "Telling the Bees," however, he took a different approach, expressing sadness for lost joy in this world rather than hope for the next. Although it is not overtly about Abigail Whittier, "Telling the Bees" expresses the feelings her son experienced at the time of her death.

Critics generally consider "Telling the Bees" one of Whittier's best works. Much of his poetry was occasional, written for specific situations, and it has not always been admired by later readers. Much of what is still well known, such as Whittier's numerous religious poems, was similarly written for specific audiences. However, "Telling the Bees" relies upon such basic experiences as a beautiful spring day and the expectation of a happy reunion to emphasize the suddenness and absoluteness of death. By employing such universal events, the poem draws its force from the basic shock of the contrast of life and its end.

Paul James Buczkowski

TELYRIC

Author: Andrei Codrescu (1946-   )
Type of poem: Lyric
First published: 1987, in *Cottonwood Commemorative: River City Portfolio 1987*;
   collected in *Alien Candor: Selected Poems, 1970-1996*, 1996

The Poem

In thirty-four lines the narrator of "Telyric" describes being prepared for an outdoor television presentation. A television performer, the narrator is clearly poet Andrei Codrescu himself. Elsewhere, Codrescu has explained that he wrote the poem while working on a documentary about baseball for a Minneapolis television station.

In the poem a "professional TV person" tells the narrator where to stand and shields him from the sun with a "silver shield"—presumably a metallic umbrella, such as is used for reflecting sunlight in outdoor shooting. The "nuclear-trained soundman" wires the narrator to himself and brags about the "top-secret clearance" he once had while "shut four years inside a sewer pipe," when he indulged a drug habit. An old man stops to ask whether the narrator is famous. He spits in a monumental fountain built by the Immigration and Naturalization Service. The fountain is reputed to have been controversial in an earlier time, when its ornamentation shielded terrorists. The British cameraman shooting the narrator proudly wears a T-shirt immortalizing the life of a Scandinavian plastic surgeon, Tord Skoog, that is worn "from Patagonia to Maroc."

The narrator feels the self-consciousness of the performer, his media personality on display in the sunshine as if he were a large puppet. He mentions a sports hero also on display, Dennis Martinez, the "new national hero of Nicaragua" (a Baltimore Orioles pitcher whom Codrescu interviewed for the documentary). Public notice and adulation conceal rather than reveal, distorting the narrator's sense of self. The electronic connections to the media equipment allow the narrator to communicate with the outside world, but they provide no psychological or intellectual understanding, no "sense." A television person waves to the narrator, signaling him to begin his performance. The narrator walks toward her, overcoming his lack of familiarity in his youth with the conventions of television performance. He puts on his television personality and delivers his first line into the bright light of the sun. His "tinfoil trembles like Skoog's fjord."

Forms and Devices

The language of "Telyric" synthesizes and blends complex experiences into units of poetic discourse. An example of this technique is the title, which by this process of blending forms a new word as "television lyric" becomes "telyric." Such formations are known as portmanteau words—words formed by telescoping pairs of existing words, such as "electricity" and "execute" to make "electrocute" or "breakfast" and "lunch" to make "brunch." However, Codrescu's title is also humorously oxymoronic in that "television" and "lyric" usually suggest contradictory contexts. "Lyric" connotes music and deep emotions—a far cry from the utilitarian banality of television.

Apart from the poem's title, the blends in "Telyric" connect the awkward social and psychological feelings involved with being in the camera's eye with the events of the production itself. The narrator's observations and memories are linked to the physical setting of the production, as when the fountain in which the geezer spits triggers memories of a long-past (and absurd) contretemps [the fountain] "said years ago/ to have been an object of controversy/ capable of shielding terrorists."

Codrescu is a master of a comic *reductio ad absurdum*, carrying the seemingly straightforward if silly—"capable of shielding terrorists"—into the completely ridiculous: "in the goldfish rolls of its Dubuffet clusters." (Jean Dubuffet was a French artist who designed large sculptures noted for their apparent disorder and spontaneous vigor.) The T-shirt worn by the British cameraman not only promotes a Scandinavian plastic surgeon—an unlikely subject in itself—but follows his life from "humble beginnings/ to an obituary in the *Scandinavian/ Journal of Plastic Surgery*"—a publication most people may be excused for never suspecting existed. The comedy is capped by the Scandinavian doctor's notoriety via T-shirt "from Patagonia to Maroc" (which are separated by the Atlantic Ocean).

The synthesizing language merges the narrator's "telyric self" and "large puppethood," the metaphor suggesting how awkward, graceless, and controlled the television self feels while under the control of the wires (literally audio cables) of the production crew. The solitary narrator "bends" like a puppet in the glare of the sun, as if on stage in a spotlight. However, the setting is outdoors, perhaps prompting the baseball comparison ("A window of light is in the dugout roof . . ."). The baseball allusion continues when the narrator "throw[s] the first pitch into the sun," punning on the idea of a television pitchman and on his role of pitching his own television performance, which is itself a documentary about baseball. The narrator's "tinfoil," recalling the "silver shield" which the producer used to shield him from the sun in the first lines, "trembles," suggesting his nervousness. This, in turn, recalls another association, the sunlight shining on the water in the fjords of Scandinavia, a reference to the Scandinavian plastic surgeon, Skoog.

The mind of the poet links experiences and associations, even if they have little in common except surface features. The narrator, here surely identified with Codrescu, who grew up television-deprived in communist Romania, walks toward the producers in the convention of the casually strolling television commentator, across the "narrows/ of the TV-less childhood." "Narrows" suggests the strait or constricted passage between two different pieces of land or countries, here possibly two different ways of life, the media-less land of Codrescu's youth and the modern American broadcast culture.

Exaggeration is also used as a comic technique. The sound man is "nuclear-trained," with "top-secret clearance." He claims to have spent "four years inside a sewer pipe," apparently doing military surveillance. His self-promotion is an ironically skewed boastfulness technically proficient persons might be tempted to indulge.

In response, the narrator challenges the engineer with an ironic question, "Top-hat clearance?" Playing on "top clearance," "top-hat" suggests the absurd image of a vaudeville performer, rather than a daring spy. The laconic answer, "our army's stoned and theirs is drunk," is a classic cynical exaggeration about the Cold War standoff between Americans and Soviets.

Command forms of verbs accentuate how little control the narrator has over his public self, as he is told to "stand here," "go on," and "put on the shield." The poem also builds on the idea of things seeming to be open while remaining closed. The narrator is "shielded" from the sun; the sound man has spent four years in a sewer pipe; Dennis Martinez is "concealed" in a dugout; the narrator is "bent" and constricted by the "narrows." Again these references reinforce the two selves in the poem: the apparently open tele-self and the closed reality of each individual. Unexpected echoes and resonances link the disparate imagery. The umbrella-like shield of the opening comes up again in the verb "shields," referring to protecting terrorists. The narrator "bends" in the sunlight while Skoog "rises." The British cameraman "shoots" the narrator while the terrorists presumably might try to shoot from the protection of the fountain.

Themes and Meanings

Codrescu's "telyric self" is at odds with the narrator's inner being. Like a puppet, he is manipulated and maneuvered into the best physical position for his performance. The narrator's relationship with his production crew is thus purely utilitarian and mechanical, as no one asks about the content of his presentation. The old man's question, "He somebody famous?" sums up the situation: The telyric self is famous; however, the inner self is unconnected to sense but rather connected to a situation rich in a feeling of fraudulence and replete with chaotic images, from Skoog's history as a plastic surgeon to baseball player Martinez to the passing "geezer" to the production crew.

The multiple nationalities represented in the short poem suggest both the confusion of many unconnected cultures and their being brought together by television. The Romanian Codrescu, Nicaraguan Martinez, the British cameraman, the Scandinavian Skoog, Patagonia (Argentina), and Maroc (Morocco). The connection between the fountain and the Immigration and Naturalization Service seems appropriate given this multicultural cast.

Whether "Telyric" reveals Codrescu's heartfelt feelings or is merely another witty performance—a poetic performance commenting on a television performance by a media-wise commentator—is immaterial. From the reader's perspective, the poem's value lies in its evocation of the awkward, uncomfortable feeling of being in the spotlight. The real self becomes a bogus one when an unnatural role is required; random thoughts and observations, "real" though they may be, are unacceptable when acting as conventional commentators must in their television personas. Codrescu himself refers to the "weirdness" of television and his beginner's wonder at it. The poem thus raises the theme of honesty in the roles people play and emphasizes the disjunction between immediate sensations and the consistency that is expected in social situations.

Andrew Macdonald

10 JANUARY 1934

Author: Osip Mandelstam (1891-1938)
Type of poem: Lyric
First published: 1964, as "10 yanvarya 1934," in *Sobranie sochinenii*; English trans-
lation collected in *Selected Poems*, 1974

The Poem

The poem "10 January 1934" is about the distinguished Russian poet, novelist, and thinker Andrey Bely, one of the leading Symbolists in the first two decades of the twentieth century. Although Osip Mandelstam subscribed to a different poetic creed, he respected Bely's poetry highly, and the two became close friends for a brief time in 1933. When Bely died soon thereafter, Mandelstam wrote a cycle of seven poems in honor of his friend and fellow poet; "10 January 1934" is the central poem of the cycle. Like so many of Mandelstam's poems, it was published posthumously.

The poem consists of nine stanzas. The title itself precisely locates the poem in time—the day of Bely's death. Mandelstam's subjective persona reveals immediately how he felt about the loss of his friend, being "haunted by a few chance phrases" of the departed poet. He speaks of "the rich oil of my sadness," borrowing the metonymy from the old Russian epic *Slovo o polku Ígoreve* (c. 1187; *The Lay of Igor's Campaign*, 1919), thus retracing the roots of Bely's heritage back several hundred years. A striking metaphor follows: "the dragonflies of death." They are black, and, even though their eyes are blue, the blueness is black at the same time. Through a series of rhetorical questions, Mandelstam comments on the essence of Bely's poetry. Mandelstam asks where a leading poet ("the first-born") belongs now that he is gone, wondering at the evaluation criteria and hinting at Bely's place among the foremost of Russian writers. Where, now, is the "tiny hawk" of soaring flights of Bely's spirit? Mandelstam then emphasizes Bely's erudition and his deep study of Russian verse, the firmness of his beliefs, and the straightforwardness of his words "honestly weaving back and forth"—an undisguised barb at the rigidity of thinking of the Soviet officials who caused Bely much suffering in the last two decades of his life. His path was paved by centuries-old wisdom of his predecessors ("solutions of three-layered salts"), by idealistic German philosophers who had a significant influence on his thinking, by Russian "mystical" thinkers, and, finally, by the Russian thinker-poet Vladimir Solovyov, who honed his thought and chiseled his verse.

In the fifth stanza, Mandelstam suddenly shifts his attention, as if rudely awakening from his reverie. The funeral music "leapt from ambush" like a "tiger . . . hiding in the instruments"; its impact was not so much to be heard and to soften things but to jar everyone and direct attention to the deceased. (In the Russian burial custom, the casket is left open until it is lowered into the grave.) As if removing the mask from the dead, the music brings back to life the muscles, "the drumming/ forehead," the "fingers holding no pen," "the puffed lips," "the hardened caress," and "the crystallized calm and goodness." While the other funeral participants seem to react normally under the circumstances (there is even an engraver in the crowd to make a death mask), Mandelstam is grieving, "hanging on my own eyelashes." He turns, increasingly, to his own feelings, "swelling, ripening, reading all the parts of the play/ till I'm picked." With the final words of the poem, Mandelstam identifies fully with his departed fellow poet, expecting to follow him along the same sorrowful path because "The plot is the one thing we know."

Forms and Devices

The poem "10 January 1934" consists of nine quatrains rhymed *abab* in Mandelstam's customary interchange of eleven (*a*) and ten (*b*) syllable lines. The poem teems with images and metaphors, as do most of Mandelstam's poems. The most expressive metaphor is the aforementioned dragonfly, a colorful, translucent insect that is a frequent symbol in Bely's poetry. In "10 January 1934," it is a dragonfly of death, befitting the occasion. Here, it represents the effervescence of Bely's talent; the irony of it is that it is very much alive even as the poet lies dead (his poetry survives him). Another metaphor is a "tiny hawk that melts deep in the eyes," a reference to Bely's powerful gaze. Nadezhda Mandelstam, Osip's widow, also speaks, in *Hope Against Hope* (1970), of the luminescence and electric charge of his eyes, of the electrifying effect he had on those he came in contact with, and of his ability to inspire new and exciting ideas in them. The swiftness of Bely's mind is depicted by the metaphor of a skater leaping into a blue flame, indicating his fearless forays into dangerous territory. His thoughts and words were sharp like "blades in the frosty air" and sonorous like "the clink of glasses in a glacier," crackling with lucidity and precision and "weaving back and forth" with astonishing dexterity and speed. The mourners gather at Bely's funeral, shoulder pressing shoulder, the fur on their coats breathing. Their health ("red ore boiling"), blood, and sweat are used as a contrast to the immobility and finality of death.

Finally, the predicaments of both Bely and Mandelstam are presented as a play with an all-too-familiar plot. Mandelstam sees the fate of Bely, as well as his own, reflected in an imaginary play, a tragedy, no doubt, as reflected in his comment about himself hanging "on my eyelashes"—a symbol, borrowed from Italian poet Dante Alighieri, of unspeakable suffering.

Themes and Meanings

The main theme in "10 January 1934" is the role and fate of a poet. By writing this requiem to Bely, Mandelstam writes not only an apotheosis of him but also a sad commentary on his difficult and even tragic fate in the society. By enumerating Bely's great achievements, he makes the forlorn appearance of his funeral stand out all the more. In this eulogy of a man who was among the leading poets of the beginning of the twentieth century, only to be neglected and hounded out of existence after the Bolshevik Revolution, Mandelstam sums up the callousness of a system that frivolously throws away its best people. Thus, the fate of a talented, independently minded poet is decided by the indifference and callous practicality of the modern age. Indeed, the poem is, in effect, "the effigy of the dying age," as Omry Ronen observes in *An Approach to Mandelstam* (1983). There are a number of poems in which Mandelstam addresses this theme: "The Age," "Wolf," and "Ariosto" come readily to mind. In all fairness, he was interested in this theme before he became the target of persecution, as attested in his book of prose, *Shum vremeni* (1925; *The Noise of Time*, 1965). He was also concerned with the impact of the modern age on the development of Judeo-Christian civilization, primarily on the spiritual plane and independent of political factors. In "10 January 1934," however, his preoccupation with the age syndrome culminated after he became aware of the destructive impact that "the age of the wolfhound" had on Russian culture in general and on poets in particular. For Mandelstam, this interaction became, literally, a matter of life and death.

Coupled with the castigation of the modern age is the theme of Mandelstam's own fate. He spent the last years of his life warning about the pernicious effects of tyranny and eventually became consumed by it, both figuratively and literally. It is not coincidental that he subtitled one poem from the Bely cycle "My Requiem," which, as it turned out, was a clear premonition of his own death. Jennifer Baines writes in *Mandelstam: The Later Poetry* (1976) that Bely's death made Mandelstam visualize "the possibility that he would be thrown unceremoniously into a hole in the ground, with none of the last respects or funeral rites accorded to Bely." Unfortunately, this is exactly what happened to Mandelstam four years later in a concentration camp in Siberia; his grave has never been identified.

The entire poem is a minute record of Mandelstam's impressions of and reactions to Bely's funeral, as if he were looking at his own burial. This is clearly indicated in his matter-of-fact statement of resignation at the end of the poem, "till I'm picked." Thus, by binding his fate to that of Bely, Mandelstam universalizes the sacrifice they made at the altar of struggle against tyranny and elevates the heroic role of the poet in his ruthless society to the level of a modern Greek tragedy.

Vasa D. Mihailovich

TENEBRAE

Author: Paul Celan (Paul Antschel, 1920-1970)
Type of poem: Lyric
First published: 1959, as "Tenebrae," in *Sprachgitter*; English translation collected in
Poems of Paul Celan, 1988

The Poem

"Tenebrae," a poem in free verse, consists of twenty-two lines. The Latin title refers
to the period of darkness prior to the death of Christ. The term also points to the idea
of an eclipse, the cause of such darkness, as well as night and death. In this context,
although with no specific reference, the association to Nazi death camps, an experience elemental to Paul Celan's life and work, cannot be avoided.

The poem begins with a declaration of apparent proximity to God. The use of "we"
as the subject pronoun provides a tone of universality. The second line clarifies this
relationship as one not only of proximity but also of attentiveness. This idea is further
developed in the second stanza. Line 3 implies that this connection is the result of a
process, a means to an end, perhaps toward some higher purpose. In line 4, however,
the reader finds that the process is one of defilement. Bodies are clawed while those
same bodies claw in anguish. Furthermore, the poem compares this experience to
God's experience, an apparent reference to Christ on the cross.

In line 7, God is called upon to pray. In the following line, the plea turns slightly
surreal, roles are reversed, and God is instructed to direct his prayers "to us." As line
9 refers back to the first stanza, it becomes clear that such proximity and the horrific
condition described are in some measure related. In the fourth stanza, the bodies are
twisted. Still, the exclamation "we went" implies that they have arrived at this
condition of their own volition. They are bent down as if having submitted themselves
at this crater. The fifth stanza, a single line, reveals that the purpose of gathering there
is to be watered like lambs or cattle.

In lines 14 and 15, the reader finds that it is blood that fills this watering hole, blood
shed by God himself. In line 16, another single-line stanza, the pool of blood radiates
with light. Now God's image is reflected in the blood and cast into the eyes of those
huddled there. In line 18, eyes and mouths are "open and empty," drained of life.
Finally, lines 19 and 20 tell of drinking from the trough and consuming both the blood
and the image cast in it. "Tenebrae" moves toward its conclusion by repeating the
directive "Pray, Lord." In the final line the repeated declaration of proximity takes on
new meaning. Clearly, the "nearness" alluded to in the poem refers not to a closeness
to God but to something horrible eclipsing this sense of immediacy.

Forms and Devices

"Tenebrae" uses several devices common to Celan's poetry. A sparsity of words as
well as the poetic tone suggest absence more than presence. Five of the nine stanzas
contain one or two lines, contributing to the barrenness of its appearance on the page.

Multiple meanings balance the thin word usage and add to the poem's complexity. Common also are the new meanings that a single word or its root take on as the poetic voice proceeds. For example, in a few brief lines readers go from being at hand to having been handled to hands clawing. Thus what begins as a reference to attentiveness is quickly transformed into violation by a single allusion.

Celan also describes events in terms of their opposites. In the darkness of the poem, images, scenes, and roles are inverted and confused. This takes on seemingly strange proportions when describing the relationship with God. He appears without omniscience. Although the idea that "we" are near provides a sense of movement toward God, he is directed to "pray to us." While the poem is clear that "we went," implying that arrival at such a state is of "our" own free will, the reader may ask if events are running contrary to God's will. What challenges the reader's sensibility is the dilemma of attributing the situation to God's absence or his apparent indifference to humanity.

The most striking inversion is that of the Christian imagery presented in the poem. The association of Tenebrae to the Passion of Christ is represented in the Catholic liturgy of the same name performed during Holy Week. Both the victims' suffering compared to the suffering of God and the common essence that the image of God and the blood itself take on evoke Christian symbolism. Because such images are easily associated with Christianity, some critics have concluded that the scene in the poem relates directly to the Crucifixion. However, this one-dimensional understanding draws the reader to surface conclusions that correlate neither to the poem's angry tone nor to the circumstances it describes.

Celan's poem constructs the horrific with the vocabulary of Christianity, the vocabulary accessible to him yet distinct from a Christian construction. The use of this imagery serves to express a marginal syntax with a central language. Yet because the vocabulary is recognizable, the reader is easily drawn to accept the obvious that eclipses a deeper explanation. In "Tenebrae," the ornaments that decorate the world may be Christian, but it is the juxtaposition of Christianity with Jewish symbolism, as well as surreal forms and existentialist doubts, that heighten the poem's meaning.

Themes and Meanings

"Tenebrae" is a poem of shadows, of multiple meanings eclipsing one another. This juxtaposition of meaning using single images provides it with layers of context. Beyond the Christian facade are Jewish underpinnings. Likewise, behind the symbolism of normative Judaism one finds reference to the Kabbala, the Jewish mystical and esoteric tradition. Finally, both Surrealism and existentialism play important roles.

The poem reads like a strange, surreal prayer. Anger and loss predominate in describing the relationship with God. The use of the pronoun "we" flows naturally in Jewish thought and practice, in which regulations strictly mandate communal prayer. *Ashamnu*, literally "we have sinned," is the prayer that runs alphabetically through the list of transgressions asking for forgiveness on Yom Kippur, the Day of Atonement. The use of "we" establishes the importance and culpability of all people in the face of God.

It is not clear that the condition described is the result of any specific sin. In fact, the angry tone of the poem implies that an injustice has been done against humanity. As the poem proceeds, it seems that "we" have acted out of obedience to God. "We" are near, and "we" went to the trough like cattle, bent over, submitted to be watered, and drank as directed. Yet this violation continued. The Lord, the shepherd, shed the blood of his own flock. "We" even drank it in obedience to God. The drinking of blood is an important allusion because it carries radically different significances for Judaism and Christianity. In Christian doctrine the blood of Christ gives life, while in Judaism the consuming of blood is strictly forbidden. Thus in a Jewish context, to drink blood at the crater is to violate one of God's commandments.

Thus not only is God's covenant with Jews eclipsed by the revelation of Christ, but also the Christian notion is eclipsed by the overriding existentialist tone realizing the absence of God. For the existentialist, this absence is a point of departure not toward nihilism but toward constructing new meaning. The poem reads: "your image into our eyes, Lord." The image of God and the faces of those staring into the pool become one. Likewise, when the eyes and mouth appear empty, God too is drained of life—another eclipse. Finally, the people depicted in the poem drink not only the blood but also the image in the blood, their own image, which in the poem inverts creation back to humanity as it sees itself and the God it created.

The multiple eclipses of "Tenebrae" are found not only in the juxtaposition of imagery but also in the language of the poem used to construct it. While in Christianity Christ is the incarnation of the Word in the flesh, within Judaism (accentuated in the Kabbala) words, the letters that form them, and even the spaces between them are thought literally to make up creation and the mystery behind it. The construction of the poem, Celan's use of a minimal number of words, and, more important, the use of a single vocabulary to describe seemingly contrary explanations all reflect a deep sense of distance from the dominant notion of God. If the central eclipse evokes the Passion of Christ, in Celan's poem it is the mythic Passion that is eclipsed—not only by a seemingly Godless reality but also by the realization of humanity's role in constructing it.

Steven Clotzman

THE TESTING-TREE

Author: Stanley Kunitz (1905-   )
Type of poem: Poetic sequence
First published: 1971, in *The Testing-Tree*

The Poem

"The Testing-Tree" is a poetic sequence divided into four sections, each written in supple free verse with no stanza breaks. The lines themselves are prepositional phrases or noun clauses and are generally enjambed, giving the reader a sense of flowing, forward movement. The title, the same as that for the entire volume of poetry in which it was originally published, is mythic, suggesting the biblical Tree of Knowledge where Adam and Eve are tested and Ygdrassil, the tree of wisdom from Norse mythology. The title is also specific, being emblematic of the tree where the narrator played games and in which he carved his name. Each sequence within the poem operates on both levels—the mythic and the local.

In section 1, the narrative "I" recalls the imaginary games and challenges of childhood in which reality, "the Academy ballpark/ where I could never hope to play," is juxtaposed against the imaginative life in which "magic Keds" bring "the prize of the mastery" and the speaker is the "world's fastest human." The speaker recalls these imaginative visions with concrete nouns ("flying skin," "crouching start") and makes these experiences vivid for the reader, while the quotidian events of daily life are only hinted at in the first three lines of the section before being abandoned in favor of the imaginary, which offers more potential and fulfillment. It is the "magic" that is able to project the speaker beyond a rather banal present into a realm of imagination; the speaker is master over the "given course."

Section 2 opens with a renewed search for this magic that takes the narrator away from home. Instead of leading toward the ballpark and imaginary fame, the magic in this section leads the narrator down a secret path leading to the woods. The path leads away from the "drainage ditch" of society and civilization of the first section to nature and solitary sojourn reminiscent of American Indians and legend. The trail is a "right of passage" and the narrator practices his "Indian walk." The magic conjures up in the narrator a sense of communion with nature, and the "umbrageous trail" leads away from the pressures of school and home.

In section 3, the trail leads the narrator, who walks with "deliberate" steps, through an abandoned quarry into a clearing where the "testing-tree" of the title stands. The narrator has inscribed his name in the tree as if to claim ownership. Yet despite this "ownership," the boy is "in the shadow" and prays for a blessing. The boy imaginatively plays a symbolic game of life in which he seeks to hit the tree "for love, for poetry,/ and for eternal life." Taking stones from his pocket, the narrator hurls them at the tree, his "tyrant and target," hoping to hit it and secure for himself the illusory joys unavailable to him in sections 1 or 4.

A mythic reading of the poem gains more resonance as, in section 4, a "recurring dream" haunts the narrator in which the family life of childhood metamorphoses into natural images: The mother appears "wearing an owl's face." The sacred space amid the vegetation of section 3 is invaded again by a presence from society. These figures of his family make him feel guilty, and he asks, "why should I be blamed?" when he notices the dirt sifting slowly down into a well "where an albino walrus huffs." The mother figure points with a "minatory" finger, and the narrator seems to attempt to avoid this finger of blame by escaping back into his sacred world of the "umbrageous trail" and his "testing-tree"; the dream, however, keeps recurring and will not let him return. The figures of family and society relentlessly pull the boy away from his solitude in nature.

Forms and Devices

References to mythic symbols abound in Stanley Kunitz's poem. The primary recurring image is that of various types of paths: a "stretch of road" in section 1 and an "umbrageous trail" in section 2; though there is no direct naming of a path in section 3, its presence is implied as the narrator winds by the stone quarry into a clearing. This clearing is the end of the trail, and "the inexhaustible oak" stands as the final test for the narrator. For the moment, the metaphor of paths is suspended as the narrator enters the shadow of the great tree and throws his stones of destiny in an attempt to wrest a blessing from it. The relapse is momentary, however: In section 4, the poet returns to the metaphor of paths. This time it is in the form of a highway unfurled, and the narrator instead wishes for the trail. The highway is associated with a mechanistic element of society that has so far been absent in the poem: A Model A car and a military tank with turrets dominate this path. Combat and industrialism intrude into the haven of consciousness offered by nature in section 3. The repetition of the road imagery indicates its centrality to the meaning of the poem, and it becomes a metaphor for the journey, the heroic quest, on which the narrator embarks.

The poem's imagery, however, is not limited to that of a journey. In section 3, the "target," or the end of the trail, is reached. This section abounds in rich symbols: an oak, stones, acorns, and a watchtower. Some of the symbols are made explicit (the stones "changing to oracles," for example), but many are left implicit, to be decoded by the reader. Traditionally in Celtic mythology, acorns were seen as seeds of prophecy: If a seer ate them, he could be given the voice of prophecy. Such a reading, with both biblical and Celtic overtones, is underscored by the presence of the name Jehovah, the highest name that can be invoked for prophecy and wisdom within the Hebraic tradition of prophets. "Bless my good right arm" the narrator asks of an absent figure who represents both a physical father and God the Father, Jehovah. The poem functions on a literal level with a boy, stones, and a tree, and on a symbolic level with a narrator, oracles, and the tree of wisdom.

Themes and Meanings

"The Testing-Tree" is a poem about humanity as a paradox, dwelling in the mortal reality of time and space yet cognizant of the infinite and "eternal life." A child's innocent games and flights of imagination and a mature man's quest and his fight to hold on to memories portray the narrator's effort to combat the ephemeral nature of humankind. He is both flesh and spirit, and the journey of this poem seeks to transcend the limitations imposed on the spirit by the flesh through receiving prophetic power at the base of the proverbial oak of wisdom. This search bears a resemblance to William Wordsworth's search in his epic poem *The Prelude: Or, The Growth of a Poet's Mind* (1850) for a way in which the mutable consciousness of humanity can imprint itself into the immutable realms of nature. The "inexhaustible oak" contains the blessings and secret wisdom that are the object of the quest in all the various paths, trails, and highways within the poem.

Another central tension in the poem is that between society and the individual. In the opening section, the narrator feels the pull of society as he imagines himself a baseball hero or a world-class runner, yet all this disappears as the boy crosses the "nettled field" and enters the "long teeth of the woods." The mossy, dark woods offer solitude broken only by signs of "rabbit life." The narrator must undergo a test of solitude and face the forces of legend contained within the oak. Again, the road is a significant image in this drama between self and other. It is straight and confined, and it implies the presence of a purpose or a final destination. Once the narrator has reached his "tyrant and target" in the clearing, he must return to family and society as evidenced by the figure of his mother in the opening of section 4. He realizes that "It is necessary to go/ through dark and deeper dark/ and not to turn." His escape from time, exemplified by his crossing of the field of wild nettles on no given path, is brief. The narrator rises up out of time and out of societal space when entering the clearing, but he can do nothing else except fall back into them in section 4. As a human being, he is limited by the circumstances of family and history. The tragedy of this reality is expressed in the words "dark" and "deeper dark" and the chilling term "necessary." In desperation, the narrator asks, "where is my testing-tree?" Finally, in the closing lines, the self of the poet reiterates a hopeless demand to return his stones. The self longs to return to the tree and hurl its oracles against the tree of wisdom in an anguished attempt to transcend mere matter and to play a game of keeps with eternity.

Tiffany Werth

THOSE WINTER SUNDAYS

Author: Robert Hayden (1913-1980)
Type of poem: Lyric
First published: 1962, in *A Ballad of Remembrance*

The Poem

"Those Winter Sundays" is a short lyric in which the speaker remembers a moment in his childhood and thinks about the sacrifices his father made for him then. This split or double perspective of the poem provides its power, for the poem's meaning depends upon the differences between what the boy knew then and what the man—a father himself, perhaps—knows now.

The poem begins abruptly. The second word of the first line, "too," in fact, assumes actions that have gone before—that the father got up early on other days as well as Sundays to help his family. In this first stanza the reader learns about the father rising in the cold to heat the house before the rest of his family gets up. The last line of the stanza contains the first hint of one of the poem's central themes: "No one ever thanked him."

In the second stanza, the narrator recalls waking as the cold, like ice, was "splintering, breaking" as a result of his father's having lit a wood fire to warm the house. And "slowly" he would get up and dress—in the stanza's last and the poem's most difficult line—"fearing the chronic angers of that house." At this point the reader can only guess at the source of those angers. The third and final stanza continues the actions of the narrator, who speaks "indifferently" to the father who has worked so early and so hard to heat the house for his family and has "polished my good shoes as well." It is Sunday, and probably the boy and his father (and other unnamed family members) are going to church.

In the concluding couplet of the poem, the adult narrator, who has been implied throughout the poem, suddenly steps forward with his final poignant question, "what did I know/ of love's austere and lonely offices?" If the body of the poem deals with the gap between the father and his son, the poem's focus in the last two lines is clearly on the gap between the boy, so indifferent to the father's sacrifices then, and the adult narrator who in his repetition of the question—almost like some incantatory prayer— reveals the pain this memory holds for him: "What did I know, what did I know . . . ?" I was a child then, the couplet implies, and I did not realize what it means to be a man, a father, and to perform the "austere and lonely" duties that family love demands. I never thanked my father, and I cannot today.

The last stanza, and especially those concluding two lines, hardly resolve the tensions of the poem. Rather, the reader is only now fully aware of the real conflicts the poem has described—not only between the indifferent child and the hard-working father, but between the narrator as a boy and the man he has become, who now knows what he missed as a young child. "Those Winter Sundays" is a poem without resolution, a poem with its pains redoubled rather than resolved. The speaker's final question,"What did I know?" can only elicit the answer "nothing" from the reader. In addition, the mystery of line 9 about the "chronic angers of that house" remains unsolved. Are these the angers of any house with young children? Are they only the angers that result from dragging reluctant children to church? The reader cannot be certain.

Forms and Devices

"Those Winter Sundays" is a fairly direct and accessible short lyric. Its language is clear and precise, its metaphors are those of everyday life, and its metrics present no particular difficulties. The form of the poem fits its content closely, and its poem's power comes from this almost perfect fusion.

One interesting thing about the poem is that it is fourteen lines long; poems of such a length are usually called sonnets, but Hayden's poem—instead of having an octave and a sestet, or three quatrains and a concluding couplet, as most conventional sonnets do—violates the sonnet form by having three almost identical stanzas of 5, 4, and 5 lines. Yet the spirit of the sonnet form (which often poses and then tries to answer a question or problem) lies beneath the poem's lines in this three-part structure. The first five lines describe the father's actions, the next seven the boy's response (or lack of response) to those actions, and the concluding two the final agonizing question that the narrator, now grown himself, is left with. Thus the sense, if not the structure, of the sonnet form is replicated in "Those Winter Sundays."

Even more noticeable than the stanzaic form of the poem is its language. Rarely in such a short lyric do readers find such intense imagery. The "blueblack cold" of the second line evokes a picture of ice, which is "splintering, breaking" four lines later. The cold is rendered vividly in such an extended image. Likewise the "cracked hands" of line 3 imply that the father is a laborer of some sort, which makes his work for his family even more difficult: His hands are already roughened by his efforts to support his family; now, every morning, they suffer more from working in the freezing cold. The alliteration of the repeated *k* sounds in the poem—"blueblack cold," "cracked," "ached," "banked," "thanked," and so on—reinforces the discomfort. (At the same time, the assonance and internal rhyme of the poem softens this harshness somewhat.)

Finally the poem's last line, "offices," reverberates with meaning. An office is a job, a duty, but it also carries the idea of a form or service of religious worship, and that sense clearly exists in the poem. Family love demands "austere and lonely offices" (austere denoting ascetic self-denial), for a family member's actions may never earn any kind of acknowledgment. And yet, as in any religious service, family love also carries a spiritual and transcendent meaning—and it is, after all, Sunday morning when the poem's actions take place.

Themes and Meanings

"Those Winter Sundays" benefits from biographical and historical interpretation. Robert Hayden was a mid-twentieth century African American poet who rarely called attention to racial issues. In fact, he was often criticized in the decades before his death by younger and more political black writers for not using racial themes more overtly.

The themes are there nonetheless. Hayden grew up in Detroit in the 1920's as that city was being transformed by the migrations of hundreds of thousands of blacks moving from the South to the industrial North for work. His neighborhood was changing daily. In addition, his own family life was a difficult and unstable one. His parents abandoned him as a baby, giving him to neighbors to raise. He believed that he had been adopted by the Haydens, but they were only his foster parents. To complicate matters even more, the woman who used to come to stay with the Haydens when he was young, Hayden later learned, was in fact Robert's biological mother. Such a strained family situation undoubtedly created tensions for all involved.

This background gives new meaning to the poem, and especially to line 9 and the unresolved question of the house's "chronic angers." Hayden spent his early years in a home full of family secrets and in a city undergoing its own incredible transformation. The angers may be explained, in part at least, by the complex personal and sociological changes going on within and around the house.

This background can thus provide context for the poem's central meaning, the tension between the child who is so indifferent to the sacrifices, the "offices," his father performs almost invisibly, and the man who recognizes now what they meant. In the poem's present time, it is implied, the speaker is a man; perhaps he is a father himself. He has, in a sense, become his father. Now he knows what family love and devotion mean, and he can appreciate the complex tensions and relationships in any family. He also knows the full story of his painful and complicated family history. The poem suggests that it may be too late, however; apparently the speaker cannot thank his father (or foster father) or tell him what he now feels. As so often happens, the poem suggests, family members miss the opportunity to express their gratitude until those who should be thanked are dead and gone.

Hayden created a poem that describes a universal human situation, but he drew from his own personal history for the texture of the work. The result is a short and powerful lyric that gives its readers a sense of the pain and suffering life often inflicts but only rarely resolves.

David Peck

THE THREE MAGI

Author: Stanisław Barańczak (1946-   )
Type of poem: Narrative
First published: 1977, as "Trzej Królowie," in *Ja wiem, że to niesluszne: Wiersze z lat 1975-1976*; English translation collected in *The Weight osf the Body*, 1989

The Poem

"The Three Magi" is a poem of twenty-four lines of varied length. The title refers to the wise men who visited the infant Jesus with gifts denoting kingship and holiness and whose coming is traditionally celebrated on Epiphany (January 6). "Epiphany" literally means "shining forth" and refers both to the holiday and, more generally, to any moment of profound insight. The title is sardonic, comparing the Magi with the three government agents who appear at the door of the man to whom the poem is addressed; however, the police who come to the door of the "you" of the poem bring only threats and despair rather than gifts. The poem has no epiphany in the usual sense of an important realization, just as there are no gifts. There is also no trace of respect or honor given to the recipient of the agents' visit. The agents of the old Communist government of Poland have come to question the man, evidently an author, perhaps about the book he tries to push under the couch without their noticing it. At the end of the poem, the officers, instead of departing from the author as the wise men departed from Jesus, take the man away for questioning, perhaps never to return (hinted at ominously by the last line, "Wasn't this a vast world").

The poem reflects the difficulty under which many writers found themselves during the days of Soviet domination of Eastern Europe, when writing the "wrong" things could be disastrous and being caught with banned books was a crime. It is noteworthy that although the original collection of poetry in which "The Three Magi" first appeared is in Polish, it was first published in Paris, France. The oppression Stanisław Barańczak describes was so real he could not publish his work in his native country; not only would official censors have prevented the book's publication, but also Barańczak himself would have been subject to arrest and probable imprisonment by the government.

Forms and Devices

Most of the force of the poem comes from contrasting the traditional image of the Adoration of the Magi with the unwelcome visit of the coldly polite but intrusive agents. The Magi are conventionally pictured as coming at night following a star; the officers arrive just as night gives way to morning, jarring the author they have come to interrogate from a sound sleep by banging at his door. The only star these "Magi" have is on an official identification they flash at the door while demanding entry. Like the wise men, whose visit is commemorated in the first week of the year, the police always seem to come shortly after New Year's Day. The Magi (called *Królowie*, or "Kings," in Polish) are the representatives of the world outside the village of Bethlehem who came to reverence and acknowledge Christ. In a parallel fashion, the government agents, although not kings, come into the writer's home from the large, outside world of Communist bureaucracy as official representatives of the government and its disapproval to acknowledge him as a source of dangerous ideas who must be silenced. While Mary and Joseph are usually pictured as being dazzled by the visit of the wealthy foreigners, the recipient of the agents' visit is dazed and shaken by the abrupt intrusion of the highly paid government officers. Further heightening the satiric comparison, the man is compared to a newborn baby, helpless and unable to think clearly when the agents begin to interrogate him.

The biblical Magi brought three gifts: gold, frankincense (sometimes generically called "incense"), and myrrh. The man, contemplating his visitors, thinks distractedly that they indeed have gold (the expensive watches they wear) and incense (the cigarettes, implicitly foreign and costly, they smoke) but that they have no myrrh. Like many modern readers of the biblical story, he even is unsure what myrrh is and promises himself that he will look it up in a dictionary when he has the time. This promise suggests a sad irony, since the man is unlikely to be able to do so for a long while. Just as Mary and Joseph had to flee to Egypt to escape King Herod's persecution after the Magi left them, the "Magi" visiting the man insist "You'll come/ with us, sir," interrupting his thoughts about myrrh. While Mary and Joseph reached safety by leaving their homeland, the man is taken from his home into custody by his visitors.

The poet also suggests a contrast with the conventional images of the Magi, depicted by artists since the Middle Ages as wearing rich, vibrant colors appropriate to royalty visiting a newborn king. This image, unspecified in the poem but so much part of the conventional image as to be suggested simply by the reference, is contrasted with the colorlessness of the cold January morning on which the well-dressed but mundane agents arrive. The light is gray, and, as the man is led out, he muses first on the whiteness of the snow and then on the blackness of the car into which they load him. Other than the gold of their watches, no other color is mentioned in the poem. Instead, everything is bleak and uninspiring. The bleakness is further emphasized by repeating the same sentence structure three times: "Isn't this a" gray dawn, white snow, or black Fiat. This leads to the final thought, which changes the thrice-repeated wording into the past tense: "Wasn't this a vast world."

Themes and Meanings

"The Three Magi" contrasts a well-loved part of the Christmas story, particularly popular in dominantly Catholic Poland, with the cruelty and fear associated with an oppressive government. The worship and nobility of the Magi are set against the official coldness of the representatives of the dictatorial regime. The exotic, royal presence of the Magi also contrasts with the ordinariness of the men who come on the gloomy morning, emphasized by the man's recognition that one of the visitors is an old schoolmate who has changed little from days gone by but who now treats him without warmth or recognition. What should be, in any normal situation, a joyful reunion is aloof and unfriendly, heightening the quiet brutality of a government that operates by such tactics and making an ordinary man seem less appealing or impressive than commonplace humanity. Although prosperous, the agents lack any trace of the regal qualities usually associated with the true Magi.

A further grim threat to be feared is implied by the aftermath of the Magi's visit in the Bible. The foreign visitors unintentionally awaken Herod's jealousy, causing him to send his soldiers to kill all the boy babies of Bethlehem so he will be sure he has slain the infant king the Magi were seeking. Mary and Joseph barely escape, but there is much suffering in the village of Bethlehem as those who remained mourn their murdered children. This suggests a dark future for the unfortunate detainee, for, in his case, the government representatives did find the person they were sent out to apprehend. Like Herod and his soldiers, the government the agents represent believes any measure, however drastic or callous, is justified if it maintains the existing state of affairs. "The Three Magi" is not entirely harsh, however. The episode of the man wondering about myrrh and resolving to find out more about it provides a lighter touch, for many readers have wondered about the same thing. Similarly, his musing that his old friend might have gained a little weight reminds the reader of normal experience. In the end, though, the softer, almost amusing side of the poem reinforces the overall sense of unfairness as the man with whom the reader has come to sympathize is carried off by his visitors to an uncertain future.

The poem was dedicated to Lech Dymarski, a writer, theatrical figure, and critic of the government of Poland during the middle and late 1970's. The "you" of the poem, the man who is taken away, is in a position in which both Dymarski and Barańczak were fully aware they could have found themselves, for writers were frequently questioned by the government in Poland at that time. The interrogations could end with only minor punishments such as reprimands and fines, but there was always a risk of imprisonment, exile, or worse. It is the threat that men and women such as Barańczak and Dymarski faced that Barańczak commemorates and describes in "The Three Magi."

Paul James Buczkowski

THREE MOMENTS IN PARIS

Author: Mina Loy (1882-1966)
Type of poem: Poetic sequence; satire
First published: 1915; collected in *The Last Lunar Baedeker*, 1982

The Poem

"Three Moments in Paris" is a three-poem sequence in free verse, each poem numbered and titled. "One O'Clock at Night" contains twenty-nine lines, and both "Café du Néant" and "Magasins du Louvre" contain thirty-six. Stanza lengths vary in all three poems. The point of view also varies; Loy uses a first-person voice in the first and third poems, and a third-person voice in the second poem. The shift in voice can best be understood in the light of the title's significance and of developments in art at the beginning of the twentieth century. Cubist painting rendered its subjects as collages of geometric shapes; Futurist painters added dynamic juxtapositions and urban imagery to this approach. Like Gertrude Stein, Loy applied these visual concepts to her writing. In "Three Moments in Paris," she creates a verbal collage that satirically examines modern male-female relationships in the wake of increasing social autonomy for women.

The female speaker in "One O'Clock at Night" is leaning against her lover in the chair they are sharing, and she is falling asleep as he argues about Futurist aesthetics with his brother. She awakens when her lover clears his throat and is able to catch "the thread of the argument." The speaker then claims that its issues—"dynamic composition" and "plastic velocity"—mean little to her, and her waking signals her recognition of the difference between men and women. The focus of the poem is on the nature of that difference. The poem abruptly closes with the words of the male lover, who cites the speaker's exhaustion as a reason to end the argument and go home.

In "Café du Néant" ("Café of Emptiness"), the field of vision shifts from the café as a whole, to a pair of young lovers, to an individual female. A sense of futility permeates the poem. The decadent atmosphere of the café reflects the state of human relationships found there. Communication between the sexes has decayed into lies, silence, and meaningless language. Behaviors fall into predictable roles, in which the male is controlling and the female passively tolerates his control. The female figure who closes the poem presents an image of death in contrast to the modern life outside the café.

"Magasins du Louvre" ("The Shops of the Louvre") returns to a first-person speaker, though the reader is not aware of the speaker's participation in the scene until late in the poem. The opening line, "All the virgin eyes in the world are made of glass," is repeated twice—a third of the way through the poem and at its end. It provides closure, serving as a refrain that draws attention to the poem's emphasis on perception. The poem places readers in a shop where lines of dolls sit throughout the store and hang from the ceiling. Within this surreal atmosphere, the speaker observes two apparently unrelated events. In the first event, a man sets out to flirt with and possibly harass the shop girl. In the second, the speaker observes two cheaply dressed young women who examine the dolls and then exchange knowing glances; they see themselves, like dolls, as commodities to be bought in a sexual marketplace. The poem juxtaposes blind innocence and the perception that comes with experience.

Forms and Devices

Several characteristics associated with free verse give "Three Moments in Paris" a modern look and sound: lack of exact rhyme and end rhyme; lack of consistent line length and meter; lack of punctuation; extra spacing within the line; sentence fragments; and words that are completely capitalized. Assonance, alliteration, and slant rhymes replace exact rhyme, and at times these are found, along with the use of anaphora, at the beginning rather than at the end of the line. Loy's line lengths vary from one word to seventeen. The spacing within the lines, which at times creates the pause normally provided by punctuation, and the use of sentence fragments contribute to the poems' collage effect. Urban settings, characteristic of this sequence and of most of Loy's poems, provide another modernizing touch. Loy renders her scenes with precise description and multisyllabic diction that at times draws on a scientific or intellectual vocabulary.

The paradox in the opening lines of "One O'Clock at Night"—"Though you had never possessed me/ I had belonged to you since the beginning of time"—suggests the irony and satire to come. Although the speaker claims she understands nothing about her lover's Futurist argument, the poem is clearly influenced, in both form and content, by Futurism's precepts, most of which were set down by Loy's one-time lover, Filippo Marinetti. Thus, the poem's literal depiction of a woman intimidated by male intellect is an ironic facade. It is not Futurism the speaker fails to understand, but rather the male tendency to engage in endless intellectual disputes. The poem's subtle satire comes at the expense of the speaker's lover and his brother.

The juxtapositions in "Café du Néant" are central to the poem's irony. In a café where candlelit tables look like coffins and lovers wearing black resemble corpses, Loy collides images of light and darkness; youth and decay; stale values and modern ones; and artistic pretension and everyday living. Finally, life and death become capitalized emblems of the exaggerated, pretentious behavior of the café patrons. Given the bohemian atmosphere, the patrons could be parodies of *fin de siècle* artists and intellectuals who, like the bourgeoisie they reject, rely on conventional role-playing in their courtship.

"Magasins du Louvre," which opens and closes with the same line and is thus an envelope poem, also draws heavily on juxtaposition. The innocence suggested by the dolls provides a striking contrast to the sexually experienced "cocottes" (prostitutes) in the shop and to the lecherous man who pursues the shop girl. This juxtaposition invites comparisons to William Blake's "Songs of Innocence" and "Songs of Experience," though Loy's poem is thoroughly modernized in that it deals with sexuality from a woman's point of view. Here, as in all three of the poems, Loy allows the juxtapositions to offer their significance without providing authorial explanation.

Although satire is a didactic form, Loy manages to produce satire in a very nondidactic way.

Themes and Meanings

Like a number of early twentieth century women poets, ranging in style from Dorothy Parker and Edna St. Vincent Millay to H. D. (Hilda Doolittle) and Laura Riding, Mina Loy was concerned with the nature of romantic attachment between men and women. Why, in an age that seemed otherwise so modern, did men remain dominant in relationships while women continued to be overly dependent upon them? This age-old "battle between the sexes" was no longer limited to husbands and wives; it now included lovers outside marriage as well as writers and artists of both sexes positioning themselves on the intellectual landscape. Loy's response to this issue was somewhat complicated by her attraction to Futurism, with its underlying strain of misogyny. Although she would later reject this aspect of Futurism, Loy appears to hold both sexes accountable in "Three Moments in Paris."

An emphasis on vision, through the use of withheld and explicit images, pervades all three poems in the sequence, suggesting that the first step in the transformation from flawed relationships to successful ones is clear perception. The female speaker in "One O'Clock at Night" cannot recognize the differences between men and women until she awakes and has to adapt herself to the male world of intellectual argument. Yet given the poem's irony regarding the speaker's knowledge, even these differences are satirized, since the poem is itself an argument against male posturing.

The lover's eyes in "Café du Néant" are also eyes lined with kohl; their darkness parallels the atmosphere of decay that permeates the café and its patrons. Unable to see themselves clearly, the patrons are doomed to repeat their old patterns of courtship even as modern life, in the form of a cab, moves on outside the café. Both men and women participate in a *fin de siècle* facade that offers little relevance to male-female relationships in the second decade of the century.

Three sets of eyes appear in "Magasins du Louvre." The eyes of the dolls are the "virgin eyes of the world," suggesting not only blindness among the sexually inexperienced but also that there is "nothing" to see "through the human soul." All humans have is what the physical world provides them. Thus, the next two sets of eyes—those of the cocottes and those of the speaker who observes them—are all too human. Embarrassed by the juxtaposition their presence in the doll shop produces, these human eyes become averted and secretive, mirroring the type of communication that typifies and complicates male-female relationships. At the same time, the mutual recognition that both female innocence and female experience via sexuality are salable provides a Joycean epiphany in the poem: What passes for modern love remains strangely tied to old habits.

"Three Moments in Paris" sketches a world of romance as oblique and difficult to understand as any reality of romance one is likely to encounter. Yet Loy's poem functions within the best tradition of satire. Clearly embedded in its images of boredom, decay, and avoidance is a voice that insists on a better, though yet undefined, alternative to love as it is generally understood.

Rhonda Pettit

TITLE DIVINE—IS MINE!

Author: Emily Dickinson (1830-1886)
Type of poem: Meditation
First published: 1924, in *The Complete Poems of Emily Dickinson*

The Poem

"Title divine—is mine!" is a short poem of fifteen lines written in 1862 and first published in *The Complete Poems of Emily Dickinson*. The poem's metrical formula and rhyme scheme are irregular but loosely follow those used in hymnals. The word "divine" in the title has a religious connotation as it calls the reader's attention to a power structure that has been notorious in placing women at the bottom of the social totem pole and suggests the congeneric connection between two social institutions the poem addresses: religion and marriage.

The narrator in the poem is apparently a newlywed. On her wedding day or shortly after, the narrator reflects on her marriage and on women's lives in general. Typical of Emily Dickinson's poems, "Title divine—is mine!" starts with affirmation. The tone in the opening of the poem is almost euphoric. The narrator is overwhelmed. She appears very excited about all the titles and accolades the wedding has bestowed upon her ("Title divine—is mine!/ The Wife—without the Sign!"), and she is thrilled about the new possibilities marriage has promised her ("Acute Degree—conferred on me—/Empress of Calvary!"). The first part of the poem, however, ends with an ominous note. The word "Calvary" reminds readers of both the place where Jesus Christ was crucified and an experience similar to that of the Crucifixion, an experience of extreme suffering. As the narrator looks beyond all the titles the wedding has brought her, she starts to see something different: She is "Royal—all but the Crown"; she is "Betrothed," regardless of whether she has experienced "the swoon"; and, because of her gender, she is relegated to a group of people who allegedly are only attracted to material possessions, things ranging from "Garnet to Garnet" and from "Gold—to Gold." From birth to marriage and then to death, this pattern would never change.

The next three lines ("Born—Bridalled—Shrouded—/ In a Day—/ Tri Victory") play a pivotal role in the poem: They represent a turning point where the narrator must face how she feels about the wedding and what it portends. In appearance, the wedding day represents a victory for the narrator. As the midpoint between birth and death, marriage is supposed to represent the peak and consummation of a woman's life. However, when the narrator notices the clichéd pattern of a life that a woman is too powerless to change, she starts to question whose victory it really is. It is a life replete with monotonous and pernicious repetitions perpetuated by both the way women are treated by others ("God sends us Women—/ When you—hold—Garnet to Garnet—/ Gold—to Gold—/ Born—Bridalled—Shrouded—/ In a Day—") and the way they treat themselves ("'My Husband'—women say—/ Stroking the Melody—"). The poem ends with the narrator questioning whether this is "the way."

Forms and Devices

Similar to Dickinson's thematic approach, the predominant form of her poems also epitomizes a paradox. Many of her poems follow, with some variations, the standard hymnbook metrical formula and rhyme scheme. However, unconventional punctuation, unorthodox capitalization, and irregular metrical beat all highlight an effort to break away from the established grammatical and literary conventions. Dickinson frequently uses a dash where a comma should be. In doing so, she is able to control the rhythm and flow of ideas, accentuating those she deems important. In the opening line of "Title divine—is mine!" for instance, the dash not only accentuates the phrase "Title divine" but also reveals the narrator's hesitation and inexperience in dealing with the situation. Similarly, by playing with the capitalization of the key words in her poems, Dickinson invites readers to participate in the process of creating tropes. The word "Calvary," when spelled with a capitalized *C*, refers to the place where Jesus Christ was crucified. When the letter is lowercase, however, it also suggests an experience similar to that of the Crucifixion, an experience of extreme suffering. Since Dickinson capitalizes her nouns almost as whimsically as she accents her lines, the word "Calvary" used in the poem is as much a reference to how the narrator feels she is treated on her wedding day as to what weddings have portended to many women for centuries.

Dickinson's poems celebrate individual spirit, freedom of choice, and social equality. They condemn oppressive social institutions, establishments, and structures. The syntax, punctuation, and capitalization of her poems correspond to her thematic concerns, calling for change and urging people to find ways that can accurately portray, describe, and represent human experiences. The form of Dickinson's poems in general and that of "Title divine—is mine!" in particular, therefore, is the message. The poem's circular movement suggests both emotional and physical confinement. The conflict between the narrator's emotional response to the occasion and her keen observation and rational reflection remains unresolved. The glorious accolades do not conceal the fact that the marriage has contributed to more of the stigmatization that the narrator has been experiencing throughout her life. She is put on a pedestal without being fully understood and appreciated. She must carry signs that are placed on her whether she likes them or not. She must behave the way she is expected to behave by society.

Themes and Meanings

Dickinson's thematic approach in "Title divine—is mine!" is as ironic as it is paradoxical. In appearance, the wedding day is the biggest celebration in the narrator's life. It brings her recognition and titles. It represents a "Tri Victory" connecting the past and the future. However, the narrator gradually realizes that she is a person who has been acted upon rather than one who has acted, a person who has been forced into the role of a passive receiver rather than an active participant. The emotional conflict the narrator reveals in the second half of the poem is, in fact, embedded in the very beginning of the poem: She is given a title by someone who apparently is more powerful than "divine," she is given the sign "Wife" with or without her consent, and she is conferred the "Acute Degree" that makes her the "Empress of Calvary." If the narrator's reading of history is accurate, the end is, indeed, in the beginning.

Thematically, "Title divine—is mine!" is firmly anchored in and representative of a large group of Dickinson's poems that protests against society's discriminatory treatment of women and condemns a system in which people are treated not as individuals but as types. In "They shut me up in Prose," Dickinson portrays a female teenager who, because of her gender, is questioned about her natural poetic talent. In "My Life had stood—a Loaded Gun," the narrator complains about a metaphoric marriage in which her volition, thanks to her social status, has been deprived to the point where although she has "the power to kill," she does not have "the power to die." "Title divine—is mine" follows the same thematic line, calling the reader's attention to the pernicious impact of a social institution that has physically imprisoned and emotionally tormented women for centuries. All the accolades the narrator has received do not conceal the fact that there is no true mutual understanding and respect between two human beings as long as one of them is judged not by who she really is but by who she is supposed to be. The titles are as nominal and empty as the prejudice against women is strong. They are as misleading as the stereotypes and preconceived ideas that people use to judge other people.

What distinguishes "Title divine—is mine!" from Dickinson's other poems with similar thematic preoccupations is its juxtaposition of religion and marriage. The poem abounds with words with religious connotations such as "divine," "the Sign," and "Calvary." The juxtaposition of two established social institutions challenges oppressive power structures in general. Marriage can function the same way as religion if the power structure is not built on equity and justice. In "Title divine—is mine!" readers are forced to confront a reality that suggests exactly the opposite of what they expect out of both institutions.

Qun Wang

TO A WATERFOWL

Author: William Cullen Bryant (1794-1878)
Type of poem: Lyric
First published: 1818; collected in *Poems*, 1821

The Poem

Both lyric and didactic, "To a Waterfowl" creates a natural scene in order to derive a moral lesson from it. The poem consists of eight quatrains, or four-line stanzas. Each stanza is written in pentameter and trimeter verse with an alternating rhyme scheme. The poem subtly blends descriptive scenes with inward reflections on them. The poem's title indicates an unspecified waterfowl, which some critics have suggested must be a goose. By not specifying the waterfowl's species, the poet suggests a more universal image that will help in conveying his theme. The poem opens with a question and the interrogative form is used in both the first and third stanzas.

The whole poem encompasses the flight of the waterfowl from two viewpoints. It appears to the poet at dusk as it gently floats overhead and gradually disappears into the horizon. The poet also projects the journey of the bird over vast territories as it flies from its winter abode to its summer home. The immediate image of the bird has the poet reflect on the bird's destination and the nature of its flight. In his whimsical meditating, the poet addresses the bird directly as though to open up a dialogue between nature's creature and the poet's inner soul. However, it is not until the last stanza that the poet reveals himself and speaks out his message in the first person.

The poem is organized clearly around the scenic images alternating with the poet's reflections. The first three stanzas describe the bird's flight and possible destination, while the fourth meditates on a "Power" that guides the bird's flight. The fifth through seventh stanzas return to the description of the bird's excursion, and the last stanza comes back to the guiding Power and brings out the poem's message. Thus, the poem twice repeats three descriptive stanzas followed by a meditation.

The poem opens at sunset as the sky glows red and evening dew falls. The poet sees a bird flying alone in the distance and muses that it is safe from any would-be hunter who would do it harm. The bird, alone and solitary, is silhouetted across the evening sky. As it floats smoothly by, the poet wonders where it is going. Is it headed for the edge of a lake in an area covered with weeds? Does it seek the margins of a wide river, or is it heading for the oceanside, "chafed" by the constant beat of the surf?

Then, the poet feels that some Power is leading the bird over coastlines that have no path, over a wide aerial expanse. Because this Power guides the bird, it can wander alone without ever getting lost. The bird will be flapping its wings the whole day, far above the earth in the cold, thin atmosphere. The bird may be weary, but it does not land even when night comes on. Nevertheless, the poet realizes that the bird's tiring journey will soon come to an end, and that the bird will be able to rest in its summer home, make noise among the other birds of the flock, and have the reeds cover its nest. The poet tells the bird that it is gone, that it is "swallowed up" in the heavens.

However, the image of the bird leaves a message in the poet's heart. The poet feels that the same Power that guides the bird from one area to another will guide him in the right path in his solitary journey through life.

Forms and Devices

This poem, like most of Bryant's poems, is filled with nature imagery. Bryant felt that the American poet should capture all the wonders of the American landscape and should also bring forth his own personal expression. This poem satisfies both goals. Bryant captures the natural scene of the bird at sunset. He shows how the sky glows with "the last steps of day." This metaphor unites the temporal with the spatial as day is seen in steps. There is also a unifying theme introduced in the poem's very last stanza, which states that the Power that guides the bird will "lead my steps aright." The metaphor of the "last steps of day" combines with images of the "crimson sky" and "rosy depths" to add the color of the natural sunset and to highlight the silhouette of the bird "darkly seen." The imagery and figure of speech help to create a vast and shaded background. However, the movement is graceful as the figure "floats along."

In describing the bird's journey, Bryant again paints a vast American landscape using vivid nature imagery, such as "plashy brink/ of weedy lake," "marge of river wide," and "chafed ocean side." Rivers, lakes, and oceans emerge in an immense vista. The bird becomes a compelling force in the sky that Bryant compares to a "desert" empty and vast; so high is the bird that the coast is "pathless." The bird has "fanned" the air with its wings as it continues on its strenuous journey. Bryant also uses dynamic auditory imagery to show the mood of the bird when its journey is over. When it reaches home, it shall "scream among" its "fellows." The use of "scream," instead of a word such as "cry," accentuates the bird's exhilaration. Moreover, the sibilant alliteration of "scream," "shall," "soon," and "sheltered" adds to the dynamics of the bird's homecoming.

In the final image of the bird, Bryant uses the metaphor of the throat in which the "abyss of heaven/ Hath swallowed up thy form . . ." This disappearance of the bird as a natural image lays the groundwork for the analogy between its flight and the life of the poet. Also, in showing the journey of the bird and comparing it to the life of a person, the poem focuses on a figure that is "Lone wandering, but not lost." "Lost" literally means not being able to find one's way; here, however, it also signifies the damned, those who are morally lost. The imagery and figurative language of the poem show a natural journey and compare it to an inner spiritual journey.

Themes and Meanings

According to one of his biographers, Bryant was inspired to write "To a Waterfowl" when he was a twenty-one-year-old aspiring lawyer on his way to a new town. As he walked through New England hills, sad and concerned about what would happen to him in his new life, he saw a solitary bird flying against a sunset and wondered about its destiny. When he stopped at an inn, he wrote what became the poem's last stanza.

Bryant not only wrote in the tradition of the Romantics, who saw sublime images in nature, but also followed the American Puritans, who saw natural events as signs of spiritual import. Like the Puritans, he read Nature as God's book, which can deliver insightful messages about the spiritual world. His poem depicts the figure of the solitary bird in its natural pattern of migration. He shows how it has no map to lead it across the "pathless coast"; yet it is "not lost." The solitary bird pursues its way tirelessly; even through the night, it does not land to rest. It continues on its way until it reaches its home or shelter. From a moral point of view the poet sees the flight of the bird as a metaphor for his own life. Like the bird, he is alone, a solitary wanderer, unsure of his path through life. Moreover, just as the bird is guided by a Power, the poet is also in the hands of providence, a benign power who would watch him "tread alone" and would "lead" his "steps aright."

Not only does this poem deliver a personal message that life is not aimless or left to chance, but it is also an argument for God or providence by use of design. The argument of design holds that the world and all its parts are so well designed and so well run that there must be some designer who put everything in order and keeps it that way. Because the migratory bird has such a "certain flight" over vast regions, there must be some Power to design and control its flight. The corollary to this argument is that the same power influences humans on their journey through life.

Like much early American literature, this poem also celebrates American individualism. The bird is not flying within a flock, but alone. The poet also is walking his journey alone. Individuals are responsible under the guidance of divine providence to walk their own paths, not to follow the herd. There are no institutions, governments, or social organizations to bolster individuals as they seek their destinies. As well as celebrating the power of divine providence, the poem acknowledges the individual's lonely struggle to discover himself anew. The solitary individual, nature, and divine providence are at the core of Bryant's poem.

Paul Rosefeldt

TO ALL GENTLENESS

Author: William Carlos Williams (1883-1963)
Type of poem: Lyric
First published: 1944, in *The Wedge*

The Poem

Gentleness, even all gentleness, may sound restrictive, but the poem "To All Gentleness" asserts that apparent opposites are akin. The first simile, likening "pink roses bending ragged in the rain" to a plumber's silvered cylindrical tank, posits a relationship between apparent incomparables. The speaker encounters both on a trip through the rain, the cylinder advertising a plumber's shop. Both, the speaker finds, invoke "enduring" gentleness. Surrounded by rain, the roses support a cylinder of raindrops above them, linking them surprisingly but with the clarity of geometry to the plumber's tank. The soft, organic, and vulnerable and the hard, mechanical, and indestructible are thus seen to be related. Indeed, the rose plant itself, to protect its tender flower, produces thorns and is thus a combination of gentle beauty and the threat of violence.

His contemporaries, the speaker reflects, ignore the lessons of nature about survival depending upon complementary contraries, the soft and hard, the gentle and fierce. People foolishly distinguish between high art—opera and the classics—and the everyday, the "anti-poetic." That distinction is, the speaker asserts, "Garbage." Poetry should not divide the world but should, like an old painting of the biblical prophet Isaiah's ideal, the lion and lamb lying down together in peace, cause one to see the unity of what otherwise seems opposed. People aim too narrowly, failing to see relatedness. An archer regards her ability as a route to prizes and a teaching job. Others exercise themselves in law courts to avoid intimate human relationships. Still others engage in business as a wedge that unnaturally divides their heads, creating oppositions within them. They buy nature instead of appreciating and living in it. With World War II raging, the speaker mentions a fighter plane that crashed. Even violent mechanical failure can, if the pilot falls into the sea, result in seawater salving his wounds. Gentleness and fierceness are linked, even as a wave rising and a wave turning into foam are one. That young pilot, a native of Seattle, would be able to return home alive. The speaker asks, Why separate astronomer Copernicus and musician Dmitri Shostakovich from what they accomplished; why separate the "occasion" from them? Such differences are like distinctions between halves of an apple. The wave that lifts and the wave that dashes down, death of one creature and provision of food for another, are parts of a unity. Caught up in only half their lives, people ignore the beauties of nature, "blind to/ the sun and moon, the brilliant/ moonlight leaves."

Military violence and the "packed word," encrusted with acquired connotations that shroud clarity, prevent humans from discovering relationships. They must understand through physical presence at opportune moments, presented in cleansed language. "Strength/ thrust upon weakness, the convulsive ecstasy," images of sexual union, the thrusting male and soft receiving female, should be seen as evidence of the constructive union of apparent opposites, not as violent images of conquest. Neither violence nor gentleness is the "core" of being; both are—even as milkweed and an embankment, a plant "reaching up from sand and rubble" are—elements of a single reality.

The speaker refers to a thin, pregnant woman who is a forewoman at the ship foundry, a valuable worker during wartime. She has had three miscarriages, and her husband married her in order to produce sons. That slender pregnant woman is tough, impervious to pain—gentle enough to be a calming place for violence, to embody the unification of opposites as do the cylinder and thorny rose with which the poem began.

Forms and Devices

Readers do not know specifically whom the poem's speaker is addressing. Perhaps they are simply overhearing a soliloquy, or perhaps the speaker is actively trying to persuade the reader. The poem takes a form appropriate to talk—paragraphs of free verse. The form and diction of much of Williams's poetry, a selection of everyday words in an arrangement free from formal strictures, was sometimes called "anti-poetic," but such a judgment is simplistic and misleading. The poem is shaped by an inner logic. The importance of "enduring," for example, warrants a full line, the space of many words, because endurance is long-lasting, often despite adversity. The form responds to content. The thought of paragraph 1 is not quite done, so the paragraph that follows "enduring" is hemi-stitched to it, a subparagraph picturing the indissoluble union between flowers and a boiler, two objects of the first paragraph. Physical form in this kind of poetry both enhances and depends upon meaning. Significance determines its own formal embodiment. Thus the seemingly "free" verse is shaped by the content it conveys, the significant elements of the whole.

In Williams's poetry, those significant elements are communicated through objects, events, and representations of people's thoughts: wilting roses, a plumber's tank, the misguided thoughts of opinionated people, the ambitions of an archer, the tribulations of a fighter pilot, the penetrating and receiving aspects of love and sexuality. The poems speak through "concrete" references, abiding by Williams's dictum that truths should be sought "in things." This commitment to inherent truth identifies Williams as a modernist. His wedding of truth in things to everyday words, allowing him to address a broad audience, identifies him as an inclusive modernist. His democratic values spring to life in both the content and the forms of his poetry, helping to shape the free, sinewy, and meticulously ordered poems in which he embodies his thoughts.

Themes and Meanings

Williams's commitment to concrete, "embodied" meaning was shared by many of his contemporaries, including the poet Ezra Pound, a fellow student at the University of Pennsylvania, where Williams obtained his medical degree. Pound argued that poems should be a "presentation" rather than a telling, that they should communicate through "images." He and another contemporary, Amy Lowell, were largely responsible for Imagism, an approach to the writing of poetry that entailed communication through concrete language. The novelist Joseph Conrad had a comparable belief that "all art . . . appeals primarily to the senses." The young James Joyce, working to create "epiphanies," moments of sudden insight built up out of mundane events, concurred, and T. S. Eliot wrote of the need for "objective correlatives" that convey through the senses the significant content of a work of art. What lies behind such dedicated attempts to ground truths in physical evidence is the realization that received beliefs are frequently wrong.

Even received words seemed to Williams suspect. He not only preferred everyday words to the presumptuous terminology of intellectuals but also sought to cleanse his words of "packed" connotations, falsifying associations that attach to them over time. "To All Gentleness" is part of a volume he called *The Wedge*, a title he associated with "LangWedge"; language, he thought, if misused, can divide people within themselves, separate them from one another, and keep them from understanding.

On the other hand, precise language provides access to truths, glimpses of what nineteenth century philosopher Immanuel Kant called the numenal world. Those opposite possibilities, both derived from language, help one to see from yet another perspective the essential point of "To All Gentleness": that opposites, properly approached, interpenetrate constructively. As the experience of the pilot thrown into the water from his crashing war plane demonstrates, both death in nature and being sustained and saved by nature are features of existence. Williams himself, the child of parents who combined Basque, Dutch-Jewish, English, and French heritages, was composed of apparently contradictory sets, an American melting pot in microcosm.

The term "anti-poetic," to Williams's chagrin, was used by his friend and contemporary, poet Wallace Stevens, to describe his poems. Stevens, like Williams, functioned in both the practical daily world and the world of art: Williams was a physician; Stevens was an insurance executive. However, Stevens distinguished between the two worlds he occupied, whereas Williams saw them as unified. As this poem demonstrates, a pregnant factory worker is no more or less poetic than a rose, a fighter pilot, or a plumber's tank. The seemingly contradictory elements in the factory worker and in her life actually form a unity, and her sinewy strength has a beauty that poems should aspire to attain. "To All Gentleness" wonderfully presents the paradoxes and urges readers to resolve the contradictions of their own lives in quest of a better world, created and peopled by an accepting and generous humanity.

Albert Wachtel

TO DISAPPEAR ENHANCES—

Author: Emily Dickinson (1830-1886)
Type of poem: Narrative
First published: 1890, in *Poems*

The Poem

In this twenty-line poem comprising five four-line stanzas, Emily Dickinson deals with the topics that she most frequently addresses in her poetry: death, loneliness, the hope (but never the promise) of immortality. She begins with the observation that the man who runs away, who disappears, is enhanced by his having left, because his memory lingers and perhaps is softened by his absence. He is, in Dickinson's words, "tinctured for an instant/ With Immortality," which is Dickinson's initial hint that the poem will be concerned ultimately with death.

Yesterday's vagrant today resides in memory, where he takes on a "superstitious value" as those who knew him tamper with their memories of him, adjusting those memories to suit their own consciences. In the first two stanzas, Dickinson toys with the notion that distance alters memories. Her capitalization of "Immortality" lends an enhanced importance to the word, often the most significant word in her poems.

The phrase "We tamper with 'Again'" at the end of the second stanza implies that the man who runs away, the vagrant, is better gone. This leads into the word "Never" in the next line, where the anonymous "we" in the poem cannot cherish the man but can adorn him with memories softened by his departure.

By the beginning of the fourth stanza, it is clear that the poet is talking about more than just a man who runs off, a vagrant who disappears, because in this stanza she introduces "Death," with a capital *D*, prominently in the first line. As soon as readers encounter this word, their minds leap back to the first stanza's "tinctured for an instant/ With Immortality."

As is usual in Dickinson's poems, the poet leads her readers into the poem on a literal level but quickly moves to a more metaphorical level that is related in subtle ways to the initial literalness of the poem. She clinches the metaphorical meaning in the fourth stanza, then she moves on with considerable whimsy to the final stanza, which can be taken in a variety of ways.

The "Fruit perverse to plucking" can be read as a person unready and unwilling to die, but it can also be read more personally on a Freudian level to suggest something about Dickinson's own sexuality. She was the quintessential virgin, the unviolated woman with volcanic passions that, in her time and in her social situation, she dared not expose except in her poetry. Her poetry is redolent with sexual innuendo if one chooses to read it in that way. Certainly the bases for such interpretation exist within many Dickinson poems.

It is clear that this poem is about loss, but the poem does not bemoan the loss. Rather, it accepts the loss as the basis for creating memories that are perhaps more agreeable than the actual presence of the one who disappeared. Proximity does not always breed appreciation. Whereas physical beings frequently act independently of others, when such beings cease to be present, others completely control their own memories of them. Dickinson seems comforted at the thought that such control is possible. In this poem she sets up an interesting dichotomy between reality and memory, between proximity and distance.

Forms and Devices

The short stanzas and overall brevity of this poem typify much of Emily Dickinson's verse. Her longest poem ("I cannot live with You—") consists of a mere fifty lines. Few of her poems exceed twenty-five lines. The economy of words in all of Dickinson's verse is notable. Like most accomplished poets, Dickinson regularly calls upon a single word to do double or triple duty.

This poem is more abstract than some of Dickinson's other poems and as a result has less of the visual imagery that one finds in a poem such as "I taste a liquor never brewed—" or "I like to see it lap the Miles—." "To disappear enhances—" deals essentially with nonvisual things: disappearance, honor, memory, immortality, excellence, delight—things of the mind. Even words that usually evoke visual images, notably "fruit," "man," and "vagrant," as used here are so metaphoric that their visual qualities are diminished, an effect that Dickinson intended.

The rhyming patterns exemplify the various kinds of rhyme with which Dickinson experimented constantly. In the first stanza, she uses imperfect rhyme when she ends line 2 with "away" and line 4 with "Immortality." Dickinson does not stray from perfect rhyme because she is incapable of achieving it. Indeed, her manuscripts, detailed in Thomas H. Johnson's edition, *The Poems of Emily Dickinson, Including Variant Readings Critically Compared with All Known Manuscripts* (published by the Harvard University Press in a three-volume edition in 1955), reveal that she often achieved perfect rhyme only to alter it consciously into imperfect, suspended (saw/now), or so-called eye rhyme (one/lone). In this poem, one finds eye rhyme in the second stanza, where "lain" and "again" look more similar than they sound.

In the third stanza, Dickinson stretches even further when she ends line 2 with "thing" and line 4 with "adorn," where the only auditory link is the *n* sound. In the following stanza, she creates a similar situation, ending line 2 with "discern" and line 4 with "then," again using the *n* sound as the most prominent commonality between the two words.

Dickinson pushed poetry to new limits because she consciously and continuously strove to avoid the conventional, monotonously rhyming poetry that is often the mark of popular but not very accomplished poets. One might call Dickinson a minimalist whose impact is subtle but striking. She likes to select words that will explode in readers' imaginations. The key word in this poem is "tinctured," which evokes visual and olfactory images in many readers, who, upon encountering the word, think immediately of something such as tincture of iodine, with its sharp, characteristic smell and its typically deep orangish color.

Themes and Meanings

It is interesting that in the first stanza, Dickinson, who is a conscious wordsmith of unquestionable competence, refers to "the Man *that* runs away" rather than to "the Man *who* runs away," which would be the more usual relative pronoun to use in this instance. By using "that" rather than "who," Dickinson decreases the humanness of the man in question, making him more of an abstraction than he would be had the more usual pronoun been selected.

On one hand, the theme of this poem is concerned with the loss of a person. On the other hand, it is concerned with control because the "we" in the poem can re-create the lost individual, the vagrant, simply by tampering with their individual memories of him. Whereas Dickinson begins by applying this control to someone who has gone away, she quickly moves toward universalizing it by introducing Death in the fourth stanza, making it clear that subtle overtones of death lurk barely visible even in the first two stanzas. The first two lines of the second stanza seem funereal after one has read the fourth stanza, although they might not strike one that way initially. The term "superstitious value" in the second stanza assumes ghostly tones when read in the light of the fourth stanza.

The "we" in the poem is a collective we, a Greek chorus kind of "we," reflecting the conscience of a community in regard to loss, separation, and ultimately death. The quotation marks around "Again" and "Never" in stanzas 2 and 3 emphasize two opposites, as does Dickinson's idiosyncratic capitalization of these words. Her terminal punctuation—dashes rather than periods, and not even many dashes—undergirds the theme of continuance that the poem suggests by its emphasis on memory, which in this case becomes a virtual synonym for conscience.

The last stanza of "To disappear enhances—" is a curious one. It is infused with sexually charged words, notably "plucking" and "ecstatic." The choice of "perverse" in this context suggests but does not clearly state Dickinson's views on her own sexual restraint and virginity. This suggestion is buttressed by the words "unobtained Delight," used with considerable irony at the poem's end. Dickinson during her lifetime had platonic attachments to several men; it is speculated that she was in love with at least two of them, Thomas Wentworth Higginson and Judge Otis Phillips Lord. This poem can perhaps be read within the context of her unfulfilled love as well as within the context of the imposed sexual restraint of her era and her society.

The final stanza is about as puckish as Emily Dickinson ever becomes, particularly in line 2, where she implies an openness to love and, indeed, to sexual encounter, although one must probe far below the literal surface meaning of the poem to arrive at such an interpretation. In many ways, the last verse of "To disappear enhances—" is a maverick verse, close to but not quite being a free-standing poem unto itself.

R. Baird Shuman

TO GO TO LVOV

Author: Adam Zagajewski (1945-   )
Type of poem: Lyric
First published: 1985, as *Jechać do Lwowa*; English translation collected in *Tremor: Selected Poems*, 1985

The Poem

"To Go to Lvov" depicts an imaginary journey, a dream journey, to Lvov, the city of poet Adam Zagajewski's birth. Lvov was in a district that was appropriated from Poland by the Soviet Union after World War II; in consequence, Zagajewski's family moved into western Poland where the poet grew up. This poem thus involves looking backward into the lost world of childhood, but it implies that everyone possesses such a landscape that is simultaneously lost and always available in memory. The poem consists of eighty-three lines of free verse in one long stanza. The lines have roughly ten syllables, although many are longer and at the last five are noticeably shorter than the rest of the poem. In its translated version, it has no metrical pattern. Instead, its organization rests on its consistent tone and on certain elements that are repeated in the course of its descriptions of Lvov.

The poem begins with the speaker's invitation to the reader to make the journey to Lvov, although from the very beginning it hints that Lvov may not exist at all except in dream. That is why the poem seems uncertain about whether this journey is taking place in September or March and even about which station is the right one "for Lvov." The speaker goes on to describe the natural landscape of Lvov with its poplars and ash trees. In line 18, the speaker introduces an architectural element of the city: the Roman Catholic cathedral "as straight/ as Sunday." It is one part of the city's religious heritage that also includes Russian Orthodox Christians as well as Jews. The details that describe the cathedral are embedded in other pictures of the gardens and botanical life of the city, including weeds, Queen Anne cherries, and forsythia. In line 25, the speaker says that "there was always too much of Lvov," an idea that becomes a sort of refrain in the central part of the poem.

In line 42, the speaker begins to describe memories of his family, his aunts and their family servants, and his philosophical uncle; he also includes fragments that hint at their home life. Once again the speaker asserts that "there was too much/ of Lvov" and that it constantly overflowed every attempt to contain it, but, in line 59, the speaker modifies the refrain: There may have been "too much of Lvov" in the past, but "now/ there isn't any." It has been cut away just as a child cuts out a paper figure, leaving all its inhabitants to bid farewell and to die and leaving its exiles to feel like Jews seeking Jerusalem. However, the speaker asserts at the end that Lvov survives as a place to which one may travel at any time.

Forms and Devices

The logic of childhood memories, like the logic of dreams, is often built on surprising associations. The poet who is attempting to recapture some of the sense of childhood's landscape often uses those associations as an organizational technique. In this poem, the speaker first establishes that the journey being described is not to be taken literally. "Which station/ for Lvov," he wonders and then says one can make the journey "only if Lvov exists,/ if it is to be found within the frontiers and not just/ in my new passport." Such a statement is relevant, of course, only if it is possible that the city does not exist. From that point, the poem piles on images in the confused way one's mind might call them up when one remembers a place from one's childhood. The images are interwoven, but they form several strands. One concerns the plant life of the area, another details the religious setting of the city, and a third pictures the speaker's family.

Botanical imagery permeates the poem almost from its beginning. The speaker thinks of the poplars and ash trees that stand like lances and breathe aloud "like Indians"; he thinks of the burdocks and weeds in the city's gardens, the plants that the Jesuits "baptized," and the roses, forsythia, soft ferns, and Queen Anne cherries. The wealth of detail suggests rich growth in a city where there is "always too much." The religious detail forms another strand of imagery. Lvov is the home of a Roman Catholic cathedral and nuns whose cone-shaped headdresses let them sail "like schooners." It is also the home of a Russian Orthodox church with its own silence, different from that of the cathedral. References to Lvov's religious life flicker through the poem as they flicker through the memory of the speaker.

It is the people, however, who form the most vivid of the speaker's recollections. He recalls his aunts who "couldn't have known/ yet that I'd resurrect them" in a poem. He recalls the servants and an uncle who "kept writing a poem entitled *Why,/* dedicated to the Almighty." He thinks of the small events that formed their lives, recalling a visiting lecturer, a family Bible reading, and someone sleeping "on a sofa beside the Carpathian rug." In the end, the speaker acknowledges that Lvov has been snipped away from reality as neatly as a child might cut out a paper animal, keeping to the dotted lines. The scissors cut away "fiber, tailors, gardeners, censors/ cut the body and the wreaths." The same passion for detail that loaded the town with greenery and relatives now lists a variety of cutting implements, but all of them lead to the same result—the speaker's permanent loss of those who have been sliced away.

Themes and Meanings

On one level, "To Go to Lvov" seems intended to call up a childhood home that is now lost to the speaker. Although it is cast in the form of directions for going to Lvov, the speaker's uncertainty about whether Lvov even exists, along with the dreamlike refrain that asserts the wealth of the city ("too much of Lvov"), seems more intended to invite the reader into the dream than to instruct the reader about going to a real place. The illogicality of dreams allows the speaker to assert things that do not make sense on the literal level. Thus he can say "joy hovered/ everywhere, in hallways and in coffee mills/ . . . in blue/ teapots, in starch." The surreal sense of dreams is particularly active as the poem moves toward its end. The scissors and other sharp implements (penknives and razor blades) that first cut away "too much of Lvov" next seem to cut the very inhabitants away from each other as surely as death.

In line 76, as the speaker pictures Lvov's people saying good-bye to each other, the separation asserts that it is indeed death that does the cutting: "I won't see you anymore, so much death/ awaits you." That death may refer to Lvov's troubled political history, but in a more general way it can easily refer to any childhood home and the deaths of family and friends that inevitably occur as the years pass, separating the one who was once a child in the place from the people and events of childhood. Line 78 links Lvov to Jerusalem: "Why must every city/ become Jerusalem and every man a Jew?" the speaker asks, suggesting that Lvov (and by extension every lost home) is like Jerusalem to the Jews, an object of love and longing, a spiritual home even if the exile has never been there physically.

Throughout the poem, the speaker has directed the reader to pack a suitcase hurriedly and go to Lvov. In the last five lines, just after suggesting that Lvov is as unattainable as Jerusalem, the speaker uses words that recall the poem's opening lines in urging the reader to "go breathless . . . to Lvov, after all/ it exists." On this new level, the uncertainty about Lvov disappears, and the speaker uses one more botanical reference to describe Lvov: "quiet and pure as/ a peach." The last line asserts what the reader has come to assume about Lvov. In saying "It is everywhere," the speaker suggests that the city can take on the character of anyone's childhood home, a place that might be both lost and always present, always approachable through memory that stores the detail that the speaker has offered in this dream journey to Lvov.

Ann D. Garbett

TO MARINA

Author: Kenneth Koch (1925-   )
Type of poem: Meditation
First published: 1979, in *The Burning Mystery of Anna in 1951*

The Poem

"To Marina" is a long autobiographical free-verse poem of approximately four hundred lines devoted to the woman of the title, with whom the poet had an affair twenty-five years before. She also served as the inspiration for many of Koch's best-known early poems, several mentioned by name or alluded to in this poem. The second-person addressee of the poem, the "you," is Marina, and much of the poem recounts events in the long-ago lovers' affair: who said what, when, and how the poet felt, though he cannot know exactly how Marina felt. Since the affair produced many poems by Koch, he has retained evidence of their love and of the creativity to which great love and negotiation of differences may give rise.

The fact that Marina was Russian is introduced early, via comments on her accent (in her speech, "The quiet, dry Z/ Leaped up to the front of the alphabet"), and many of the lovers' differences arise over the question of nationality. Marina is from a nation with more direct experience of the hardships of war, and she is more serious and realistic than the younger, naïve American Koch. For the poet, these differences are exotic and exciting, suggestive of experience and providing a muse, as is indicated in an early section of the poem where Marina points out Kenneth's naïveté, and the poet reponds with desire rendered in lyric imagery: "Oh Kenneth/ You like everything/ To be pleasant. I was burning/ Like an arch/ Made out of trees."

The reader should be aware while reading the poem of a split between two different Kenneths: the younger poet whose experiences with Marina are recounted and the older poet of today who remembers and makes sense of these experiences. While the poet is remembering his lover and speaking to her, he is also remembering himself, remembering youth and inexperience after a life of experiences. Certain moments of the poem act almost as snapshots of earlier moments in life, as when Koch describes a day with Marina in New York a quarter-century earlier in the present tense: "We have walked three blocks. Or four blocks. It is New York/ In nineteen fifty-three. Nothing has as yet happened/ That will ever happen and will mean as much to me. You smile, and turn your head." The event described in this memory is less important than the state of mind the poet remembers being in when it occurred, just as a photograph from one's past may not have meaning for someone else but is deeply meaningful to the one who knows when it was taken and can remember long-since-outgrown feelings it recalls. The remembered smile cannot be called significant, except that it has been recalled for more than two decades and corresponds in the mind of the poet to a time emblematic of his youth and corresponding feelings of potential, possibility, and joy.

Marina represents experience for the young Kenneth; their love is "illicit," Marina already married and having to deal with consequences Kenneth does not after the two have begun their affair. At other junctures of the poem she represents erotic danger (telling him, "Kenneth you are playing with fire") and a love whose pain in ending paradoxically makes the poet feel truly alive. In the end, while he laments, "You were the perfection of my life/ And I couldn't have you," he also realizes that little else remains but poems from this time—"I am over fifty years old and there's no you—/ And no me, either"—a time when experience was fresh and became permanent in the beauty of poetry.

Forms and Devices

The reader is advised to take a look at some of Koch's early lyric love poems, especially those mentioned in the poem, such as "To You," "Spring," and "In Love With You." While the author does not expect every reader to be familiar with every poem he alludes to, some familiarity with his earlier work is assumed and will help the reader comprehend that Marina in this poem is as important as a muse as she is as the poet's former lover—and perhaps more so.

Like other poets of the so-called New York School (such as Frank O'Hara and John Ashbery), Koch frequently writes about what might not seem to be serious poetic subject matter—daily events from his own life. O'Hara called such poems "I do this, I do that" poems, because events frequently follow upon events without the poet explicitly telling the reader what they are supposed to mean. This is meant to mimic formally daily experience, in which the things that happen to one on any given day do not conform to a particular subject heading, but simply happen. In "To Marina," Koch pushes some of this formal experimentation further by varying line lengths, distorting syntax, and employing odd, even surreal, juxtapositions in order to approximate the feelings that the lines are meant to convey. The second stanza begins, "It is wise to be witty. The shirt collar's far away./ Men tramp up and down the city on this windy day." The sing-song rhyme conveys a mood of ebullient, even flippant, joy. Norms of grammar and syntax are deliberately altered: "A clock rang a bird's song rattled into my typewriter." Koch is a firm believer in nonformulaic verse, to the point of adopting all manner of devices even in free-verse lines. He takes great pains to rid himself of anything that would smack of routine. Some stanzas are punctuated according to rules of standard usage; others have little or no punctuation. The attempt is to write a poem that is never lazy, retains fidelity to different aspects of human experience and conveys that fidelity through forms designed to express different states of mind, settings, and events.

Themes and Meanings

It is interesting that while Marina is older and more experienced than the young Kenneth of the poem, he now realizes that through her he was able to gain access to childish wonder, which transferred itself to poetry. The poem ends with the poet calling his time with Marina his "Renaissance," "when I had you to write to, when I could see you/ And it could change." The suggestion of these lines is one familiar to readers of William Wordsworth and other Romantic poets, that poetry is a function of "childlike" perceptions—that as we grow into adults and become familiar with the world, we lose the magic of youthful sight. "The things which I have seen I now can see no more," wrote Wordsworth in "Ode: Intimations of Immortality from Recollections of Early Childhood." Koch himself devoted two books (*Wishes, Lies, and Dreams*, 1970, and *Rose, Where Did You Get That Red?* 1973) and much of his teaching career to teaching poetry to children. "Renaissance" means, literally, "rebirth." Now, the poet laments, the ability to perceive afresh in verse is no longer second nature to him. That the time is gone when an undefined "it" "could change" indicates that life for the poet has become less surprising, more domesticated and routine, and that consequently to write poetry—the type of poetry Koch once wrote, which called routine its enemy—is now a struggle.

Perhaps this situation helps explain the variety of line lengths, styles, and approaches employed in "To Marina": The poem is perhaps an energetic attempt to recoup some of that which has been lost. Alternatively, if like the years themselves this ability has been lost forever, it may be an attempt to call upon artificial means to reproduce something that once came more naturally. This interpretation adds depth to the pain of reflection upon the poet's lost love: He has lost not only youth, not only the beauty of his beloved, not only the unexpectedness of her character and the insights it gave him, but his very self, his occupation. It can still get him from place to place, but without the same joy and ease, as when normal human locomotion is replaced by movement in a motorized wheelchair.

If this is the state of the despairing mind of the poet at the end of his meditation, it discounts neither the excitement he once felt at love and poetry nor the ways in which "To Marina" succeeds as poetry. It can serve as both an introduction to Koch's work—introducing the reader to themes and devices at work throughout Koch's poems—and, on its own, as a meditation on a poet's lost muse. While writing would seem to be an individualistic occupation, Koch's remembrance of his muse makes clear that no writer ever achieves greatness entirely alone.

Ted Pelton

TO NO ONE IN PARTICULAR

Author: Marvin Bell (1937-   )
Type of poem: Lyric
First published: 1976; collected in *Stars Which See, Stars Which Do Not See*, 1977

The Poem

"To No One in Particular" is a poem in free verse. The title functions much like the "To Whom It May Concern" salutation of a letter that carries a message to anyone that can make use of it. It is written from a first-person perspective with nothing to indicate that the poet is speaking through a persona (a character distinctly different from the poet who functions as the narrator of the poem). Both the voice and the ideas expressed in the poem are consistent with those in many other poems by Marvin Bell, so it seems reasonable to assume that there is no philosophical difference between the "I" of the poem and the poet himself. With no stanza breaks and no extra spacings or peculiar formatting, the poem's fifty-five lines appear on the page like one long, narrow paragraph; however, there are some easily distinguishable sections of the poem.

The first two lines of the poem, "Whether you sing or scream/ the process is the same," prepare the reader, like the thesis statement in an academic essay, for an exploration of "the process" behind human vocalizations. The next eight lines act as an introduction to a comparative analysis of two very different types of human speech–learned and instinctive. They also point out crude aspects of the actual vocal instrument–"spittle and phlegm."

In lines 11 through 22 the poet speculates that if one were to grab someone by the throat and beat him, someone else would almost certainly try to record the event in minute detail, right down to the individual utterances made by the victim. The problem, as the poet explains it, is that the person recording the events would embellish on what he or she had heard and would try to gloss the sounds made by the victim "in one of those languages/ revered for its vowels./ But all the time, it's consonants/ coming from the throat."

In the third section, lines 23 to 35, the poet focuses on the victim, "still gagging out the guttural ch–/ the throat clearing, Yiddish ch–/ and other consonants." He then follows the victim home, where the victim in turn victimizes his wife. Once he has exhausted himself, he falls asleep and snores, and the poet tells the reader that "all the time/ he hasn't said a word we can repeat./ Even though we all speak his language."

In the fourth (the last and longest) section of the poem, Bell returns to the more ecclesiastical voice he uses at the beginning of the poem, questioning even the possibility of understanding our most basic sounds. His questions come rapidly: "Who will write down this language?/ Who will do the necessary work?/ Who will gag on a chicken bone/ for observation?" and so on, until he concludes by telling the reader that everything of real importance in his life "occurred in another language."

Forms and Devices

Marvin Bell is well known for creating free verse that has the deceptive appearance of prose broken into lines; however, a keen ear or eye soon recognizes that his work is pure poetry. He uses very few quickly discernable devices in this poem. The most obvious of these are juxtaposition and anaphora. The poem begins with the juxtaposition of two human sounds—singing and screaming. He states that the "process" of creating these two sounds is essentially the same and that both of them use "spittle and phlegm." The difference stems from fear causing the throat to constrict. The juxtaposition of "consonants" and "vowels" is so prevalent that it becomes a theme of the poem.

Anaphora is the practice of repeating the same word or phrase at the beginning of lines, clauses, sentences, or stanzas. Bell makes back-to-back uses of this device in the last half of the poem. Beginning at line 35 he starts three consecutive sentences with "Even though," and immediately begins the next four with "Who will." Probably the single most famous use of anaphora in the English language is the Beatitudes of the Bible, nine statements attributed to Christ, each of which begins with "Blessed are." Although Bell's reasons for using this device may differ from the biblical author's, the effect is essentially the same; it establishes a strong tone of authority, a voice that simply will not be ignored. Unlike the biblical use of the device as an introduction to a sermon, Bell uses it near the end of his poem, providing a dramatic burst of speed and energy.

Most of this poem's imagery centers on the throat. When the throat constricts, "the back of the tongue/ can taste the brain's fear." To give someone a good beating, one should start by grabbing him "by the throat." People try to clear their throats with "the guttural ch–," the "Yiddish ch–." In the morning we feel "the toast in our throats." We "gag on a chicken bone." The shape of the poem relies more on syntax than on lineation. Many of the line breaks ignore obvious phrasing in favor of limiting either the length of the lines or the number of stresses in particular lines.

"To No One in Particular" ends, as many of Bell's poems end, with a personal memory, real or imagined, and a direct statement to the reader—a statement that carries some mythic or mystic message for human beings in general. "The Self and the Mulberry," "Gradually, It Occurs to Us . . . ," and "The Mystery of Emily Dickinson" are good examples from this same volume by Bell that have this type of ending.

Themes and Meanings

Like any good work of art, this poem has several things to offer, but one in particular is the notion that a common language can be a common problem. Language is a major theme throughout Bell's work, and in this poem he tries to show that humans have two types of language. First, we have natural language, the utterances that we, as animals, instinctively make—the guttural sounds and consonants that squeeze out of our throats. We give no thought as to how we make them, why, or what they mean. They are instinctual, products of evolutionary processes.

The other form of language is synthetic, a system of utterances developed to help communicate more complex and detailed ideas. At its best this type of language is a tool that facilitates cooperation among humans. No matter how far we think we have evolved, no matter how detailed and protean our synthetic language has become, we are still animals. In times of stress, frustration, fear, anger, or any other situation that engenders emotional response, we revert to our first language, a language that is not tied to "an alphabet meant to make sense."

Throughout the poem Bell makes references to instinctive language as guttural, squeezed, or primarily composed of consonants, whereas he depicts the synthetic type of language as musical and "revered for its vowels." Inextricably tied to this theme of two types of language is the notion that humans must never allow—as if it were possible—their tendency to analyze things to replace or destroy their ability to feel things. Analysis is often the practice of "some fool" whose elaborate glosses take people further and further away from what they actually feel.

The great irony here is that synthetic language is the meat and potatoes of every poet. In no way does this fact invalidate this poem, however. In fact, it demonstrates that not even poets can tame that language that sometimes explodes to the surface from deep down inside us and exposes, for the moment, who we really are.

Edmund August

TO THE HOLY SPIRIT

Author: Yvor Winters (1900-1968)
Type of poem: Lyric
First published: 1946; collected in *To the Holy Spirit*, 1947

The Poem

"To the Holy Spirit" is written in rhyming trimeter divided into four stanzas of varying lengths. The expansion of the stanzas—from ten lines in the first, to twelve lines in the second and third, to fourteen in the fourth—reflects the development of the subject of the poem. The title suggests a prayer or a petition to the Holy Spirit. This part of the Holy Trinity traditionally is a source of hope, inspiration, forgiveness, and consolation for humans. The Holy Spirit is the mediator between God and humans. The poem is written in the first person, and the speaker is calling on the Holy Spirit to come to his aid as he tries to believe in God.

The poem's epigraph, "from a deserted graveyard in the Salinas Valley," sets the poem in California. It also allows the speaker the opportunity to mediate on life and death in a serene environment. The graveyard is abandoned, and the speaker of the poem has arrived there in late morning. Once there, the speaker observes how nature and death possess powers that humans cannot easily comprehend. The graveyard setting lends itself to contemplations of the limits of reason and ultimately of human mortality. While the speaker does not seek immortality, he does appeal to the Holy Spirit to guide him in understanding how God and he can coexist in the world.

In the first stanza, the speaker arrives in the graveyard on a hazy, not too warm summer day. He seems to be surprised to have encountered the site on his walk. As the speaker surveys the scene of neglected graves, he contemplates how death is the great equalizer: "the bones/ Beneath are similar:/ Relics of lonely men,/ Brutal and aimless, then,/ As now, irregular."

The speaker recognizes individual dignity ("relics") in these graves and is forced to consider the relationship between life and death that is a part of all humans. The speaker's acknowledged problem in stanza 3 is how to think about the Holy Spirit and God, abstractions in which he feels compelled, irrationally in the presence of death, to believe. In stanza 4, he longs for the blind faith he presumes the dead have. He then concludes the poem by suggesting that whatever his thoughts are on life, death, immortality, and God, they are irrelevant in the face of the reality of mortality. In his own mind, through his meditations, the speaker has established a reason to believe in God. His position is theistic—that is, a belief in the existence of God, who reveals himself to humans.

Forms and Devices

Imagery, language, and meter are carefully chosen to produce the meaning and effect of "To The Holy Spirit." Winters was particularly attracted to the barren ordered beauty of the desert landscape and the open spaces of New Mexico and California. He spent his twenties in New Mexico and later moved to California; he was a college professor at Stanford University for over thirty years. The images of the desert, with its wordplay on "deserted," are created in the first two stanzas of the poem. They yield a sense of limitlessness and some discomfort in the dry heat, dust, and sand. Although the poem has an emphasis on landscape, it is not a Romantic poem. Instead of images of lush, fertile, friendly nature, this landscape is harsh, yet uniquely beautiful; the mood is tense, and the speaker struggles to find reconciliation in nature.

The language is clear and direct. The use of older forms of address in stanza 3, "Thou," "thee," and "thine," lend seriousness to the speaker's reflections. They carry the weight of tradition. The image patterns in the poem move from obscurity to clarity. In the first stanza the haze blocks the speaker's ability to see the vista he suspects is before him. In the second, with the advent of noontime, the haze begins to clear. By the third stanza he sees more clearly in his mind the nature of his problem with belief in God, and in the fourth his physical eyes and his mind's eye see the truth of his situation.

The poem's vocabulary is specific yet rich in connotation. The first two words, "Immeasurable haze," create an image of vastness, a picture of an open landscape marked only by a few paltry trees. They give an immediate sense of the limits of sight but not of imagination. Measurement is a precise activity, and the speaker recognizes the haze as "immeasurable." The haze, which engulfs the speaker and obscures his vision, is not cloud or fog, but particles of water vapor, smoke, or dust; again, natural elements symbolize the speaker's condition and how he has defined himself in nature. A third word that carries precise meaning is "graveyard." While the dictionary shows cemetery and graveyard as synonyms, Winters chose the latter to name the poem's setting. Cemetery's root word, from the Greek, means "to put to sleep," whereas graveyard is an Anglo-Saxon compound noun. It includes the word "grave," which means several things besides a burial place for the body. Of special note are its meanings as an adjective—describing situations or places filled with great importance, filled with danger, or solemn and dignified. In this one word the reader perceives the poem's content as active, not passive, and as serious, not lighthearted or superficial.

The poem is written in the three-foot line known as trimeter. A nice choice as the three beat line keeps the three-person God in focus. Trimeter was popular with some British Romantic poets as well as with the Irish poet, William Butler Yeats (1865-1939). Using trimeter allows Winters to participate in the tradition of writing about nature's role in leading humans to certain understandings of the world.

Each stanza rhymes irregularly. Couplets are used in stanzas 1, 2, and 4. Stanza 3 is the climax of the poem, and here Winters uses alternating rhymes (*ababcdcdefef*) to echo the speaker's indecisiveness. As a formal poet, one who used rhyme and meter, Winters was aware of the value of traditional versification in giving structure to verse. The variations in rhyme combined with the metrical steadiness create a feeling of ambivalence while promising resolution.

Themes and Meanings

"To the Holy Spirit" is concerned with the logical conflict of faith with reason. The speaker, until the last stanza of the poem, is trying to comprehend how he can know an unknowable, and he is uncomfortable in exchanging sensory truths for acts of faith. Yet he feels limited in knowing that the end of life is only death. He settles on the realization that what he thinks will not affect his ability to believe in the power of the Holy Spirit and the existence of God. Only the living are preoccupied with the meaning of death; the dead are experiencing it. Only the living worry about what there is to know, and the speaker appears, at the end of the poem, to be solaced by his awareness that when death comes, he will be rationally and spiritually prepared because he has had God revealed to him in the graveyard. It is important to recall that Winters's speaker accepts the existence of God but makes no claims for the validity or purpose of any particular religion. This speaker is ultimately satisfied with a hierarchical worldview in which he is a rational believer in the existence of a higher power.

"To the Holy Spirit" is acknowledged by critics as among Winters's best poems in both form and content. John Finlay wrote of the poem as "a summary of Winters' entire poetic career, one which began in free verse, imagism, and aesthetic relativism and which ended in traditional meter, classicism, and theistic absolutism." In becoming a critic of his own desire to have faith, the speaker challenges himself to deal with cultural assumptions about the limits of reason and the need to believe in the existence of anything greater than humanity. When he leaves the graveyard, the speaker has driven away the irrational facet of faith and replaced it with a reasonable observation: "And I, alas, am bound/ Pure mind to flesh and bone,/ And flesh and bone to ground."

Beverly Schneller

TOUCH ME

Author: Stanley Kunitz (1905-   )
Type of poem: Meditation
First published: 1995, in *Passing Through: The Later Poems New and Selected*

The Poem

"Touch Me" is the final poem of *Passing Through: The Later Poems New and Selected* (1995), published on the occasion of Stanley Kunitz's ninetieth birthday. Kunitz, who among his many honors has received the Pulitzer Prize and the Bollingen Award, had a long and distinguished career as poet and teacher. Unlike many of his earlier poems, "Touch Me" does not have a particular stanzaic form; instead it moves down the page in thirty short, tightly controlled lines of free verse. The poem begins with the words *"Summer is late, my heart,"* from one of his earlier poems, "As Flowers Are," written in 1958. The speaker remembers the feelings that sparked the earlier poem when he was younger and "wild with love." Now, nearly forty years later, he finds that it is his "heart" that is late, that he has already had his "season." He has spent the afternoon gardening, listening (almost as when he was a boy) to the sound of the crickets, marvelling at their very existence, questioning the nature of creation. So now, in the present-tense voice of the poem, lying in bed listening to the wind and rain, he goes back over the afternoon, reaching for the man he used to be.

When asked about his recent poems, Kunitz replied, "What is there left to confront but the great simplicities? . . . I dream of an art so transparent that you can look through and see the world." "Touch Me" represents just such an art; the poet's desire to fix the moment in memory means that the reader is asked to see every detail through a shaping eye. Haunted by wind and rain, by the branches thrashing against the windowpanes, the poet sees through to the heart of things. The poem is meditative, however, not visionary. Turning to direct address, the poet speaks to his wife— "Darling, do you remember/ the man you married?" The line break is crucial. If she remembers, then he has identity; if she remembers, she connects with the person who was "wild with love"; if she remembers, she is the link between the old man, his younger self, the child, the cricket, and the very earth in which he has been gardening all afternoon.

The title is interesting in that, instead of opting for the more universal concept of "touch," Kunitz has particularized it—"Touch Me." The "me" functions in several ways. It limits the act, both temporally and spatially. Following his directive, his wife can reach across the bed and touch him to "remind" him not only of his former self but also of the power of love. With great honesty and vulnerability he admits to a need for another to restore him fully to a sense of himself, a self rooted firmly in the present tense: "who I am." Again, the "me" (as recipient) resonates with the persistent questions of who he is and where he fits in the larger "garden." The underlying question of identity rests on the simple question of being.

Forms and Devices

The first thing one notices in "Touch Me" is its extreme simplicity. Its monosyllabic lines—"when I was wild with love" and "It is my heart that's late, / it is my song that's flown"—are comparable to those of Robert Frost. At the same time, these lines reveal an underlying iambic rhythm that is characteristic of Kunitz. The churning question—"What makes the engine go?"—is more effective because of its regular stresses, and the answer to the question is reinforced through repetition of meter as well as of the word itself: "Desire, desire, desire." The procreative force has been reproduced not only in the cricket's song but also in the sounds on the page.

At the same time, Kunitz sometimes cuts across his regular cadences, using trochaic or spondaic rhythms to undercut the essential optimism of the poem: "scatter like leaves" and "under a gunmetal sky." The old longing for the dance (echoed in the rhythms of the poem) is mitigated by the poem's one broken line: "One season only,/ and it's done."

The tone of "Touch Me" is informal; it is filled with contractions that suggest a spoken voice. Still, it is an internal voice, one overheard and internalized by the reader. Although informal, however, "Touch Me" has a tight structure. The reader learns early that it is a night of "whistling wind and rain" and so is not surprised when the poet returns from reverie to the present weather of the poem. This pattern of memory and memory recollected allows the poet to become "like a child again," to look at everything through fresh eyes. This looking produces a circular movement, from recent past to present to remembered past, which is broken by the phrase "and it's done." Only then can the poet fully enter the present, breaking out of his own meditation to speak to his companion.

"Touch Me" displays an intricate network of rhymes—more a crocheted pattern than a woven one. The slant rhymes create a pattern like the fluid course of a soccer ball as the players move it down the field: rain/flown/afternoon/down, and, later, again/machine/done, or the initial "air" echoed in clear/pour/desire. Then, as in a reprise, "air" is caught up again in "remember"—the operative word of the poem.

Themes and Meanings

"As one who was not predestined, either by nature or by art, to become a prolific poet, I must admit it pleases me that, thanks to longevity, the body of my work is beginning to acquire a bit of heft." This sentence, from the author's note to *The Poems of Stanley Kunitz, 1928-1978*, was written nearly twenty years before the publication of "Touch Me." By his ninetieth birthday his longevity had led to an even more substantial body of work, of which "Touch Me" is perhaps emblematic.

"Touch Me" gives the reader, above all, a sensibility. It is an old man's poem, a poem of looking back, of putting a lifetime in perspective. Yet it is also a poem of continued renewal, very much of the present. The ending is not elevated; it does not try to make language fill the void. The poet falters at the edge of the visionary, where the song has "flown," pulling back from the urge to fabricate in favor of the urge to resuscitate. At the exact moment when Kunitz's earlier poems would have made a transformative leap, this poem settles back. The poet forgoes rhyme and rhythm in favor of statement, a deflated kind of poetry that makes the ending both terrifying and poignant. Moving quickly from contemplation to a moment of action, or implied action, the poet connects to his past and his future simultaneously. The emotional moment has already been completed, and the poem is recapitulation. "Remind me," he says, not "tell," or "show." The act (the touch), if it comes, will remind him of what has already been fulfilled.

In some ways, "Touch Me" is about poetry itself and its regenerative, life-giving powers: "The longing for the dance/ stirs in the buried life." The "buried life" of the garden is echoed in the poet's buried past, brought to life through memory. His need to give and receive love has been reactivated through coincidence—the intersection of memory and geography that gives rise to the poem. There is, however, some implied equivocation: Poetry can only do so much. Thus "Touch Me" is a poem of completion and incompletion; it makes the link for the poet (as in his memory of his earlier line), but that is not sufficient. His wife can reconnect him to his life through touch, the physical act no poem can reproduce. The gesture of poetry is superseded by one of human contact.

Speaking of poetry as a form of blessing, Kunitz tells readers (in an introduction to *Passing Through* that he called "Instead of a Foreword") that "it would be healthier if we could locate ourselves in the thick of life, at every intersection where values and meanings cross, caught in the dangerous traffic between self and universe." In "Touch Me," Kunitz has located himself at that intersection. If he is the equivalent of the "battered old willow," then he is also the man who can turn to his wife with an endearment and rekindle love. If the speaker is merely "passing through," as the title of the entire collection suggests, then what is the meaning of an individual life? Stalled in the memory of youthful emotion, Kunitz admits vulnerability. Yet the title of the poem is reciprocal. In asking her to touch him, he touches others through his poem. In its very uncertainty, "Touch Me" is affirmative; as the poet finds himself asking all the old questions, he sees through them to where, although life has "one season only," he is happily and healthily still in the thick of it.

Judith Kitchen

TRANSLATIONS

Author: Wing Tek Lum (1946-   )
Type of poem: Lyric
First published: 1987, in *Expounding the Doubtful Points*

The Poem

"Translations" is a poem in three parts that considers the ways in which provoca-
tively descriptive language influences and reflects attitudes toward cultural communities located outside of conventional representations of life in the United States.
Speaking with the thoughtful, reflective voice that is characteristic of his work, Wing
Tek Lum begins the poem with the word "Ghosts," a focal point for an exploration of
the manner in which the terminology chosen by a people to describe themselves may
differ significantly from the words used by outsiders to refer to them. The first lines
of the poem recall the innocent pleasure of a child's delight in the thrill of the
supernatural, a series of images evoking the harmless fun of "running around in/ old
bedsheets," enjoying the reassuring comic-book fantasy of the friendly Caspar, and
then "marveling at/ the trick/ camerawork" in a television show about Cosmo G.
Topper. These familiar, pleasant vignettes from popular culture are placed in sharp
contrast with Lum's adult perspective on ghosts as the second section of part 1 begins
with the word *Gwái,* a Chinese term for "demon" or "devil." The transition to a term
loaded with negative connotations introduces a darker, more sinister element to the
poem, which Lum amplifies by references to "Shaw Brothers horror/ films" and "rites
of exorcism" before concluding the section with a cryptic comment about "Old
Demons who wear/ white skin/ and make believe/ they behave/ like men."

The second part of "Translations" moves away from Lum's closely personal
account of his changing perspective on the word for "ghost" and toward an omniscient
position in which the poet proceeds as the voice of communal experience. Summariz-
ing decades of cross-cultural confusion and intrasocietal clashes, Lum states that "The
Chinaman" (a stereotype) gave "the Demon" (another stereotype) "what/ the former
thought/ the latter thought/ were things/ Chinese." This mutual misconception resulted in "a comedy/ of errors" that Lum, maintaining a degree of distance from the
humiliation involved, describes as "part fawning, part/ deception and contempt" for
both groups. He concludes part 2 with a mordant observation, pointing out that "There
is no/ word for/ fortune cookie in Cantonese," a statement that effectively undercuts
one of the most prominent assumptions about Chinese life held by many non-Chinese.

In the third part of "Translations," Lum somewhat ruefully recalls the name that
Chinese Americans gave to their home: *Tòhng Yàhn Gāai* ("China-People-Street").
As an indication of the pressures placed on an ethnic minority by a dominant culture
indifferent to the nuances of their lives, Lum says that Chinese Americans eventually
"mimicked/ Demon talk" and began to use the term *Wàh Fauh* for their address. This
is the predominant descriptor in many American cities, the "China-Town" that is
regarded primarily as an exotic tourist destination. In conclusion, Lum explains that

the difference in names is obvious. "The people" (that is, the soul and spirit of the community) have "disappeared," or, in a unifying trope that reaches back to the first word of the poem, they have become ghosts.

Forms and Devices

"I have always been slow in my verbal skills," Lum commented while discussing his processes of composition. "Since the fourth grade I have resigned myself to plodding along with the written word," but then he realized that "by nature poets choose their words carefully" and that what seemed like a limitation could be an aspect of his strength as a writer. Rather than the "razzle-dazzle of the flow of words," Lum's poems often provide what he calls "epiphanies of passion, of something deeply-felt" that he deems "important to share." Consequently, Lum has emphasized "the clarity of the image" so that in a poem such as "Translations" the political element that he has always recognized in his work emerges from the juxtaposition of the images that he presents.

The controlling image of "Translations" is that of ghosts rendered first in terms of a child's delight with features of a magical cosmos then darkened by the adult's realization that there is a component of psychic danger in horror films and exorcism rites. The establishment of the twofold nature of the ghost phenomenon enables Lum to begin to examine the ramifications of the ghost/*Gwái* polarity, a division in which the demon's "white skin" is a disguise camouflaging its nonhuman behavior or attributes, an inversion of the friendly nature of Caspar, whose white ghost form covers a humane disposition. This doubling of the human/devil image expresses Lum's opinion that white people have sometimes acted with demonic malice and ignorance in transcultural matters.

The clarity of the ghost imagery permits Lum to place a conundrum at the core of the poem. The intricate reversal and inward reflection of his assertion that "The Chinaman gave/ the Demon what/ the former thought/ the latter thought/ were things/ Chinese" is a tightly wrapped enigma that demands close attention but that contains a kernel of meaning that becomes accessible in accordance with the previous presentation of imagery. Even as the general idea becomes comprehensible, however, it remains elusive, which is part of Lum's point: The thinking of both groups is muddled and biased, and the "things Chinese" are subject to misinterpretation and misconception. Lum's designation of this as a comedy of errors somewhat softens the force of the language he uses to describe the postures of the participants in the play (their "fawning," "deception," and "contempt" are not conducive to any kind of admirable human interaction), while his matter-of-fact observation about the absence of a word for "fortune cookie" in Cantonese epitomizes his exasperation at assumptions that avoid any comprehension of a complex reality.

The poem concludes with a fusion of word and image that is reminiscent of the characters used in the Chinese written language. Lum's recollection of the original name for his neighborhood, *Tòhng Yàhn Gāai*, is translated into English as "China-People-Street" as if each word is also an image representing its meaning. Then, as he and his neighbors accede to "Demon talk" and write only *Wàh Fauh*, the alteration and the absence of the key word for "people" has literally changed the appearance of the place, both in written language and in the way in which language shapes perception.

Themes and Meanings

In the special dedications for the poems in *Expounding the Doubtful Points*, Lum says that "Translations" is "for Jeffrey Paul Chan in appreciation of his letter to the editor, *New York Review of Books*, April 28, 1977." Chan's letter was written as an explanatory corrective to a review (significantly entitled "Ghosts") by Diane Johnson in which Johnson discussed Maxine Hong Kingston's *Woman Warrior: Memoirs of a Girlhood Among Ghosts* (1976). The thrust of his critique is that Johnson "knows nothing about Chinese-American society" (which he demonstrates with considerable historical support) and that her contention that "Chinese-Americans are a notably unassimilated culture" is nonsense. Contrary to her claim that "generations go nameless," Chan explains that to comply with immigration regulations many Chinese American families give their children both an American and a Chinese name in a subversion of the "white Christian missionary invention of the double name system to break down the hold of Chinese language and culture on converts." In other words, the question of identity is contested on linguistic grounds since the entire history and heritage of a people is threatened with extinction if ancestors become amorphous, ghostlike entities.

Lum's goal in "Translations" is to explore the complex nature of the assimilation process in terms of his understanding of his "ethnic self" as "first neither Chinese nor American." He is determined to resist all of the stereotypes perpetrated by opportunists and exploiters from both cultures, the fawning by phonies pretending to appreciate each other's exotic characteristics, which disguises the contempt they actually feel for anything differing from their own world. The "Chinaman" and the "Old Demon" who scuttle around trying to anticipate each other's preconceptions are Lum's figures for fools locked in a dance (thus the circular arrangement of part 2) of deception so that the people behind the caricatures have essentially disappeared. As Lum has eloquently put it in an essay on Asian Americans, "Denial and deceit are some of the hallmarks of the self-hatred which so often is the survival response" in the face of insidious stereotypes.

Lum's efforts in "Translations" and many other poems to overcome the "self-hatred" he deplores and to support what he calls "an ethnic identification, an understanding that there is a group of individuals who share . . . common sensibility, culture and tradition" is based on his conviction that he cannot let the people of "China-People-Street" disappear. His method stems from what he calls "an honest acceptance of who we really are." In "Translations," this means a return to the poem's opening in which a significant part of a Chinese American childhood is recalled in terms that most people would regard as entirely separate from the Asian experience that is supposed to be its defining frame. Just as he marveled at the trick camerawork of mysterious ghost stories, Lum would like his readers to look with fascination rather than fear at the unfamiliar facets of a community whose strangeness does not imply hostility.

Leon Lewis

TRANSMIGRATION

Author: Brendan Galvin (1938-   )
Type of poem: Narrative
First published: 1982; collected in *Winter Oysters*, 1983

The Poem

"Transmigration" is a mid-length narrative poem with irregular stanza lengths and meter. The poem's title suggests the transmigration of the soul, the theological idea that after death one's soul migrates to exist in another creature, human or animal. In the case of Brendan Galvin's poem, the transmigration referred to is of a middle-aged man who jogs to lose a paunch gained from overeating. The jogger has "sat out easy rains" and has not worked very hard at becoming healthier. Ironically, instead of becoming healthier, he dies on the beach, and his soul enters a seagull. The title also introduces the concept of migration, an idea that Galvin plays with throughout the poem. The onset of winter is traditionally associated with death, but it is also the time when birds migrate. Thus, Galvin conjoins the idea of a soul's migration after death with a bird's natural instinct to migrate when the days grow shorter. The poem begins precisely at the moment of death as the jogger's soul leaves his body and reawakens in the seagull.

Much of the poem charts the orientation of the soul to its new body. The man, now a bird, is afraid and lands immediately on a tree, its "new feet gripping." Getting in touch with "instinct," however, he is able to acclimate himself to the new body. The man enjoys the new perspective, which is both visual and spiritual. Visually, the soul sees things differently, looking "for the first time" at the world from above. Spiritually, the soul knows the secret that humans do not, that death is another beginning, though one of a different sort than most suppose.

Although the poem begins with the man's soul entering the seagull's body, there are many retrospective moments within the poem where readers glimpse his previous existence as a human. One poignant example is the memory of Ryder beach, where he and "one summer's girl" were surprised on the shore by a construction crew. However, Galvin reminds readers that "such memories are useless," and the beach holds no nostalgic human associations but has become a place for the bird to hunt for fish. At the end, as the bird flies above the town, he hears the organ playing at his own funeral, though from where he flies it sounds "thin as a harmonica." He follows the cars of the funeral procession, but Galvin tells him that he "can't feel" for what he trails. The bird, or soul, or man experiences the "simple rightness of things" and knows he could never explain it to "that veiled woman/ and downcast kids" he sees below at the cemetery.

Forms and Devices

The most notable poetic device in "Transmigration" is the use of the second-person pronoun "you." Galvin addresses the soul of the man that has entered the seagull, but the effect of the "you" is to position the reader in the man's place. Readers become the "you" that is addressed and see from the bird's perspective, experiencing a "bird's-eye view" of life from the position of a participant. This is the ultimate transmigration of the poem. The poet's task is to cause readers' souls to transmigrate from their own bodies to absolute identification with the "you" of the poem. The "vowels of love" Galvin refers to are, in some sense, his statement about poetry. The sound and sense experience of the poem should move one into a direct experience of it, a loving transmigration from reader into participant.

"Transmigration" is notable, as is Galvin's work in general, for a rich use of simile and metaphor. Given the subject matter, it is interesting how human the comparisons are. The poem opens, for example, with the simile "When your bones turn/ loose and light as a deck chair." Like the seagull, the deck chair is part of the seascape, but unlike the bird, it is part of the human world. Galvin compares the hollow-boned lightness of a bird to the tubular construction of a deck chair and, in very human terms, tries to convey what it feels like to suddenly have one's soul reawaken within a bird. As a bird seeing the world from above for the first time, the soul still experiences things in human terms. The runway of an airport, for example, "could be/ a dropped paperclip." The metaphor places readers in the position of the bird, which views the runway from a great height, but also reminds them of the man's previous life and suggests he may have held a job in an office. Similarly, when he hears, from his position in the sky, "Crackles of speech/ as off a police radio," the simile visually reminds readers not only where and what the man is now but also what he used to be. The police radio and the "money talk" he overhears suggest the complications of human society and contrast with the uncomplicated life he now leads. Conversely, some of the poem's metaphors reflect on how animalistic the man was before his death and how heavy he was compared to the lightness of the bird. He jogs because he has been to "too many troughs" and is "trying to shake off a pelt."

In writing a poem about what it feels like to become a bird, Galvin is forced by human circumstances to rely on metaphors emerging from human experience. Such a move, though perhaps necessary, is also successful and constantly keeps before the reader the transmigration that has occurred from man to bird. Some of the visual imagery places the reader firmly into the position of the bird. Readers see common things in an uncommon way, "from above" like a bird. Simple things that went unnoticed such as the beauty of a plowed field ("the art of tractors") are now seen "for the first time." Above all, spatial orientation has altered dramatically. The bird experiences a different relationship to the sun, moon, earth, sea, and sky. Flying so high he can sense the curvature of the earth, the seagull watches until the "last light/ drops off the planet's/ easy curve."

Themes and Meanings

"Transmigration" first appeared in *The New Yorker* but has been reprinted in three collections. In each case, it occupies a significant position in relation to the collection as a whole. In *Winter Oysters* (1983), for example, "Transmigration" occupies a separate section unto itself; in *Great Blue* (1990), it occupies the final place in the first section. Most significant is its appearance in *A Birder's Dozen* (1984), in which it is the thirteenth and final poem. All the poems in *A Birder's Dozen* are about birds: "The Birds," "Chickadee," and "The Grackles" are representative titles. However, "Transmigration" comes last and is about a man's transformation into something that he had previously only observed. Galvin's point in positioning the poem at the end seems to be a desire to migrate, through poetry, from observer to participant. Reading his twelve poems about birds, the reader becomes transformed into one in the thirteenth.

In some sense, however, the poem is not about a man becoming a bird but about what it feels like to become a soul. The contrast between the man's physical heaviness and the bird's lightness is a significant one. The heaviness suggests the burden of being human, of the "weighty" decisions and responsibilities. The lightness of the bird is a removal of those things, and, unchained, the soul is free to fly in a kind of immediate contact with the natural world. The new relation to space and time is part of that contact, as the bird has no real concept of time passing other than flying higher in the sky so the sun will stay out longer. It is no wonder that the poet watches longingly and asks, "What are you, a soul?"

Near the end of the poem, the bird listens and watches as his funeral procession leaves the church and wends its way to Memorial Lawn cemetery. Although the bird knows the "simple rightness of things" the transmigration has caused, he cannot entirely forsake his human life and thoughts. In the dramatic climax of the poem, the soul sees his wife and children below, but they become "that veiled woman" and the "downcast kids." His connection to them is severed, and he knows that he could say no words of comfort to explain the "rightness" of things as they are. Still, though his existence as a bird is liberating, he knows he will never be able to leave his human life behind. He will haunt Main Street "for snatches of the inconsequential/ that bind person to person/ and day to day below." Though liberated, his soul is still bound, and the poem ends with the man/seagull/soul flying with exhilaration and sadness into the night sky.

Joe B. Fulton

TRAVELS IN THE SOUTH

Author: Simon Ortiz (1941-   )
Type of poem: Narrative
First published: 1976, in *Going for the Rain*

The Poem

"Travels in the South" is a three-part poem in free verse, its sections divided by geographical location: "East Texas," "The Creek Nation East of the Mississippi," and "Crossing the Georgia Border into Florida." As the title suggests, Simon Ortiz, a member of the Acoma Pueblo tribe of American Indians, takes readers on an emotionally charged journey through several southern states beginning with an early morning departure from the Coushatta people in Alabama and ending in a state park in Florida. Using first person throughout, he skillfully situates these travels within the context of the narrator's heritage, culture, family, and community.

The first part, "East Texas," establishes a warm connection with the Coushatta people who feed and emotionally nourish the narrator on this leg of his journey. While the poem begins here, readers sense that his travels actually began earlier and that this locale is merely where he begins his tale, which is, in essence, a quest to find Native American people. It thus constitutes the narrator's search for identity. A humbling stop at the Huntsville State Penitentiary and a talk with the American Indian prisoners there completes his Alabama trip. When Ortiz turns his attention to Texas, the tone shifts; in fact, the narrator admits he does not want to be in Dallas, Texas, where the Bureau of Indian Affairs relocation official cannot even say how many American Indians live in the city. Witnessing much suffering, including a jobless Navajo and "an Apache woman crying for her lost life," the traveler moves on to Lake Caddo, named, according to the park ranger, for "some Indian tribe." There, much to his delight, he happens upon two seventy-year-old black women with whom he spends the rest of the day fishing and laughing.

Part 2, "The Creek Nation East of the Mississippi," begins at a hot dog stand in Pensacola, Florida, where the narrator asks for the names of local Native Americans. The vendor directs him just across the state border to Chief Alvin McGee's home in Atmore, Alabama, where he is surprised and heartened to recognize McGee as the same American Indian he had seen in pictures in old history books. While the venerable chief reminisces about famous local American Indian leaders and laments the devastating losses indigenous communities have experienced over the years, the two men watch the election news on television. When George Wallace is once again elected governor of the state, they clearly sense another loss for Native Americans as well as other people of color. Attempting to lift the old man's spirits, the narrator urges, "please don't worry about Wallace, don't worry." His words ring hollow, for as he travels on to his next destination, he hears a radio broadcast about the National Guard killing college students at Kent State University and must pull off the road despite, or perhaps because of, a sign that says "NO STOPPING EXCEPT IN CASE

OF EMERGENCY." Tired and depressed, the traveler begins to ponder the demoralizing results of his search for identity and community in a hostile country.

The final section, "Crossing the Georgia Border into Florida," chronicles several difficulties in Atlanta, Georgia, where the young narrator's long hair and dark skin elicit nervous glances and discriminatory practices from local white people. Reeling from such injustice, he empathizes with African Americans who experience abuses regularly but lack the opportunity to move on, which contrasts with his mobility when the American Indian meeting at the Dinkler Plaza ends. Settling finally at a campsite in a Florida state park "noted for the Indians/ that don't live here anymore," he seeks respite in nature. The poem concludes with a surprisingly apt image: The traveler offers crumbs of bread—"white, and kind of stale"—to the squirrels and birds. When they refuse such tasteless and paltry handouts, he understands why.

Forms and Devices

"Travels in the South" is a poem about recovery. It centers on one man's efforts to reclaim his Native American heritage by retracing the steps of his ancestors in the South. Sadly, the reader learns that many American Indians are merely a nameless memory in the minds of white people who now claim the land for their state parks and recreation areas. The American Indians that he does manage to locate still struggle to exist amid hostility. Yet Ortiz retrieves the tribal names—Coushatta, Caddo, Creek, Navajo, Apache, Acoma—and in doing so reclaims for himself an important part of his identity. Language, specifically the power of naming, becomes the catalyst for the poem's powerful message: Native American survival today depends upon a strong link with the past. Herein lies continuance.

By using names from both the past and the present, Ortiz creates a paradoxical mix of traditional Native American and what he calls "Mericano" culture. Each section of the poem and thus each mile of his journey unearths these surprising linguistic juxtapositions. He finds that the dominant culture is killing his people. Instead of living in harmony with the land, they are prisoners in the "State Pen" or unemployed welders in Dallas. He learns of an elder's whereabouts when he buys a hot dog and a beer, and, as they watch television together, they see their civil rights steadily erode. Significantly, however, at each stage of his journey, the narrator is sustained by the rising of the sun and by the language and wisdom of his elders. Two old black women, in a symbolic gesture, teach him about the stubbornness and perseverance of turtles and thus about his and all oppressed cultures' need for resistance and persistence. As he receives a traditional blessing from Chief McGee, he remembers his grandfather and "the mountains, the land from where [the narrator] came."

A final, illuminating mix of the old and new occurs in the third section when the narrator, a modern American youth wearing the styles of the 1970's, worries about the potential harassment he might encounter in the deep South because of his long hair. This concern calls to mind his grandfather, named "Tall One" by the Acoma, who also had long hair. Thus, while Ortiz merges the "Mericano" and Native American cultures, it is not with a sense of despair but rather a conviction that the traditions and heritage provide security in the present and an empowering solidarity with all op-pressed peoples.

Ortiz saves the most meaningful situation, which illustrates the chasm between the old ways and the new, for the end of the last section in which the narrator's "brothers," the squirrel and red bird, refuse the crumbs of white bread he offers, a symbolic rendering of the "too little, too late" offerings of white society. The American Indian beliefs that animals are relatives and that their presence in life offers messages humans would do well to heed are instructive: Their refusal suggests that the narrator, too, should decline the "leftovers" of mainstream culture and thereby defy the tacit degradation accompanying such gestures.

Themes and Meanings

Ortiz is a storyteller, a fact to which he alludes in the second stanza: "Once, in a story, I wrote that Indians are everywhere." His travels in the South attempt to prove that Indians do indeed live in every part of the United States and thus debunk the popular "vanishing Indian" stereotype. Growing up in the oral tradition, his commit-ment to the Acoma tribe is strong. He believes that culture survives because of the story, which in turn generates poetry that tells the life of the people. Yet as a young man he was struck as if by a revelation by the writings of the Beat generation. He recalls being overly impressed by Jack Kerouac's prose. Indeed, many of Kerouac's themes are echoed in "Travels in the South": a focus on struggling people, a search for identity, and an on-the-road experience that ultimately exposes America's rough edges and dark underside.

These motifs are repeated in his books of poems published after *Going for the Rain*, especially *A Good Journey* (1977) and *Fight Back: For the Sake of the People, for the Sake of the Land* (1981). His poetic works chronicle "red power" activism and an awareness of the extended problems created by society's decimation of American Indian lands. Ortiz's poetic vision is clear in this early poem: Society's caretakers of the land, the park rangers in Texas and Florida, lack a basic understanding of its history and significance. This deficit is highlighted further in the second stanza when the narrator meets Chief McGee, who shows him his garden and fields. Speaking of the white oppressors, Chief McGee says, "There ain't much they don't try to take." In the final stanza of the poem, the traveler pays $2.50 to enter the space once owned by his people, a painful and ironic commentary on how successful white society has been in their greedy quest for land.

"Travels in the South" offers readers a series of images that illustrate how one man can feel like an outsider in his homeland. Ortiz cleverly contrasts the deep spirituality of the Acoma tradition with the shallow surface of contemporary society. Pueblo oral tradition includes stories, advice, and counsel, the priceless legacy the narrator inherits from his elders and, in effect, passes on to the readers.

Carol F. Bender

TRIVIA

Author: John Gay (1685-1732)
Type of poem: Poetic sequence
First published: 1716

The Poem

The full title of this poem is *Trivia: Or, The Art of Walking the Streets of London*, and the word "trivia" here is easily misunderstood. In the modern sense of "insignificant details," it would seem to indicate a poem about a congeries of minor matters. However, to readers of the eighteenth century who were steeped in the classics, it would be understood in the Latin sense of the intersection of three roads or as the plural of *trivium*, the three subjects of traditional education (grammar, rhetoric, and logic). It might even be seen as an allusion to the three-headed goddess Hecate, or Diana, who ruled over day, night, and the underworld and was sometimes referred to as Diana of the crossways. Accordingly, the poem is organized in three cantos, or books. *Trivia* offers a liberal education in urban sociology.

Book I, "Of the Implements for Walking the Streets and Signs of the Weather," is prefaced by an advertisement, or notice to the reader, to the effect that the author owes "several hints of it to Dr. Swift," the celebrated dean of St. Patrick's Cathedral, Dublin and author of *Gulliver's Travels*. That Swift and the other members of the Scriblerus Club (including Alexander Pope) thought highly of *Trivia* is supported by their letters. Swift's "Description of the Morning" (1709) and "Description of a City Shower" (1710) are clearly models for Gay's much longer compositions; Gay's *Rural Sports* (1713) and *The Shepherd's Week* (1714) were preliminary and highly regarded experiments in the same genre. *Trivia*, *The Beggar's Opera* (1728), and *Fables* (1727) established his fame, and he was accorded a burial in Westminster Abbey beside Chaucer's tomb.

The opening lines of *Trivia* parody those of Vergil's *Aeneid* (transcribed c. 29-19 B.C.) and thus set the mock-heroic tone; instead of declaring his subject to be "arms and the man," Gay states that it is "How to walk clean by day, and safe by night." Accordingly, his first substantive stanza is on the choice of shoes, which should not be foreign or fashionable but "firm, well-hammered" ones that will be serviceable in snow, rain, or sleet. Shoes too wide, he says, may cause a sprain; those too short will cause corns or blisters.

Next the poet evaluates various types of overcoats and cautions against Bavarian ones or those with lace; he recommends a simple, inexpensive wool that will allow the wearer to "brave unwet the rain, unchill'd the frost." The potential walker is advised to carry a cane—not like those of the city beaux, which are amber-tipped and used for show, but a practical one—one that, if sturdy, will chase others away from building walls and will attract the attention of carriage drivers.

In a long stanza Gay describes the perils of walking in foreign cities and bemoans the increased street traffic in Britain, augmented by "coaches and chariots" as well as sedan chairs so that no longer "Rosie-complexion'd health thy steps attends,/ And exercise thy lasting youth defends." Then he provides a dissertation on the weather, with special attention given to cold, fair, and rainy days and a list of superstitions to be disregarded. This consideration of rainy weather leads logically into a recommendation that ladies should wear pattens (shoes elevated by metal cleats) and carry umbrellas.

The preliminaries of Book I run to 282 lines; Book II, "Of Walking the Streets by Day," is 468 lines; and Book III, "Of Walking the Streets by Night," is 416 lines. Since few walkers ventured onto the streets of London at night, clearly the proportions of the poem are quite appropriate.

Gay recommends the morning for walking: "For ease and for dispatch the morning's best:/ No tides of passengers the street molest." There are dangers, however: Barbers, perfumers, and bakers can soil black clothes; chimney sweeps, coal merchants, and dustmen can bespoil lighter clothing, and tallow men, chandlers, and butchers can spot any clothes. Likewise, the fop with his powdered wig and the miller should be avoided, but the bully should not be demurred to: He may mutter curses, but he will yield. Should the walker lose his way, he should seek directions from a tradesman rather than a boy—and never from a woman, for she may be a pickpocket.

A second edition of *Trivia* (undated, but probably 1717) contains an addition (lines 99-220) on the rise of the shirtless shoe-shine boy, an illegitimate son of the goddess Cloacina, whose image was found in a sewer by Tatius, king of the Sabines. The celebrated Dr. Samuel Johnson judged this addition "nauseous and superfluous." The interpolation contains the memorable couplet, "But happier far are those (if such be known)/ Whom both a father and a mother own"; nevertheless, inorganic and irrelevant, the addition lacks merit.

The remainder of Book II cautions against walking in narrow streets and those that house chandlers, fishmongers, and butchers—or walking where masons are at work or boys are playing football. It reminds the walker that Mondays and Thursdays are "days of game," when bull- and bear-baiting can be seen, and that Wednesdays and Fridays are fasting days so that seafood can be seen in the stalls. The fruits of the seasons are enumerated. Gay reminds the walker to be charitable to widows and orphans, the lame and blind, for walkers are blessed: They are immune to jaundice, coughs, asthma, gout, and stones. Accordingly, they should never envy those in coaches or in fine clothes. To his fellow walkers he says, "give me sweet content on foot."

Book III cautions against walking near noisy crowds, where pickpockets usually congregate—often aided by ballad singers or girls with pretty faces—and offers advice on eating oysters, avoiding cheats, identifying whores and rakes, bribing watchmen and policemen, and avoiding the numerous terrors of the night, including fires. It comprises what Gay calls "Useful Precepts," among which are:

> Let constant Vigilance thy Footsteps guide,
> And wary Circumspection guard thy Side;
>
> . . . .

Thou gh you through cleanlier Allies wind by Day,
To shun the Hurries of the publick Way,
Yet ne'er to those dark Paths by Night retire;
Mind only Safety, and contemn the Mire.

Forms and Devices

The epigraph of *Trivia* is the opening line of Vergil's ninth eclogue: "Where are you off to, Moeris, walking on the road to town?" The quotation illustrates both Gay's indebtedness to the classical tradition and his plan for what might be termed a city eclogue, a poem in which conversation about current matters, spiced with proverbs and advice, takes place between an older, sophisticated person and a younger, inexperienced auditor. The prefatory motto is taken from Vergil also, and it preempts criticism of the poem by addressing any potential gainsayer as "ignoramus as you are." That is, Gay regards himself as *the* authority on walking the streets of London and thus is inhospitable to cavilling criticism. He is the model for modern city tour guides, pointing out buildings, homes, and institutions of interest. He warns his audience against the pitfalls of disregarding his directions and suggests the delights of further exploration and examination. The accuracy of almost all the topics of *Trivia* can be verified by consulting two twentieth century collections of historical illustrations, *The Thames About 1750* (1951) and *Engravings by Hogarth* (1973), which substantiate even the minor details of Gay's remarkably memorable descriptions of persons, places, and practices.

The classical model is borne out by the frequent allusions to Greek and Roman notables, both civil and mythological: Ariadne, Orpheus, Oedipus, Phaeton, Pythagoras, Regulus, Scylla and Charybdis, Theseus, and Vulcan are among them. The comprehensiveness of the guidebook aspect of *Trivia* is impressive: The reader is beguiled by pithy comments on such places as Cheapside, Covent Garden, Charing Cross, St. Clement Danes Church, Drury Lane, Fleet Ditch, Ludgate Hill, and the Thames bridges. Clearly, Gay's apprenticeship to a London silk mercer provided him with the opportunity to see more of the side streets, the fashions, and the employments of London than most poets, so his poem is marked by its social realism and by its frank admission of the unsavory aspects of early eighteenth century British urban life. While many poets painted only the atypical upper social stratum, Gay took as his subject the whole spectrum of London life: prostitution, poverty, pickpocketing, and pilferage as well as fops, fashions, food, and fairs.

Both the comprehensiveness of his overview and its reliability (as tested by more particular contemporary commentaries) are deserving of admiration. All the sounds, sights, and smells of the city are conveyed with verisimilitude. One twentieth century literary critic, George Sherburn, wrote that Gay, "like many realists, stressed the gutter to the neglect of more pleasant prospects; but for his foot passenger, his warnings were vivid and sage. Like Hogarth he paints the grotesque realities of London life." This is high praise, really, because painter and engraver William Hogarth is greatly admired for his penetrating vision of city life in his day, which counterbalanced the misleading representation offered by upper-class artists and writers. Part of Gay's strength is derived from his effective juxtaposition of morning and evening, walking and being carried (in chaise or carriage), males and females, refinement and depravity, bucolic and urban, rich and poor, indolence and industry, beauty and sordidness. He is concerned, it is clear, not with a particularly partisan presentation but with presenting a comprehensive portrait of London. The effect of *Trivia* is comparable to viewing one of Canaletto's panoramic scenes of the Thames and its environs.

In his early poems Gay made frequent use of alexandrines and triplets for variety; these characteristics of verse composition were condemned by Pope, and Gay subsequently abandoned them for the most part, even revising some lines of *Rural Sports* and *The Fan* to eliminate these solecisms. Gay's poetic technique was normally a mixture of the established and the original; he is more rigid in his adherence to the heroic couplet than Pope, yet he uses a more demotic language than his mentor, and his sentence structure is less complex.

Burlesque, a form of parody that imitates the form and style of a serious work but makes the imitation entertaining by the disparity between the subject matter and the method, is basic to *Trivia*, in which many of the aspects of street life are compared to famous incidents in classical mythology. Accordingly, Gay compares the rustic in awe of the city to Theseus in the Cretan labyrinths, horses straining up Ludgate Hill to the Parthians throwing their javelins backwards, the walker caught in a street brawl to Laius slain by Oedipus at a crossroads, and moisture on church monuments to Niobe dissolving into tears. Not all these allusions and comparisons are meaningful to a present-day reader, but their force would have been apparent to Gay's readers.

It has been observed that Pope was prepared to sacrifice truth for a brilliant epigram or a brilliant antithesis. Such was not Gay's practice, though his self-composed epitaph indicates that he was as capable as Pope in this most demanding form of composition: "Life is a jest, and all things show it./ I thought so once, and now I know it." Perhaps the best epigram in *Trivia* is the following, occasioned by writing on the great frost of 1715: "Ah Doll! All mortals must resign their breath, / And industry itself submit to death!" Or this, doubtless written tongue-in-cheek: "Death shall entomb in dust this mould'ring frame/ But never reach th'eternal part, my fame." Even the final line of the poem has the merits of brevity and pithiness: "This work shall shine, and walkers bless my name." In his use of classical allusions, juxtaposition, the many forms of imagery, adherence (but not slavery) to metrical forms, and epigrams within the burlesque form, Gay exhibits enviable compositional skills.

Themes and Meanings

Although Gay was evidently aware of the pitfalls associated with writing a mock-heroic poem on the simple topic of walking the streets of London and entitling it an art (inviting his readers to compare it with Horace's *Ars Poetica* (the art of poetry, c. 17 B.C.), he clearly saw his endeavor as having some utilitarian value for country folk and others who were less familiar with London thoroughfares than he was. His intent was to be of help to the uninitiated and the inexperienced, and he acknowledged toward the conclusion of his poem, "Yet shall I bless my labours, if mankind/ Their future safety from my dangers find." His didacticism is therefore quite clear: He wants to be a guide, to be helpful—a commendable intention for a poet or a friend when in need. The reader is thus well disposed toward the poet and is ready to accept his guidance and even his predispositions and prejudices.

The issue or concern at the heart of the poem is the safety of a neophyte tourist in London, sightseeing on foot by day or night, in all the seasons. While the subject might seem devoid of poetic possibility, Gay's selection of particular subject matter provides the basis for the poetry—rather than mere verse—to be found in almost all sections. Edgar Allan Poe argued in *The Poetic Principle* (1849) that there is no such thing as a long poem—that in actuality a long poem is a series of minor poems, each deserving that name only to the extent that it excites by elevating the soul. There are numerous exciting and elevating sections in *Trivia* that complement the ironic and bathetic sections, and over the centuries the preponderance of critical reaction has been that the former are the more numerous.

Trivia has been praised as a literary burlesque and as a serious social document, a detailed picture of eighteenth century life in a great metropolis. It was drawn by a writer with considerable life experience at both extremes of the social scale, one acquainted both with life in rural Devonshire and with the manners and affectations of the aristocracy.

It has been declared to be the finest mock-georgic in English and to be the greatest poem on London life in English literature. Perhaps these descriptions are somewhat too generous in their praise, but it must be allowed that Gay's accomplishment is great: He shifted the subject of poetry from the country to the city, from the ancient to the contemporary, from the exalted to the lowly, and he did so with clear-sighted realism, a refreshing cynicism, and a tolerable irony. Moreover, he never forgot that the social classes are interdependent, a theme that pervades his *Fables* and *The Beggar's Opera* as well.

A. L. McLeod

THE TRUTH IS

Author: Linda Hogan (1947-   )
Type of poem: Meditation
First published: 1985, in *Seeing Through the Sun*

The Poem

"The Truth Is," a poem in free verse, comprises forty-seven lines arranged in six stanzas of unequal length. It depicts the speaker's conflicting emotions about her dual heritage. The speaker, in this case, is the poet's alter ego and reflects her own background: Linda Hogan's father is a Chickasaw Indian, and her mother is a European immigrant from Nebraska. Hogan uses the first person and, later, addresses herself by name, both of which clearly indicate that the poet is speaking of her own predicament.

The first stanza brings out the conflict. Normally, the two hands of an individual work in harmony to accomplish tasks. In this case, however, her hands, symbols of her ancestry, refuse to cooperate. The left hand represents the Chickasaw part of her heritage and the right that of her white lineage. Their separateness is so distinctive that the speaker needs to reassure herself that both hands, hidden away in each pocket, are indeed hers. She describes herself as a woman who "falls in love too easily" yet "sleeps in a twin bed"—in other words, she maintains her single status. The emptiness of her pockets indicates the absence of material possessions. The fact that she walks with her hands in her pockets further suggests her reluctance to advertise her ancestry. She informs us that if she ever puts her hands in someone else's pocket, it is "for love not money."

The speaker continues her meditation on her peculiar state in the second stanza. She would like to envision herself as a grafted tree bearing two distinct yet equally appreciated types of fruits—perhaps apricots and cherries. The unfortunate truth, she realizes, is that the grafting, in this case, has not been successful: She finds that both branches "knock against each other," creating unwarranted tension. Yet, this constant warring is not what they desire; they "want amnesty."

The tone changes from reflective to conversational in the next stanza. The speaker admonishes herself—"Linda, girl"—to stop fretting about history. After all, nothing would be gained by going over the record of wrongdoings (by the white ancestors) or of loving generosity (of the Native Americans). The sense of her disharmonious existence is further conveyed by her comparison of herself to an old Civilian Conservation Corps member from the days of the Depression. The phrase "taped together" evokes the image of an object barely held together: She sees herself in a similar predicament. Her empty pockets, devoid of "coins and keys," the accoutrements of modern life, reinforce the absence of tangible wealth. She finds consolation in the fact that since wealth blinds the soul, hers remains unfettered by material bondage.

In the fifth stanza, the speaker recounts further the dangers of being "a woman of two countries." Her hands remain sheltered in the dark, empty pockets; in other words, she remains ignorant of both heritages that they represent. While she pretends to act nonchalantly, she cannot escape the "enemy." She desires to forget the gory history of the relationship between the white settlers and the Native Americans, to stop thinking of "who killed who." However, it is difficult to forget it all when she is constantly reminded of "that knocking on the door/ in the middle of the night"—a reference to the thoughts about continuing acts of violence originating from mainstream society.

Resolution, for the speaker, comes not in achieving a state of amnesty between the warring elements of her being but in the acceptance of her struggle. As she shifts her attention from hands to feet and shoes, the dilemma continues, for the right foot is still white and the left is still Chickasaw. In other words, "the truth is" that she will have to learn to live with this ever-present tension as she journeys through life.

Forms and Devices

Lacking a formal structure, the poem is deftly held together by metaphors, similes, symbols, and imagery. Hogan's use of hands to denote her heritage is a rather unusual metaphor, suggesting the emphasis on actions rather than thoughts. That these hands are hidden away in the pockets is a reminder of the unseen but powerful forces of heritage. Furthermore, the emptiness of the pockets reflects the speaker's state of existence: Her heritage has not, as yet, brought her any material or spiritual riches. Phrases describing the woman, who "falls in love too easily," who "sleeps in a twin bed," and who "walks along with hands/ in her own empty pockets/ even though she has put them in others/ for love not money," evoke the image of a vulnerable woman in search of peace and love.

The metaphor of a grafted fruit tree in stanza 2 is a powerful one. Normally, the process of grafting produces new varieties. If the grafting is successful, it is difficult to distinguish between different branches. In this case, however, this is not so. The grafting of the two cultures has not worked well; the speaker's dream that the tree would bear two fruits, each distinctive in itself, has not been realized. The phrase "It's not that way" tersely reveals the truth. The image of branches that "knock against each other at night" contrasts the reality with the speaker's erstwhile dream of peaceful coexistence. "Who loved who" and "who killed who" allude to the history of relations between whites and Native Americans, which has been dominated by violence.

In the fourth stanza, the use of simile, imagery, metaphor, and symbolism further advances the idea of the failure of an emergent composite identity. The speaker compares herself with an old worker from the Depression era and evokes another powerful image of herself as a "taped together" relic of the past. The pockets are depicted as "masks/ for the soul," serving as blinders that hide the soul. The coins and keys clearly symbolize material wealth and possessions. Their absence leaves the pockets free of jingling elements; their continued emptiness, however, suggests her failure to fill them with other riches.

The next two stanzas draw upon the earlier metaphors and allusions in reiterating the ever-continuing conflict. The pretense of not being concerned or afraid cannot go too far. The line "you better keep right on walking" clearly suggests moving on without being debilitated by the state of inertia. The poem thus succeeds in using these figures of speech effectively in establishing the mood of the speaker.

Themes and Meanings

One's identity is an amalgamation of many ingredients, the most important of these being, perhaps, one's heritage. Harnessing the forces of heredity and environment has never been an easy task. It becomes even more complicated when one does not belong to the mainstream of society. Having a mixed ancestry further compounds the problem, especially when those two elements are derived from a mutually adversarial relationship. Such is the context of Hogan's "The Truth Is."

The speaker's desire to reconcile the Native American and the European parts of her heritage permeates her life. If only she could create a distinctly new identity from this mix, life would be peaceful and simple for her. However, it does not happen this way. She realizes that the underlying, persistent clashes that are revived by the memory of historical wrongdoings, and, occasionally, by interruptions from the present will continue to be a part of her existence. Her reassurance to herself that she should forget about the past and live in the present helps her to accept the situation.

Ignoring the existence of this tension is of no avail; she cannot carry the pretense of being unconcerned for too long. The solution, then, is to acknowledge the truth and keep treading one's path. In her own life, Hogan seems to have achieved that equilibrium. In *Winged Words: American Indian Writers Speak* (1985), she admits that though her mixed heritage creates "a natural tension that surfaces" in her work, she has learned to use it to her advantage to strengthen her imagination.

Discussing Native American poetry, scholar Brian Swann observes, "Most poems reach for balance, for sanity in a mad world, in the face of antagonism, past and present. One sees a desire for wholeness—for balance, reconciliation, and healing—within the individual, the tribe, the community, the nation" (*Harper's Anthology of 20th Century Native American Poetry*, 1988). Hogan's poem reflects this tradition. "The Truth Is," in the end, transcends the speaker-poet's feelings and speaks to all those who share her experience of struggling to reconcile the different strands of their heritage.

Leela Kapai

TURNING

Author: Rainer Maria Rilke (1875-1926)

Type of poem: Lyric

First published: 1927, as "Wendung," in *Gesammelte Werke*; English translation collected in *The Selected Poetry of Rainer Maria Rilke*, 1982

The Poem

"Turning" is a poem of fifty-four lines divided unevenly into ten stanzas. The title suggests a turn or change in some important issue, and that is, indeed, the focus of the poem: a turning away from the poet's previous vision of the task of poetry to a new phase in his development as a poet. The poem is written in the third person, a device often used to distance the poet from the speaker or subject of the poem. In this case, however, it is clear that the poet is Rainer Maria Rilke himself. He sent the poem to a friend, saying that "it portrays the turning that will certainly have to come if I am to live." This poem can be read as a history of Rilke's poetic focus on observation of the outer world and a transition to bringing his vision inward.

The poem opens with a slightly altered quote from the philosopher Rudolf Kassner, a friend of Rilke: "The way from intensity to greatness leads through sacrifice." The quote is quite appropriate, as the poem represents a time during which Rilke was turning away from his intense exterior observations to look into himself for poetic inspiration. The poem can be divided into two main sections. The first, longer section describes his former way of seeing and creating poetry. The second section, beginning with the sixth stanza, reveals his doubts of his earlier perspective and describes his new intentions for his poetry.

Rilke lets his reader know from the very first line that a change is imminent: "For a long time he had achieved it with observing." The act of *Anschauen* (watching, observing) is now in the past, but, before he lets it go completely, Rilke lists his earlier achievements. The power of his look could force nature and inanimate objects to submit to him: "stars collapsed on their knees," and towers were "filled with terror." This power was not entirely negative since a landscape could "rest in his calm perception," animals and birds trusted him, and flowers returned his gaze as they did to little children. The very rumor of such an observer, a seer, stirred up women. In all these cases, the poet shows, even boasts about, how he could will everything to his unique poetic vision.

The poem then begins its transition from the proud declaration of earlier victories to an overriding feeling of doubt. A lonely, anonymous hotel room is evoked along with an air of depression. This is a scene he has been through many times (in fact, Rilke traveled and lived a great deal abroad, often in difficult financial circumstances). He avoids the mirror, perhaps to avoid looking at and into himself. The bed torments him, due not only to its probable poor construction but also to his own doubting consciousness. He is painfully alone with his thoughts and heart—a heart that still beats painfully, desiring to feel love. The poet can no longer avoid his moment of truth:

He does not have love in his heart. The turning point of "Turning" comes when the poet realizes the limits of his former successes. He must go forward with himself and his poetry because the world can only mature and be nourished in love. The "work of the eyes is done," and he must now go forth and "do heart-work" on the very images he had earlier submitted to his gaze but still does not truly know. The poem's last lines are a plea for him to look within and learn from the feminine inside himself to discover her multiple natures so that he might finally learn to love.

Forms and Devices

The structure of "Turning" is more difficult to grasp than Rilke's earlier poems, which had regular meter and rhyme patterns. "Turning" has no rhyme pattern and has a very irregular meter, though iambic meter dominates. The stanzas are divided unevenly, the longest containing thirteen lines and the shortest containing one line. This irregular structure is appropriate for "Turning" when one considers that the poem is a criticism of the unemotional, objective vision that the poet now rejects in favor of listening to his emotional side that is striving to be released. A poem that was highly structured, following a strict rhyme and meter pattern, would betray the very purpose of what the poem is trying to say.

One structure that Rilke does use repeatedly in "Turning" is the present participle. Examples abound throughout the poem, including *knieend* (kneeling), *weidende* (grazing), and *ein Schauender* (one watching). This grammatical form has the same effect in German as it does in English; there is a sense of an ongoing process, a flowing movement both in sound and meaning. That this grammatical structure is used in German much less frequently than in English makes it all the more noticeable in the original. When reading the poem aloud, there is little that is musical or rhythmic due to its lack of rhyme and regular meter, but the present participle slows down the language and softens the proselike effect of the poem's message.

One device used frequently in "Turning" is personification (giving human characteristics to animals, inanimate objects, or abstract qualities). The objects that the poet has conquered through his gift of observation take on human characteristics or actions. The stars he mastered with his look "collapsed on their knees," the towers he stared at were "filled with terror," the landscape "sank to rest" in his calming observations, and the flowers "gazed back into him." During the difficult transition period in his art, the rooms he stays in during his wanderings also take on a personality. They are "distracted, alienated, . . . moody," and the very air in the rooms becomes filled with voices discussing his work and, finally, judging it and him to be without love—a judgment that will lead to a crisis and a turning point in his poetry.

Themes and Meanings

"Turning" is more than a poem; it is Rilke's self-critique of his work up to that time and a declaration or manifesto of how he intended to change his vision of poetry. It marks a new stage in his efforts to combine art and life. To understand the change he desired, one must first understand how Rilke saw the world through his writing. His perception revolved around the idea of *Schauen* (observation, seeing, watching), a skill he consciously cultivated that reflected his personal philosophical view of the world. This perspective developed out of his lifelong love of art.

The interest in pictures came early to Rilke, beginning in his childhood with a love of the visual arts. He later studied art history (among other subjects) at universities in Prague and Munich, traveled to Florence (a city rich in art) in order to develop precise observation skills, and, as a young man, lived in the artists' colony at Worpswede near Bremen, Germany. There he became involved with several artists, befriending the painter Paula Modersohn-Becker and marrying the sculptor Clara Westhoff, and developed his skill of observation. Later in Paris he also worked for the sculptor Auguste Rodin, about whom he wrote a monograph. For most of his life he was interested in and exposed to the visual arts and the theories and techniques of artists. He looked at poetry as a craft to be honed and polished.

This artist's vision is evident in the first part of "Turning" as the poet proudly lists his conquests of animals, buildings, nature, even the cosmos while bending the outer world to his will. Then he begins to doubt himself and his method. Rilke wrote that his "gazing outward" had "eaten him empty" and had no true relation with the outside world. He would have to turn completely away from his earlier convictions, which were cold and impersonal, and make "a devoted effort to achieve inner intensity." In the latter half of the poem, he acknowledges the limits of his method of observation and realizes he must begin on a new journey to find love and "do heart-work" on the images he sees. He has suffered through a crisis about himself and his poetry but has successfully turned to a new, inward-looking direction for his future work.

Shoshanah Dietz

28

Author: Philip Levine (1928-   )
Type of poem: Narrative
First published: 1986; collected in *A Walk with Tom Jefferson*, 1988

The Poem

Based on Philip Levine's own experiences when he traveled to California on a fellowship to study with the well-known poet and scholar Yvor Winters, "28" is a long narrative poem. In the opening line, the poet describes himself as twenty-eight years old and faithless, a statement that will be repeated throughout the poem. No exact meaning of faithless is given, forcing the reader to speculate about the poet's intention. He then describes driving across the country while under the almost hallucinatory influence of a fever, seeing birds appear, then vanish, along the roadside.

Time and place are fluid in the poem. Levine shifts back and forth between the present and various time periods in the past. After setting the reader off on the cross-country trip that took place twenty-eight years ago, Levine moves ahead in time to an unspecified period, when he was injured in a motorcycle accident when a station wagon accidentally forced him off California Highway 168 (Tollhouse Road). The description realistically conveys vivid, fragmentary details remembered from the accident: the children's open mouths, the long slide across the asphalt, the motorcycle tumbling away. A sense of mortality and death, which recurs throughout the poem, is first introduced here. This accident is an image that reappears several times, a warning of death. As the section ends, the poet returns to the present and describes how, even today, the scars on his arm return him to the awareness of life's fragility that he first experienced on Tollhouse Road.

The second section continues the trip, through Squaw Valley to the San Francisco area, where narrative details lead to further speculations on mortality. At the beginning of section 3, Levine again returns the reader to the present. It is a gray day in New England. The poet, looking out of his window, watches children outside; once again, his memories slip back to near death on the road. In the fourth section, Levine resumes the trip with his arrival in California and subsequent meeting with Arthur, who is introduced to the reader as he tends his garden, a place where he is "almost happy." (Arthur is the poet Yvor Winters who was Levine's teacher and mentor in California.)

The next two sections describe details of his life in California, recounting his relationship with Winters. He mentions that he is still faithless, not yet part of a family of five, not having received the lesson of the mountain road. The sixth section, which describes Arthur, is poignant. At fifty-six, Arthur sees the Nothingness that waits ahead and deals with it by reciting French Breton poetry.

The final section begins in April, when Levine is twenty-nine and traveling from place to place throughout California, then shifts to the present and the poet's house in New England. He realizes that he is the same person today as he was twenty-eight years ago. He watches the children outside, filled with poetic images of the past and present. He understands them no more now than he did at age twenty-eight; he doesn't know why the accident happened in the past or the why the small blond girl waves at him today.

Forms and Devices

The poem is told in the first person, and the details are clearly autobiographical. In fact, Levine has written a prose account of the same experiences that inspired "28" in an essay, "The Shadow of the Big Madrone." It has been collected in Levine's memoirs, *The Bread Of Time: Toward an Autobiography* (1994). This essay is extremely helpful in understanding the narrative details in "28"; in addition, it gives a glimpse into Levine's poetic process since he includes his first draft of the poem in the essay.

In "28," Levine combines strong, narrative details, which describe the people he meets and the places he travels, with lyrical, almost mystical, language used to describe nature and emotions. His descriptions of nature are rich with metaphor and simile. One evocative metaphor declares that the sea at Bondy Bay, which runs underneath his house in California, possesses the power to erase the "pain of nightmares." Levine begins section 3 with another vivid metaphor describing nature. The sun threatens to withdraw its affection, a bleak image with which the reader can easily identify. Levine, however, extends this image by adding narrative detail in an extended simile. The pale sky becomes "bored" like a "child in the wrong classroom"—or like a man of twenty-eight, who forgets the names of the trees he has been taught (a reference to another incident Levine mentions in "The Shadow of the Big Madrone"). The connection between nature and the poet's emotional state is clear.

Similar connections between autobiographical, narrative detail and poetic imagery describing emotional discoveries fill the poem. In one long sentence stretching over nine lines of poetry, Levine moves from a factual description of writing to his wife to a metaphor comparing the voice of American writer Kenneth Rexroth to the one God uses to lecture to Jesus Christ. He then switches metaphor and theme as he speculates about "the cold that leaps in one blind moment/ from the heart to the farthest shore." He is amazed that he ever believed allergy pills (or any of man's devices) could be proof against the mortality that comes to all nature, even creatures that he never knew existed. Such dazzling combinations of fact, imagery, and emotion keep the reader moving quickly through the varied times and places in the poem. In fact, these rapid shifts in subject, these unexpected mixtures, help to create the emotional power of the poem.

This emotional power is particularly noticeable in the portrait of Arthur/Winters. Levine recreates Winters's voice, ruined and graveled, for the reader. The garden, where he "was almost happy," is filled with "wounded tomatoes" and "elusive strawberries." Such details lead into the fact that the dying Winters is preparing for Nothingness, while reciting Breton poetry.

In his first books, Levine's poetry was formal and metric. He frequently employed a seven-syllable rhymed line. He later, however, experimented with the length of his line. The poem "28" is written in free verse using the natural rhythms of speech. He uses long poetic lines to bind images together, often creating complex pyramids of images.

Themes and Meanings

As Levine combines narrative and lyricism, he also combines themes, incorporating a number of motifs into the poem. It is impossible to ignore his richly detailed snapshots of American life. Levine has frequently been compared with nineteenth century American poet Walt Whitman for his democratic portrayal of working-class America. Indeed, Levine grew up in working-class Detroit and incorporates those experiences into much of his poetry. Like so many of his poems, "28" presents brief, vivid, instant flashes of Americana: towns such as East Palo Alto, home to "divorcees and appliance salesmen" and people such as the Okie Sunoco station attendant on Pacheco Pass.

Levine also intends the poem to be a tribute to Yvor Winters. In the introduction to his memoirs, Levine expresses his need to honor the memory of those persons who helped make him the writer and thinker he became. Clear, narrative details based on Levine's own experiences provide the vital emotional backdrop for "28." For Levine, these portraits are intimately tied with poem's main theme, the inexorable passage of time and the progression to Nothingness. The poem's title refers to Levine's age when he met Winters. Winters, twice that age, was dying. Now that Levine has reached fifty-six, the same age, he reexamines his life and relationship with both Winters and mortality. As the poem returns to Levine's youth, the reader is also shown Winters's preparations for death, the "final cold, a whiteness like no other."

A sense of mortality fills the poem in many other ways. Even before the reader is introduced to Winters, Levine introduces the subject of death. In the first section, when Levine describes his motorcycle accident, he prefaces it with the line, "I have died/ only twice." Death is a constant motif. The Sunoco station attendant warns him that an entire family had been killed on the road the day before. Nature, too, reflects this sense of inevitability. The sea creatures shudder from the cold that travels outward from the poet's heart; the black roses in his backyard are "battered, unclenched."

However, "28" is not a poem about hopelessness and tragedy. Death is seen as part of the natural progression of life. The last line describing Winters proclaims, "he was dying and he was ready." In contrast to Winters's preparations for death, the poet's third child is about to born. Life and death are both present. In the present, the poet, now fifty-six, watches children from his window. The poem ends with a joyous, graceful image as an eight-year-old blond girl waves to the poet before cartwheeling away. Levine no longer repeats the poem's opening line, "I am faithless." Family, relationships, and memories bring faith.

Mary E. Mahony

UNCONSCIOUS

Author: André Breton (1896-1966)
Type of poem: Narrative
First published: 1932, as "Sans connaissance," in *Le Revolver à cheveux blancs*;
   English translation collected in *Poems of André Breton*, 1982

The Poem

"Unconscious," a poem in free verse, consists of fifty-five lines. The title refers to that category of the mind outside conscious experience; the original French suggests both "unacquainted" and "unconsummated" as well. The poem is inexact in its subject matter: The poetic voice moves in and out of the poem with no consistent pattern, and changing points of reference, broken thoughts, and the absence of punctuation further complicate the reader's comprehension. Furthermore, it is unclear whether the protagonist of the poem is the narrator, although both reader and narrator share the experience as more than implicit observers. Such lack of clarity lends itself to the dreamlike atmosphere of the text.

The poem begins by reminding readers that the incident about to be described, whether real or imagined, has already occurred. The first ten lines establish a memory of an "odd attempted abduction" of a fourteen-year-old girl standing in an elevator. Line 3 begins the idealization of the girl ("Hey a star and yet it's still broad daylight") that continues throughout the poem. Lines 4-10 emphasize the early pubescence of the girl that entices the narrator. Her age is described as "Four more years than fingers," and her breasts, which the narrator imagines he sees bared, resemble "handkerchiefs drying on a rosebush." These images are important in establishing the virginal representation of the girl and are contrasted by the reminder that her parents are "firmly" beside her. Lines 11-14 tell of the location of the scene in Paris; it is a place the narrator says he remembers no matter where he is. Line 15 returns to the girl and her predicament. The elevator is stuck between floors. Lines 20-23 describes the array of images occupying the third-floor landing below: "light-colored boards the eel of a hand-rail" and blades of grass painted on the wall that resemble a man's clothing. In such a state, the girl "compares herself to a feathered jack-in-the-box." From line 24 onward, the narrator follows the girl's eyes, greener "than angelica green usually is," where they meet the eyes of a man, eyes that burn with the yellow flame of boron. Above the landing, he notes her calves under a fine dress from Paris. "That is enough," readers are told in line 28, "for these two creatures to understand each other."

Lines 28-48 provide a montage of images as the backdrop to a sexual encounter. The tentativeness of the situation is overcome as "excitement works wonders." Shadows move around them on the wall, the pendulum of a clock derails, thunderbolts flash from the street, and the girl smiles "between fear and pleasure," her heart skipping a beat like the first bud of spring exploding on a tree. With one word, readers are reminded in line 40, this dream can be undone. As in the poem's introduction, line 49 recalls the conclusion. A gunshot sounds and blood leaps down the stairs, but neither is quick enough to stop the assailant. He vanishes in the night, lighting a cigarette. The poem describes him as a handsome man, "Sweeter than the pain of loving and being loved."

Forms and Devices

"Unconscious" is a Surrealist poem. As a founder and primary theorist of this movement, André Breton typically created works recognized more for their exemplification of his notions of what art should be than for their intrinsic literary value. To the Surrealist, poetry is a way to access the unconscious mind with the goal of reuniting the conscious and unconscious realms of experience, the world of dreams and the world of reason, to create "absolute reality" or surreality. The Surrealist devices employed in the poem include the shocking juxtaposition of conflicting or contradictory images and the constant shifting of mood and color.

The strongest contradiction, perhaps, is that the poem takes place outside social norms as it describes a sexual encounter between a man and a fourteen-year-old girl. The dominant metaphor of "Unconscious," that of the elevator resting between the floors, physically draws the mind's eye of the reader to dichotomize the girl's predicament as the central theme. She is on her way up to the fourth-floor apartment of her parents, although in line 10 their presence seems more immediate: She exists between her father, "a post firmly set in the shadows," and the light of her mother. Below, on the third-floor landing, stands the protagonist. However, as the title indicates, this is not a poem in which conscious choices are made. Such tension, derived as much from the shock of the reader as from the text itself, is a Surrealist construction that deceives the reader into drawing a simple conclusion.

The sexual imagery that makes up the poem is bold and abundant. Line 25 tells the reader how the girl's "calves glisten, they are two dark birds that must be warmer and softer than all the others." The man's "boron" eyes burn with excitement. As line 31 focuses on "a parasol being shut," the phallic image of the closed parasol reveals itself. A rush of adrenalin is illustrated by shadows of charging horses and lightning bolts. In line 39, the girl's heart skips a beat as "the first bud" leaps from a chestnut tree. Allusions to nature abound in the poem: Line 15 refers to the girl as Euphorbia, a large genus of plants that includes several species used in food and medicine; the man's eyes burn like the chemical element boron; and the man's hand moves up her dress, which "rises" like a fuchsia. Although the scene transpires in an elevator, the "two creatures" join in a hut during a tropical storm where "excitement works wonders." This device serves to temper the shock to the reader's sensibilities in an effort to convince the reader that the scene is, in fact, quite natural while at the same time reinforcing the notion that what is taking place is, at its core, sexual. However, readers should not be misled: The primary device remains bound to the title. As the poem mixes and matches these images, they are only natural in combination outside the realm of what is rational.

Themes and Meanings

The main theme of "Unconscious" is the awakening of one's sexuality as a vehicle for exploration of the unconscious mind. In approaching the place where the world of dreams and reality meet, the poem reflects the process as well. This overriding quest of Surrealism reveals a debt to Austrian psychoanalyst Sigmund Freud, who defines the characteristics of unconscious processes to include timelessness, an exemption from mutual contradiction, and the replacement of external reality by psychical reality; all these elements are present in the poem.

Read carefully, this is not a poem about a young girl's sexual awakening but of a man's fantasy of awakening a young girl's sexuality. The girl is an object. Stranded in the elevator, dangling between floors, she is a helpless little bird, a "feathered jack-in-the-box." When the two finally join, line 29 explains the experience as something not only natural and exotic but also deriving from a primal collective unconscious. The experience is surreal not because it takes place outside what is rational but because it does not take place at all. Against a backdrop of rationality, from the "abduction" to the man's getaway, the poem shocks the reader with a rape fantasy. However, the scene occurs in that part of the mind where rationality is displaced by the dream, a key to understanding the process.

One of the most telling references in the poem occurs when the narrator calls the girl Euphorbia. At one time, several species of Euphorbia had medicinal value as a laxative or a vomit-inducing agent. The automatic processes such as free association employed by the Surrealists in an effort to unlock the unconscious mind are akin to a mental regurgitation. Normal poetic conventions such as meter and rhyme only constrain the poet to rational modes; the Surrealist forsakes such conventions to allow what lies deeper in the mind to flow unfettered just as the presence of the girl, Euphorbia, induces the overflow of primal sexuality. Thus the opening line, "One has not forgotten," refers not to something real that has happened but to what, for the poet, continues to happen in the unconscious mind. What this means is not clear. For the Surrealist, says one critic, there is no message, only an invitation to explore the possibilities. Enigmatic as this is, it assists the reader in understanding the distance between normal poetic conventions and Breton's poem in which contradiction and the absurd stand on equal ground with reality.

Steven Clotzman

UPON NOTHING

Author: John Wilmot, Earl of Rochester (1647-1680)
Type of poem: Satire
First published: 1679; collected in *Poems on Several Occasions*, 1680

The Poem

"Upon Nothing" has always been regarded as one of the earl of Rochester's most important poems. Samuel Johnson called it "the strongest effort of his Muse." In seventeen short stanzas, it moves from philosophical satire on the vanity of human attempts to comprehend the meaning of existence to social satire on particular human pretensions to importance. In the end, Rochester implies, nothing means anything, because in the end, as in the beginning, there is only Nothing.

The first seven stanzas offer a brief, difficult account of the process by which the known universe of things came into existence. "Nothing," the primeval reality, is established as a character. Rochester presents three similar, but not identical, descriptions of the emergence of Something: Nothing "begets" Something (stanza 2), Something is "severed" from Nothing (stanza 3); Matter is the "offspring" of Nothing (stanza 5). Stanza 4 focuses on the moment when abstract Something particularizes itself into individual created things: "Men, Beasts, birds, fire, water, Ayre, and land." However, as stanza 3 had asserted, all particular things, like their abstract source Something, are only a temporary aberration in the universe. All must inevitably fall back into their source, "boundless" Nothing. Stanzas 5 through 7 describe the creation process in terms of political revolt undertaken by a new set of philosophical abstractions. Matter, Form, Time, Place, and Body form a conspiracy of existing things united in opposition to Nothing. Then one of the allies—Time—turns against his fellow conspirators. Things require time to exist, but Time also relentlessly measures their progress into disintegration. In the end, all things dissolve back into Nothing's "hungry wombe."

The middle stanzas of the poem (8 to 12) "move" from abstract philosophical satire to the personal, social satire that ends the poem. In these middle stanzas Rochester directs his attack upon three types of pretentious thinker: the theologian ("the Divine"), the philosopher ("the wise"), and "the Politician." These are precisely the individuals who hold themselves to be the knowing intermediaries between high abstract truth and ordinary minds. The latter—"Laick Eyes"—remain happily ignorant of the envelope of Nothing that surrounds their existence. The theologian pretends to superior knowledge—which is, Rochester implies, really a knowledge of Nothing. Nothing is the reward of both good and evil; as a result, the virtuous may expect the small consolation of not being punished ("Nothing" will be taken away from them), while the wicked, who might expect punishment, may rejoice at receiving the identical fate. In stanza 10, Rochester turns to philosophers, mocking their methods and terms: "Enquire, define, distinguish, teach, devise"). Nothing, which is the ultimate answer to all questions, repudiates all analyses. Finally, when the most pragmatic of thinkers, the politicians, attempt to apply high-minded philosophy ("Is or is not . . ./ And true or false") to practical matters, they too are frustrated. The "least unsafe and best" solution to these philosophical questions seems to be a nihilistic belief in Nothing.

In the final five stanzas of the poem, Rochester moves to a more familiar Restoration satire of social types. Having established Nothing as a positive character, he can wittily describe the king's counselors as fit for "nothing." Moreover, he notes that "Something" (gold, although he does not use the word) is absent from the king's treasury. (Charles II's exchequer was often in an embarrassing state, and "Upon Nothing" was probably written at the time of a 1672 declaration of bankruptcy.)

England's "Statesmen" also lack "Something"—intelligence. Stanzas 15 and 16 extend the satire beyond the center of the realm to include the categories already touched upon and to expand beyond England. Bishops ("Lawn-sleeves"), noblemen, scholars, and judges ("ffurrs and Gowns") are full of pompous Nothing. The prides of the French, Dutch, British, Irish, Scots, Spaniards, and Danes prove equally vacant. Rochester concludes by leveling three more items, the gratitude of a great man, the promises of a king, and the vows of a whore: All are equally empty. In making the whore his ultimate instance of nothingness, Rochester emphasizes his contempt for all attempts to inflate the importance and the permanence of human achievement.

Forms and Devices

"Upon Nothing" is a panegyric that celebrates the universal significance of nothing. It is composed as an apostrophe, with Rochester addressing the personified abstraction, "Nothing." The character of Nothing is, however, ambiguous; its sex, for example, is uncertain. In stanza 1, it is a "brother" who "begets," but in stanza 7 it has become a mother with a "hungry wombe." The confusion here, like that caused by the three slightly differently phrased accounts of creation in the first seven stanzas, may constitute a deliberate parody of what Rochester saw as the fatal inconsistencies in the biblical account of creation.

There is a paradoxical aspect to the phrase "hungry wombe"; wombs should produce, not consume. Paradoxes abound in the poem. "Fruitfull Emptinesses" (stanza 4) is, in effect, an inversion of "hungry wombe." In another paradox, "Rebell-Light" does not enlighten but rather "obscures" (covers over, darkens) the dark face of Nothing. The phrase "Rebell-Light" also recalls the two most common names of the devil in the Christian tradition: Satan (adversary) and Lucifer (light-bearer). Rochester's satanic Lucifer, however, is the enemy not of the Creator but of uncreative Nothing.

The end of the poem is openly paradoxical, as Rochester ironically praises the empty knowledge of philosophers, the empty treasury of the king, the empty veracity of the French, the empty courage of the Dutch, and the empty content of the king's word. This avalanche of particular paradoxes is rooted in the core paradox of the poem, the idea that "Nothing" is a thing that may act and which may be addressed.

Rochester develops two principal patterns of imagery in the first half of the poem as he narrates the actions of his personified abstractions. The first is the imagery of sexual generation, beginning with the metaphor of Nothing "begetting" Something and a probable obscene pun on "what" (punning with "twat") in stanza 2. It continues with references to Nothing's "offspring," "embrace," and "wombe." The introduction of "Rebell-Light" in stanza 5 begins a pattern of references to politics and revolt: Nothing's "foes" join in "Leagues"; Time is a traitor whom Nothing bribes into betraying his allies back into Nothing.

"Upon Nothing" is composed in rhymed triplets, a relatively rare form in a period when the heroic couplet had established itself as the standard for poetry. Scholars have pointed to the verse letters of John Donne and the *Divine Emblemes* of Francis Quarles as possible sources. Lines 1 and 2 of each stanza are iambic pentameter; with the exception of stanzas 4 and 14, the third line is an Alexandrine (iambic hexameter). The additional syllables of the concluding line emphasize Rochester's use of the stanza as an end-stopped unit of thought.

Themes and Meanings

"Upon Nothing" has been described as one of the most nihilistic poems in English literature. It may well be; it seems to assert that nothing matters because Nothing is the alpha and the omega of the universe. Yet it also illustrates an inescapable paradox of nihilistic art: Is not a work of art in itself an assertion that something—art—does matter? Is not Rochester's intellectual and linguistic cleverness an assertion of some aesthetic value? And does not his disparagement of the illusions promoted by theologians, politicians, the French, the Dutch, and others necessarily imply an assertion of some moral standard?

"Nothing" figures both positively and negatively in the poem. On one hand, "Nothing" acts like a thing: It is "a being"; it can beget and embrace and bribe; it can be described as a "brother" or a "self"; it has a face, a bosom, hands, and a womb. On the other hand, "Nothing" is the absence of all things: It is the formless, substanceless vacuum from which, according to Judeo-Christian tradition, God created the universe. Rochester conspicuously omits God from his account of the creation of the world and of its eventual dissolution. No providential deity plans the lives of humans or the fate of the universe. Creation and destruction are equally self-generated; the first is spontaneous, and the second is inevitable. Rochester deliberately rejects the pieties of his age. Most specifically, he mocks the pious poems "Hymn to Light" and *Davideis* by his celebrated contemporary, Abraham Cowley. Until his own conversion to Christianity prior to his early death, Rochester was strongly influenced by the atheistic, materialistic philosophy of Thomas Hobbes.

There is a sharpness to the last lines that is characteristic of Rochester's satire. His reduction of the great man's gratitude, the king's promises, and the whore's vows to equal emptiness is a pointed gesture. The circle of aristocratic wits to whom he circulated the poem—none of Rochester's verse was published by him—might comfortably share his jibes at the delusions of the self-righteous metaphysicians, but even they, as "Great men" themselves, should have been pricked by the sting of these last lines.

J. K. Van Dover

V-LETTER AND OTHER POEMS

Author: Karl Shapiro (1913-   )
Type of work: Book of poems
First published: 1944

The Poems

V-Letter and Other Poems is Karl Shapiro's second major collection of poetry, written from 1942 to 1944 while Shapiro was on active duty in the U.S. Army during World War II. As Shapiro notes in the book's introduction, all the poems except "Satire: Anxiety" were written while he was stationed in Australia and New Zealand. As described in his 1988 autobiography *The Younger Son*, he left the selection, editing, and arrangement of *V-Letter and Other Poems* to his first wife Evalyn Katz because the rigors of serving as a combat medic prohibited much involvement with the actual making of a book. While one might suspect that the war would most definitely shape the poetry, Shapiro states that he guarded "against becoming a 'war poet.'" Shapiro remarks that he had not "written these poems to accord with any doctrine or system of thought or even a theory of composition." Furthermore, he states, "I have nothing to offer in the way of beliefs or challenges or prosody."

Despite Shapiro's modest self-effacement, *V-Letter and Other Poems* established him as one of the most important American poets, prosodists, and poetry critics of postwar American literature. He may have been isolated in the small, war-torn terrain of New Guinea for twenty-six months writing his poetry in his more than occasional lonely solitude, but when he returned to the United States after the war he discovered he was famous. *V-Letter and Other Poems* not only won the Pulitzer Prize in poetry, but it also enjoyed a large readership (including being placed on all U.S. Navy ship libraries), and it launched for Shapiro a long, distinguished career in American letters. Ultimately, the book's publication led Shapiro to become the first poetry consultant to the Library of Congress (the position is now titled United States Poet Laureate), the editor of the prestigious *Poetry* magazine, and a tenured professor at the University of Nebraska at Lincoln, where he edited the literary journal *Prairie Schooner*. Thus, Shapiro did indeed have something of value to offer.

Much of Shapiro's poetry, including the lyrics found in *V-Letter and Other Poems,* tends to cast the poet as an outsider, an iconoclast. As Shapiro once noted in an interview in *The Paris Review,* "The poet is in exile whether he is or he is not. Because of what everybody knows about society's idea of the artist as a peripheral character and a potential bum. Or a troublemaker. . . . I always thought of myself as being both in and out of society at the same time." While *V-Letter and Other Poems* seems to exhibit a poet who embraces the conformity of traditional forms and prosody, the nonconformist vision is certainly most evident. One will notice, for example, that the poet seems more like a voyeur than a participant despite his actual involvement in the war as a medic. Yet this detachment may have arisen largely from his Jewish heritage: He was a conscientious objector and did not carry a gun; therefore, he observed the violence of war firsthand and assisted in rescuing wounded participants, but he did not himself participate in the making of violence. Thus, his poems very often place him outside the scene looking in while the violent world is dropping shells all around him. Additionally, his use of traditional forms and meter might suggest his conformity to past designs; however, close scrutiny of the work reveals Shapiro's innovative departures from poetic tradition. For example, the lead poem of *V-Letter and Other Poems*, "Aside," is a long lyric poem of six sexains or sestets (six-line stanzas). As Shapiro himself notes in his *Prosody Handbook* (1965), "the stave of six is an iambic pentameter or tetrameter stanza rhyming *ababcc*." However, rather than specifically employing the English stanzaic conventions, Shapiro embellishes. He recasts the stanza's first four lines into a brace or envelope quatrain rhyming *abba*, which is then followed by the rhyming couplet. Interestingly, the brace quatrain is rarely found except in the writing of the Italian sonnet octave. Thus, the iconoclastic poet is simultaneously adhering to and departing from tradition.

In "Aside," Shapiro, as an observer, focuses upon the significance of mail day to soldiers who face combat on a daily basis. The poem is not merely a celebration of mail day but an illustration of how mail day is an occasion for renewal as if the soldiers had stumbled upon an oasis. The "war stands aside for an hour"; as a result, "demo-bilized for a moment, a world is made human." Peace is renewed in the souls of the men despite the fact the battle rages elsewhere. For the moment, they will "Say no more of the dead than a prayer" because "there is nothing alive / Except as [mail day] keeps [them] alive, not tomorrow but now." His detachment from the scene allows readers to more thoroughly enter the scene, to know more immediately what it is to still breathe despite the fact that death has been near and will yet be near.

Much of what holds *V-Letter and Other Poems* together is the way Shapiro focuses not so much on the war itself as on what it is that keeps the men alive. While this is surely a thematic concern, it is also consistent with the lyric quality of the collection. Shapiro neither praises war nor casts aspersion toward it. He does not idealize the heroes or make them romantic and, consequently, unreal. When Shapiro utilizes the heroic quatrain (four lines rhyming *abab*), he does so not to invoke the hero of old but to denigrate the nonheroes of his and the soldiers' world. For example, Shapiro prefaces the ballad "The Intellectual" with the line "What should the wars do with these jigging fools?" Clearly, "The man behind the book may not be man,/ His own man or the book's or yet the time's." The intellectual is Shapiro's nonhero. On the other hand, the poet advocates the man, the soldier, or the artist who will "Do something! die in Spain or paint a green/ Gouache." He says, furthermore, that he would "rather be a barber and cut hair/ Than walk with [the intellectual] in gilt museum halls." If the intellectual is Shapiro's nonhero, the detestable man, then clearly his heroes are the outcasts as shown in the poems "Jew" and "Nigger." In the former example, the Jew is one of the world's active people, though despised and destined to die: "The name is immortal but only the name// Our name is impaled in the heart of the world on a hill/ Where we suffer to die by the hands of ourselves, and to kill." The poem "Nigger," on the other hand, explores the prejudices endured by black men, who are admirable in comparison to the intellectual. This particular poem is filled with active verbs, elevating its character above those who do nothing:

> When you boxed that hun, when you raped that trash that you didn't rape,
> When you caught that slug with a belly of fire and a face of gray,
> When you felt that loop and you took that boot from a KKK,
> Are you coming to peace, O Booker T. Lincoln Roosevelt of grape?

Not only does Shapiro show readers the injustice of a prejudicial world in which the black man is punished for crimes he did not commit, in which he has had to fight battles he did not start, but the poet also shows how black men have been killed by the South's cultural politics. What is a black man's peace, perhaps, but death? Even then, however, Shapiro questions peace in death: "Did the Lord say yes, did the Lord say no, did you ask the Lord/ When the jaw came down, when the cotton blossomed out of your bones?"

Readers may wonder why poems such as "Jew" and "Nigger" are included in a collection composed during and written about World War II. Likely, Shapiro intends for readers to see that all soldiers are "Jews" and "niggers." Soldiers are immortal in name only; in "bondage of murder and shame" ("Jew"), they die and fight upon the hills, bringing to mind the famous portrait of the Marines at Iwo Jima. Soldiers catch slugs fired from the gray, ambiguous politics that find wars necessary; they feel the noose about their necks and hope that Jesus will "cut that cord" ("Nigger"). If this is the case, these poems stand as allegories for the soldier's condition and perhaps the reader's as well. If Shapiro's heroes are people such as barbers ("The Intellectual"), if they "do something," are people not, in the majority, "soldiers," "Jews," and "niggers" too?

Granted, darkness frequents Shapiro's lyrics; yet his poems are not mournful songs as one might suspect when reading a volume about war. They are songs that breathe with the experience and significance of the war itself. Take, for example, "Troop Train," a long lyric of five octaves (eight-line stanzas) written in either a nonrhyming or coincidental rhyming pattern. The soldiers are "clustered" on themselves and "hang as from a cornucopia/ In total friendliness." The image is one of the horn of plenty, a celebration of life's sustenance, a Thanksgiving scene. While this image creates situational irony (how can troops, gathered together, perhaps traveling toward death, sustain life or be thankful?), the effect is understood. They are thankful to be alive, if only currently, and thankful for the closeness when, once the soldiers arrive at the battle, they must ultimately face death alone: "Luck also travels and not all come back." Yet while the trains lead "the march to death," they may also lead to "that survival which is all our hope."

Perhaps one of the most engaging and horrific pieces in the collection is "The Gun." The poem personifies the soldier's gun: "You were angry and manly to shatter the sleep of your throat." In this poem, comprising five brace or envelope quatrains, the reader discovers an image of the close relationship, almost worshipful, the soldier has with his gun. "I savour your breath like a perfume," the poet writes; "I grip you";

"Come with me"; "You are only the means of the practical humor of death/ Which is savage to punish the dead for the sake of my sin!" Interestingly, the words chosen almost suggest a sexual bond between the soldier and his gun; if the gun "comes" with the man, both have experienced the simultaneous orgasm of fear and courage, life and death. The soldier persona, who does not wish to place the blame of violence upon the gun, says, "I absolve from your name/ The exaction of murder, my gun. It is I who have killed." Significantly, Shapiro recognizes the human, passionate aspect of warfare and, furthermore, how the soldier clings to the "god" or lover that might save him.

Forms and Devices

Shapiro is a master of poetic form and devices. Much of his professional career was dedicated to studies of poetics and prosody, as found most impressively in *A Prosody Handbook*. In *V-Letter and Other Poems*, Shapiro's ability to manipulate form and reinvent it is unmistakable. His favorite form in this particular volume seems to be the terza rima, as found in "Movie Actress," "Jew," and the sequence "The Interlude." The terza rima is an Italian form composed of interlocking tercets, or three-line stanzas, ending with a couplet. For example, the rhyme pattern for Shapiro's poems is *aba bcb cdc ded gg*. An antique form, it was introduced into English poetry from Dante Alighieri's *La Divina Commedia* (c. 1320; *The Divine Comedy*). Perhaps Shapiro's use of this form is a matter of "form as an extension of content," a design suggested by American poet Robert Creeley. If Shapiro borrows this form from *The Divine Comedy*, he may be suggesting the divine comedy of the war itself.

Not only does Shapiro utilize the terza rima in *V-Letter and Other Poems*, but he also uses the Italian sonnet form frequently, as in "The Sydney Bridge," "Christmas Eve," "Lord, I Have Seen Too Much," and "On Reading Keats in War Time." An Italian sonnet is composed of an octave (eight-line stanza) and a sestet or sexain (six-line stanza). Typically, the Italian sonnet's rhyme pattern runs *abbaabba cdcdcd*. Shapiro, however, makes many adjustments to this basic pattern, sometimes opting to fashion other rhyme combinations. Among other forms are rhymed or unrhymed quatrain or ballad stanzas ("New Guinea," "Sunday: New Guinea," "Fireworks," "Nigger," "Franklin"), sexain stanzas ("Aside," "Red Indian," "The Synagogue"), and cinquain or five-line stanzas ("Jefferson"). Of particular interest, however, is the ambitious form of Shapiro's ottava rima variations ("Piano" and "Christmas Tree"). The ottava rima is a very difficult poem to write, following a standard rhyme pattern of *abababcc*. Shapiro, however, modernizes the form by displacing the couplet from its final position and embedding it elsewhere. The rhyme pattern of "Piano," for example, is *ababccab*. What Shapiro gains from reinventing the form is displacement of the expected, which is metaphorically equivalent to the displacement of those soldiers from their other lives. In "Piano," the music of both the piano and the poetic form allows the soldiers to "Escape, escape, escape."

Among the more playful forms Shapiro handles expertly is the ballade, as found in "Ballade of the Second-Best Bed." According to Shapiro's *A Prosody Handbook*, the ballade is a "Gallic importation" consisting of "three stanzas and a four-line envoy (a kind of conclusion or dedicatory stanza). The ballade uses three rhymes, and each stanza uses the same rhyme sounds; the scheme is *ababbcbc*. The last line of the first stanza is used as the last line of the other two stanzas and of the envoy." The overall effect is whimsical; so much repetition of sound renders even the most serious of topics humorous. In Shapiro's ballade, the persona, English playwright William Shakespeare, is giving orders for his will. "Good wife," Shakespeare says, "bad fortune is to blame/ That I bequeath when I am dead,/ To you my honor and my name,/ A table, a chair, and the second-best bed." Its place in *V-Letter and Other Poems* is clever and, once the riddle is solved, unmistakable: Just as Shakespeare must prepare his last will, so must a soldier. Furthermore, in reality a soldier's wife is left with as little as Shakespeare's wife; thus, one might as well find humor in the poverty of living. One additional note about "Ballade of the Second-Best Bed" is merited: Shapiro does not ever mention, among the items of Shakespeare's will, a "best bed"; ironically, the best bed is doubtless the grave because it is there that all battles stop.

This discussion about Shapiro's use of poetic form should in no way minimize his other abilities as a poet. He is a master of English metrics, he has a clear eye for imagery, he understands the subtleties of rhythm, and he constructs metaphors that are both startling and exhilarating. As Shapiro once stated in a seminar in creative writing at the University of Nebraska at Lincoln, every poem ought to have an "alligator," something unusual in it that will bite and hold the reader. Shapiro does this without exception in the whole of his work.

Themes and Meanings

V-Letter and Other Poems is a collection of poems about war, written in a time of war by a mind occupied by the effects of war upon his real-people heroes. However, Shapiro's collection neither celebrates war nor condemns it; it is not a patriotic call to arms, and it is not a protest against violence as is so often found in Vietnam War-era poetry. Rather, *V-Letter and Other Poems* examines the human dimension of warfare, from the brotherhood of "Troop Train" and the realization that any one of those friends playing cards may be traveling toward death to the love poem "V-Letter," which clings hopefully and furiously to the security of love.

Perhaps love is a primary theme of *V-Letter and Other Poems*. While the poet may not necessarily love the war, he loves the human aspect of the war: the human isolation, the human discovery of unusual and unnatural relationships ("The Gun"), the human need for pragmatic heroes, the human stage of the movie house and of locale, and the human dignity despite the indignity of death. Shapiro's purpose is to embrace his world and the life in it despite the destruction raining down upon him and his comrades. It also seems to be his desire to use his poems to write home about the war experience. Historically, the "v-letter" was a correspondence mailed home from the front, read and censored by military personnel before being sent to the United States. The actual, graphic details of war never made it across the ocean, locations were never specified, and secrets were kept secret. However, through Shapiro's metaphors and language, his poetic "v-letters," he tells readers more about war and the human position in war than the most realistic account. The war is a mood, a tone, a shadow settled in people's souls. It is a dark humor and a deep, lasting love. In "V-Letter" he writes, "I pray nothing for my safety back,/ Not even luck, because our love is whole/ Whether I live or fail." This is Shapiro's "v-letter" to all of humanity.

Mark Sanders

VENDÉMIAIRE

Author: Guillaume Apollinaire (Guillaume Albert Wladimir Alexandre Apollinaire de Kostrowitzky, 1880-1918)
Type of poem: Meditation
First published: 1912; collected in *Alcools*, 1913; English translation collected in *Alcools*, 1964

The Poem

Guillaume Apollinaire's poem "Vendémiaire" takes as its title the name of the first month of the new calendar adopted in the wake of the French Revolution. This month, corresponding to September 22 to October 21, was named for the grape harvest (*la vendange* in French, as opposed to *la moisson*, for harvest in general). Thus themes of wine, drinking, and even drunkenness permeate the poem along with the gathering in of the harvest.

"Vendémiaire," the last poem in Apollinaire's collection *Alcools* (alcohols), parallels the opening poem "Zone" and continues the street scenes of Paris that recur throughout the collection. "Zone" began with an image of the Eiffel Tower as a shepherdess of the bleating flock of Parisian bridges. In contrast to the sights of Paris that dominate the earlier poem, Apollinaire turns in "Vendémiaire" to a general evocation of Paris that emphasizes the sounds of voices.

The opening quatrain focuses on the poet himself rather than his surroundings. Apollinaire situates his life "à l'époque où finissaient les rois," at the time when the new calendar of the revolution had replaced the time of the monarchy. In accord with the title, he walks through Paris in late September, where, during nights filled with grapevines, he awaits "the harvest of the dawn." The harvest, however, will be composed not of grapes but of song. One night, he hears Paris sing: "I am thirsty for the cities of France, of Europe and of the world." This thirst of Paris, which all other cities attempt to satisfy, affirms the dominant position of the capital both within France and in the world beyond.

To this initial voice, seven others reply, as other cities respond to Paris. The first to answer are three cities from Brittany—Rennes, Quimper, and Vannes. This choice underlines the identity of this harvest as something other than the literal production of wine. Brittany is the part of France least capable of producing wine, but this maritime climate produces "reason" and "mystery" that satisfy an intellectual thirst.

The next three voices, those of northern cities, Lyon, and southern cities, reply from within France to pay homage to Paris. The industrial north offers the song of its "holy factories," while Lyon and the south make more emotional contributions. Then from outside France come voices from Sicily, Rome, and Koblenz. The song of Sicily draws on pagan mythology, invoking the danger of antiquity with references to Ixion, who earned the wrath of Zeus, and to the sirens tempting sailors to their doom. This threat is in the past, but that of Rome extends to the present, as Rome with its "imperious voice" seems to challenge Paris. Still, the pope's triple crown falls to the floor, allowing Rome to be exploited by enemies. Finally from Koblenz comes only prayerful silence. As the night ends, Apollinaire sees himself as the "gullet of Paris," drinking in the knowledge imparted by the songs that have come from the rest of the world.

Forms and Devices

Several elements place "Vendémiaire" at the beginning of modern poetry. Many of its lines retain the twelve syllables of the classical French Alexandrine form, but some are cut shorter. Many couplets rhyme, but other lines are unrhymed. Also, this was the first poem Apollinaire published without punctuation, a form he continued in his later, freer verse. In keeping with this advent of modern style, the opening section of the poem contains echoes of Charles Baudelaire, who developed a use of imagery that would become modern Symbolism. In his prefatory poem to *Les Fleurs du Mal* (1857; *Flowers of Evil*, 1931), Baudelaire describes a descent into hell, where he sees "Satan Trismégiste." Apollinaire uses the same adjective to describe the "three-times-power-ful" kings who were nonetheless dying.

The poet, according to Baudelaire, descends into the sinful temptations of the world seeking the inspiration that will form his poetry, the evil from which he will derive poetic flowers. Central to this experience is drunkenness. Here Baudelaire was continuing a definition established by the Romantic poets, for whom *ivresse* was not mere physical intoxication but any intense experience, physical or emotional, that led to a form of enlightenment.

Apollinaire uses multiple references to this concept as he describes Paris "at the end of September" (the autumnal season Baudelaire also favored) as a place where vines "spread their light over the city," while overhead "drunken birds" peck at the "ripe stars." Baudelaire had also used the flight of the bird as emblem of the inspiration of the poet and described the birds in flight as being drunk. Apollinaire, however, makes these images especially suggestive of poetic productivity because of the light pro-duced and the ripeness of the stars, which parallels that of the grapes.

The wine produced by the harvest of "Vendémiaire" makes the poet drunk with his own inspiration. Thus the birds are "de ma gloire," the talent through which the poet knows that by morning he will reap the harvest of poetic insight. If physical intoxica-tion produces hallucinations, it follows logically that Apollinaire hears voices. The poet's gift, however, calls forth both insightful utterances and voices that "sing" in the sense of providing the material of poetry.

The imagery of grapes and harvest frames the poem. At the end, Apollinaire returns to the concept that he has "drunk the whole universe." The various voices use other images, many of which again recall motifs of Baudelaire's poetry. The cities of the north especially, with their metallic imagery of factories, echo Baudelaire's substitu-tion of urban scenes for rural imagery in lyric poetry. The mythological theme of Ixion, repeated by the northern cities and by Sicily, parallels a similar use of repeated figures in Baudelaire's "Le Voyage" ("The Voyage"), in which the mythological characters, such as Ixion, represent mistaken choices.

Themes and Meanings

A strong religious theme joins the imagery of wine throughout the poem, drawing on the role of wine as the blood of Christ in Communion. The power of religion places the poet in an ambiguous role, for while as a visionary he dominates his world, he must also recognize the superiority of the divine.

Again the poem is divided between the enclosure segments where, with the dominant wine imagery there are references to the poet's authority, and the voices of the cities that advance religious themes. In the opening line Apollinaire addresses "men of the future" who should remember him. The theme of his own poetic immortality continues in Apollinaire's later poetry written on the battlefields of World War I. In the 1917 poem "Merveille de la Guerre" ("Marvel of War"), for example, he leaves his own story as a "legacy to the future" and continues the universal perception he claims in "Vendémiaire," saying that he "was at war but knew how to be everywhere." The poet's vision allowed him to escape the harsh context of battle.

Explicit religious imagery arrives with the songs of the various cities. Though all seem to give a form of tribute to centrally located Paris, they simultaneously lay claim to forms of transcendent power. The towns of Brittany establish the religious theme with the image of hands forming steeples and then refer repeatedly to mystery, culminating in that of "another life," the afterlife that no man can know.

The industries of the northern cities and of Lyon are described as "holy," with "angels" at Lyon weaving the cloth for which the city was famous. The question of religious authority returns, however, in the voices of the southern cities and of Sicily, which resolve the dualism of dominance and submission. The southern cities say that Paris and the Mediterranean should "share our bodies, as one breaks communion wafers." Clearly, with the example of Christ, it is possible for the victim of a sacrifice to retain a dominant position. Similarly, Rome asserts its power through its "vin par deux fois millénaire," which shares the age of the sacrament established by Christ but must also witness the fall of the pope's triple crown.

The end of the poem reasserts the power of the poet. Because he has drunk all the elements of the universe, he has gained universal knowledge. In his confidence in his poetic role, Apollinaire sets aside the biblical prohibition that men must not aspire to the knowledge of good and evil. As he urges future generations to "listen to my songs of universal drunkenness," he affirms his role in transmitting a divine message. The sun rises on a new day as the poet emerges from his night of visions with a new truth.

Dorothy M. Betz

VERSES ON THE DEATH OF T. S. ELIOT

Author: Joseph Brodsky (1940-1996)
Type of poem: Elegy
First published: 1970, as "Stikhi na smert' T. S. Eliota," in *Ostanovka v pustyne*;
English translation collected in *Selected Poems*, 1973

The Poem

"Verses on the Death of T. S. Eliot" is a poem in three parts modeled on W. H. Auden's 1939 elegy "In Memory of W. B. Yeats." The classic elegy of Western tradition is a meditation on death, be it the death of a particular person or death as the inevitable end of all things mortal. At the same time, it "finds consolation in the contemplation of some permanent principle" (*Princeton Encyclopedia of Poetry and Poetics*, 1974). Brodsky's elegy, like Auden's, mourns the death of a poet; unlike Auden's, it takes considerable comfort—even exults—in the power of memory and poetry.

Thomas Stearns Eliot, American expatriate and British subject, died in England on January 4, 1965. Joseph Brodsky, Soviet citizen in exile in Russia's far north, learned of the elder poet's death a week or so after the fact. Part 1 begins with the flat statement of when and where Eliot died: "at the start of the year, in January" in a city of streetlights, entryways, intersections, and doors inhabited by darkness, cold, and snow. The city seems concrete enough, a real and practical place haunted by eternal but practical concerns. The question of inheritance is raised, but, in a shift to another plane, Eliot's heirs are the Muses, who can hardly complain that he has left them bankrupt. Poetry may be orphaned, "yet it breeds within the glass/ of lonely days," echoing like Narcissus's lovesick nymph and visible in the rhythm of time and the "rhyme of years." Death takes the singer, not the song; it has no need for the fields or seas or well-wrought lines in a poem. Eliot the Anglican convert may have managed to live through Christmas into the beginning of the new year, but the new year itself marks the end of the old year and its holiday; the calendar rhythm of the year, like the rhythm of ocean waves, bears him away from his own high holiday. Time and tides rather than God pull him out to sea, leaving the rest of humanity on dry land.

Part 2 continues in the same meter and on the same vast scale of seas and continents. However, the realistic cityscape is replaced by a funeral tableau, a scene straight from a Greek or Roman bas-relief. Magi, prophets and priests of antiquity, are called in to hold the halo while two mournful female figures stand downcast on either side of the grave (that is, the ocean). They are America, where Eliot's life began, and England, where it ended (in Russian, *Amerika* and *Anglia*, both feminine nouns). The final line of part 2 is a single sentence set apart that acts as a conclusion: "But each grave is the limit of the earth." Part 3 shifts meter and rhyme scheme. The poet invokes the god Apollo to cast down his own wreath at Eliot's feet as a marker of immortality in the mortal realm. The footsteps and songs will be remembered by the trees and the land, by wind, by every sheaf of grain. What he has left behind will be felt, invisibly but tangibly, in the same way that love is felt after the loved one disappears forever. Just as the body recalls touch, memory recalls words.

Forms and Devices

Brodsky's initial and most obvious device is his choice of models: Auden's poem on the death of Yeats. The poem is not a narrative, so the three parts are not chapters forming a beginning, middle, and end. Instead, they vary in formal structure and in tone, changing the stance of the person looking at this poet's life and work. While Auden eschews rhyme and strict meter in the first two parts, Brodsky observes them. (The English translation, though more regular in meter than Auden's poem, is not as traditional in form as Brodsky's original version.) The formal likeness is greatest in part 3, in which the meter (trochaic tetrameter), regular rhyme scheme (*abab*), choice of stanza (quatrain), and use of repetition give the whole section both regular movement and finality.

Yet Brodsky's poem is not an imitation; rather, it uses Auden's reflection on a poet's life, death, and art as a framework for a different sort of monument. For example, Auden's three parts reflect stages in Yeats's poetry, last to first: realistic, sober, and urban in his last years; ironic and emotional in the middle; Romantic, balladic, and folkloric in the beginning. Brodsky uses his divisions differently; they mark not progression but a shift in angle of vision that is linguistically expressed as style. Connecting links are arranged not in time but in space, using imagery often found in Eliot's own work: bleak cities, landscapes, and seas. There are echoes of Eliot's themes, especially the likeness of beginnings to endings and the connections between poetry and death that run through his *Four Quartets* (1943): "the end is the beginning,/ And the end and the beginning were always there/ Before the beginning and after the end./ And all is always now." ("Burnt Norton") and "Every phrase and every sentence is an end and a beginning,/ Every poem an epitaph" ("Little Giddings"). There are also allusions to other poems, including "The Coming of the Magi" and "The Cultivation of Christmas Trees." Aside from allusions to Eliot himself, the poem contains classical pastoral imagery of wood and water as well as allusions to Narcissus and the lovelorn nymph Echo, Aeolus the wind, the Roman poet Horace, and finally, triumphantly, Apollo, god of poetry, patron of the arts. Through the classical allusions, imagery, and rhyme also come echoes of Russian poets Alexander Pushkin, Osip Mandelstam, and Anna Akhmatova.

Themes and Meanings

An elegy, by definition, deals with death and life, the ephemeral and the eternal. It need not deal with anyone famous or powerful, but when it does, it often makes a point of just how fleeting fame and power are. In the case of tyrants and warlords, the elegy may act as a warning that earthly victories and treasures, however glorious, cannot be taken into the afterlife. In the case of poets, the message is a different one: Beginning with Horace and his ode "Exegi monumentum aere perennius," poets have spoken of the monument that will last as long as art and human memory that other poets have built and that they hope to build for themselves.

At the same time, poets (Eliot included) are mortal, and when they leave this earth they leave forever. For all the play in part 1 on endings equaling beginnings, on cycles and rhythms, the living are orphaned, left behind. Part 2 ends with the unequivocal statement that "each grave is the limit of the earth," and Eliot's departure in part 3 is as final as the end of love. Still—and this is Brodsky's contribution to the tradition—the love may no longer be visible, but it is tangible. The body remembers touch, and the ordinary things of earth—footsteps, grass, wood—remember sound. Words, even if never carved in stone, have weight and mass and continue to exist as part of this world.

If poets are mortal, poetry is not. Horace's ode was translated by Russian poets Gavrila Derzhavin and Alexander Pushkin and so became part of the Russian tradition just as Russian poetry became part of the classical tradition. Brodsky's mention of Horace automatically brings in Pushkin and Derzhavin, and, by incorporating some of Eliot's own imagery and sensibility and alluding to Mandelstam and Akhmatova, Brodsky connects them all and connects himself, in turn, to them. His choice of subject (Eliot) and his choice of model (Auden on Yeats) brings in English-Irish-American speech as well, adding another link to the connection or another strand to the web of association called context. In his famous essay "Tradition and the Individual Talent," Eliot talks about tradition not as "blind adherence" to what others have done but as a historical sense, a sense that the past is both past and present. "The feeling that the whole of the literature of Europe from Homer and within it the whole of the literature of his own country has a simultaneous existence and a simultaneous order" is what gives writers a sense of their own time and their own place. Meaning does not exist in a vacuum but rather in a context. Brodsky both pays tribute to the tradition and changes it by his presence.

Jane Ann Miller

VIEW WITH A GRAIN OF SAND

Author: Wisława Szymborska (1923-   )

Type of poem: Meditation

First published: 1986, as "Widek z ziarnkiem piasku," in *Ludzie na moście*; English
translation collected in *View with a Grain of Sand: Selected Poems*, 1993

The Poem

"View with a Grain of Sand" is a poem of thirty-seven lines grouped into seven
stanzas that range from four to seven lines each. In both Polish and English, the poem
exhibits occasional irregular rhymes, although these are not the same lines in both
versions. (For example, the fourth stanza rhymes the second and fourth lines in Polish
and the first and second line in English.) Like much of Wisława Szymborska's poetry,
the language in "View with a Grain of Sand" sounds like everyday conversation,
differing from prose or ordinary speech only in very subtle rhythms and patterns of
sound.

The speaker of the poem may be Szymborska herself, although such an identification does not affect the meaning conveyed or the impression formed by the poem. This
speaker pictures a lake and its surroundings, beginning with a grain of sand from the
shore. She mentions that the sand is complete in and of itself and that it is not affected
by people touching it, talking about it, or dropping it on a windowsill; these things
pertain solely to human experience. The speaker then considers the window that
overlooks the lake but that has nothing to do with the lake itself except in human
perception. The poem reminds its readers that the "wonderful view" exists only in the
individual mind, as do colors, sounds, odors, and, most strikingly, pain. Szymborska's
speaker goes on to say essentially the same thing about the lake, that it knows nothing
of the attributes people associate with it. She adds that the lake lies beneath both a sky
similarly unaffected by human thoughts or feelings and the sun that "hides" behind
clouds and "sets" beyond the horizon but which, she reminds readers, neither truly
hides nor actually sets. By bringing up these two particular figures of speech, common
not only in Polish and English but also in many other languages, Szymborska quietly
suggests that human perceptions of "reality" often prove to be highly illusory in nature
since the sun only seems to behave as human beings describe it as behaving. Citing
such a commonly known fact strengthens the message Szymborska conveys: People's
ideas are not accurate reflections of the world around them.

Finally, the speaker discusses the passage of time, which seems to rush by as if
carrying an important message for someone, but again she points out that such
perceptions are the result of human imagination. Time does not rush; it simply exists
as do the lake and sun. The personification of time is merely the result of human
thought at work. Through repetition, the poem reinforces the thought that it is the
human desire to appreciate and understand the world that is responsible for the
interpretations people place upon the physical universe. In his afterword to Szymborska's poetry collection *Nothing Twice* (1997), translator and poet Stanisław Barańczak

explains that Szymborska is a poet who often asks questions that she does not attempt to answer. Instead, she seems to focus on challenging her readers' assumptions as if the questions themselves are more interesting than any possible answers. In "View with a Grain of Sand," she makes readers wonder if the ideas they associate with the world around them have any meaning at all and ask why humans tend to see only themselves in the rest of the universe.

Forms and Devices

The poem exhibits a subtle musicality of language, as when Szymborska writes of the glass in the window that is "colorless, shapeless,/ soundless, odorless, and painless." Besides an implied pun (in English) on "pane," the repeated syllable "less" provides a rhythmic feel for the reader. This rhythm is further emphasized by occasional rhyme, as in stanza 4, in which Szymborska writes "The lake's floor exists floorlessly,/ and its shore exists shorelessly," pairing not only the final adverbs in each line but also their corresponding nouns "floor" and "shore." The use of sound echoes (not always true rhymes but repetition of sounds within words such as "sky" and "skyless" in the fifth stanza) enlivens what would otherwise seem almost like simple prose. Although there are noticeably more such rhymes and echoes in Polish, where conjugations and declensions provide many words with the same final syllables and thus make rhyming somewhat easier, enough of the strategy survives in English to give a free, almost floating quality to the verse. The diverse lengths of the lines also reinforce this impression: In English, the lines vary from three to fifteen syllables in length (which resembles the original version's range of five to fourteen syllables per line). The unfettered quality of the poetry suggests private reflection or reverie, especially appropriate to the subject of the mind considering its own perceptions.

The subject, beginning with a tiny grain of sand and moving through increasingly large concepts to time itself, creates a perception similar to that established in motion pictures when a camera changes focus from a small detail to a vast panorama in one movement—the microcosm has been replaced by the macrocosm, and the reader is encouraged to reflect that all existence is similar to that of the items, both small and large, that Szymborska has mentioned. What she claims for a grain of sand, a lake, the wind, the sky, the sun, and even time might equally be said of anything in the universe. Just as the casual-sounding language is given shape and rhythm by careful arrangement of sound, the insight into existential philosophy that forms the content of the poem is made far more accessible by Szymborska's use of specific physical objects and places to anchor and clarify what otherwise might be too abstract to present in an effective poem.

Themes and Meanings

In "View with a Grain of Sand," Szymborska stimulates her readers to question their interpretations of the world around them. Viewers of the lake might normally watch the waves lapping at the shore, but readers of the poem are reminded that the waves and the shore in themselves signify nothing except that the wind has ruffled the surface of the lake and that the water ends at a certain point. The refreshment, serenity, or pleasure usually associated with such perceptions have nothing to do with the lake itself but only with the people who view the lake. The poem encourages readers to remember this as they consider their own responses to such scenery. If the water, shore, and wind that humans see as beautiful are untouched by human thought, they also lack any inherent meaning for human beings. The same is true of the sky and sun, which only obey their own natures and do nothing of what humans believe them to do. By implication, the only meaning is that which people make for themselves in their thoughts about the world. Even the passage of time, essential to thought and human consciousness, has no essential meaning for humankind. People may perceive it as purposeful or fast, but that is only because of their capacity to deceive themselves. Time, in the final line of the poem, truly bears an "inhuman" message, one that people could never understand because it is totally alien to them. The human perception of time will always be in human terms. It is as if human nature forever cuts humanity off from the rest of existence because people seek meaning and sense where none exists and find only themselves, their thoughts, and their feelings.

Szymborska's assertion that the human mind's activities and attempted interpretations of the world reflect only human reality resembles some of the insights offered by Buddhist and Hindu doctrines: The world is essentially an illusion, and profound understanding of existence must come through the mind itself. However, Szymborska does not offer teachings about the true nature of knowledge or the mind but only suggests that no one may fully grasp the inhumanity of the universe. She has mused over the emotional implications nature scenes have for many observers and has suggested that there are no meanings or essential emotions to be connected with such scenes. She implies that the human habit of contemplating their place in the world is best answered by suggesting that people may truly have no place in existence except for whatever places they create in their own thought.

Paul James Buczkowski

VOLTAIRE AT FERNEY

Author: W. H. Auden (1907-1973)
Type of poem: Meditation
First published: 1939; collected in *Another Time*, 1940

The Poem

"Voltaire at Ferney" is a short poem consisting of thirty-six lines divided into six stanzas. Each stanza contains two or three sets of lines that rhyme. A casual reading of the poem and its title suggests that the author is merely portraying a scene in the life of François-Marie Arouet, better known to history as Voltaire. In fact, Auden had reviewed books about the famous French philosopher. (He assumed that the reader was familiar with the life and times of Voltaire and therefore did not provide any background information.) A thorough reading of the poem reveals that Auden essentially constructed an epigram in which he attempted to develop a psychological profile of Voltaire. His approach is analytic and conceptual, and there are no dramatic scenes. The poem, however, takes on additional meaning when one considers the period of time in which it was written as well as the changes that were taking place in Auden's own life.

In the beginning of the poem, Voltaire is surveying the ancient estate of Ferney, located in the county of Gex, which borders on Switzerland. In 1754 he had settled in Geneva, being *persona non grata* in both France and Prussia. In 1758 he had acquired Ferney when his relationships with the leaders of Geneva were becoming strained. (Voltaire's friend and associate Jean Le Rond d'Alembert had published an article on Geneva that revealed the personal failings of its Calvinist clergymen.) Ferney was in France, but it was only three miles from Geneva, thereby allowing Voltaire to avoid its Calvinist leaders—or flee to Switzerland should the Catholics in Paris (re)issue orders for his arrest. To safeguard his investment against confiscation, he purchased the estate in the name of his niece. Shortly thereafter, Voltaire added, by a life purchase, the neighboring seigneury of Tournay and could legally call himself a lord and even display a coat of arms. As the first stanza indicates, Ferney was a working estate employing eight hundred people in agriculture, weaving, and watchmaking.

The blind old woman of the second stanza is Marie de Vichy-Chamrond, Marquise Du Deffand. The greatest minds in Europe came to visit her salon in Paris. She liked Voltaire as much for his fine manners as for his great mind, and their correspondence remains a classic of French literature. The marquise lost her sight in her mid-fifties but heeded Voltaire's advice to go on living to a ripe old age because "nothing is better than life." At the very least, she could enrage those who paid her annuities. Voltaire ultimately concluded that life is worth living in order to fight "against the false and unfair" as well as to garden and to civilize others. In Voltaire's 1759 novel *Candide*, Professor Pangloss, Voltaire's parody of the philosopher Gottfried Leibniz, tells his young pupil how the unfolding of tragic events clearly proves that this is the best of all possible worlds. Candide agrees, but she insists on cultivating their garden, if only to protect them against the three great evils—idleness, vice, and want. To Voltaire cultivating one's garden could only be considered a beginning when so much was amiss in the world.

Forms and Devices

To Auden ideas were not vague abstractions of the mind. They were real things that shaped the terms and conditions of the unending struggle for democracy and socialism. Auden's affectionate portrait of Voltaire attempted to capture both his relatively unimportant personal failings as well as his larger contributions to the important causes of reason and justice. It was at Ferney that Voltaire learned of the arrest, torture, and murder of the Huguenot Jean Calas by the Catholic authorities in Toulouse and began his struggle against the abuses and ineptitude of France's *ancien régime*.

In the third stanza Auden assumes a subtly critical attitude toward the motives, methods, and character of Voltaire and his philosophical contemporaries by describing them as a group of rebellious schoolchildren who want to defeat "the infamous grown-ups." Voltaire is presented as "the cleverest of them all," who does not hesitate to lie when necessary and is willing to bide his time until the moment is right. In the fourth stanza Voltaire reflects upon those who might have been effective allies in his crusade. These include d'Alembert, who compromised himself by drawing a pension from the court, the "great enemy" Blaise Pascal, the "dull" Denis Diderot (who espoused an unacceptable system of materialistic atheism), and the weak and sentimental Jean-Jacques Rousseau.

Voltaire did not seem to care if anyone took offense at his scandalous conduct. He carried on a scientific partnership and openly adulterous affair with Gabrielle Émilie Le Tonnelier de Breuteuil, Marquise du Châtelet, who is mentioned in the fifth stanza. His relationship with his niece, Marie Louise Mignot Denis, can only be described as disgraceful even by the standards of the court of Louis XV. Yet Auden is not entirely without sympathy for Voltaire's desire for the more sensual pleasures. At the end of the fifth stanza, he writes that Voltaire had "done his share of weeping for Jerusalem" and that "it was the pleasure-haters who became unjust." However, Auden may also be suggesting that Voltaire was too confident about his chances for success and that his lack of humility and sense of propriety detracted from the larger causes.

Themes and Meanings

Auden wrote "Voltaire at Ferney" during what he described as the third period in his career, which covered the years between 1939 and 1946. During this time, Auden underwent profound changes in his religious and intellectual perspectives. After an earlier visit to Spain during its civil war, he became disillusioned with the political Left and began his return to the Anglican faith. In 1939 he settled in New York City and eventually became an American citizen. His works from this time often raise questions concerning the nature of existence, thereby suggesting his reaffirmation of Christianity. They also contain lighter and more romantic verses, some of which lack the unusual style and vigor of his best earlier works.

In one sense the poem is autobiographical. Auden, like Voltaire, had wandered from one country to another and had finally settled down in a distant part of the world. Both men had made personal and intellectual mistakes in their lives. Both had matured and retreated from the more radical ideas of their respective youths. However, maturity did not mean that they had abandoned their most cherished beliefs. Now, both men must gear up for the most important struggles of their lives. Both will use their talents of the pen to further their causes. Many of Auden's poems from this time express strong antiwar sentiments.

The parallels between the situation in Europe before the French Revolution and the outbreak of World War II are obvious; large-scale violence and bloodshed were about to be unleashed, changing the face of history. In the last stanza, Auden states that "the night was full of wrong,/ Earthquakes and executions." In Voltaire's time, an earthquake on All Saint's Day in 1755 had destroyed Lisbon. Christians wondered how God could have permitted this disaster to happen at a time when so many people were praying in the churches. One Jesuit priest proclaimed that the earthquake was God's punishment for the vices that were permitted to flourish in the city. Rousseau, however, argued that fewer people would have been killed had they not abandoned the more natural life of the villages. He added that people must remain optimistic and continue to believe in the goodness of God; everything in the end would be right. The only alternative was suicidal pessimism. These kinds of explanations seemed absurd to Voltaire, and they helped prompt him to write *Candide*. Likewise, a series of miscarriages of justice in France resulted in the execution of several men accused of crimes against God—as well as in the burning of books written by Voltaire, Rousseau, and other philosophers—and persuaded Voltaire to declare war on the Church.

Auden's final remark about "the uncomplaining stars" appears to acknowledge a certain futility. There are limits to what one person can do to advance the causes of reason and justice. He, like his eighteenth century counterpart, had hope—if little reason for optimism. Nevertheless, they "must go on working." At that time Auden could not foresee that he, like Voltaire, would return to his native land at the end of his life and be showered with honors.

Peter A. Schneider

THE WAKING

Author: Theodore Roethke (1908-1963)
Type of poem: Meditation
First published: 1953, in *The Waking: Poems 1933-1953*

The Poem

"The Waking" is the final poem in the collection *The Waking* (1953), for which Theodore Roethke received the Pulitzer Prize in poetry in 1954. In a departure from the free verse of much of his earlier work, this poem is composed in the form of a villanelle, a nineteen-line closed verse form consisting of five successive tercets rhyming *aba* followed by a closing quatrain rhyming *abaa*. Two key lines that contain the theme of the poem are repeated alternately at the end of each stanza and then again together in the last stanza. The title suggests the central idea of the poem: a discovery of the fundamental paradox of human life. The "waking" to which the poet refers involves the broad assertion that life leads to death. More precisely, the poet has grasped the insight that living (waking), which involves coming to new awarenesses, ultimately leads only to dying (sleep). By using several examples, the speaker reveals that this truth is not overwhelming or even essentially negative. Rather, "The Waking" describes the poet's revelation of life as an organic and somewhat mysterious process; the poem portrays the refinement and gradual confirmation of this truth. Hence, for him life is a process in which individuals move unhurriedly ("waking slow"), trusting nature to take them through the seemingly contradictory processes of coming to life and moving toward death. The poem is written in the first person, and the poet speaks to readers directly about his own experience. In this way, Roethke makes use of a rich tradition in lyric poetry in which the poet speaks on his own authority and in his own voice directly to the reader. The poet also employs another tradition, an old American penchant for the slightly didactic voice of the "seer" or "visionary" who has seen, who now knows, and who wishes to impart his understanding.

In the first stanza, the poet speaks from within the darkness (as readers learn by the third stanza) as he chants his awareness that life leads to death: "I wake to sleep, and take my waking slow." He ventures to say (in lines 2 and 3) that this fact cannot make him afraid because he is aware these are the necessary processes of nature. In the second stanza, he amplifies the idea that abstract knowledge is not frightening but is even irrelevant because he, like the Metaphysical poets of the seventeenth century, would rather "think by feeling," basing his life upon the stream of experience rather than abstract ideas. The third stanza presents a vivid example that illustrates why he is unafraid of the awareness that life leads to death: When he senses the presence of someone he cannot clearly see (perhaps, for Roethke, his dead father), he feels the holiness of nature and the rightness of nature's plan.

Two more examples are offered in the fourth stanza: "Light takes the Tree" and "The lowly worm climbs up the winding stair." Both examples depict the miraculous and wonderful growth in nature. These two examples of life processes are contrasted to the central idea in the fifth stanza that nature has "another thing" to do to human beings (death). Thus in stanzas 4 and 5 he exemplifies the two processes that he has set out in the first stanza—growth and decay, or living and dying—and challenges the listener with the *carpe diem* theme to "take the lively air," to live fully in the time remaining. In the sixth and final stanza, the poet sets forth the justification for his trust in nature's plan: Whatever seems to die still remains. He says, "What falls away is always," and so the reader sees the poet's vision: Life does indeed lead to death, but death does not entail a complete severance. Rather, everything (and everyone) abides.

Forms and Devices

The form of the poem is the villanelle, a verse form that can be traced back to Italian folk songs of the late fifteenth through the early seventeenth centuries. In the sixteenth century, French poet Jean Passerat gave the poem its current form. One distinctive quality of the Roethke villanelle is the contrast between the precision of this complex, closed form and the loose process of association that so clearly marks the poem.

The poem contains two central metaphors—waking and sleeping—and connotations hovering around these two metaphors express much of the ambiguity of the poem and the richness of the poet's vision. In a narrow sense, the antithesis of waking/sleeping suggests gaining consciousness and losing it, growing and diminishing, and living and dying. The poem's title itself suggests another meaning of "waking": the dawning of the idea that the process of waking/sleeping does not involve a horrible reality. That is, the metaphors of waking and sleeping describe the life cycle, and the waking that the poet wants to describe for the reader is the new awareness that this life cycle is to be feelingly lived and loved rather than feared.

Every metaphor in the poem—the light, the tree, the air, the worm, and the winding stair—plays a part in clarifying the poet's vision. The light taking the tree and the worm ascending the stair represent two images of growth. The suggestion to "take the lively air" presents a direct invitation to the reader to enjoy life, particularly the things that bring great pleasure and joy, while the time remains to enjoy them. A final, important image of things "falling away" contains the fundamental reason for the poet's acceptance of and trust in life. He avows, "What falls away is always." Hence, what dies only seems to pass away from human presence at times, for the poet senses the presence of absent things and people even though they cannot be clearly apprehended by the senses. The atmosphere of this poem is celebratory as the poet paints a backdrop of night, loss, and death only to lead readers to an awareness of the presence of departed friends and an ultimate acceptance and trust in nature.

Themes and Meanings

In simplest terms, the poem's theme is acceptance of nature's cyclical and seemingly contradictory plan for the living. Seen in this way, life is a natural, organic process of growth and decay, perhaps recalling for some William Cullen Bryant's poem "Thanatopsis." Related to this view of life is the invitation to enjoy life while one has it, to make use of the limited amount of time one has to grow. However, the poem suggests much more about the nature of the actual experience of this life. Human beings "think by feeling"; that is, their lives begin in feelings and senses, and all thought and knowledge naturally follow from and are intertwined with feeling. Armed with this awareness, the human being is free to "dance from ear to ear." In other poems, Roethke centers on what he suggests here: the divine, mad dance of the person/poet who is in love with this brief, contradictory life.

Life, then, is not a problem to be solved or a process to endure; rather, it is a mystery, a paradox to which people must open their trust, for "What falls away is always. And is near." In this poem, Roethke speaks from within the idealist American Romantic tradition of Bryant and Ralph Waldo Emerson and the English Romantic vein of William Blake, William Butler Yeats, and even William Wordsworth. This poem does not spiritualize the poet's grounded experience; it does not take readers beyond the natural world. Rather, it describes the holiness of the "eternal now" as it teaches readers what Roethke himself declared during a panel talk on the poem "Identity" at Northwestern University in 1963: "'We think by feeling. What is there to know?' This . . . is a description of the metaphysical poet who thinks with his body . . . and it is one of the ways man at least approaches the divine . . . for there is a God, and He's here, immediate, accessible."

Jeffery Galle

WAKING EARLY SUNDAY MORNING

Author: Robert Lowell (1917-1977)
Type of poem: Lyric
First published: 1967, in *Near the Ocean*

The Poem

"Waking Early Sunday Morning" is a long lyric poem, a meditation on mortality in fourteen eight-line stanzas. The title invites comparison with Wallace Stevens's poem "Sunday Morning," and indeed the poem may be read as Robert Lowell's pessimistic, Puritan-tinged reply to Stevens's celebration of an earthly paradise. Stevens evokes a lushly fertile world in which the "balm and beauty of the earth" is heaven enough, but, in Lowell's vision, the earth is no longer a garden but an exhausted volcano, its violence all but spent, "a ghost/ orbiting forever lost" in a universe empty of meaning. The poem is written in the first person, both singular and plural, so that the speaker is sometimes "I" and sometimes "we." The speaker, implicitly Lowell himself, moves from the personal to the prophetic, expressing first a desire for freedom, then a wistful longing for lost religious faith, and finally regret for the doomed planet and its children fated to fall "in small war on the heels of small/ war."

"Waking Early Sunday Morning" is an internal journey through the thoughts of the speaker as he awakens. The poem begins with a dreaming image of freedom and escape, the wish to "break loose" like a salmon swimming against the current, leaping and finally clearing the waterfall to reach its native stream. Yet the image carries its own darkness: The salmon braves the current only to "spawn and die." The second stanza finds the speaker waking from his dream and feeling the childlike joy of a Sunday morning's leisure ahead, "squatting like a dragon on/ time's hoard before the day's begun"—a line that echoes seventeenth century English poet Andrew Marvell, whose "The Garden" is also recalled by the rhymed octosyllabic couplets of Lowell's poem.

The poet's awareness moves from himself to his surroundings, from mice and termites in the walls to the harbor view outside his window, from a glass of water at his bedside to the "new electric bells" calling worshipers to Sunday church service. Through several stanzas, the poet explores this lost connection to the "Faith of our fathers," to the white steeples of New England now reduced to "vanishing emblems" of a salvation no longer assured. This Puritan faith, recalled in the lines of hymns still sung but not believed, was not without its own terrors, yet it gave to its followers a sense of order and a chance for redemption, a "loophole for the soul."

In the closing five stanzas, Lowell explores the condition of a people whose only god has become the god of war, of the United States as a Philistine empire of excess and military might without true direction. Again, in stanza 12, there is the longing to break free, to find redemption in some pastoral summer. However, the poet allows no return to innocence, no escape from this wounded earth: "Pity the planet, all joy gone/

from this sweet volcanic cone." Humanity is left forever in the ruins of the paradise it has destroyed.

Forms and Devices

"Waking Early Sunday Morning" uses a relatively strict and demanding metrical form: the iambic tetrameter or four-beat couplet. Each of its fourteen stanzas contains four couplets or eight lines. Though the form and meter echo Marvell's "The Garden," Lowell's poem is modern in its diction and subject matter, and the regularity of form is varied by Lowell's use of off-rhyme. In stanza 3, for example, Lowell rhymes "night" with "foot" and "sun's" with "dawns." These slight irregularities, together with Lowell's use of three seven-syllable lines in the last stanza, give the poem an edge that keeps the reader from being lulled by its musicality.

The word pairs Lowell chooses for rhymes and even his line breaks often challenge the reader's expectations. "Waking Early Sunday Morning" does not actually break poetic rules, but it defies poetic conventions, as when the speaker, in the midst of a visionary exhortation ("O to break loose"), suddenly breaks in with "Stop, back off." The voice abruptly becomes more casual, more intimate. There are similar shifts in diction throughout the poem. Sometimes the speaker is musing, personal, and intro- spective; sometimes he is almost biblically oratorical; and sometimes he is almost comradely or Whitman-like, addressing readers and pulling them into the "we" of the poem. These shifts in rhetorical style reflect the speaker's shifts in perception from dream state to consciousness, from casual observation to philosophical speculation, and from wry amusement to despair.

Language in the poem is playful yet precise. Lowell delights in using words that resonate with other poems he has written, with works of other writers from Roman poet Horace to Marvell to Stevens, and with figures and events from history. Thus the description of the nocturnal animals in the third stanza—"obsessive, casual, sure of foot"—recalls Lowell's own "Skunk Hour" and its mother skunk and kittens search- ing for food in the moonlight. The "rainbow smashing a dry fly" in stanza 2 is clearly a trout but also calls to mind the last line of Lowell's poem "The Quaker Graveyard in Nantucket," which in turn refers to the biblical story of Noah with its comforting story of God's covenant. That comfort is subverted in "Waking Early Sunday Morn- ing": There is no promise that the world shall not be destroyed; what God may not do, humanity will.

Biblical imagery and literary allusions abound in "Waking Early Sunday Morning." The glass the poet gazes through in stanza 5 and the line "Each day, He shines through darker glass" in stanza 9 echo the biblical metaphor "For now we see through a glass, darkly" (I Corinthians 13:12). Elsewhere in the poem, U.S. military forces are seen in terms of an army of elephants, recalling Hannibal, whose exploits are recounted in Lowell's translation of Roman poet Juvenal's tenth satire. Other phrases suggest events from more recent history: The reference to chance assassinations is surely the poet's response to the violent events of the 1960's. "Waking Early Sunday Morning" is a poem that seems constructed in layers, broadly referential yet personal, dense with many meanings yet still accessible on an immediate, physical level.

Themes and Meanings

A descendant of Puritans who at one point converted to Catholicism, Lowell was a student of the classics who was fascinated by ancient Rome. He saw history as a continuing process; *Near the Ocean* (1967), the collection in which "Waking Early Sunday Morning" first appeared, contains original poems by Lowell as well as his translations of works by Horace, Juvenal, and others. In an introductory note, Lowell speaks of "the greatness and horror of [Rome's] empire," then adds, perhaps slyly, "How one jumps from Rome to the America of my own poems is something of a mystery to me." Actually, there is little mystery in the metaphorical connection Lowell draws between Rome near the end of its empire and America in the latter half of the twentieth century. In "Waking Early Sunday Morning," Lowell evokes a sense of living in "fallen" times, referring to both the fall of an empire and humanity's original fall from grace. The poem is thus one observer's reflections upon a particular time and place as well as a metaphorical recasting of ancient myth.

Lowell was not only a poet steeped in history but also a poet of his times. During the 1960's, much of his work reflected his political concerns and moral beliefs; poems in *For the Union Dead* (1964) touch upon ethnic segregation and nuclear war, and *Near the Ocean* continues this mingling of public issues with the exploration of private concerns Lowell had pioneered in his autobiographical *Life Studies* (1959). He opposed the Vietnam War and, in 1965, refused an invitation to read at a White House arts festival as a protest against President Lyndon Johnson's Vietnam policy. Certainly Lowell had Vietnam in mind when he wrote of "man thinning out his kind" through a succession of small wars in "Waking Early Sunday Morning," and certainly Lowell's public repudiation of Johnson echoes in the poem's portrait of the president "swimming nude, unbuttoned, sick/ of his ghost-written rhetoric"; yet the image also recalls Lowell's father singing in his bathtub in "Commander Lowell." By showing these figures of authority literally stripped naked, Lowell at once satirizes and humanizes them. They are flawed, perhaps even destructive, but they are not monsters.

"Waking Early Sunday Morning" has something of the mood of an elegy. The voice in the poem is not that of a thunderous Jeremiah of the Bible or the fierce Puritan Jonathan Edwards preaching doom but rather the quiet voice of a rueful observer who hopes for the best even as he expects the worst. Understanding of human weakness and compassion for the troubled human species permeate its melancholy yet often lovely stanzas. The personal despair and loss of faith treated in Lowell's earlier, more explicitly "confessional" poems such as "Skunk Hour" are transmuted in "Waking Early Sunday Morning" into a gentle pity for all humanity and for the fate of the earth itself.

Kathryn Kulpa

WALKING TO SLEEP

Author: Richard Wilbur (1921-   )
Type of poem: Meditation
First published: 1967; collected in *Walking to Sleep: New Poems and Translations*,
   1969

The Poem

At 143 lines, "Walking to Sleep," the longest of Richard Wilbur's poems, is the title poem of *Walking to Sleep*, 1969, in which it was first collected. As the third part of that book, it concludes the section of original poems, with a number of translations following. In an interview with William Heyen (*Conversations with Richard Wilbur*, 1990), Wilbur confesses that the book represents eight years of work. Because poets give a great deal of thought to the placement and arrangement of poems, the placement of this poem implies that its ideas embody a sense of finality which transcends mere bodily sleep. The poem is written in the first person, and the speaker is barely distinguishable from Wilbur himself. The speaker assumes an air of authority and seasoned wit as he addresses the reader.

"Walking to Sleep" opens on a note of grave confidence which the speaker establishes and continues throughout the poem. Suggesting that the reader step off into the "blank of your mind," he assures the reader that such confidence is absolutely necessary for the journey—which will be both imaginary and real. The journey begins in the realm of the imagination as shaped by the real. The speaker warns the reader, however, that frustrations occur, especially if the reader attempts to control the direction and outcome of the journey. What follows is an interplay of images and specific directions.

As if the speaker becomes aware that he may be frightening the reader, and finding the reader still awake, he suggests that the reader forget all that the speaker has said and begin again. The poem itself seems to begin again at this point; this time the reader starts in the real world, allowing the imagination freedom to shape experience. Finally, Wilbur ends the poem by averring that the most fruitful journeys are those which remain open to the real and the imaginative experience, with no attempt at control.

Forms and Devices

By using direct address as the vehicle for advancing the poem, the poet establishes an intimate relationship between the speaker (essentially the poet himself) and the reader, involving the reader in the argument of the poem. The reader mentally hears the speaker, reacting as if the reader and the speaker were in close communication, indeed, in the same room. Wilbur reinforces this tone by stepping outside the flow of images to ask questions, give advice, or warn the reader. The effect of direct address is to strengthen the conversational resonance.

Wilbur is the master of the iambic pentameter line, which is composed of five poetic feet—an unstressed syllable followed by a stressed syllable. The lines "Detach some portion of your thought to guard/ The outside of the building; as you wind," taken from well within the body of the poem, seem to sing with the strength of the iambic beat. Through the use of the five-stress line, the poem emphasizes the walking pace which the reader and speaker assume. To avoid a sing-song effect, Wilbur varies the placement of the stresses. For example, the first two lines of the poem end with an unstressed syllable, while the third line ends with a stressed syllable: "Step off assuredly into the blank of your mind." By emphasizing "mind," the poet underscores the role that the mind plays in this journey, which the poem elucidates.

A formalist poet, Wilbur uses form adeptly, not as adjunct to the poem, but to emphasize the meaning of his lines. The long lines stretching across the page shape the poem into one stanza with no break, except for the slight pause implied by the indentation of "What, are you still awake?" Wilbur therefore controls the pace at which the reader reads the poem, drawing similarities to both a leisurely reading and taking a walk.

Characteristic of a poem by Wilbur, the images are intensely beautiful and sensual. After the poem takes the major twist when the speaker tells the reader to forget everything he has said, the speaker conveys the great possibilities that nature provides for helping the reader to understand the journey through a series of images. He advises the reader to rub his or her eyes as if waking up and to see: "The phosphenes caper like St. Elmo's fire,// Let all things storm your thought with the moiled flocking/ Of startled rookeries, or flak in air,/ Or blossom-fall." In such lines, Wilbur's poem recalls the iambic lines that William Wordsworth uses as he walks through the English countryside. These and other images reveal the order in disorder which the poem seems to defend.

Themes and Meanings

In a conversation with John Graham (*Conversations with Richard Wilbur,* 1990), Wilbur states that this poem speaks about someone giving advice to someone else about how to get to sleep. The first line, "As a queen sits down, knowing that a chair will be there," provides an image for the confidence with which a person should enter the land of dreams. Although such an idea may have provided the impetus for the birth of the poem, its singularity gives rise to the idea that the poem is uncharacteristic for Wilbur, as suggested by its length. The poem reads as if the poet would make his readers understand, once and for all, his writing process as well as its effect on him. The use of vivid, almost surreal imagery mimics the fragmentation that the personality undergoes as it yields control of the journey to the process of journeying itself. Thus, while the poet's interpretation sheds light on the poem, there are other ways of reading it.

Another possible way of understanding the poem "Walking to Sleep" is understanding "sleep" as a metaphor for death and the journey as the process of dying. Certainly the fact that the poem is the final one in the volume's section of original poems suggests that possibility, as if the author were telling his readers that death is the end of the journey for everyone. Such an interpretation would suggest that the interplay between the imagination and the real world culminates in the release of control, which the speaker calls for, leading to the acceptance of the inevitability of death. Indeed, such undertones exist in the poem, but another interpretation arises as well.

The poem also seems to speak of the poet's own struggle with the sources of the creative process itself. When the poet, in creating a poem, steps off into the "blank" of his mind, anything can happen. No one can maintain a blank mind for very long; consequently, the poem begins a catalog of dreamlike images that occur to the poet. Just as a queen risks falling when she "sits down, knowing that a chair will be there," the "Potemkin barns" in eighteenth century Russia existed in a village of facades erected to deceive Empress Catherine II. Such images may emerge from dreams, hallucinations, or other subconscious sources.

The poet allows that such sources are most fruitful when there is little attempt to control them. If there is too much control, "what you project/ Is what you will perceive; what you perceive/ With any passion, be it love or terror,/ May take on whims and powers of its own." The poet, then, must allow the process to take him where it will.

The poem continues to intersperse guidelines and vivid imagery as if to suggest a cause and effect relationship. Sometimes the warnings take on the tone of a governmental official: "Should that occur, adjust to circumstances/ And carry on, taking these few precautions." The reader learns that there is nothing that can be done to foresee with any accuracy what will happen as the mind journeys. Whether the reader seeks shelter in the Great Pyramid that Cheops erected or in an iron shed in a military barracks, both are temporary and subject to invasion, whether by grave robbers or enemy soldiers.

The poet suggests that even pleasant images can distract the reader from the journey. Thus the poem counsels the reader to avoid beautiful rooms with beautiful women in them and to continue doggedly in pursuit of "The kind assassin Sleep." At this point, the poem twists as the speaker asks "What, are you still awake?/ Then you must risk another tack and footing./ Forget what I have said." Instead of using the imagination as the vehicle for travel, the poem suggests that the reader look closely at the ordinary things in ordinary life. At this point, the poem celebrates nature as revelatory of whatever truth the reader seeks.

The final image, that of Vishnu sleeping by a pool, alludes to the story told about Vishnu, the Preserver, the chief god worshiped by the Vaishnava as the second member of the trinity in Hinduism, which includes Brahma, the Creator, and Shiva, the Destroyer. As Vishnu slept, wrapped in "maya," the illusions of the flesh, the images that crossed his face contained all of history—past, present, and to come. Yet he received these "as they came," with no particular importance attached to or difference made among them. Wilbur suggests that the poet should imitate such receptivity.

Martha Modena Vertreace

WANTING TO DIE

Author: Anne Sexton (1928-1974)
Type of poem: Lyric
First published: 1964; collected in *Live or Die*, 1966

The Poem

"Wanting to Die" is a short poem in free verse that divides its thirty-three lines into eleven tercets (three-line stanzas). Because it is written in the first person and is conversational in form, this poem has been described as one of Anne Sexton's literary suicide notes. Because it presents a speaker attempting to explain to a sympathetic listener why she wants to kill herself, some critics have also suggested that it reads like a discussion between Sexton and her psychiatrist. The use of the first person in a poem often causes readers to assume that the poet's voice and the speaker's voice are the same—an assumption that, while often erroneous, holds true for this work. Besides being suicidal herself, Sexton often used letters or personal reminisces as the foundations for her writing. "Wanting to Die," in fact, was initially a free-association addendum attached to a letter written to her friend Anne Wilder when Wilder had asked Sexton why she was attracted to suicide. Knowing that Wilder was a psychiatrist and was, therefore, unlikely to overreact to even strong imagery, Sexton addressed Wilder's very real question in poetic form.

In the opening lines of "Wanting to Die," Sexton's speaker chooses to respond honestly to the question posed to her even though the hearer may find the topic repellant. "Since you ask," she says, she will tell. The speaker describes herself as walking unconsciously through life, unimpressed and unaffected by the world around her. The only passion she feels is "the almost unnameable lust" for death. In the next two tercets, she explains further that she has "nothing against life" and no hatred for "the grass blades" that symbolize the vitality of the living world; she simply loves death's promise more. "[S]uicides have a special language," she says, and "like carpenters, they want to know *which tools.*/ They never ask *why build.*"

So far Sexton's speaker has simply discussed her life in a detached, calm manner. At this point the speaker tries to explain the attraction that death holds and to translate her concept of death into words that the hearer can understand. The next two tercets describe in brief the speaker's previous two suicide attempts; she has "possessed the enemy," death, "taken on his craft," and "rested."

The question remains, however: Why does she want to kill herself? The last six tercets seem to provide an answer, however unsatisfactory it may be to others. The first three describe a suicidal person's perception of life as a kind of "drug." Although its pleasures are "so sweet," life keeps the "body at needlepoint"; an addiction to life, like an addiction to drugs, prevents a person from seeing life's bitter reality. Living an illusion has, the speaker asserts, made her "already [betray] the body" even before she attempted suicide. Further, death has been waiting, "year after year," to "undo an old wound" and release the speaker from the body that has become a "prison." Life is a kind of suffering (the "wound") that only suicides recognize when they are "balanced there" between life and death. Even love, the ultimate reason for living, cannot provide the suicide with sufficient reason to stay alive; love is "an infection" that keeps them sick with life.

Forms and Devices

In writing "Wanting to Die," Sexton rejected the strict formal patterns that permeate her earlier volumes of poetry. Although they are occasionally present, rhyme and meter in *Live or Die* are coincidental—the most important poetic devices of the volume are intense, compelling imagery and suggestive metaphor. Many critics have observed the strength behind Sexton's creative vision; "Wanting to Die," like most of her other suicide poems, is about a woman driven insane by the intensity of her emotions. Not surprisingly, then, other critics are repulsed by the immediate anguish and intimacy of Sexton's confessional lines. They suggest that to read Sexton's poems sometimes seems like a tour through her personal hell. Sexton's imagery does tend to be repellant. The picture of the happy suicide having "rested, drooling at the mouth-hole" has a strong impact. Yet it is also a true picture of the complete "rest" that death brings. Drooling, lack of eye response, and incontinence (the image created when the speaker says, "the cornea and the leftover urine were gone") are the realities of dying, however disgusting they may seem.

"Wanting to Die" is also a highly metaphorical poem. For the suicidal speaker, the desire for death is not easily explained to outsiders. The metaphor of the carpenter (with its suggestion of Christ, who himself could be seen as a kind of suicide in that he willingly chose to die) is used to describe why suicides do not seem to consider the impact of their actions before they act. Carpenters do not ask why they build—they presume that the act of building has a purpose. The carpenter's only concern is which tools to use. Similarly, suicides do not ask why they wish to die; they, too, only need to know which "tools" to use.

For a normal person, death is tragic, even repugnant—the typical reader may not really want to know how the most disgusting qualities of death can be so compelling. Only the careful use of metaphor can overcome repulsion's barriers by comparing what is visually acceptable and understandable to what is gross and incomprehensible. When the poem compares life to an addictive "drug," the use of metaphor effectively explains why the suicide does not want to keep on living: He or she wants the power to choose life or death rather than be compelled to live by an addiction to the pleasures of living; "dazzled, they can't forget a drug so sweet." "Wanting to Die" may not make this rationale acceptable to normal readers, but its use of metaphor makes the suicidal person's obsessions more understandable.

Themes and Meanings

Sexton's major accomplishment in "Wanting to Die" is how clearly and powerfully she expresses the feelings of the emotional suicide. Unless one has faced the miasma of emotions that cause one to consider suicide, one may have difficulty in understanding how someone can choose to commit suicide. Sexton makes this choice comprehensible when she presents the reader with the suicide's view of life as being spent facing trivialities and making no impression upon the world: "I walk in my clothing, unmarked by that voyage." Life under these conditions is meaningless and full of pain. Suicidal people's "clothing," their way of thinking and reacting, does not cover their emotional nakedness. Without the normal person's psychological strength, suicides are vulnerable to the smallest hurts; "something unsaid, the phone off the hook" are witnesses to the suicide attempt as well as goads that drive one to suicide. Most painfully, the relationships of the suicidal person seem unreal and unreliable: "the love, whatever it was, an infection."

For the normal person, life is to be enjoyed. For the suicide, death is a rest from the constant trivialities that stab at them. Anne Wilder's letter to Sexton celebrated the fact that life abounds in the world—even the life within the blades of grass was to be wondered at and cherished. Human companionship, as represented by the "furniture . . . under the sun"—lawn chairs, perhaps—is treasured by those who love living. "Wanting to Die" acknowledges the attractiveness of these things; it is not the pleasures of life that she cringes from, but rather the fact that these pleasures pale in comparison to the restful cessation of "raging" and sorrow that death provides. Suicides, Sexton seems to suggest, are born with the tendencies that they will act upon later in life. The fact that they are alive rather than dead does not negate their essential morbidity; "Still-born, they don't always die."

Although this way of thinking, like Sexton's imagery, may be repellant to the average reader, it is an accurate reflection of suicidal thinking. Most seriously depressed people think of their lives as a meaningless struggle that they are incapable of changing. Others, suffering from long-term depression, report that they have always been depressed and have thought of death as a comforting option.

Julia M. Meyers

WASHING DISHES LATE AT NIGHT

Author: Kathleen Norris (1947-   )
Type of poem: Lyric
First published: 1981, in *The Middle of the World*

The Poem

"Washing Dishes Late at Night" is a poem in free verse consisting of just seventeen lines, only three of which contain more than five words. The setting is the poet's home, and the title further limits the action to the kitchen. The title also indicates the time, "late at night," when it is natural to be tired, to have one's defenses down. The speaker is busy washing dishes, a task so routine that it leaves her thoughts free. There is another person in the room, whom she sometimes addresses. Since both the poetry and the prose that Kathleen Norris writes are highly autobiographical, one can be fairly certain that her companion, who is described as living with her, is her husband.

Although the poem is divided into three parts of almost equal length, it does not develop chronologically or even logically. Each section provides more information about the action while, at the same time, interpreting it.

Thus, after beginning with a simple, factual title, the author, in the first section of the poem, turns subjective, asserting that a "room tips." This comment is followed by some relevant facts: The room about which the poet is thinking has just been "rearranged." A logical explanation for her unease could be that, looking at the new arrangement, she feels that it has some aesthetic defect, perhaps a lack of symmetry or balance, which would, indeed, make one feel that it was tipping. On the other hand, the poet might just need time to get used to the changes. After this down-to-earth reference in the second line of this section, however, the present disappears and, with it, so does the real world. In the last three lines of the section, the poet harks back to a time that she admits seems like a "fairy tale." The use of the past tense is significant; evidently, that golden age is now no more than a memory.

The second part of the poem begins with explicit references to sensual experiences. Now, however, there is a conflict: While the room clings to these memories, the man addressed is eliminating them by hanging "new pictures." Meanwhile, the poet is working at her own chore.

In the first line of the final section, there is a dramatic change of subject. It now appears that the writer's primary concern is not furniture arrangement but the creative process. The poem about "faith" that she was trying to write has been blocked, evidently because of something in the atmosphere. The poem ends with the husband and wife again together, but what they share is uneasiness and fear.

Forms and Devices

"Washing Dishes Late at Night" is written in a terse, uncluttered style. The words are simple and commonplace. Norris uses nouns such as "room," "lovers," and "arms and legs," and verbs such as "tips," "rode," and "dip." Because so many of her words are monosyllabic, the poem has a terse, even an abrupt, quality. In the first line ("The room tips"), for example, two of the three syllables are stressed. Although there is more of a lilt in the occasional longer lines in the poem, such as "Where we have rearranged it" and "Their unencumbered arms and legs," most of the lines resemble the initial one. The last three lines of the poem are heavily stressed: Out of eleven syllables, six, perhaps even seven, are accented, and of ten words, all but one are single syllables. As a result, although the poem concludes without a solution, it does end with a strong statement. There is no doubt about the doubt the two characters are experiencing at the end of the poem.

Similarly, there is nothing unclear about Norris's images. The dirty dishes, the pictures, and the "pale light," as well as the room, whose importance is indicated by the fact that it is referred to in each section of the poem, are all, quite evidently, drawn from the poet's own everyday experience. Even the "arms and legs" of the naked "lovers" and the fairy tale "dragon" or "horse" are hardly obscure. It is important to note, however, that while all of the images are concrete and familiar, some of them represent the world of the here and now, and others represent the realm of memory and imagination.

Another stylistic device that has thematic implications is the frequent shifts from one personal pronoun to another. "Washing Dishes Late at Night" begins with a reference to the couple's uniting: "[W]e" worked together on the room. Then, in the second section, there is a rather surprising shift. The "lovers" of the preceding stanza are spoken of in the third person, not once, but twice. The poet immediately proceeds to a description of the present, with "You" (presumably her husband) involved in one activity, "I" in another. The final section brings them back together, with "our," "we," and "Both of us." It is evident that the pronouns in this poem were not selected by accident. Instead, they are clearly meant to serve as directional signals, signifying the development of thought and feeling from line to line, section to section.

In prose works such as *Dakota: A Spiritual Geography* (1993) and *The Cloister Walk* (1996), Norris has emphasized one of the important lessons she has learned during her own spiritual awakening: If life is understood as being, above all, a matter of one's relationship with God, everything in this world is significant. This faith is reflected in Norris's poetry. One should never think that her imagery and syntax might be merely incidental or ornamental. For Norris, the purpose of form is to illuminate theme just as the purpose of everything in God's creations is to demonstrate His goodness and His power.

Themes and Meanings

Though, at first glance, "Washing Dishes Late at Night" appears to be a poem about change, loss, and alienation, the primary theme of the poem is, in fact, religious doubt. However, the poet does not indicate her subject until the final section of the poem, and, even then, she does so obliquely. Up to that point, she has set up a pattern of contrasts, whose real purpose does not become evident until the very end of the poem.

Dominating the poem is a sense that none of the changes that have taken place are for the better. The new arrangement of the room makes the poet uneasy. Moreover, much has been lost, not only a sense of stability, for we assume that, in the past, the room did not seem to "tip," but also the kind of magic that made the lovers, presumably the poet and her partner, feel that they lived in a fairy-tale world. There is also the suggestion of a loss of innocence. In the past, even a "dragon" was tame enough to be ridden, but that time has vanished. It is also pointed out that all traces of the lovers' sensual activities, which, in an unfallen world, have their own kind of innocence, are being eliminated.

Although the couple, at first, joined in making changes, it is significant that the two are now separated. The poet's partner is energetically eliminating the past, replacing it with something new, while the poet stands alone, washing away the remains of a communal meal, symbolically washing her hands not only of the past but also of her own unhappiness.

As soon as Norris explains that she had intended to write about faith, however, it becomes clear that this is not merely a poem about change and the loss of stability or about alienation and the loss of love but about something more basic, the source of all uncertainty: doubt of God's presence in the world. The alienation between the lovers, as well as between them and the past, is both a metaphor for a spiritual malaise and a symptom of it. Again, one is reminded of the Fall: After they became separated from God, Adam and Eve immediately turned on each other.

Nevertheless, "Washing Dishes Late at Night" does end with a degree of hope. The poem does not end in total darkness but in a "pale light," though not in the full radiance of God's presence. Moreover, the fact that it is night implies that morning will eventually come. Most important of all, the couple is once again together, though, at present, all they have in common is their sense of instability and a common fear.

It is a mark of Norris's stature as a religious poet that she does not take refuge in easy answers. She writes about temptation, as in "The Monastery Orchard in Early Spring," which refers to Saint Augustine's boyhood sin and to the allure of sensuality; she writes about the ever-presence of death, as in "The Blue Light" and "Desert Run Scenario"; and, as in this poem, she writes about the terror of doubt. However, the dawn does break, the desert does bloom. In many of her poems, Kathleen Norris voices a faith that is even stronger for having dealt with darkness.

Rosemary M. Canfield Reisman

THE WATCHERS

Author: W. H. Auden (1907-1973)
Type of poem: Pastoral
First published: 1945, as "Not All the Candidates Pass," in *The Collected Poetry*; collected as "The Watchers" in *Collected Shorter Poems, 1927-1957*, 1966

The Poem

"The Watchers" is a short, forty-line poem in eight five-line stanzas reminiscent of the medieval French form known as a cinquain, which used a five-line stanza with a variety of meter and rhyme schemes. It was written in February, 1932, but not published until 1945. The speaker or persona of the poem is an observer who is watching a sleeping world from his window late at night. A yellow clock face and a green pier light eerily illuminate "a new imprudent year" as the night's silence "buzzes" in the poet's ear. Except for the clock, the light, and the buzzing silence, the poet is alone in his window; "The lights of near-by families are out."

The speaker then observes various objects and phenomena in the night, describing them in a manner that invokes a feeling of watchfulness and apprehension. He describes a dormant lilac bush as being "like a conspirator" that "Shams dead upon the lawn." The "Great Bear/ Hangs as a portent over Helensburgh," and the "influential quiet twins" (a reference to the Castor and Pollux constellation) "look leniently" upon the sleeping populace.

The scene becomes more ominous when the speaker describes the "keepers of a wild estate" as stocky men carrying guns. On the surface, these keepers are there to ensure the safety of the town's estates, yet they keep the peace "with a perpetual threat" to any intruder. The unknown intruders are given the characteristics of moles that burrow in the earth, peacocks that transform themselves from plain to proud, and rats possessed of "desperate courage." The intruders need these characteristics to trick the keepers and escape detection; the reader may well wonder why people would be forced to escape detection in their own world.

The answer comes as the year moves "Deeper towards the summer" and the poet poses the question of what would happen if "the starving visionary" were to see "The carnival within our gates." Describing the "wild estate" as a carnival suggests a scene of wild riot and unrelenting chaos, and the reader sees that the estate keepers must watch for human intruders who would report on the carnival—the chaos that has taken over the pastoral world where peace and tranquillity should reign. The last two stanzas reinforce this point when the poet implores the estate keepers to use their power: "We need your power still: use it, that none,/ O, from their tables break uncontrollably away." Fearful of uncontrolled behavior that would bring danger and damage, the poem abruptly ends by depicting the carnival of intruders "Mopping and mowing through the sleepless day."

Forms and Devices

"The Watchers" is based on the medieval French cinquain form, which originally had a variety of meters and rhyme schemes. Auden's rhyme scheme varies from stanza to stanza, and he uses both exact rhyme and slant rhyme effectively. The rhyme scheme of the first stanza is *aabbc*, for example, and the second stanza rhymes *abccd*. The rhyme scheme for the third, fourth, and sixth stanzas is *aabba*. In other stanzas of the poem Auden uses slant rhyme, or near rhyme. Slant rhyme uses assonance (repeated vowel sounds) or consonance (repeated consonant sounds) to produce an end rhyme. For example, in the second stanza the poet creates a slant rhyme with "stir" and "conspirator." Slant rhyme is also employed in stanzas 2 and 7. Stanza 7 uses consonance to repeat the closing *ts* sound in "gates" and "streets."

Beyond such recognizable formal devices as rhyme, Auden imbues the poem with a quality of mysterious ambiguity. The watchers—the "stocky keepers" of the estate—are never clearly defined or described, and in fact the speaker notes that they are not exactly real; they are his thoughts about "forms" he saw in a dream. The watchers, then, these shadowy, unseen forces, may reflect a paranoia within the speaker as much as anything in the outside world. They seem like soldiers or sentries, posted in doorways or atop ridges, yet they also have an aspect of ambushers ("'Of late/ Here . . . They lay in wait'"). The precise meaning and boundaries of the "wild estate" itself are also left open to interpretation. The speaker's attitude toward the watchers is also ambiguous, ambivalent. They keep the peace, but only by being armed with guns and carrying a "perpetual threat." The speaker alternately is trying to trick them himself and urging them to use their power to keep order. In the last lines they take on a particularly oppressive cast, protecting the status quo against minor transgressions: one person lunging dangerously about a room and another "out wild-/ly spinning like a top in the field." The first may pose some momentary danger, but the second, although perhaps eccentric, would seem to pose no real threat. As is true in other of Auden's works, the very obtuseness or obscurity of the poem adds to its feeling of indefinable unease and apprehension.

Themes and Meanings

"The Watchers" is a poem about contradictions, about the appearances of things and their realities. Auden contrasts pastoral images—the lilac tree, constellations, the seasons—with mechanical images, such as the yellow clock face, the green pier light, the estate keepers' guns, and the carnival, which intrude upon nature's peacefulness. Mechanical images are characteristic of Auden's poetry and identify him as a member of a 1930's group of young, liberal poets called the Pylon School; this group also included Cecil Day-Lewis, Louis MacNeice, and Stephen Spender, all of whom used mechanical images.

As a pastoral, the poem describes a rustic setting, including the estate keepers and references to a copse, a bridge, and animals. However, because Auden wants to depict contradictions, the images take on extra meaning. The opening stanzas show the opposition of the quiet night to the intrusion of the light and the clock face, both of which are mechanical objects that impart contrived sequences upon nature—the glowing clock measures artificial hours, and the light artificially lights the darkness.

An estate keeper's job is to maintain the land, yet these keepers carry guns, mechanical objects that can inflict injury and death. Because nature is pastoral, and because Castor and Pollux, the "influential quiet twins," are looking "leniently upon all of us tonight," the intrusive keepers are particularly jarring to the scene. Although the person at the window and the constellations looking down are watchers, the estate keepers are the most significant watchers in the poem, and their guarding is not reassuring but threatening, even dangerous.

Through images containing contradictory meanings, Auden presents worlds in conflict with each other. One is natural and filled with pastoral images, while the other includes humans who come as intruders to subvert pastoral nature into a violent and mechanical environment. Humankind, intruding upon nature, is watched in its watching, a situation that lends irony to the poem. "The Watchers" reflects the uncertainty of England and Europe in the 1930's, with fascism on the rise.

Dennis L. Weeks

WE SHALL MEET AGAIN IN PETERSBURG

Author: Osip Mandelstam (1891-1938)
Type of poem: Lyric
First published: 1922, as "V Peterburge my soidiomsia snova," in *Tristia*; English
translation collected in *Tristia*, 1973

The Poem

Osip Mandelstam wrote "We Shall Meet Again in Petersburg" in 1920 and published it in his collection *Tristia* in 1922. In the title, the persona addresses unnamed friends, vowing to meet them again in Petersburg, a former capital of Russia. (Originally Saint Petersburg, the city was renamed Petrograd during World War I, Leningrad after Lenin's death, and Saint Petersburg again in the 1990's; popularly, it has always been known as Petersburg.) Mandelstam spent the best years of his youth in Petersburg, publishing his first poems there and making several close friends among the poets, primarily the Acmeists; it is these poets Mandelstam addresses as "we." During the Bolshevik revolution, Mandelstam was forced to lead a turbulent life, often changing his abode but returning to Petersburg whenever he could. After the revolution had uprooted thousands of people, the poet was confident that he and his fellow Acmeists would renew their friendship in Petersburg. "We Shall Meet Again in Petersburg" is his nostalgic anticipation of that meeting.

The poet envisions his joy of seeing his fellow poets again, but the meeting acquires the sense of a mission. It is as though they had buried their sun there and they will now do what they had always wanted: utter for the first time their "blessed and meaningless word" so that the "black velvet of the Soviet night" and the resulting emptiness will not stop the women from singing or the everlasting flowers from blooming. They will not be deterred by the oppressive mood of the capital, "arched like a wild cat," by the ubiquitous police patrols, or by an angry car echoing frighteningly through the desolate night. The poet does not need a pass, and he is not afraid of the sentries. Instead, he will courageously pray in the Soviet night for the sake of that "blessed and meaningless word."

The poet further imagines how the ugliness of the present is overcome by a theater performance during which beautiful female voices and Aphrodite's roses inspire the art lovers, so that they warm themselves by a bonfire (the flames of the revolution) instead of being consumed by it. In such bliss, ages will pass and "the beloved hands of blessed women will gather the light ashes" of the sun they had buried in Petersburg. Amid the sweet-sounding choirs of Orpheus, the radiant dark eyes of the singers, and programs fluttering down from the gallery like doves, the poet once again expresses his defiance in defense of more exalted things in life. He ends his poem by warning the powers of darkness that they will not succeed with their sinister designs. They may extinguish the candles, but they cannot stop "the blessed women" from singing. The unshakable truth is that those dark forces are incapable of seeing "the night sun" and are therefore destined to ultimate defeat.

Forms and Devices

"We Shall Meet Again in Petersburg" is written in one of Mandelstam's favorite forms, the eight-line stanza (*vosmistishye*). The poem has four stanzas of varying meters rhymed *ababcdcd*. Images and metaphors are the main vehicles of Mandelstam's poetic craft, as seen in his other poems as well. From among his most striking images, a buried sun in line 2 and the night sun in the last line both refer to the great Russian poet Alexander Pushkin. The repeated image of "blessed women" engaged in artistic performances with their kindred eyes and rounded shoulders adds an almost religious quality to the poem. Immortal flowers and Aphrodite's roses represent love and beauty expressed through arts. The poet uses all these images to emphasize the beautiful, harmonious, and healing power of the arts.

These positive images are contrasted to the negative ones culled from everyday reality. An arched cat expresses anger and the unfriendliness of life in Petersburg during the revolution. A ubiquitous patrol stands on the bridge as if inhibiting the passage from one part of the town to another, thus underscoring the loss of freedom. An angry car speeds through the gloomy night and cries like a cuckoo in eerie silence, a sign either of terror or of mourning. The "black velvet of the Soviet night" not only expresses the dark, oppressive atmosphere of Petersburg in 1920 but also symbolizes the life-threatening effects of the revolution, recalling an executioner's block draped in velvet. The bonfire itself represents the flames of the revolution; the opponents of the Bolsheviks use it, ironically, to warm themselves despite their opposition, as if to say that the arts conquer all evil. Finally, the image of the candles that the dark forces may extinguish symbolizes life and the enlightenment of the arts threatened by "the black velvet of the world's emptiness."

These powerful images are reinforced by equally striking metaphors. The metaphor of the buried sun representing Pushkin has already been mentioned. Toward the end of the poem, the "blessed women" are gathering the ashes in an almost religious ritual, as befits the burial of the great poet. Women are playing the role of beauty enhancers and peacemakers. Mandelstam extends that metaphor by imagining a theater performance in the twilight of civilization brought on by the revolution. The theater itself, as Steven Broyde remarks in his *Osip Mandel'stam and His Age* (1975), separates with its curtain the world of art and beauty from the real world that has turned ugly. The theater motif is frequent in Mandelstam's poetry, but he uses it in "We Shall Meet Again in Petersburg" to counteract the destructive force of the revolution. Additional metaphors are to be found in the use of Aphrodite as a goddess of love and beauty, who stands for the beauty of the arts pining against the world of drab reality and cruelty. Orpheus is also used as a metaphor for an archetypal poet, specifically for Russian poets endangered and threatened with oblivion.

Themes and Meanings

The basic theme of "We Shall Meet Again in Petersburg" is the mortal clash between two worlds: the world of beauty and artistic freedom and the world of everyday reality and coercion. The poet's firm declaration at the outset that "we shall meet again" implies certain disruption. Mandelstam summons his fellow poets, presumably Nikolay Gumilyov and Anna Akhmatova, with whom he had formed, at the beginning of the twentieth century, the powerful poetic movement known as Acmeism. Being apolitical and nonutilitarian in their poetic creed and devoting all their attention to the purely artistic aspects of poetry, they were branded by the revolutionaries as being antisocial and inimical to the revolution. (Gumilyov was executed during the revolution and Mandelstam himself was executed twenty years later.) The revolutionary chaos disrupted these poets in their favorite activity and, in effect, rendered them useless. Despite all this, Mandelstam promises his fellow poets that they shall meet again and speak "the blessed and meaningless word"—a reference to the unfounded pillorying of their poetry on the part of the Bolsheviks, who advocated an engaged, useful, tendentious, and politically oriented poetry.

Mandelstam characterizes the reunion in the poem as a solemn burial of their favorite "sun" (Pushkin), who he considered to be their teacher and poetic God, since Pushkin was also wronged by the society (he was killed in a senseless duel that should have been prevented) and was buried in Saint Petersburg on a winter day similar to the one depicted in the poem. However, the invocation of Pushkin's name is not limited to him individually; it applies to the entire Russian cultural heritage, which, to be sure, is often personified best through Pushkin. By identifying himself and his fellow Acmeists with the great Russian poet, Mandelstam does not so much intend a comparison with Pushkin as he does an avowal of their alliance with true artistic creators and against the destroyers of art such as the Bolsheviks. Mandelstam uses the theater performance not only to glorify the intrinsic value of the arts but also to contrast them with the destructive force of those who are either indifferent or inimical to them or want to use them for their own purposes.

The strongest statement in the poem is contained in Mandelstam's determination to meet again with his fellow poets despite all the dangers and obstacles. Considering how difficult it was for the Acmeists (as well as for other poets not sympathizing with the Bolsheviks) to exist in the midst of revolutionary turmoil, let alone write poetry according to their own creed, Mandelstam's defiance and his nostalgic belief in something that seems to have vanished forever is courageous indeed. By defying the revolutionaries and the prevailing spirit of the time and by declaring that the poets shall meet again, he is saying prophetically that artistic beauty will triumph over the forces of the "velvet night," thus ending the poem on a highly optimistic note.

Vasa D. Mihailovich

WHAT THE DOCTOR SAID

Author: Raymond Carver (1938-1988)
Type of poem: Meditation
First published: 1989, in *A New Path to the Waterfall*

The Poem

In "What the Doctor Said," the speaker is recalling the most traumatic experience of his life. His doctor tells him he has terminal lung cancer. The fact that it is inoperable is indicated by the doctor's statement that he quit after counting "thirty-two of them." Twice the doctor refers to "them" as if avoiding calling "them" what they really were: malignant tumors. He does not suggest any treatment such as radiation or chemotherapy, nor does he suggest, as doctors often do, that his patient seek a second opinion. The doctor is trying to be kind but wants to make it clear that there is no hope for a cure. Both doctor and patient feel awkward, and the speaker is more aware of the doctor's feelings than his own. He will have plenty of time to experience his own complex feelings when he is alone with the grim, inescapable fact that he is very gently being handed his death sentence. The doctor quite understandably asks the patient if he is a religious man, presumably hoping he has some faith in a higher power that will give him consolation. This question, however, only makes the patient's grim fate more certain because it is as if the doctor is saying, "There is nothing medical science can do for you; you had better prepare to meet your maker."

The poem ends with a very puzzling statement. The speaker seems almost grateful that the doctor has just given him "something no one else on earth" has ever given him. The speaker deliberately terminates the interview by jumping up and shaking hands with the doctor. Realizing that there is no more to be said or done in that claustrophobic office, he wants to get away. The awkwardness of the interview is underscored by the fact that the speaker recalls that he may have even thanked the doctor—although under the circumstances it would be nearly as inappropriate to do so as for a prisoner to thank the judge who has just sentenced him to be executed. The reader can relate to the patient because it is force of habit to say something such as "Thank you, Doctor" at the conclusion of an office visit. The speaker is obviously experiencing a wild mixture of feelings. What is so strange is that these mixed feelings seem to include gratitude and relief. He regards the doctor's fatal pronouncement as a gift, "something no one else on earth had ever given [him]." The reader is left wondering how such a diagnosis could have any mitigating overtones. It would seem that the speaker sees some ray of hope when the doctor alludes to religion and love of nature. Apparently the speaker feels that although he has only a short time to live, he may still be able to achieve spiritual enlightenment.

Forms and Devices

"What the Doctor Said," a poem of only twenty-three lines, is typical of a popular school of modern poetry. Its members have abandoned all traditional poetic devices, including rhyme, meter, and "poetic diction," and write in a simple, straightforward, conversational manner. The poem is also completely lacking in punctuation. Raymond Carver has even departed from the convention of capitalizing the first letter in each line. There are no quotation marks around the words spoken by the doctor or patient, and there is no question mark at the end of the sentence in which the doctor asks if the speaker is a religious man who prays for spiritual guidance. There is not even a period at the end of the last line. The elimination of conventional punctuation marks makes "What the Doctor Said" seem like a stream-of-consciousness narrative and makes readers feel as if they are eavesdropping on very private thoughts and feelings. A longer example of this kind of interior monologue can be found in the last chapter of James Joyce's famous novel *Ulysses* (1922), often called "Molly Bloom's Soliloquy," which consists of one sentence running for forty-five pages without a single punctuation mark.

It is especially noteworthy that the poem is factual and prosaic except for lines 7-11, in which the doctor appears to be using poetic imagery and metaphysical terminology. These lines stand out in sharp contrast to the others in the poem. The speaker's recollection is sketchy: It seems likely that most of the words he attributes to the doctor in those lines (especially "mist blowing against your face and arms") are not really part of "what the doctor said" but rather thoughts and images aroused in the speaker's own mind. The device of having a few lines of vivid imagery stand out against a backdrop of deliberately prosaic utterance can be found in some of Shakespeare's sonnets. It always has the effect of making the imagery more intense by contrast. A good example for comparison with Carver's poem is William Shakespeare's Sonnet 29, which contains the famous lines:

> Yet in these thoughts myself almost despising,
> Haply I think on thee, and then my state,
> (Like to the lark at break of day arising
> From sullen earth) sings hymns at heaven's gate.

Themes and Meanings

Carver's poems, like his short stories, are usually personal and autobiographical. "What the Doctor Said" deals with an actual incident. In September of 1987, Carver, who had been a heavy cigarette smoker for many years, was diagnosed with lung cancer. Two-thirds of his left lung was removed, but, in March of 1988, the devastating disease recurred—as it often does—as a brain tumor. He underwent seven weeks of full-brain radiation, but by June the doctors found many more new malignant tumors in his lungs, and he knew he had only a short time to live. He died on August 2, 1988.

The most unusual statement in the poem comes as a surprise ending. The patient acts grateful for the bad news. He jumps up, shakes hands, and perhaps even thanks the doctor. The reader is left wondering what priceless gift it is that the speaker feels he has just received. There is something very strange about this deceptively simple, factual poem. The doctor should be offering consolation, but it seems that the patient is more sensitive and aware than the doctor, who is a sympathetic but unimaginative man of science. The speaker realizes that the doctor feels uncomfortable in that awkward situation. The patient actually ends up comforting the doctor, trying to make his ordeal easier. This subtle reversal of roles is a Carveresque touch of humor that gives the poem an added dimension. It is also ironic that while the patient uses only the most prosaic language, the doctor uses "poetic diction" and metaphysical concepts when he speaks of forest groves and blowing mist and asks for understanding of the meaning of life and death.

The idea that death can be a blessing has often been expressed in literature. For example, in the famous soliloquy that begins with the words "To be, or not to be" in Shakespeare's play *Hamlet* (1603), Hamlet says that death is "a consummation devoutly to be wished." In one of Emily Dickinson's best-known poems, she says: "Because I could not stop for death/ He kindly stopped for me." Algernon Charles Swinburne, in his poem "The Garden of Proserpine," writes:

> From too much love of living,
> From hope and fear set free,
> We thank with brief thanksgiving
> Whatever gods may be
> That no life lives forever;
> That dead men rise up never;
> That even the weariest river
> Winds somewhere safe to sea.

What Carver means by the doctor's "gift" is susceptible to multiple interpretations. Perhaps the only person who can be sure of understanding the multifaceted emotion in question is one who, like Carver, knows that his or her own death is imminent and inescapable.

Bill Delaney

WHO LEARNS MY LESSON COMPLETE?

Author: Walt Whitman (1819-1892)

Type of poem: Lyric

First published: 1855, untitled in *Leaves of Grass*; "Lesson Poem," in *Leaves of Grass*, 1856; "Leaves of Grass No. 11," in *Leaves of Grass*, 1860; "Leaves of Grass No. 3," in *Leaves of Grass*, 1867; "Who Learns My Lesson Complete?" in *Passage to India*, 1871 and in *Leaves of Grass*, 1881

The Poem

Because "Who Learns My Lesson Complete?" appeared in the first edition of *Leaves of Grass* (1855), underwent numerous revisions, assumed its final form in 1867, and remains in the final edition of *Leaves of Grass* (1892), it is safe to say that Walt Whitman placed considerable importance on this poem. "Who Learns My Lesson Complete?" is a short poem in free verse with twenty-six lines of varying lengths divided into nine stanzas. The title asks a rhetorical question that may be simply paraphrased as "Who are they who are most likely to master the lesson taught throughout *Leaves of Grass*?" or perhaps, more cogently, "Who stands in greatest need of the lesson taught pervasively throughout *Leaves of Grass*?" The answer to the rhetorical question is, as is to be expected, contained in the body of the poem itself: Readers—whoever they may be—are likely to learn, and stand in need of learning, the "lesson complete."

After asking the introductory rhetorical question, the poet immediately welcomes all of humanity to "draw nigh and commence": "Boss, journeyman, apprentice, churchman and atheist,/ The stupid and the wise thinker, parents and offspring, merchant, clerk, porter and customer,/ Editor, author, artist, and schoolboy." The reader will note the paired opposites included in the invitation that suggest that all humanity has been summoned to hear the "message complete" to be announced by the poet.

Ironically, however, the "message complete" is ultimately beyond the ability of the poet to communicate to others: "I cannot say to any person what I hear," the poet says, adding that "it is very wonderful." What he has heard are "beautiful tales of things and the reasons of things" that are "so beautiful" he nudges himself "to listen." Though the poet tells readers that he lies "abstracted" (that is, intellectually focused and emotionally intent) upon these beautiful tales, it quickly becomes apparent that the poet sees nature and the universe not as phenomena to be explained but rather as wonders to be celebrated.

What exactly, then, is the "lesson complete" that the poet attempts to communicate to the reader of this poem and to the student of *Leave of Grass* in general? The lesson, readers are told, is "no lesson—it lets down the bars to a good lesson,/ And that to another, and every one to another still." If the lesson is not really a lesson but a removal of obstacles to the reception of a lesson, of many lessons perhaps, then the brunt of the message is that all of humanity can be students of nature and learn the "lesson complete" while free of the usual impediments to knowledge associated with conventional learning experiences. The fundamental lesson transmitted by the poet is quite simply the experience of wonder—hence the recurrent nouns "wonderful" and "beautiful." However, wonder and beauty lie quite beyond explanation; they are emotions to be experienced, not phenomena to be explicated. Who, then, learns the "lesson complete"? The poet has already supplied the answer to the rhetorical question: "The stupid and the wise thinker, parents and offspring, merchant, clerk, porter and customer,/ Editor, author, artist, and schoolboy," that is to say, all of humanity can learn the "lesson complete" if they approach nature in the right spirit—the spirit of wonder.

Forms and Devices

Whitman's poem essentially has a question and answer structure. The question announced in the title "Who Learns My Lesson Complete?" is answered throughout the remainder of the poem. As a writer of free verse, Whitman avoids rhyme and regular meter, preferring the parallel structures observable in the King James Bible and the persuasive prose of the New England Transcendentalists (Ralph Waldo Emerson and Henry David Thoreau, for example). The persuasive nature of the poem makes these repetitive structures quite viable. One might observe the first four words of the final five lines of the poem as a lesson in parallelism: "And that my soul," "And that I can," "And that I can," "And that the moon," and "And that they balance." The student learns to look, in other words, not at the ending of lines for rhymes but at the beginning of lines for emphatic repetitions.

It may be that Whitman had an ironic pun in mind when he titled his poem "Who Learns My Lesson Complete?" The word "lesson" is pronounced identically with the word "lessen." In brief, the poet announces a lesson that lessens the work normally expected of the student; it is the assumption of a sense of wonder, not a scholarly absorption in facts, that will constitute "the lesson complete." This ironic lessening is in reality a mystical increase in the student's appreciation of natural phenomena.

Themes and Meanings

The central theme of the poem is the understanding of the most important type of knowledge, that is, knowledge that cannot be communicated except through a shared sense of wonder. The "lesson complete" is the lesson felt, experienced, and endured; it is not a lesson learned in textbooks or in lectures. The most important kind of knowledge is gained through a relaxation of the soul, making possible the understanding of the wonderful nature of natural phenomena.

As the poem's title suggests, the great poet functions as a great teacher. The poet as teacher is a common nineteenth century figure. The poet does not instruct so much as he shows the way through his own example. Readers of *Leaves of Grass* will recognize the theme of the difficulty of communicating the sense of wonder as pervasive in Whitman's work. The short poem "When I Heard the Learn'd Astronomer," to cite a familiar example, narrates two scenes: The first scene shows the poet attending an astronomy lecture, while the second scene relates the narrator's departure from the lecture to stare "in perfect silence at the stars." The lecture leaves the poet "tired and sick," but he is refreshed when he looks up at the stars, having escaped "the charts and diagrams." The relief from such depression consists in the sense of wonder awakened by simply staring up at the stars. True learning comes about as a result of the sense of wonder rather than formal education.

The theme of equality, of the essential nobility of all human beings whatever their occupation, educational level, economic status, or location is, again, one that all readers of *Leaves of Grass* have come to expect from the great poet of democracy. Another theme, the assertion of immortality and the sense of wonder associated with the belief in immortality is, to most critics and scholars who have commented on this poem, insufficiently developed. As one of the most important doctrines of *Leaves of Grass*, it is more satisfactorily treated in poems such as "Song of the Rolling Earth" and "Salut au Monde!"

James T. F. Tanner

WICHITA VORTEX SUTRA

Author: Allen Ginsberg (1926-1997)
Type of poem: Mock epic
First published: 1966; collected in *The Fall of America: Poems of These States, 1965-1971*, 1972

The Poem

"Wichita Vortex Sutra" is a long poem (690 lines) in free verse that is divided into two main parts. Part 1 (156 lines) was actually written the day after part 2 (534 lines); the poem was written on February 14 and 15, 1966. The word "sutra" in the title is the Sanskrit word for thread, connective cord, or rule, and is used in a religious context to denote any of the sermons of the Buddha. Situated near the geographic center of the continental United States, Wichita, Kansas, is, for Ginsberg, also the cultural heart of the country. Overwhelmingly white, Christian, and conservative, Wichita is the quintessential expression of mainstream America, the metaphoric axis of its violently whirling vortex. In terms of sound sense, Wichita (though an Indian name) evokes the word witch, thus conjuring images of sorcery, witchcraft, evil portents, and America's Puritan heritage. So, taken as a whole, the title employs alliteration as it ironically juxtaposes Buddhism and Christianity, order and chaos, prayer and violence, and suggests an incantation or sermon meant to admonish, and possibly even exorcise, America.

Written in the first person, the poem describes a 250-mile bus ride (south on Route 77) from Lincoln, Nebraska, to Wichita, Kansas, on a bleak Sunday afternoon in midwinter. (Indeed, the route from Lincoln to Wichita traces a kind of sutra—a thread or connective cord—between the two cities.) In terms of narrative strategy, the poet shifts between vivid descriptions of the rural midwestern landscape, quotations from contemporary newspaper reports, free-associative meditations on the Vietnam War then raging, the larger history of the Cold War, and the state of America's soul. The form of the poem, philosophical meditation thinly disguised as travelogue, may owe something to "Travels in North America" by the Nebraskan poet Weldon Kees, a native of Beatrice—one of the towns that the bus passes through on its way to Wichita.

Rife with hyperbolic, angry, and plaintive exclamations arranged in uneven lines spread over long, loosely structured stanzas, the poem does not offer a concise or neatly defined argument. Nonetheless, it does manifest a coherent polemic. As is characteristic of so much of his poetry, Ginsberg starts out by lamenting the sexual and emotional repression that is at the root of the terrible loneliness of American life: "to speak my lonesomeness in a car,/ because not only my lonesomeness/ it's Ours, all over America." He then echoes his hero, Walt Whitman, in calling for a renaissance of joyful feeling: "No more fear of tenderness, much delight in weeping, ecstasy/ in singing, laughter rises that confounds/ staring Idiot mayors/ and stony politicians eyeing/ Thy breast,/ O Man of America, be born!" Ultimately, though, the poet's main concern is with language, particularly its grotesque misuse in the service of militarism: "I search for the language/ that is also yours—/ almost all our language has been taxed by war." Much of the poem is concerned with exposing and denouncing "language abused/ for Advertisement,/ language used/ like magic for power on the planet." However, the poem also envisions positive alternatives. Counterpoised against the distorted language of the media, politicians, and "U.S. military spokesmen," the poet offers as exemplar the visionary language of his friend, Bob Dylan: "His youthful voice making glad/ the brown endless meadows/ His tenderness penetrating aether,/ soft prayer on the airwaves,/ Language, language, and sweet music too."

Forms and Devices

Ginsberg's poetic approach might be best described as historical stream-of-consciousness. Like Whitman, Ginsberg starts with the consciousness of the individual self and expands its purview to encompass the putative consciousness of American society as a whole—and, by extension, of the entire universe ("I am the Universe tonite"). As a poem ultimately about the United States, much of the imagery of "Wichita Vortex Sutra" consists of precise and telling descriptions of the American landscape: "Prehistoric excavation, *Apache Uprising/* in the drive-in theater/ Shelling Bombing Range mapped in the distance,/ Crime Prevention Show, sponsor Wrigley's Spearmint,/ Dinosaur Sinclair advertisement, glowing green—." Here and elsewhere, the scenery is charged with metaphoric significance; seemingly banal landmarks act as synedoches for American commercialism, militarism, police repression, and the exploitation of resources and other peoples.

As Ginsberg gets closer to Wichita, "the heart of the Vortex,/ where anxiety rings," his concern with the degradation of language becomes more urgent. Accordingly, he summons his bardic powers to effect a ritual transformation of the language through his own utterances: "I call all Powers of imagination/ to my side . . . to make Prophecy . . . Come to my lone presence/ into this Vortex named Kansas/ I lift my voice aloud,/ make Mantra of American language now,/ I here declare the end of the War!"

As it nears culmination, the poem gathers momentum and takes on aspects of a shaman's chant as the word "language" is more frequently interjected: "U.S. Military Spokesman/ Language language/ Cong death toll/ has soared to 100 in First Air Cavalry/ Division's Sector of/ Language language/ Operation White Wing near Bong Son/ Some of the/ Language language/ Communist/ Language language soldiers/ charged so desperately/ they were struck with six or seven bullets before they fell." Thus, the poet uses the very word "language" as a kind of linguistic solvent to destabilize and overturn that which the word (self-reflexively) denotes. False, degraded language must be deconstructed and banished before a more truthful language can be uttered in its place.

Themes and Meanings

Though on one level it is certainly an antiwar poem, "Wichita Vortex Sutra" transcends both its genre and the specific historical circumstances that occasioned its creation. A fundamental premise of the poem is that language, though a simple tool, is also a tremendously powerful and potentially dangerous tool, much more powerful and dangerous than is generally assumed. More than merely expressing consciousness, language shapes consciousness and therefore controls history.

As an example of the reality-transforming power of language, Ginsberg cites an utterance by President John F. Kennedy's secretary of defense, Robert S. McNamara, who "made a 'bad guess'/ 'Bad guess?' chorused the Reporters./ Yes, no more than a Bad Guess, in 1962/ '8000 American Troops handle the/ Situation.'" McNamara's sloppy and infelicitous use of language may or may not actually have helped to precipitate the disastrous U.S. involvement in Vietnam. Ginsberg dramatizes McNamara's statement because he sees it as typical of a chronic pattern of U.S. government deceit, exaggeration, misapprehension, and misstatement that marked the entire history of the Cold War: "Communism is a 9 letter word/ used by inferior magicians with/ the wrong alchemical formula for transforming earth into gold." In the mouths of such men, language ceases to have any mimetic significance; it is reduced to gibberish, an abstruse and secretive currency of power. Indeed, as if language were not debased enough, new terms are coined to obscure reality further: "General Taylor *Limited Objectives/ Owls* from Pennsylvania/ Clark's Face *Open Ended/* Dove's *Apocalypse*."

Ginsberg also asserts that America's corporate media is ideologically all of a piece, and is at one with the government, in the creation and dissemination of lies and distortions that further oppression and war: "N B C B S U P A I N S L I F E/ Time Mutual presents/ World's Largest Camp Comedy:/ Magic in Vietnam—/ reality turned inside out." Yet against such concerted and powerful forces of mystification, the lone poet also has enormous power: the power to name evil. The evil that Ginsberg identifies as underlying America's war on language, on nature, on its own and other peoples, is a Puritanical, life-denying strain that is integral to the American character.

Engaging in the sort of instructive hyperbole that marked his treatment of the McNamara statement, Ginsberg closes the poem with an arresting assertion: "Carry Nation began the war on Vietnam here/ with an angry smashing ax/ attacking Wine—/ Here fifty years ago, by her violence/ began a vortex of hatred that defoliated the Mekong Delta—." The idea that Carry Nation (the famous midwestern temperance advocate who marched into barrooms and smashed bottles and fixtures with a hatchet) somehow instigated the Vietnam War is, of course, not literally true. What is true is the *spirit* of the statement—its equation of prohibitionist fervor with interventionist arrogance. To Ginsberg's way of thinking, both events come from a characteristically American intolerance of difference, an insatiable desire to control or to destroy.

Robert Niemi

THE WILD COMMON

Author: D. H. Lawrence (1885-1930)
Type of poem: Lyric
First published: 1916, in *Amores*; revised in *The Collected Poems of D. H. Lawrence*,
   1928

The Poem
   "The Wild Common" is, in D. H. Lawrence's own terms, "a good deal rewritten."
Among his earliest writings, it was composed in 1905 or 1906 at a time when he was
"struggling to say something which it takes a man twenty years to be able to say."
Lawrence finally got that said when he published his extended version of the poem—
twenty percent longer and with more than fifty percent of the original reworded—
as the opening poem in his *Collected Poems* of 1928. The forty-two-year-old poet
changed little of the basic scenario, or even of the rhyme scheme and rhythm, of "The
Wild Common" from the version he wrote at nineteen. The content of the poem,
however, matures markedly.
   Critical consensus prefers the revised poem, with its increased detail and clarified
focus. The earlier version is almost never anthologized. Some commentators consider
the improvements over the first version as substantive as William Butler Yeats's
sweeping revisions of his poems. Whereas the original is more of a personal effusion
on the beauties of the English countryside, the later poem zeroes in on issues of
substance and shadow, celebrating the corporeal present in an exultant "I am here! I
am here!"
   "The Wild Common" in its final form consists of ten four-line stanzas, each stanza
following a regular *abab* rhyme scheme. The rhythm is irregular, and that prosodic
irregularity is compounded by alternating short and long lines. The title aptly prefaces
Lawrence's paean to life's natural beauty, beauty both physical and spiritual. This
English "Wild Common" fairly bursts with warm sunshine and inviting water, with
ecstatic larks and rejoicing peewits (birds also known as lapwings), with blossoming
shrubs and lively flowers. The poem is written in the first person, a perspective that
helps sharpen the poignancy of the poet's personal encounter with the natural world.
   On its most fundamental level, the poem is an ode to nature's beauty. Lawrence
writes simultaneously as an observer from the periphery of the natural world and as
an active participant in nature. The speaker is at first an observer, content to paint
impressions of the common, but as the poem progresses he becomes a participant,
immersing himself in the inviting atmosphere of the common. Lawrence's description
invites the reader to accompany him in that rich sensory immersion.
   It is in the second stanza that the poet first enters the wild common. He interrupts
a tranquil scene of rabbits resting on a hill. Questions in rapid succession—"Are
they asleep?—are they living?"—move the poet to startle the rabbits into motion.
Lawrence's excitement pulsing through these images charges his punctuation, where
the sparks of exclamation points begin to fly. Though the third stanza returns the poet

to passive observation of the common, he manages even in quiescence to enliven the ordinary with crackling details, with kingcups (buttercups) that "surge to challenge the blossoming bushes" and a "streamlet" that, however lazy, "wakes again, leaps, laughs, and gushes."

The beginning of the fifth stanza marks a crucial shift in the poet's thought, raising philosophical issues that broaden the significance of "The Wild Common." Observing his own shadow on the common turf triggers for the speaker crucial questions about the meaning of his life. He ponders the significance of death, which causes him to wonder how physical realities relate to spiritual ones. That thought in turn raises for the speaker the question of how consciousness and unconsciousness interact.

In the final five stanzas Lawrence explores possible answers to those questions. He finds his most satisfying answers in his plunges into the sensuous delights of the wild common. Lawrence makes it clear that the physical and spiritual interweave as thoroughly as the landscape knits together the plants, the birds, the weather, and the light of the common. The poem's climactic concluding image interweaves at deeper levels the sensual and the metaphysical: The poet immerses himself in the common's pond to find in its waters answers to his deep questions from stanza 5.

Forms and Devices

That experience of integration, like most experiences in D. H. Lawrence's poetry, is richly physical. The reader can taste in this poem the sweet substance of felt life and relish Lawrence's incomparably responsive eye for natural detail. It seems significant that Lawrence in his revising of this poem shapes the sensuousness away from the erotic toward the religious. The earlier poem featured a central image of "soul like a passionate woman," with closeups of intimate love running "ecstatic over the pliant folds rippling down to my belly from the breast-lights."

The images that replace those erotic visions in the final version are, in contrast, strikingly incarnational, even liturgical. Lawrence sees a beatific sun whose "substance" transubstantiates into "yellow water-blobs." He makes simple peewits angelic, "wings and feathers on the crying, mysterious ages." The climax of the poem is explicit incarnation: "All that is God takes substance!" A rabbit stands in for the priest at this "confirmation," while in the background lark songs—a decidedly liturgical seven lark songs—are "pealing" like church bells. The underlying emphasis on religious ceremony consecrates the youth's dive into the pool as emblematic baptism into life.

It is intriguing that the question of Lawrence's materialism is so much debated among critics. Some readers see him as limited by his focus on natural phenomena to the exclusion of spirit. Perhaps that perception of materialism is more a response to Lawrence's insistence on the personal. Lawrence's ultimate poetic technique goes beyond religious emblem and even sensory detail to insistence on personal presentation.

Lawrence wrote frankly from his own experience. What many readers admire in Lawrence's poetry is not so much the poetry as Lawrence himself; they are drawn to the human feeling rather than the sometimes awkward phrasing. His poetry in general, and this early poem in particular, has been condemned by critics for inept phrasing and frowned upon as imperfectly articulated. Lawrence came out of the Georgian era at the beginning of the twentieth century, sharing with other Georgian poets habits of stodgy syntax, heavy rhyme, and predictable subjects taken from nature. Yet Lawrence also came out of that era in a different sense: His reaction to the natural world seems more deeply felt than that of the usual serene Georgian; it is both emotionally and prosodically more intense.

"The Wild Common" is central to Lawrence's poetic canon; he comes close in his essay "Poetry of the Present" to suggesting it as a kind of exemplum of the essence of his poetic statement. The poem speaks to the heart of Lawrentian concerns, returning the reader—through the plunge of the speaker into the water and the immersion of the reader into the countryside—to a sense of the divinity inherent in life, to a feeling of the divine nature in all things. Even those who dislike "The Wild Common" think that it has affinities with the best in Lawrence. A companion poem of shared theme and similar method, "Red Moon-Rise," is seen by many as the finest poem in Lawrence's volume *Love Poems*.

Themes and Meanings

Appropriately set in late spring or early summer, "The Wild Common" is an effusion of life, which explodes everywhere in its vivid imagery—light "leaping" from the bushes, birds "sweeping" above the "turf" while water "gushes" from the gorse. The overflowing of life approaches resurrective proportions. Rabbits quiescent as "handfuls of brown earth" on the "mournful turf" come to dramatic life when the speaker lifts his arms in blessing and "the hill bursts and heaves under their spurting kick!"

All that fecund life stirs the urgent question: "What if . . . I were gone?" Behind that poetic pondering on death lies the deeper question of how we can be sure we exist in the first place. Amid the teeming life of the common the speaker sees his own "white shadow." It is that uncertain "quivering" reflection of himself in the waters of life that makes him aware "how splendid it is to be substance." Outer reflections can be key to inner identity.

Burgeoning life becomes in the poem a kind of revelation of personal being: "You are here! You are here! We have found you!" shout the peewits and the rabbits and the "seven larks singing at once." The "naked lad" dives into the fertile water and merges with that oxymoronic white shadow which is his own soul, finding himself, body and soul, in nature. He is integrated, whole, "No longer shadow!" The poem's ultimate affirmation—"All that is right, all that is good, all that is God takes substance"—is not only the central theme of this poem but also the underlying theme of Lawrence's *Collected Poems* as a whole.

Steven C. Walker

WILDFLOWERS

Author: Richard Howard (1929-   )
Type of poem: Dramatic monologue
First published: 1973; collected in *Two-Part Inventions*, 1974

The Poem

With the publication of *Untitled Subjects* (1969) and *Findings* (1971), Richard Howard was acknowledged as a master of the dramatic monologue, a one-sided verse conversation during which the reader gains insight into the character of the speaker. With "Wildflowers" and the other five lengthy poems in *Two-Part Inventions*, however, he explores the possibilities of a new form: the dramatic dialogue. "Wildflowers," for example, attempts to render a conversation between two great figures of nineteenth century literature: the American poet Walt Whitman, author of *Leaves of Grass* (1855), and the Irish-born poet and dramatist Oscar Wilde.

Subtitled "Camden, 1882," the poem purports to re-create what was said when Wilde first visited Whitman in the latter's residence in New Jersey. However, Howard takes certain liberties with historical fact. Although he did seek out Whitman during his 1882 tour of the United States, Wilde actually visited the American poet twice, the first time with his friend, the Philadelphia publisher J. M. Stoddart, and the second time alone. Howard makes Wilde's second visit his first and sets the confrontation in Whitman's Mickle Street residence, a home that he did not purchase until two years later in 1884. Wilde actually visited Whitman in the Stevens Street home of Whitman's brother George. Probably, for dramatic purposes, it suited Howard better that Wilde meet Whitman in the home he lived in by himself except for his housekeeper Mary Davis, a sailor's widow who worked for the poet in exchange for a rear apartment. Over the course of his long literary career, Whitman was the center of a considerable circle of discipleship, and many of his readers made pilgrimage to Camden after he retired from a series of federal government positions in 1874.

As the poem begins, the sixty-three-year-old Whitman is preparing to meet his twenty-eight-year-old admirer from across the ocean. He puts on a red tie and rereads the letter from his Canadian follower Dr. Richard Bucke that first brought Wilde to his attention. Fresh from his tour of the American West, *"dashing between/ coyotes and cañons,"* Wilde has come to pay homage to a man that he sees as "America's great voice." They talk in Whitman's "ruin" of a room, made infamous by his biographers for its disorder. The far-ranging conversation between these two poets is the substance of the poem.

Forms and Devices

The title of the collection *Two-Part Inventions* is a reference to the fifteen keyboard pieces written by German composer Johann Sebastian Bach in two-part counterpoint, a technique of combining two individual melodies to make a harmonious texture. Similarly, the poem "Wildflowers" takes two very different perspectives and weaves them into a unified dialogue. On one hand is the young, Old World poet who speaks of "form" and artifice in poetry and in life; on the other hand is the elderly New World poet whose gospel is natural freedom. Yet during the course of their exchange of ideas, they reach a level of mutual understanding. Whitman realizes that Wilde really needs an answer to the question of his place in the scheme of things, and Wilde believes that Whitman has provided that guidance in his assertion that a person finds himself by giving himself away. Thus real poetry is deemed sacrificial. In this regard, Whitman's self-confessions in *Leaves of Grass* prefigure Wilde's in *De Profundis*, the latter's 1905 letter from prison.

As the title indicates, one of the poem's unifying image patterns involves flowers. In addition to the pun on Wilde's surname, there is the tributary visit that provides the basic situation of the poem and the floral offering that Wilde makes to Whitman at the end. Known for holding a flower in his hands while lecturing, Wilde presents the older poet with a heliotrope, a small, fragrant, purple flower that turns toward the sunlight. In this case, it is Wilde himself who turns toward Whitman as his guide and prophet.

There is also the comparison that Wilde makes between Whitman's *Leaves of Grass* and French poet Charles Baudelaire's *Les Fleurs du Mal* (1857; *The Flowers of Evil*, 1931). He calls both works his "sacred botany," the sacred texts of his time. Baudelaire has taught Wilde the lesson of the artist who suffers for his art; Whitman will teach him the lesson of the artist whose art transcends suffering. Also providing a subtext for the conversation between these two poets is the story of the fisher king. In medieval legend, a desert land is ruled by the fisher king, made sterile by a curse. The king will be cured and his land made fertile only by the sacrifices of a hero who is brave and pure of heart. Prior to Wilde's arrival, Whitman thinks he hears "something like rain, off in the distance." Wilde tells Whitman that he comes to him as one who consults a man "*whose twig bends near water.*" Both Wilde and Whitman look to each other for redemption of a sort. Identifying with Wilde's quote from Baudelaire ("I am even as the king of a rainy country, rich but impotent"), Whitman laments the defection of some of his young disciples who grow "old and cold" and looks to Wilde, "a great boy," as a promising acolyte. For his part, Wilde hopes to find in the older poet a key to his destiny.

The poem is also marked by a wealth of historical detail. Howard is noted for his ability to make the nineteenth century come alive through his engagement with the principal artists of the period. One good example is Whitman's reference to the dismissal from his job at the U.S. Department of the Interior after Secretary James Harlan, a Methodist layman and former professor of mental and moral sciences, found a proof copy of some of the poet's work. This rifling of Whitman's desk by his supervisor underscores Whitman's warning to Wilde that "It will not do to fly in the face/ of courts and conformity." To this admonition Wilde, with some of his characteristic wit, replies, "*I shall cross that bridge/ after I have burned it before me.*" This well-turned epigram foreshadows his three public trials for homosexuality and his eventual imprisonment.

Themes and Meanings

During the course of this imaginary conversation between two poets, there is, of course, much talk of the meaning of their craft. Wilde espouses the aesthetic approach of art for art's sake, and he cites the verse of Baudelaire as part of his contention that literature need not serve a moral or didactic purpose. Whitman, on the other hand, sees himself as a teacher of young men, as the proponent of such concepts as wise passivity, physical and spiritual nakedness, and the primacy of sex and manly love; all of these values he advocates through natural rhythmic cadences. In response to Wilde's recitation of one of Baudelaire's poems, Whitman recoils. To him, it is sickly self-pity organized according to "mathematical principles." This proponent of free thinking and free verse asks, "Is it not a machine,/ a kind of enslavement?"

As he would not be a slave to meter, Whitman chafes at the restraints of illness and old age. For him, his partially paralyzed body confined to a chair by the window is a kind of prison. This central image is part of a larger theme of incarceration. Wilde, for example, speaks of confronting a novel-reading inmate at a "model" prison in Idaho; Whitman terms his age and infirmity "another kind/ of model prison." For one who exalts the life of the senses and the transforming power of touch, it is a tragedy to have to admit that one's "fingers are dead."

This theme of imprisonment is naturally linked to the issue of identity. According to Whitman, one finds oneself through sacrificing or surrendering oneself to others. For Whitman, the working-class boys he nursed in military hospitals during the Civil War were the principal audience he had in mind for *Leaves of Grass*. For his self-expression he was censured by the reading public: "I expected hell./ I got it." In the context of the poem, however, Whitman's scandal is a matter of the past; old age has brought him a modicum of respectability as the "Good Gray Poet." For Wilde, scandal is still to come. His great sacrifice will be his loyalty to his lover, the unworthy Lord Alfred Douglas, and his subsequent public trials and his years at hard labor for acting on his physical affection for other men. In prison, Wilde will drop the mask of art that he donned under the tutelage of Baudelaire and discover for himself *"how a desire becomes a destiny."*

In a very basic way, Howard is the third part of his *Two-Part Inventions*. Because of his own homosexuality, he understands the position of the gay artist as outsider. In this regard, both Whitman and Wilde reach a shared recognition of their status as sexual outlaws whose desires diverge from the norm. They also realize that to give expression to these desires in the nineteenth century means scandal and censure. Yet pain can be a bridge to insight and suffering can be transcended by transforming life into art.

S. Thomas Mack

WILLINGLY

Author: Tess Gallagher (1943-   )
Type of poem: Narrative
First published: 1980; collected in *Willingly*, 1984

The Poem

Tess Gallagher's "Willingly" is a poem in free verse with forty lines divided into four stanzas. The title suggests the cheerful act of giving one's self or doing a task voluntarily; its function, however, is to establish an ironic mood. While most people would be quite pleased to wake up to the sight of their homes being freshly painted, the speaker is anything but happy. She feels violated and erased by the very action that would bring so many other people joy. Just as her house is inanimate and unable to stop itself from being painted and therefore manipulated, the speaker is just as passive and is unable to exert any will over her life at this time. The title is ironic because to give something willingly one must own and control that which is to be given.

In the second stanza, the narrator's home is bathed in a strange "new light." She reflects that even in her sleep she felt the strokes of the painter's brush, or "the space between them," bearing down on her. The poet compares those ominous strokes with "an accumulation/ of stars" that arrange themselves "over the roofs of entire cities." By equating the power the painter wields with every stroke of his brush to the unyielding strength of the universe, the painter becomes godlike. Under the incredible force of the painter's "steady arm," both the speaker and her house begin to disappear, to become changed by an immutable force.

The third stanza again shows the painter as an agent controlling the destiny of the speaker. The narrator watches helplessly as the painter's "careful strokes whiten the web" of the poet's very complicated disassociation from herself. The painter's elevated status is made clear by the fact that he is standing on a ladder far above the poet's head. On a deeper level, when the poet stands by the painter's ladder "looking up" at him, "he does not acknowledge" her. This lack of response to her presence further strengthens the speaker's feelings of uncontrollable invisibility. By the fourth stanza, the speaker has completely relinquished her house to the painter. Smelling the strong odor of the paint, she thinks, "This is ownership." The speaker did not paint the house, and therefore, in her mind, she can no longer lay claim to it. After this painful revelation, some paint falls onto her shoulder, and it feels as if it passes right through her. In the pain of feeling as if she has no control over her house or her existence, the poem concludes with the speaker trying to convince herself that she has "agreed to this," that the path her life has taken has been taken willingly.

Forms and Devices

The first nine lines of the opening stanza are written in the first person. The first-person point of view allows readers to feel as if they are eavesdropping on the speaker's thoughts and allows them to feel the poet's presence intimately. It is important to note that the last line of the first stanza and the remaining three stanzas are written in the second person. The second person is used in this poem to make the reader take the place of the first-person narrator. Readers who compare the lines "I look back on myself asleep in the dream/ I could not carry awake" to "Some paint has dropped onto your shoulder" will notice that this removal of the first-person speaker who drew them into the poem leaves them with the rather surreal feeling that the rest of the narrative is unfolding in their own minds. With each stroke of the painter's brush, the person who spoke to the readers from the perspective of the first-person point of view becomes an increasingly distant memory until she is finally erased altogether. This switch reflects the major theme of self-erasure in "Willingly."

Enjambment (the running over of the meaning from one line into the next line) is used effectively to emphasize the way the speaker interprets the events in the poem that cause her to feel as if she is a nonentity in her own front yard. For example, as the painter's careful strokes "whiten the web" of turmoil in the third stanza, the speaker "faithlessly" says that "Nothing has changed." However, the fifth and sixth lines of this stanza assert, through enjambment, that "something has/ cleansed you past recognition." These lines eloquently say that the new coat of paint on the poet's house has cleansed her to the point of invisibility and that the way she views her life has been radically changed. Also in the third stanza, the painter blots out the swirl of the house's wood grain "like a breath stopped/ at the heart." The effect that enjambment has here is to create an urgent pause. By ending the line on the word "stopped," an auditory image is created. The reader is compelled to imagine the haunting sound of a last gasp before the silence of death. If the lines were simply end-stopped ("the swirl of woodgrain blotted out/ like a breath stopped at the heart"), much of the dramatic tension the poet has created would be lost. When the paint falls onto the narrator's shoulder in the fourth stanza, the reader is told, "You think it has fallen through/ you." The pause that is created by this enjambed line allows readers to reflect on the importance of its meaning. Symbolically, the paint passing through the speaker reemphasizes that she has disappeared.

Themes and Meanings

"Willingly" is a poem about erasure. What can make people feel as if they do not exist? Lack of control? External powers that seem overwhelming? Change? Gallagher's poem implies that all these things can make a person feel as if life is nothing more than a series of inevitabilities. "Willingly" resonates with truth because it documents the way many people act when their lives take unexpected turns. They withdraw in the same way that the speaker in this poem withdraws: quietly yet tumultuously. Tortured and alone with their pain, these sufferers often see their circumstances as much larger than themselves. The speaker of this poem certainly seems helpless in the presence of the painter whom she elevates into an almost celestial being. The saving grace of this poem, which seems so utterly depressing, is that like most successful poems, it is about the survival of the spirit. "Willingly" manages to transcend the pity that readers seem to be asked to give to the speaker.

What is most important is that the creation of this poem, of any poem, is an act of grace in and of itself. Rather than wallow in sorrow, the narrator not only writes of her pain but also shares it with the world. In doing so, she rises above her circumstances and attempts to inspire her readers to do the same.

Paula Hilton

THE WIND INCREASES

Author: William Carlos Williams (1883-1963)
Type of poem: Lyric
First published: 1930; collected in *An Early Martyr and Other Poems*, 1935

The Poem

"The Wind Increases" is a short lyric poem in free verse composed of twenty-eight lines. All the lines of the poem are arranged in such a way as to suggest the motion of wind. In this sense, the poem could be said to be a shaped verse, a type of poem in which the typographical shape of the words on the page represents some part of the subject. Because the overall structural pattern of the poem is so loosely arranged, the poem has no set stanzaic form. In fact, Thomas R. Whitaker, in *William Carlos Williams* (1968), states that the way that the lines are organized encourages the reader to "not think of line-ends"; rather, the set of lines as a whole "dissolve and reconstitute the poetic line as they seek immediacy." Based upon its content, however, the poem can be divided into five parts. In the first seven lines, the poet describes an approaching storm and tells about the "harried earth," the trees, and "the tulip's bright/ tips" being tossed around by the increasing wind. The second part of the poem changes abruptly from this rather literal description of the coming storm to an admonition to the reader: "Loose your love/ to flow." This sudden shift is made all the more emphatic because it and the third part of the poem are in the form of a command. Moreover, this third part is composed of only the single verb "Blow!" At this point, the reader may believe that the poet is referring to the blowing of the wind, that he is perhaps commanding the stormy wind to blow. Undoubtedly, this is one meaning of the line, but the line also suggests that people, after "loosening their love," should allow their love to "blow" or be distributed more freely to their fellow human beings as well as to the world of nature.

The fourth and fifth parts of the poem also seem to involve an unexpected change because they are not directly concerned with describing a storm or with love. Instead, the fourth part asks a question: "Good Christ what is/ a poet—if any/ exists?" The rest of the poem is devoted to answering this question. The reader may also wonder at the quick shift in tone, for the phrases "Good Christ" and "if any exists" imply that the poet himself is both exasperated and frustrated with the difficulty of responding to his own query. There is even a hint of skepticism about whether or not poetry and poets can be developed and created. This irritation and doubt following the poet's comments about the storm and love are surprising. However, after readers finish reading the poem, they see how and why all of these parts fit together to convey the messages that a poet must produce living, moving, fresh ideas just as nature produces new growth each year and that in order to be original and creative, a poet must "loose" his love "to flow." That is, a poet must be full of love—for his craft, for his fellow humans, and for the world of nature—in order to create great art.

Forms and Devices

References to nature abound in "The Wind Increases." The word "wind" is even in the title of the poem. The picture that the poet paints of the increasing wind as well as the other images of nature found in the first seven lines serve to describe literally, albeit somewhat dramatically, the beginning of a storm. In fact, after reading such vivid descriptions of the wind and storm, the reader may wonder about the use of the verb "increases" in the title. Such a word, which is usually used in a precise, mathematical sense, lacks the immediacy and the power of phrases such as "harried earth" and "tulip's bright tips." However, Williams's choice to use the verb "increases" in his title is actually consistent with his style and form. He believed in experimentation in poetry and was not bound by the conventional rules of style or content. Thus, for him to use a word that often has a mathematical connotation in a poem about nature and the philosophy of poetry is not unusual.

Williams does not refer to nature in the middle section (lines 8-13); rather, it is here that he most openly reveals his overriding concern in the poem. He wants to address the same issue that many other poets have contemplated: What is poetry? In order to explore this topic, the poet uses a question-and-answer format. In lines 11-13, he asks what a poet is and then immediately starts to supply an answer. The first part of the answer (lines 14-17) makes no references to nature. Instead, a poet is described as "a man/ whose words will/ bite/ their way/ home." That is, a poet must seek depth of experience, symbolized by the word "home," for people's homes are usually thought of as places where they can expose their "depths." In the last part of the middle section (lines 17-19), the poet emphasizes that the words must be "actual" and yet have "the form/ of motion," that the language of the poet must be abstract yet concrete and vivid.

In the last eight lines, the poet again returns to the use of nature imagery in order to answer his question about the nature of poetry. In these final lines, the poet's essential message concerns his belief that poets must produce their own answers to the age-old questions that have perplexed and "tortured" humans throughout time. However, in order to illustrate this concept, the poet creates a metaphor about a tree: A poet must add new words to each "twigtip" and yet use words that, like the roots of a tree, "grip the ground." These words must also extend all the way "to the last leaftip." That is, a poet should use words that describe even the outermost reaches of thought and feeling just as a tree must extend nourishment to all of its parts, including its most remote leaves on its highest branches.

Themes and Meanings

The central issue of "The Wind Increases" is the subject of poetry itself. In lines 11-13, the poet very directly and almost bluntly asks, "Good Christ what is/ a poet—if any/ exists?" Throughout the course of the poem, the poet replies to his own query, ultimately concluding that there are six essential qualities that a good poet must possess. First, a poet must have an imagination that is "open to the weather." Just as a storm may arise suddenly and without warning, a poem may also arise and come unexpectedly to the poet's consciousness. The poet, however, needs to be open to such an experience in order to produce art. Second, poets must "loose" their love and allow it to flow freely if they are to fully understand and participate in life. Without permitting one's feelings to surface, a person cannot live well or write a good poem. Third, the poet must discover and use words that will "bite their way home" and express the heart and the essential truth of the human condition. Fourth, these words—which must be actual, concrete words—must also be able to capture or emulate the form of fluid, invisible motion. Thus, the language of poetry should be concrete yet capable of describing intangible feelings and ideas. Fifth, a poet must fashion and invent new ideas to add to the already existing body of knowledge. Sixth, in addition to being original, the poet must be rooted in reality and willing to explore every aspect of life and the world.

Thus it requires a combination of vital abilities and talents to become a great artist. If poets do possess all these necessary qualities, they will be able to create their own unique artistic works. According to Whitaker, Williams believed that being an artist was a high calling. Whitaker states that Williams thought that "art itself [was] important because, inviting and refreshing our attention, it [helps] to awaken us from our ordinary sleepwalking—from those habits, blockages, and illusions that produce and perpetuate man's inhumanity to man."

Jo K. Galle

WINTER HORSES

Author: Barbara Guest (1920-   )
Type of poem: Lyric
First published: 1991; collected in *Defensive Rapture*, 1993

The Poem

"Winter Horses" is a poem in four short sections of thirteen, eleven, nine, and eight lines, respectively. The first and last sections' lines are left-justified, whereas the middle sections' lines are scattered on the page. The poem's title provides a useful index to the poem as a whole: "Winter Horses" juxtaposes the idea of winter (stillness) and the idea of horses (motion). Readers can fruitfully consider the poem a meditation on the results of this juxtaposition. Seeming paradoxes are linked through logical associations which lead them to be viewed as complementary ideas instead of contradictory ones.

The first section catalogs the effects of winter on the land and the people. The first line, "placed two sticks upon a dazzling plate," suggests the movement of the poem: How will readers reconceive the ordinary (the "two sticks") on the "dazzling plate" of winter? Abruptly the poem moves from the landscape to people, invoking wars, memory, hearsay, and treachery in only two lines; apparently the emotional landscape of winter is neither still nor dazzling but turbulent and pained. The second stanza implies that readers remember the "tawny . . . splendor" of summer in glorious winter sunsets, despite the freeze that "shut[s] the moat."

The next two sections, with their lines shifting on the page, work even more associatively. The conflict between winter (bearing cold stillness) and horses (living motion) persists but now appears to operate by an associative logic rather than by seeming contradiction. Further, the details begin to probe the greater emotional depths of the connotations of these ideas. For example, as the second section's first stanza turns "sea grey cold" into "a door" and then "one boulder," the cold and the forbidding size of a boulder suggest a closed door and thus the emotional connotations of such a door. The poem thus invites the reader's fuller participation as the reader essentially rewrites the poem in trying to create a personal understanding of the associations. The emotional landscape darkens in the third section as the lines approach a more regular spacing, with some lines indented about half a line while others are left-justified. When an unidentified "they" bring the reader, posed as "you," "a fig dish," it appears as a luxury, but the next line offers a corpse. The winter appears increasingly menacing and powerful, despite its designation as *la gloire* (French for "the glow" or "glory") at the beginning of the section; hence the closing lines, "the cramped space ran/ out of breathing." Winter's compass, left unchecked, would deny life to everything that breathes.

The poem's last section brings readers to the start of the spring thaw as winter still clings. Though snow may "lance" the brightness, winter's last attempt to reign over nature will surely fail. The sun, warm enough that windows are "flung" open, will soon dominate again. This moment between seasons, during which both show their force, creates a sense of awe, a "dazzlement" that urges new life. Yet this life arises from death, for the people who come out in their boots necessarily step on the invisible creature of the air, the sylph. Poet Barbara Guest suggests that the cycle of seasons is not pure; one cannot merely associate winter with death and spring with life. Rather, Guest evokes a far more complex layering of the promise and the threat of a season in the world and in the mind.

Forms and Devices

Guest builds the poem through an accumulation of fragments, of striking phrases that might be disturbing in their incompleteness for the reader of traditional poetry. In an interview, Guest described another one of her poems as working "on several levels and [moving] back and forth . . . between levels as reality does." In Guest's poetic vision, reality is fragmented rather than unified. This is not to say that Guest does not believe there is any coherence but that coherence arises between the levels, between the fragments, in a process of association and accumulation. Guest's fragmentary style urges a high level of participation from the reader. Readers cannot simply accept a given narrative or linear logic; rather, they bring their own associations to the poem and hence find the silence on the page (what Guest does not say) as the place for their participation and understanding. This does not mean that the poem can mean anything the reader wants it to, but that the fragments allow both a greater range of interpretation and any interpretation to remain subject to reconsideration by a different reader.

Guest's use of capitalization and punctuation provide further guidance. There are no capitalized words, placing the reader *in medias res*. This evokes questions about the poem's temporality: Is the poem going on now? The alternation between past and present tense suggests some narrative progression, some relation between what has passed and what is happening now, but the fragmentary nature of these phrases leads more to suggestions than to specific answers. Guest's punctuation operates more definitively: Periods organize the fragments that came before it into a unit, and semicolons link fragments to evince a relation. At the beginning of the third section, the exclamation point at the end of the second fragment suggests that the "it" refers to winter, as the section's beginning and the exclamation point enclose what comes between them and thus relate the two fragments to each other. Guest offers *la gloire* as the reader's preconception of winter: "winter/ you know how it is *la gloire!*"

Guest's fragmented imagery provides something similar to a kaleidoscopic effect in the shifts of light, color, shape, and mood. Readers appear to view a medieval scene composed of "feudal wars," "fortifications," and a "moat" that represents the winter while being situated in it, and yet that scene constantly shifts as it accrues more detail. Some of the images require the reader's invention, as when the reader, described as remembering feudal wars, appears to have not only a historical memory but also a historical imagination; for Guest, these may well be one and the same.

Themes and Meanings

The title of the book in which "Winter Horses" is collected suggests a provocative theme for this poem in particular: *Defensive Rapture*. Where does this poem reach for rapture, and where does it appear to defend against or temper it? Is it the rapture itself that menaces, or does something else underlie and necessarily disrupt rapture? Can a defensive rapture be called rapture at all? The answer might lie in the word "rapture" itself. While the word bears the generally positive definition of "transport to ecstasy," its original Latin root, *raptus* ("to have been seized"), is a form of the verb *rapio* ("to seize"), which is the root of the word "rape." Someone experiencing rapture has been seized, and while this feeling brings the pleasure of ecstasy, it also takes possession of one's mind. A mind as aware of *la gloire* as of fortifications and wars might well find rapture impossible to maintain. Indeed, reality offers both fragments of rapture and menace, and a defensive rapture brings one not so much safety as a steady awareness that can recognize and experience both pleasure and pain, particularly through the vehicle of the imagination.

This leads to a second key theme in the poem: the relationship between reality and the imagination. People generally do not consider reality to be as fragmented as Guest presents it, which raises the question of the role of the imagination. In the poem, the reader's imagination creates coherences between the fragments. Is this also how imagination works with reality? The poem highlights the ability of the mind or the imagination to connect seemingly disparate objects and ideas and to devise meaning, revealing what might be the mind's partly conscious, partly unconscious work. Yet this does not imply that the poem ever loses its ability to disturb by the gaps that it leaves; one cannot merely connect the dots. Readers can make easier connections between some fragments than others. Some fragments contain more of a sense of emotional connotation than a precise interpretation. The poem's incompleteness continues to resonate because that incompleteness produces the necessity to rewrite or reconnect with the poem with every new reading. The period that concludes the poem might well serve as an arrow redirecting readers back to the poem's beginning to read that beginning anew in light of what the "end" has provided. As poet Tom Clark has commented, Guest's work "mimes the tenuous, evanescent sense of shimmer or mirage that life's splintered transparencies present us." Readers may revel in that shimmer, recognizing Guest's "splintered transparencies" as the view from their own lives.

Carrie Etter

WITH A COPY OF SWIFT'S WORKS

Author: J. V. Cunningham (1911-1985)
Type of poem: Lyric
First published: 1947, as #42 of "Epigrams: A Journal," in *The Judge Is Fury*

The Poem

"With a Copy of Swift's Works" is a short poem in couplets, totalling twelve lines. It is divided into two sentences; the first is a couplet, and the second is a single thought elaborated over ten lines. The title refers to the occasion of the poem. The speaker is looking at the literary works of the Irish author Jonathan Swift (1667-1745), who was best known for such satirical prose works as *Gulliver's Travels* and "A Modest Proposal." Swift also wrote poetry, contributed essays to literary periodicals, and authored a fourteen-volume *History of the Reign of Queen Anne*. The initial reference in the poem to the pseudonyms of two of Swift's female friends, "Stella" and "Vanessa," suggests that the speaker is thinking of Swift's poetry. Swift helped several eighteenth century Irish women authors, using his editorial, critical, and business skills to connect Dublin-based women writers with publishers in both Dublin and London. He also wrote poetry to Esther Johnson and Esther Vanhomrigh. Johnson was Stella, and Vanhomrigh was Vanessa. Swift's poems on "Stella's" birthdays are very well-known. The use of pseudonyms was common in verse written by both men and women in the eighteenth century.

Cunningham's poem was written in Palo Alto, California, on May 20, 1944. It became one of the forty-three poems that comprise the "Epigram Journal" of his 1947 book, *The Judge Is Fury*. Swift, too, wrote epigrams, which are short, witty poems, often satirical in tone. The Greek and Latin root words mean "to write on" or, as it is commonly taken to mean, to write an inscription. "With a Copy of Swift's Works" is an epigram which serves as an inscription to an edition of his works—akin to something that the giver of a gift might write in a gift book.

"With a Copy of Swift's Works" begins with the presentation of the book to the reader with the cheery explanation, "Underneath this pretty cover/ Lies Vanessa's, Stella's lover." The poet is making two points here. The first is that all that is left of Swift's talents and genius is bound in this book. The second is about the speculation that Swift was secretly married to Esther Johnson (Stella). There were rumors circulating in both Dublin and London society during Swift's lifetime that he was sexually involved with both women; the rumors have never been proven. In the eighteenth century, "lover" was the term for a fiancée or someone who was dating. To say Swift was a "lover" as Cunningham does here is to play off the older and the modern meanings of the term, indicating sexual involvement.

The next ten lines of the poem are its second sentence. The poet instructs the reader not to be saddened by Swift's life or death. Cunningham assumes the reader is familiar with Swift's life: He had hoped for a job in London but was rejected and thus entered the ministry and became Dean of St. Paul's, the most important Anglican church in

Dublin. He was rumored to have been very bitter about having to live in Dublin, and some of his earliest critics pointed to his dissatisfaction as the reason he was attracted to satire. The poet's view of Swift is objective and practical. It is by his success as a writer that the person to whom the gift is given or the poem is addressed should know and appreciate him. Swift was unsympathetic in his handling of satiric subjects, even tactless, and he would neither want nor deserve sympathy, states Cunningham.

Forms and Devices

The poem is written in couplets. This form is particularly suitable for writing about Swift, as most eighteenth century poets wrote in couplets. The meter of the poem is the trochaic tetrameter, a popular alternative to iambic meters. The trochee is a syllable pattern that goes from unstressed to stressed syllables, while the iamb is a stressed-to-unstressed pattern. Tetrameter has four accented syllables per line. The third couplet, which marks the second part of the poem, demonstrates the technique of catalexis—omitting the stress on the last syllable of the line to create variety in the trochaic line.

"With a Copy of Swift's Works" employs philosophically based imagery. Cunningham's construction is dependent on several strains of late seventeenth, mid-eighteenth, and nineteenth century thought. "Absolute" and "Motion" are the richest words of the vocabulary and are the keys to comprehending the balance of the poem. The third couplet states: "Who the Absolute so loved/ Motion to its zero moved." Swift's satirical vision, and why he came to write what he did, are being described. "The Absolute" was brought into philosophical vocabulary in Germany at the end of the eighteenth century. The concept had been in existence since the mid-sixteenth century in the work of Baruch Spinoza. The phrase "the Absolute," as Cunningham uses it, can be interpreted as a manifestation of God, defined as the creative source of everything real in the world. As an essence or primary source, the existence of God is known through the activities of artists, writers, and musicians, who reveal "the Absolute" to humanity. Humans, then, although mortal, are divine by nature. "The Absolute" was eventually characterized by philosophers between 1803 and 1893 as possessing freedom, reality, truth, and harmony. It is likely that Cunningham was as well acquainted with Samuel Taylor Coleridge's use of the term in his literary periodical *The Friend* (1809-1810) as he was with the work of Georg Wilhelm Friedrich Hegel, James Frederick Ferrier, and Francis Herbert Bradley, all of whom contributed to defining "the Absolute."

The depiction of "Motion" in the poem has its origins in Aristotle, Galileo, and Thomas Hobbes. Cunningham uses "motion," "moved," and "immobile" to relate the action that "the Absolute" takes in relation to Swift. The progress of the remaining couplets is Aristotelian. Aristotle defined the idea of the "Absolute," when he wrote of the unmoved mover. Motion actualizes potential which creates a form which can change in quality, size, and location. Aristotle's idea, as it regards humans, is usually taken to include his idea that humanity could achieve perfection. In the poem Swift is put into action by "the Absolute," which allows him to realize his potential as a writer; then, because he is mortal, he dies.

Galileo's (1564-1642) theory of uniformly accelerated motion adds the element of evolution over time to the poem. Galileo was interested in the description of motion based on geometric axioms, not in trying to determine the cause of motion. Hence motion moves to its "zero," and fury freezes as the anger that motivated Swift's satires diminishes. Finally, Hobbes's (1588-1679) theory of motion is based on the premise that without force or impetus there can be no motion. He posits that movement happens when the body acted on by the force resists it. At the first push of force, however, the body will yield, no matter how hard or solid it may be. Hobbes's theory, when applied to the poem, introduces the concept of tension between the external source of the force and the body it moves. Cunningham uses this notion to symbolize the power of death in life, Swift's mortality, and the reader's love-hate reaction to satire.

Themes and Meanings

The reader's satisfaction with "With a Copy of Swift's Works" depends on prior knowledge of Swift's life and works. Cunningham presumes a reader who knows Swift and would want his works. This reader is acquainted with the rudiments of Swift's life, Swift's own unpublished "Verses on the Death of Dr. Swift, D.S.P.D." (1731), his epitaph, and the philosophical theories of the mover and the moved, developed in Swift's life and expanded upon after his death.

The principal theme of the poem is that Swift's works represent him well. The "pretty cover" of the volume is deceptive, as many of his works were intended to expose the "ugliness" or vice-ridden aspects of human nature. The poet is suggesting that there is no need to feel sorry for this writer, who achieved what he intended.

Cunningham previously alluded to Swift in a 1932 poem, "The Wandering Scholar's Prayer to Saint Catherine of Egypt." In this poem, collected in *The Helmsman* (1942), Cunningham evokes Swift as a specter of death to describe the hobos in the train yards who are dying of starvation and neglect as "Swift in idiot froth." Swift was declared insane and therefore mentally incompetent in 1742 when the symptoms of Mèniére's syndrome had debilitated him beyond his ability to care for himself. He died a painful and miserable death, and his illness caused his reputation to suffer and created a lack of compassion among the public.

Cunningham, like Swift, uses the glib briskness of the satirist's stance to appear lighthearted about serious matters. "With a Copy of Swift's Works" addresses the theme of the relationship between a writer's life and the work produced. When the figure is one of the stature of Swift, it is easy for the reader to misinterpret his motives in writing satirical works and compassionate poetry. Cunningham, while relying on the reader's knowledge of Swift, implies that Swift was acting out the will of a higher power or force in his writing. His satires were not motivated by bitterness about a life that could not be, but by a soul tormented by the realization that perfection is within the grasp of humanity, which is too weakened by vice and self-interest to attain it.

When Swift realized that he had accomplished all he could with his work, fury froze within him and he died in harmony with "the Absolute," which had directed his actions to its satisfaction. When fury's force was silenced, the writer ceased to move.

Beverly Schneller

WITH THE GRAIN

Author: Donald Davie (1922-1995)
Type of poem: Meditation
First published: 1959; collected in *New and Selected Poems*, 1961

The Poem

Donald Davie's "With the Grain" is a meditative lyric of sixty-three lines divided into three sections, each with three seven-line unrhymed stanzas. The poem ponders the applicability of certain aspects of carpentry and painting to fundamental elements of romantic love and literature. The general, alternating contrast between long and short lines in each stanza as well as the lack of uniform line pattern within or between stanzas (line length varies from five to fourteen syllables) echoes the contrast between regularity, or order, and irregularity, or "cross-graining," in the poem's extended metaphor of the effects of the grain in wood on carpentry and other forms of expression.

In stanza 1 of section 1, the speaker moves from particular to general, or concrete to abstract, in a series of third-person questions about the metaphoric applicability of specifics in carpentry (graining) and gardening (tilling) to those endeavors as a whole and, more broadly, to all mental activity or thought. From musing about the application of the idea of the wood's grain in carpentry to human behavior, inherent in proverbial expressions such as "with the grain" or "ingrained," the speaker compares, in stanza 2, the carpenter and his work to romantic lovers by personifying the woodworking: "the irritable block/ Screams underneath the blade/ Of love's demand." In stanza 3 of section 1, the speaker introduces first-person references and addresses the issue of attempting to communicate through the use of various media: carpenters through wood, painters through color, and romantic lovers and poets through language. This stanza thus commences the correlation developed in the poem between lovers and literary authors, who both use language to communicate.

Section 2 moves from a comparison between communication in romantic love and communication in the "decorative arts" (especially carpentry) to a comparison between communication in romantic love and communication in the visual art of painting. Just as wood resists carpenters' blades and hue and light may affect or impede painters' perceptions and renderings of the color of their subjects, so too may the primary medium of communication between lovers (language) resist precise expression. As the painter should find an "equable light" that would not distort hue or color, so, the speaker says to his romantic partner, "we should say, my dear,/ Not what we mean, but what/ The words would mean." That is, the speaker goes on, "We should speak,/ As carpenters work,/ With the grain of our words." Nearly all people have had the experience of having something to say but not being able to find the words to precisely express it, sometimes because the words have meanings that pull in different directions from people's original intentions. The concept of undistorted color in painting (found, according to the poet, in the light of the town of Saint Ives, England) leads the speaker to the idea of a fixed color in love (mauve) that, like the white robes of the Druids in Cornwall or the blue robes of the bards in Wales, would signify devoted, undeflected constancy and commitment.

The association of lovers with bards and Druids in section 2 leads the speaker, in section 3, to call lovers a kind of "fourth estate" that is "hieratic." The imagery of carpentry and the imagery of painting are combined in section 3 in the speaker's references to lovers with true communion of emotion and language who are able to "chamfer away/ A knot in the grain of streaming light" and to the poet as the "carpenter of light" who may "work with the grain henceforward." The repetition of the first three lines of the poem in the first three lines of the last stanza gives the poem a circular or spiral structure, helping to round off the idea that the "colorful trades" of artisan, painter, lover, and poet all aspire, like Icarus, to triumph over elements of the real world that are unruly and a hindrance to their endeavors.

Forms and Devices

In addition to the striking extended metaphors drawn from carpentry and painting that are used to explore interconnections among artisan, painter, lover, and poet in how they deal with the surrounding world, Davie makes repeated use of allusion, pun, and inverted syntax. Stanza 2 of section 1 contains a humorous allusion to William Shakespeare's *Hamlet* (1603) in the speaker's recognition that the expression "in-grained habit" is metaphoric or "fanciful": "And there's the rub/ Bristling, where the irritable block/ Screams underneath the blade/ Of love's demand." Counterposed to the moody, doubtful, and philosophically contemplative Hamlet, who worries about what really may follow death ("To die, to sleep;/ To sleep: perchance to dream: Aye, there's the rub"), Davie's speaker is wittily inquisitive and philosophically contemplative about love and art. In stanza 1 of section 3, Davie alludes to a famous passage in French historian Jean Froissart's *Chronicles* (1373-1410) that vividly and poetically describes a jousting tournament during which two knights strike each other's helmets so forcefully that sparks fly from their lances. Davie's point is that lovers and poets, preferring the "equable light" of Saint Ives to alluring but misleading and sparkling words, would not succumb, like Froissart, to special effects. Indeed, the range of allusion in "With the Grain," including the history of modern painting (the Saint Ives movement), ancient Celtic lore (Druids, bards, Tristram and Iseult), medieval French literature (Jean Froissart), and classical mythology (Icarus), helps add to the philosophical breadth and scope of the poem.

The multiple puns and inverted syntax in the poem not only add to its meaning but also help convey its theme of the waywardness of words. Repeated color references in section 2 suggest a pun on "philtre" as not only the vial that might change perception but also the "filter" that might change the color of one's outlook. In stanza 2 of section 3, the "refractory crystal" that the poet attempts to ignore is "reluctant" to allow its allure to be disregarded. In stanza 3 of section 3, the "colourful trades" are "distinctive" and literally "full of color" as depicted in the poem; the "High lights" into which the colorful trades climb are simultaneously lights that are high up, brilliantly lighted areas in a painting, and distinctive features; the reference to how the ideal sun reached by the colorful trades "Dyes only more intensely" has an overtone of death through a lurking pun on "dies" since the trades have risen like Icarus, who not only rose toward the sun with Daedalus's wings but also plunged to his death because of them and his aspiration.

Following the grain of language is suggested immediately in the poem by the syntax of its first four lines, echoed in the first four lines of the final stanza. This repetition is slightly less exact in the 1990 version of the poem through Davie's change of "elevate" in line 1 in the 1959 and 1961 versions to "deviate" in the 1990 version. However, in all versions the syntax is inverted, suggesting that language, like the grain in wood, cannot always be planed into simple straightforwardness; not all sentences or thoughts begin with a subject only to be followed by a verb and then a direct object. Rather, as in the openings of the first and last stanzas of the poem, the idea has to be found by following the grain of the sentence to discover that the subject is delayed, preceded by the verb: The activities deviate into their own ideas, and the colorful trades elevate into the light of ideas. This inverted syntax is also required by the linguistic requirements of forming a question sentence that begins with the word "why," which emphasizes the poem's contemplative quality.

Themes and Meanings

Davie's interests in literary criticism and aesthetics are reflected in many of his poems, including "With the Grain." The poem reminds readers that language, literature, crafts, art, and romantic love or interpersonal relationships may be, and have been, interconnected. Because of the world's complexity, principles from any one of these areas may cross over into principles of the others; thus, a correlation is revealed in the development of proverbial metaphoric expressions, the shaping of a carpenter's block, the filling of a painter's canvas, the evolution of a romantic couple's relationship through dialogue or argument, and the unfolding of a poem's—including this poem's—form and meanings.

A crucial premise of the poem, in accord with Davie's early reputation as a modern neoclassicist, is that principles of order do indeed underlie the apparent meandering diversity of people, activities, and material objects in the world. These principles allow the poet's recognition of reflections and connections among the disparate data of experience, ranging from modernity to antiquity. The modern romantic partner addressed by the speaker in section 2 is assumed to have the wit and intelligence of the addressees of love poems in the bygone neoclassical and Metaphysical periods of English literature, who could understand and appreciate the artistry and thought of Alexander Pope, John Dryden, and John Donne. These poets, like Davie, could contemplate and find the surprising resemblances between romantic love and planing a block of wood.

Norman Prinsky

WITHIN THE VEIL

Author: Michelle Cliff (1946-   )
Type of poem: Lyric
First published: 1985, in *The Land of Look Behind*

The Poem

"Within the Veil" is composed of twenty-one six-line stanzas. The title suggests that certain conditions are being concealed, as if under a veil, and that they are not being addressed. The first line of the poem, "Color ain't no faucet," establishes that the poet is addressing racism. The poet invites readers into the poem by addressing them directly as "you." By doing this, Michelle Cliff establishes a direct dialogue between herself and readers. She also implicitly makes her readers accountable for the issues she addresses, partly through the casual, intimate tone that she employs throughout. The most immediately noticeable aspect of the poem is that it is written in blues form, with the blues' typical repetition of lines.

"Within the Veil" is a biting commentary on race relations, sexism, and social injustice. Each stanza recounts historical events or phenomena that have adversely affected black people, not only in the United States but also in the Caribbean and on the African continent. The tone of the poem is matter-of-fact, and the poet implies that readers are in the know, indicating that the poem is directed specifically toward black readers. This becomes clearer in stanza 2 and is further developed in stanzas 3 and 4, in which Cliff sets up an oppositional relationship between herself and her readers on one hand and the "whiteman" on the other, advising readers that "We got to swing the thing around." Here, as throughout the remainder of the poem, the reader is co-opted into a collective "we," implying agreement with the poet. From this point on, Cliff speaks not only for herself and about her own experience but also for the reader who supposedly shares her perspective.

Cliff explores many of the major issues that African Americans have confronted since the great migration from the South to the North after World War II. The use of "ofay," a derogatory term African Americans used when referring to Caucasians, further signifies that the poem is aimed at a black audience. Words such as "sisters" and "mama" indicate that Cliff is speaking specifically to black women. However, the poet's criticism is not only geared toward the way white people have treated blacks but also toward African American homophobia (stanzas 6 and 10) and the different hair styles they have used to divide themselves (stanza 8). When she states, "How dare anyone object/ Tell me I had better not exist," Cliff is both speaking of white attitudes and pointing out that black people must accept one another's differences.

The first ten stanzas draw a historical line from African American migration from the South, to the Harlem Renaissance, and on to the 1960's. The persona of the poem functions as a historian as well as a praise singer who recounts African American achievements. In stanza 5, for example, readers learn about Zora Neale Hurston, a Harlem writer and friend of poet Langston Hughes. Hurston was severely criticized by many male writers, notably Richard Wright, for her work. Hurston focused primarily on all-black communities, specifically her hometown of Eatonville, Florida. Hurston's classic novel *There Eyes Were Watching God* (1937) has been widely taught since Alice Walker unearthed Hurston's works in the mid-1960's. Cliff alludes to Hurston's seminal anthropological work, *Mules and Men* (1935), to defend Hurston's credibility. In stanzas 8 and 9, two other archetypes are revered. The first is Madame C. J. Walker, the first black female millionaire, who invented the hot comb to press hair. The second is Lorraine Hansberry, the first African American to win the New York Drama Critics Circle Award for the best play of the year, *A Raisin in the Sun* (1959).

Forms and Devices

"Within the Veil" fits into a genre known as blues poetry. The blues is a distinctly African American form of music and poetry that is said to have its roots in Africa, specifically Senegal. There the griot (performers whose songs and stories keep the oral history of their people alive) tradition is best represented. Blues lyrics generally recount personal stories, and the most popular blues focus on love, heartbreak, and hard times. "Within the Veil," however, fits into another category of blues, one that emphasizes sociopolitical implications. In this type of lyric, although the poem or story may seem to be about an individual's personal problems, the implication is that the seemingly isolated situation is applicable to the group.

Lyrically, the blues form consists of three-line stanzas (musically it is most often in a repeating twelve-measure or "twelve-bar" pattern). "Within the Veil," although it appears as six-line stanzas, adheres to the blues format. Generally the first line of a blues states the problem or situation, and the second line repeats it for emphasis, sometimes with a variation or twist. The third line then resolves the stanza or provides some concluding commentary on the situation. In Cliff's poem each of the standard three blues lines is written as two lines on the page, but the stanza can nonetheless be sung over the rhythmic framework of a twelve-bar blues:

> Gold chains are love-symbols
> You tell me where they are found
> Yes, gold chains are love-symbols
> You tell me where gold is found
> There are mines in South Africa
> Where our brothers sweat their lives underground.

The blues typically maintains a rhyme pattern in which the last line rhymes with the concluding word of the first two lines ("found"/"underground"). Another important element of the blues is the use of vernacular or slang and intimate references. Throughout the poem Cliff uses words such as "ain't" and adopts a casual style of speech: "We got to figure what we can do." Some of the intimate, familiar words that Cliff uses are "baby," "sisters," and "brothers," which are terms of endearment implying that all black people are connected by a common ancestry.

Another technique that Cliff exploits in the poem is the shifting of pronouns, as from the first-person singular "I" to the plural "we." She moves among pronouns, including "I," "you," "we," and "they," to emphasize inclusion or division as it suits the individual stanza and the poet's purpose. In stanza 4, for example, she says that "we" (African American women, "sisters") can call "them" (whites) names, but that "you" (listeners or readers, part of the "we" but here being directly addressed) "lie if you tell me you don't know." Furthermore, by citing concrete examples—whether of famous historical individuals, a police shooting in Boston, or the work of miners in South Africa—Cliff not only establishes credibility for the claims she makes in the poem but also presents herself as a voice of authority and a keeper of tradition.

Themes and Meanings

"Within the Veil" calls for social justice for blacks throughout the African diaspora. Cliff reveals how all black people, regardless of whether they live in the United States, in the Caribbean, or on the African continent, are connected by oppression and should therefore, as a group, be committed to a singular freedom. The poet states the importance of black people not allowing themselves to be divided by sexual orientation ("Your best friend's a bulldagger") or ethnic makeup ("Some of us part Indian/ And some of us part white"). Cliff suggests that ultimately it does not matter what an individual black person's orientation or ethnic background is; in the final analysis, all blacks are subject to the same treatment.

The poem, not unlike the protest poems of the 1960's by Nikki Giovanni and Amiri Baraka, is a call to action. By playing on the sentiments and victimization of blacks, Cliff seeks to motivate black people to act on their own behalf. However, "Within the Veil" does not have a seditious or violent tone that pits blacks against white as opposing groups. The focus is wider, and the poem's political agenda is to end social, racial, and sexual imbalances. Cliff makes it clear than she is not calling for upheaval: "If we say Third World Revolution/ The white folks say World War III." She states her desire for freedom rather than Armageddon. This biblical reference to the end of the world as a result of the final battle between nations (Revelation 16) is intended as a caution to both black and white people.

In the opening line of the last stanza, Cliff clearly states her position: "It's all about survival." The stakes are high. If black people are to persist and conquer institutional injustices, they must come together and "do it better," or they "might as well lay down and die." Although these are the closing words of the poem, the ending is not a pessimistic one. The tone throughout the poem is guardedly optimistic, its optimism accentuated by the use of the blues form, which is well suited for storytelling, social commentary, and exhortation. By citing several atrocities that have occurred to black people throughout history and around the world and showing their parallel relationships, the poet attempts to galvanize the community to act in its own defense. In the tradition of the blues, the process of identifying, naming, and sharing pain is believed to help abate it; recovery and healing can then begin. "Within the Veil" uncovers—it lifts the veil—so that constructive changes can occur.

Opal Palmer Adisa

WOLF

Author: Osip Mandelstam (1891-1938)
Type of poem: Lyric
First published: 1964, as "Za gremuchuyu doblest' gryadushchikh vekov," in *Sobranie sochinenii*; English translation collected as "For the sake of the future's trumpeting heroics" in *Selected Poems*, 1974; as "Wolf" in *The Eyesight of Wasps*, 1988

The Poem

"Wolf" is a short poem of sixteen lines divided into four quatrains. It is one of several poems written in the spring of 1931 on the same theme; they are considered by some literary historians to be variants of the same poem and are therefore known as the "Wolf cycle," "Wolf" being the central poem. Written in the first person and in the present tense, it is, like many of Osip Mandelstam's verses, highly autobiographical. In order to interpret the poem correctly, circumstances of Mandelstam's life in the late 1920's and early 1930's must be taken into account. From the events of Mandelstam's life at this time, it is certain that the poet and the persona are identical.

The title suggests a predator and, consequently, a danger to the persona. The poem opens with an assessment of the poet's position in society and history. He avers that for the sake "of the future's trumpeting heroics" and of "that exalted tribe," he has deliberately deprived himself of the merriment and honor at his "fathers' feast." Without specifically naming the "exalted tribe" or his fathers, he dwells on the degree of and reason for his sacrifice. This becomes clearer in the second stanza, in which he complains that "The wolfhound age" has jumped on his shoulders, thus introducing a feeling of mortal danger to the poet. In the next line, he hastens to add that he is not a wolf by blood, indicating that he is not in the same league with the forces oppressing him. Instead, he pleads for understanding and compassion, suggesting that he would wish to be tucked into the sleeve of a Siberian fur coat like a hat. However, the warmth and security of a fur coat are not the main reasons for his wish to be transported far away.

In the third stanza, he openly says that he does not want to witness "the snivelling, nor the sickly smears," or, more ominously, "the bloody bones on the wheel." Thus, another motif is introduced, that of the cruelty and inhumanity of man to man. Rather than witnessing all those undignified acts or, even less, participating in them, he would prefer the serenity of the Siberian nights and the blue foxes shining all night as they did in primeval times. In the last stanza, the poet pleads again to be taken to a distant region where a peaceful river, the Yenisey, flows and the pines reach to the stars, avowing again that he is not a wolf by blood. The repetition reinforces importance of the statement to the poet. At the very end, he declares defiantly that only an equal can kill him, specifically introducing the final motif of death. The last two statements disassociate him from the events around him and express defiance, even courage, in the face of mortal danger.

Forms and Devices

The poem is written in a conventional style typical of Russian poetry of the nineteenth and twentieth centuries. It is rhymed *abab* with twelve-syllable lines alternating with nine-syllable lines, resulting in a distinct, strong rhythm and a highly musical quality, which, unfortunately and perhaps inevitably, is not fully reproduced in translation. The two most striking devices used by Mandelstam are images and metaphors. The first image that strikes the reader's eye is the cup at the feast. Although the image itself is not ambiguous, its significance is somewhat unclear. It is also not clear of whose glory the poet speaks or to what "exalted tribe" he refers. Yet there is no doubt that a feast is taking place. Speaking of his preferences, Mandelstam uses a powerful image of a hat tucked into a sleeve of a fur coat of the Siberian steppes, which suggests warmth, security, aloofness, and beauty. The beauty of a peaceful river flowing through the steppes of Siberia is enhanced by the images of blue foxes shining in the night amid primeval snow by tall pine trees reaching out to the stars. These beautiful images are contrasted to "the snivelling . . . sickly smears" of the poet's surroundings, which he is forced to endure and from which he would rather escape.

There are fewer metaphors, but one of them occupies a central position. It is the so-called mother metaphor: the wolf. It stands not so much for a wolf in nature as it does for a bloodthirsty predator underlying the beastly nature of modern existence in the persona's society. This is clear from the word Mandelstam uses, *volkodav*, which does not mean simply a wolf but a wolf-dog or wolfhound, corresponding to the nature of the times depicted. Mandelstam extends the metaphor by refusing to identify with it, thus placing it in a sharper focus. Another metaphor, "bloody bones in the wheel," is even more drastic. It stands for the oppressive, torturous age in which the persona lives and for the force of a turning wheel that grinds on inexorably and, like fate, cannot easily be stopped or escaped. Thus, by reinforcing the metaphor introduced in the second stanza ("wolf") and by repeating the salient phrase ("I'm no wolf by blood"), Mandelstam creates a powerful sequence of images and metaphors that support and sharpen the quintessence of the poem.

Themes and Meanings

The main theme in "Wolf" is a defiant resistance to the persecution of humanity. On the basis of the circumstances surrounding Mandelstam's life as attested most forcefully in *Hope Against Hope* (1970), the memoirs of his widow Nadezhda Mandelstam, it is certain that his own experience, or a premonition of it, inspired the poem. The persecution of Mandelstam by the Stalinist authorities began in the late 1920's, gathered steam in the 1930's, and culminated in his death in a concentration camp in Siberia in 1938. At the time this poem was written, he was obsessed by the distinct possibility that he would be arrested, which indeed he was a short time later. Images and metaphors in the poems of the Wolf cycle hint time and again at that possibility. The use of the main metaphor, the wolfhound, for the name of the period (*vek-volkodav*, "the age of the wolfhound") unmistakably defines the poet's under-standing of the period. He strengthens that definition with frightening images of "the snivelling . . . sickly smears" and "the bloody bones on the wheel" in order to castigate cowardice and sycophancy among those helping the operation of the bloody wheel.

The poet is determined not to give in to the threats. His defiance is prefaced by a declaration of his sacrifice "For the sake of the future's trumpeting heroics,/ for that exalted tribe" at his "fathers' feast." Although these references are ambiguous, it is possible that Mandelstam is willing to forsake his Jewish ancestry for the sake of a better life for all. Perhaps he refers to the brotherhood of fellow writers, many of whom are unwilling to join the "new age," or perhaps he has in mind his own spiritual and artistic values. What matters is that Mandelstam is willing to sacrifice his future for all the lofty causes he enumerates. That the wolfhound jumps on his back just the same, eliciting a bold cry of defiance, should not be blamed on the poet. At the same time, Mandelstam expresses his yearning for peace and serenity in a distant place such as Siberia. There is a hint of resignation in his plea to be left alone and allowed to find peace far away from predators. As Nadezhda observes in her book, the use of the image of a fur coat recurs in Mandelstam's work as a symbol of the Russian winter and a cozy, stable existence. It is clear that the poet desires security, which is quite understandable under the circumstances.

While the ending of the poem remains inconclusive and the reader is left wondering what happened to the poet and whether his defiance was strong enough to overcome all the perceived threats, the real-life drama supplied the answers, attesting once again to the poet's clairvoyance. That Mandelstam finds security in Siberia is both ironic and sad, for it was in Siberia that his life ended prematurely under the most tragic circumstances. Siberia has been a place of punishment and exile throughout Russian history, but Mandelstam's premonition is nevertheless uncanny. The irony is that instead of blue foxes, he was met by the wolfhound again. Yet his defiant statement that "only my own kind will kill me" turned out to be true: While he has been physically killed by the "wolf," as a poet he remains very much alive.

Vasa D. Mihailovich

WOMAN AT LIT WINDOW

Author: Eamon Grennan (1941-   )
Type of poem: Lyric
First published: 1991, in *As If It Matters*

The Poem

"Woman at Lit Window" is a reflective inquiry in which poet Eamon Grennan considers the possibilities of accurately rendering the details and nuances of a woman he is observing from outside her window while assessing the factors that make it impossible for him to ever quite capture the full dimensions of his vision. The poem consists of three stanzas of roughly equal length (ten, eleven, and twelve lines) divided by a partition of blank space but joined by the continuation of a statement after the line break. Its mood of quiet reflection is established by the contemplative tone that the poet employs in the first line—"Perhaps if she stood for an hour like that"—which creates a feeling of extended time and suspended motion. However, in an almost immediate introduction of opposing impulses, the poet mentions that he would also have to "stand in the dark/ just looking" at the woman, something he doubts he could "stand" to do. The lure of precision carries his thoughts toward a contemplation of the possible components of his verbal portrait, details of such exquisite precision ("etch/ of the neck in profile, the white/ and violet shell of the ear") that he is held in a kind of rapture of meditation before he considers how his subject might react if she became aware of his presence.

Although he knows that he is invisible to the woman's gaze, his curiosity about what he would do "if she starts/ on that stage of light/ taking her clothes off" unsettles him as the barrier that has kept them physically separate is breached by the power of a creative imagination. At this point, the poet is unable to retain objectivity as an observer concerned only with an accurate rendition. The relationship between them—even if in his mind—has been altered so that even though she "frowns out at nothing or herself/ in the glass," totally oblivious to the observer, he cannot quite return to the mood that initiated his desire for a perfect portrait. While he still believes that given sufficient time and a lack of distraction he might be able to "get some of the real details down," he is now aware of the inevitable intrusion of some distraction that will make this impossible. As he continues to muse about the ideal conditions that would permit him to approach his goal, the woman "lowers the blind," cutting off his actual view of her in the window. As the second stanza ends, the woman is "turning away" and "leaving a blank" that is accentuated by the space between the stanzas.

The third stanza fills in the blank space, denoting it as an "ivory square of brightness," an empty frame glowing with potential. This shifts the focus of the poem, which has been wavering between the poet and the woman in the window, entirely to the poet. The energy released by the image of the woman charges the poet's mind so that everything around him is transformed by the power of vision. The poet, now the primary subject of his own contemplation and illuminated by a "half moon" that casts his shadow on the path to his home, moves amid a glow of cosmic radiance. Its source is in the natural world ("a host of fireflies") but its impact is considerably enhanced by the exultation of his creative consciousness, which sees in the features of the landscape a miraculous essence that defies description but compels an effort to convey its beauty.

Forms and Devices

In "Woman at Lit Window," Grennan moves between moments of reflection and contemplation, in which he considers the possibilities of capturing the essence of the striking image he is observing, and moments of lyric effusion, in which he is reacting directly to and then is almost consumed by the transformative power of the image itself. The poem is structured by the modulation of moods, beginning in a mood of meditation and concluding in an ethos of ecstasy, and is controlled by the alteration, juxtaposition, and intermixture of images of luminescence and darkness. The pattern of imagery is set at the start, with the poet "in the dark" and the woman in the window on "a stage of light." The woman then moves out of the spotlight, leaving "a blank ivory square"—that is, illumination without definition. This is a pivotal point in the poem, a moment of pause and a turn away from the poet's contemplation of the woman and toward a sense of himself as an illuminated object. The light that lingers flows beyond the "stage," less intense but equally captivating, a natural light issuing from the moon and from the pinpoint flashes of fireflies.

The psychological mood of the poet corresponds to the changing light, and Grennan expresses these changes by controlling the tone of the poem, beginning with a meditative, tentative utterance and finishing with a flourish of lyric exuberance but mixing both the lyric mode and the more reflective, philosophical one throughout the poem. The language that he employs at the start is conditional, his ambition qualified by words such as "Perhaps" and "might" and phrases such as "I think I could." His course of action is speculative ("I stand wondering what I'll do"), but, amid this uncertainty, his responses to the image are already vibrant, the description he envisions (and actually offers) vivid and evocative: "I might get it right, every/ fine line in place: the veins of the hand/ reaching up to the blind cord." In this description, there is a sense of subdued excitement mingled with an air of expectancy and then tinged with mild regret and disappointment at the woman's disappearance. As the poet becomes the central subject of the poem, the meditative mode is eventually submerged in the lyrical one. The philosophical cast of the poet's mind is still apparent in his cautious return through the shadowy darkness, but the ecstatic, elevated condition of his spirit is revealed by his fascination with the soft but significant light generators (the half moon and the fireflies). His sensory description of the "fragrant silence" that surrounds him, his identification with the fireflies in their "native ease," and his response to the heartbeatlike "pulse of light" produced by these fireflies illustrates the extent to which the hesitancy of the opening lines has been superseded by the light-generated powers of vision and inspiration. Grennan's description of his shadow—a projection of the self "skinned with grainy radiance"—suggests that he feels his place is still "to stand in the dark"; this darkness, however, is not total, and a keen eye can register gradations that are as interesting in the muted natural light as they are in the artificial blaze emanating from the window.

Themes and Meanings

Throughout his work, Grennan has explored the range of light across a continuum from its absence in total darkness to its fullest manifestations, both in poems written prior to "Woman at Lit Window" and in subsequent ones such as "I Lie Awake Each Morning Watching Light." Although it is not an exact equivalency, light, for Grennan, is often conceived as an analogue for artistic vision. Its occurrence affords the opportunity to see an object or subject with an exceptional clarity. In "Woman at Lit Window," Grennan is transfixed by the illuminated image he sees and is then characteristically inspired to try to capture or convey its essence in language. The persistent problem he faces is that there are always impediments to the ultimate completion of his conception, including the circumstances of his observation, the elusiveness of his subject, or, perhaps most significantly, the complex of personal responses that occur beyond his ability to predict or restrain them. This is what makes the situation so challenging and, sometimes, so frustrating.

In addition, the title of the collection in which the poem appears, *As If It Matters*, is an expression of one of Grennan's fundamental tenets. He is plagued by a sort of hovering uncertainty about the importance of his work and perhaps even the direction of his life. This is not an overwhelming obstacle, but it affects his attitude toward the world and is a factor in many poems. The title is not taken from any of the individual poems in the collection and has therefore been chosen specifically to apply to all the poems in the book. It implies that the struggle to find the language and form for what he sees not only is likely to be difficult and frustrating but also might not even be worth attempting. In "Woman at Lit Window," Grennan resists this position by proceeding as if it does matter, even if his efforts are inevitably going to come up short of his ultimate intentions. As a demonstration of the validity, or at least the usefulness, of this approach, Grennan concludes the poem with the poet suffused in a light as energizing as that which lit the woman in the window in the first stanza. The striking image of his shadow "skinned with grainy radiance" offers a complicated texture as compelling as the pure light on the woman. The effort to "get it right" has given him an opportunity to share or enter the "radiance" accompanied by the almost magical "host of fireflies" that endow the light with spiritual grace.

Leon Lewis

WORDS FOR MY DAUGHTER

Author: John Balaban (1943-   )
Type of poem: Lyric
First published: 1989; collected in *Words for My Daughter*, 1991

The Poem

"Words for My Daughter" is a six-stanza poem written in free verse directed to the poet's daughter. Although the poem tells several brief stories of the poet's past, it is not truly a narrative poem. Rather, it is the poet's first-person voice recalling events to his daughter in order to account for the violence that adults direct at children. The poem opens with scenes from John Balaban's childhood in the rough neighborhood of a Philadelphia housing project. In the opening stanza, the reader learns the story of a boy named Reds, "fourteen, huge/ as a hippo." The scene of idyllic childhood fort building is interrupted by screams from Reds's mother and Reds rushes to rescue her from his father's brutality. The litany of violence continues in the second stanza, in which another of Balaban's friends attacks the milkman who is raping his mother. The poem then turns to a girl "with a dart in her back, her open mouth/ pumping like a guppy's, her eyes wild." It can be surmised that the girl's brother has caused her pain because later the neighborhood kids, with their rough justice, try to hang him.

The third stanza, only three lines long, shifts abruptly back to Reds: "Reds had another nickname you couldn't say/ or he'd beat you up: 'Honeybun.'/ His dad called him that when Reds was little." This stanza further addresses the source of Reds's hatred for his father. The sexual connotation of the nickname suggests that Reds himself had been abused by his father. The next stanza is set off from the rest of the poem not only by stanzaic white space but also by asterisks. Here, Balaban addresses his daughter, directing his words to some future time when she will be able read. In addition, the reader finds the first of three things Balaban wants his daughter to know: "I want you to know about their pain/ and about the pain they could loose on others." The stanza ends with the assertion that "children suffer worse." This statement catapults the poet and the reader into a memory of the Vietnam War. The two stanzas are connected by the word "worse," which closes the previous stanza and starts the next. In addition, the two stanzas are connected by the idea of children suffering. In this nine-line stanza, Balaban recalls a nine-year-old Vietnamese boy on an operating table screaming and "thrashing in his pee" while Balaban tries to identify the source of his pain. The child, however, is deaf. "Forget it. His ears are blown," is the surgeon's comment to the poet.

The next scene describes Balaban and his infant daughter on Halloween. For the poet, the smell of her "fragrant peony head" launches him back to a Vietnamese orphanage filled with screaming infants. At that moment, a young trick-or-treater dressed as a Green Beret arrives with his father, who is also dressed in camouflage. That the father would put his son in such clothing infuriates Balaban, and the memories of Vietnam and his daughter's infancy merge. In the last stanza, Balaban concludes the lesson: "I want you to know the worst and be free from it./ I want you to know the worst and still find good." After presenting images of his daughter laughing and interacting with friendly adults, Balaban suddenly seems to realize that while he protects his daughter, his daughter also protects him.

Forms and Devices

Balaban uses images to great effect throughout the poem. By providing the reader with specific detail, he is able to recount the violence done to and by children. In addition, Balaban combines visual, auditory, kinesthetic, olfactory, and tactile images so that all of the reader's senses are engaged in the poem. In the first stanza, for example, pastoral visual images such as a "mulberry grove" and "the thick swale/ of teazel and black-eyed susans" are interspersed with the auditory images of the screeches of Reds's mother, "thumps like someone beating a tire/ off a rim," and the sound of Reds yelling profanities "at the skinny drunk/ stamping around barefoot and holding his ribs." In the fifth stanza, the reader is absorbed by Balaban's description of his infant daughter and her fragrance. These images, endearing and comforting, are interrupted by a memory from Vietnam of "Sœur Anicet's orphans writhing in their cribs." Again, through this device, Balaban is able to convey his primary concern of violence done to children.

Another device that Balaban uses effectively to introduce and develop his themes is juxtaposition. That is, the poet carefully places his memories in a particular order to create a particular atmosphere. In the opening scene, he layers examples of adult brutality to children and the children's brutal retaliation. In the final three-line stanza of this section, he only needs to hint at the sexual abuse of Reds for the reader to make the connection. Perhaps the most important juxtaposition, however, is the connection of his memories of children in Vietnam with his memories of his own childhood friends and with his own infant daughter. The memories, initially divided by stanzas, ultimately become one memory in the fifth stanza, in which he holds his infant daughter, hears Sœur Anicet's orphans in his mind, and sees the "tiny Green Beret" trick-or-treating at his door. Balaban is able to convey the traumatic nature of his memory by inserting that trauma into the happiest of his moments. Even in these long years after the war, his memories of his daughter are inextricably tied to his memories of injured Vietnamese children. The juxtaposition, then, serves to underscore his theme.

Themes and Meanings

"Words for My Daughter" is a poem about the damage adult violence does to children. It is also, however, a poem of adult redemption made possible by a child. Balaban's background provides some clues to his themes and meanings in "Words for My Daughter." In his book *Remembering Heaven's Face: A Moral Witness in Vietnam* (1992), Balaban recounts his days as a conscientious objector who volunteered to go to Vietnam. As a Quaker, Balaban committed his life to nonviolence and opposition to war. While in Vietnam, Balaban worked for the Quaker and Mennonite Committee of Responsibility to Save War-Burned and War-Injured Children as a field representative. His knowledge, then, of the damage done to children is born out of firsthand experience. It is also clear from reading Balaban's memoir that he roots his poetry in his own experience. "Words for My Daughter," for example, grew out of an actual incident he details in *Remembering Heaven's Face*.

When Balaban writes of his early memories of life in Philadelphia, he thematically connects incidents that concern abusive relationships among family members. Children are not only abused themselves, but they are also called upon to rescue other members of their family who are being abused, or they turn to abuse themselves. What should be loving, protective relationships are instead violent and painful. Certainly, one of Balaban's primary themes in this poem is what happens when "desperate loves" are "twisted in shapes of hammer and shard." However, even if the pain is dreadful in Philadelphia, it is worse in Vietnam. There Balaban's recollections turn to orphaned children who have no family members to protect them and who find themselves abused by members of the human family at large. In these instances, Balaban tries to protect the children just as he finds himself in a protective position with his own daughter as he faces the father and son dressed as Green Berets. The confrontation is ironic: Balaban the pacifist finds that his own love for his daughter twists his response to the other father, whom he curses. Thus Balaban arrives at another important theme: Violence can shape and twist the experience of love.

In the last stanza, the reader is introduced to yet another theme, and perhaps it is here that the meaning of the poem seems most clear. What Balaban says he wants for his daughter is, ultimately, what he wants for himself: "I want you to know the worst and be free from it./ I want you to know the worst and still find good." The ease with which traumatic memories intrude into Balaban's life suggests that he may never "be free" from them. It does seem, however, that he knows the worst and still finds some good. The last stanza, with its description of the poet and his daughter, corrects the early vision of family violence. In the last full sentence, the poem turns around. Suddenly, it is no longer Balaban who is the protector of children; rather, it is his child who redeems him. For Balaban, who often finds himself wandering in the memories of violence and despair, his daughter represents hope. She pulls him from the past and into the future, her birth a regeneration of the world.

Diane Andrews Henningfeld

YOU WERE WEARING

Author: Kenneth Koch (1925-   )
Type of poem: Lyric
First published: 1962, in *Thank You and Other Poems*

The Poem

"You Were Wearing" is a free-verse lyric poem consisting of thirteen long lines divided into two stanzas. Most of Kenneth Koch's lines appear to be two or three lines long on the page, but each one is considered a single poetic line. The title is taken from the first line of the poem: "You were wearing your Edgar Allan Poe printed cotton blouse." What follows is a series of scenes of family life and innocent adolescent flirtations between the speaker and a "cute" girl addressed in the poem as "you," with incongruous references to figures from American history and literature. These imply that the place of the poem is a resort, possibly in New England, the region of the United States that fostered both American revolutionary fervor and served as the cradle of American literature. However, the allusions are meant to be out of place and comic in their effect. To emphasize this, Koch's historical and literary references are often intentionally artificial and grammatically awkward, as in the last line of the first stanza: "And ran around in an attic, so that a little of the blue enamel was scraped off my George Washington, Father of His Country, shoes."

Though the poem does not pinpoint a specific setting, one cannot doubt that the characters appearing in the poem are all Americans, and the reader may well recognize the nationalism that celebrates all things American. This overly patriotic impulse is satirized by the poem, especially when it describes objects with unlikely adornments such as teacups "painted with pictures of Herman Melville" that depict scenes from his works. Yet such objects might well be found in tourist shops, and the American trait of making commodities out of all aspects of its culture—that is, finding ways to sell that which Americans hold dear—is likewise an object of Koch's satire.

The speaker is also a character in the poem, a young male who acts as a wry observer of this commodified world. Since his father wears a "Dick Tracy necktie" and his mother wears a "Strauss Waltzes comb" (the only non-American allusion), readers may surmise that his upbringing has been influenced both by his father's popular culture leanings and his mother's preference for European high culture. These influences, combined with the nationalistic fervor that pervades American life through the sale of these objects in the marketplace, convey a sense of the components of American culture: Comic strips and remnants of European influence commingle in a land in which respect of culture is conveyed through the surreal appearance of cultural icons on everyday objects.

Forms and Devices

Koch is most frequently associated with the New York School poets, which include Frank O'Hara, John Ashbery, and James Schuyler. They, like Koch, frequently write poems that mix high and low culture, employ surrealistic techniques (unusual or even impossible juxtapositions designed to mimic dream states rather than directly lived reality), and, especially in the case of O'Hara, utilize a kind of chatty poetic line that may not seem like poetry at all to readers more accustomed to metrically ordered lines. The New York School poets do not completely eliminate rhyme and meter, but they do want to free poets from the necessity of using these devices in every poem as a *sine qua non* without which a poem cannot exist.

The reason for this abandonment of the more formal qualities of poetry or even of traditional free verse (there is also very little in the way of metaphor or lyric imagery in this poem) is that the New York School poets want to write a more immediate kind of poetry, one that reflects modern American life and escapes the academic formalism of backward-looking poetic devices. (Koch's poem "Fresh Air" lampoons these contemporary conservative academic poets.) Koch is more interested in mimicking the odd juxtapositions the past creates for contemporary lives than he is in commenting upon the past itself. Comedy is a technique used by all the New York School poets, and, in the final lines of the poem, the clash between historical allusion and contemporary utility becomes most farcical when the narrator and his girl sits on an "Abraham Lincoln" swing: "You sat on the eyes, mouth, and beard part, and I sat on the knees." From this vantage point, they see "a snowman holding a garbage can lid smashed into a likeness of the mad English king, George the Third." At first, this might strike the reader as departing from the American context until one remembers it was this king against whom the colonists staged their rebellion. That a trash can lid would resemble such a figure becomes an additional step in the transformation of the American locale: This is not a manufactured image painted or printed on an object but one that is imagined by the speaker of the poem as one might describe the shapes that clouds appear to resemble. Yet there is no distinction made in the poem between this imagined historical reference and the overt likenesses on blouses, neckties, and teacups elsewhere in the poem. This suggests that the inhabitants of this place—this American place—have come to perceive the world through eyes that have been structured by their environment. This is not a reflective engagement with the past that allows people to apply history's lessons to contemporary life but rather a fetishization of icons from the past that allows people to believe they are learned and in tune with their history and literature simply through the act of using an object, drinking tea, or sitting on a swing.

Themes and Meanings

Koch identifies a kind of "lifestyle history" as part of the American character, and though Americans surround themselves with references to the past, Koch suggests that this is merely commodity fetishism masquerading as an understanding of their literature and history and its importance to contemporary life. While his examples, designed for comic effect, might not seem familiar to the reader (who has probably never seen a blouse divided into squares with a picture of Edgar Allan Poe in each one), every reader is likely to be able to identify similar objects in American culture.

Koch suggests that Americans seem to think that by wearing a T-shirt embossed with the image of a famous person they can take a shortcut to true knowledge and understanding. However, a certain malaise results from practicing blind reverence toward surface details of American history rather than attending to actual meanings. When the narrator smells the hair of the girl he is with, he gets a whiff of "the mould of [her] seaside resort hotel bedroom," suggesting the moldiness of the lives that pass through historical resort locales as well.

Readers see very little of substance in any of the characters in the poem; thus the "You Were Wearing" title acts as an indicator of practically everything the narrator remembers about the young girl he may have met at the resort. While there is something of a nostalgic tone conveyed by the past-tense description of the happy details of this carefree summer holiday life, there is also the suggestion of lost opportunity: The boy and girl are so immersed in the images of the past they are expected to unreflectingly revere that they discover little about each other or about history, literature, or life. Koch's poem thus acts as a caution to readers to not blindly accept what is alleged to be significant in the past but to dig toward more meaningful experiences of the past's legacy. Everyone has been in crowds of half-alert people walking through national monument sites acting reverent because they are expected to do so. While Koch's juxtaposition of important figures from American culture seems at first to detract from their importance, the final lesson of the poem is otherwise: It serves as an instruction to appreciate the significance of American cultural history, which, paradoxically, is the way people can best take possession of their own place within the culture and live lives that do not dote on icons of the past.

This is consistent with what Koch and the New York School poets are also attempting to do in poetry. Their forsaking of traditional poetic practices does not occur in a vacuum; rather, Koch is very conscious of literary history throughout his work. However, he suggests that the best way to honor the past is to live in the present. One is reminded that historical figures who are honored today were usually people who attempted to find new forms through which to convey the experiences of their own time. Blind reverence was not something that motivated Washington, Melville, or any of the other figures who appear in the poem. A true appreciation of the American national legacy demands that Americans live in their own moment, conscious of, but not trapped within, their own history.

Ted Pelton

THE YOUNGEST DAUGHTER

Author: Cathy Song (1955-   )
Type of poem: Dramatic monologue
First published: 1980; collected in *Picture Bride*, 1983

The Poem

"The Youngest Daughter" is a monologue in fifty-two lines of delicately cadenced verse divided into five stanzas of differing lengths. The speaker of the poem is the youngest daughter of her family, and she is burdened with caring for her aging parent. Her monologue reveals a conflict of emotions within her: Love and pity for her invalid mother clash with feelings of resentment and entrapment for having to deny herself.

In the first stanza, Cathy Song evokes the effects of aging upon both women. The housebound daughter describes her skin becoming "damp/ and pale," while her mother's skin is "parched" from having labored in the fields. Both images are joined referentially by sunlight or the lack of it. The daughter's condition results from being cloistered and kept in the "dark/ for many years," whereas her mother's condition results from spending too much time in the "drying sun." Thus one of the paradoxes in this poem emerges: The sufferings of mother and daughter, though different, are also similar. Another contradiction rests on the reversal of roles that continually takes place. The mother and daughter switch back and forth between being the caregiver and the cared for, the soother of pain and its cause. In stanza 2, the daughter's eyes are burning with frustration. Ironically, it is suggested that the mother, who tries to soothe her daughter's "migraine," is also the cause of it.

In stanza 3, the daughter describes an instance of her role as caregiver and reflects on her mother's plight. She attends her mother, bringing her in a wheelchair to her morning bath. As the daughter washes her mother's breasts, the imagery not only reveals the daughter's understanding that her mother's body has been used to pleasure her husband and suckle her children but also suggests the daughter's revulsion at such a fate. Song proceeds, in stanza 4, to express the odd tenderness the daughter feels toward her mother. The daughter pities the mother's diabetic body scarred by insulin injections. She realizes that the two of them have always been trapped together in the same "sunless" room in a futile unity. Neither has a choice but to be there for the other.

The last stanza describes a reversal of roles as the mother prepares a meal for the daughter. As they eat, there is an unspoken understanding between the two. The daughter thinks, "She knows I am not to be trusted,/ even now planning my escape." In the final irony of the poem, the daughter toasts her mother's health, although it is her mother's longevity that prevents the daughter from having a life of her own. Song ends enigmatically, however, with the daughter's wistful (or perhaps ominous) description of the "thousand cranes" pictured on the window curtains that "fly up," presumably to a freedom that may yet be hers.

Forms and Devices

The cadences of Song's verse are as unobtrusive as breathing. They ripple and eddy in her speaker's stream of thought that seemingly proceeds from the very heart of her being. Upon this introspective stream, Song launches intricately contrasting images that create the poem's irony and paradox. Light and heat, food, and the body are the primary sources of Song's imagery. The poem begins by contrasting mother and daughter in terms of sunlight and skin. For the speaker-daughter, "The sky has been dark/ for many years," a powerful image of long-term deprivation that suggests a seed with arrested germination. Expressed in terms of the body, her "skin has become as damp/ and pale as rice paper": overly delicate, pallid, and friable. The daughter's sunless state contrasts starkly with the mother's overexposure to the sun that has parched her skin in the fields. The mother's experience of the exterior heat and light of the sun is, in turn, contrasted with an internal fever and pain that sears the daughter's body. The daughter says that when she touches her eyelids, they feel "hot enough to burn"; her "skin, aspirin colored,/ tingles with migraine"; and "pain flares up" on her face.

These two initial stanzas intimate the long-term situation of the two women. The rest of the poem describes two specific scenes, a morning bath and an afternoon meal, that are symmetrically balanced and contrasted: In the morning, the daughter is the caregiver bathing her mother; in the afternoon, the mother is the cook making their meal. Both situations are replete with painful body images. In the morning scene, the mother is an invalid who must be "wheeled . . . into her bath." Her skin is "freckled" with mementos of pain, the "blue bruises" of thirty years of insulin injections. However, the commanding body image is of the mother's breasts "floating in the milky water/ like two walruses,/ flaccid and whiskered around the nipples." Startling and unsavory as this image is, its effect is heightened by the gustatory image that follows: "I scrubbed them with a sour taste/ in my mouth, thinking:/ six children and an old man/ have sucked from these brown nipples."

Gustatory and food imagery fills the lines describing the afternoon meal. In this scene, the women's roles are reversed, the mother becoming the cook and the daughter the diner. This role reversal completes Song's construction of the two women's relationship as a paradoxically life-giving and life-sapping one, at once symbiotic, parasitic, and codependent. Song's food imagery takes on symbolic overtones when the daughter thinks of "a slice of pickled turnip" as a "token" for her "white body." The women's "ritual" meal, then, is a communion approaching cannibalism wherein the communicants feed off the daughter's body, consuming her opportunities for life. Hence the daughter toasts her mother's health with tea, a bitter cup. At the same time, the mother knows the daughter is planning escape like the thousand cranes of the window curtain that "fly up in a sudden breeze."

Themes and Meanings

In "The Youngest Daughter," Song, a Hawaii-born daughter of a Korean American father and a Chinese American mother, elaborates upon the universal feminist theme of mother-daughter relationships and puts an Asian American spin on it. Both situation and imagery in Song's poem have Asian overtones. In traditional Asian families, it is customary for the unmarried daughter to remain with the parents and care for them as they age. In many cases, this will be the youngest daughter's lot. The title of Song's poem carries resonances of this social and familial phenomenon, the speaker being the youngest of six siblings. Of Asian provenance, too, are several of the poem's images and symbols. The ingredients of the women's meal, for instance, are Asian: tea, rice, gingered fish, and pickled turnip, the last probably being the Japanese daikon, which is blanched white in color like the speaker's pallid skin. The crane image is also a common Asian symbol that connotes health and longevity, a connotation that Song employs enigmatically at the end of the poem: "As I toast to her health// a thousand cranes curtain the window,/ fly up in a sudden breeze." Clearly, the daughter longs to take flight from this sick relationship and achieve her freedom. Readers may wonder how she envisions this happening: through her mother's recovery, her longevity, or her death?

The relationship between mothers and daughters is an enduring theme of much literature written by or about women. Filiality, which shows itself in reverence for one's parents and respect for one's elders, is also a cardinal virtue of Confucianism and a widespread subject of writing in East Asia. The Asian overlay to a fundamental element of the human experience gives Song's situation a special piquancy. The mother-daughter relationship in Song's poem is depicted through the point of view of the daughter, the speaker of the poem. Through her, Song portrays a complex and rending mix of love and hate, of gratitude and resentment. It is a relationship that sustains and destroys, nourishes and devours, emphasized by the poem's use of food and gustatory imagery. The mother has brought the daughter into life by giving birth to her, has sustained her by nursing her at the breast, and continues to nurture her by soothing her migraine and preparing her food. However, now that age is taking its course, the women's roles are reversing. The daughter increasingly plays the role of nurse and caregiver, wheeling her diabetic mother about, bathing her, and companioning her. In this role, the daughter feels trapped, deprived of the freedom to be what she wants, and is keenly aware that her filial duties are atrophying her vital energies. Since it is unlikely that the mother can recover from her thirty-year-old diabetes or arrest the process of aging, the daughter is presumably trapped in her role until her mother's death can provide a final solution to her filial bondage. Hence the poem's closing irony and ambiguity are wrought by the daughter's bitter toast to the mother's health juxtaposed against the image of the cranes escaping in flight.

C. L. Chua and Keisha Blakely

GLOSSARY

Accented syllable: See *Stressed syllable*

Accentual meter: One of four base meters used in English (accentual, accentual-syllabic, syllabic, and quantitative), accentual meter is the system in which the occurrence of a syllable marked by a *stress* determines the basic unit, regardless of the number of unstressed syllables. In other words, it is the stresses that determine the metrical base. An example from modern poetry is "Blue Moles" by Sylvia Plath, the first line of which scans: "They're out of the dark's ragbag, these two." Because there are five stressed syllables in this accentually based poem, the reader can expect that many of the other lines will also contain five stresses. (See also *Scansion*)

Accentual-syllabic meter: By far the most common base meter for English poetry, accentual-syllabic meter measures the pattern of stressed syllables relative to the unstressed ones. In the first line of William Shakespeare's sonnet 130, "My mistress' eyes are nothing like the sun," there is a pattern of alternating unstressed with stressed syllables, although there is a *substitution* of an unstressed syllable for a stressed syllable at the word "like." In the accentual-syllabic system, stressed and unstressed syllables are grouped together into *feet.*

Allegory: One of the "figures of speech," allegory represents an abstract idea in concrete imagery, almost always in the form of a humanized character. Gluttony, for example, might be allegorized by a character who eats all the time, while Christian love might be allegorized by a character who does charitable deeds. The traditional use for allegory is to make it possible for the poet to show how abstract ideas affect real people who are in contact with them, or how abstract emotions affect each other within a human being.

Alliteration: When consonant repetition is focused at the beginning of syllables, the repetition is called alliteration, as in: "Large *m*annered *m*otions of his *m*ythy *m*ind." Alliteration is used when the poet wishes to focus on the details of a sequence of words and to show relationships between words within a line. Because a reader cannot easily skim over an alliterative line, it is conspicuous and demands emphasis.

Allusion: When a reference is made to a historical or literary event whose story or outcome adds dimension to the poem, then poetical allusion occurs. "Fire and Ice" by Robert Frost, for example, alludes to the biblical account of the flood and the prophecy that the next destruction will come by fire, not water. Without recognizing the allusion and understanding the biblical reference to Noah and the surrounding associations of hate and desire, the reader cannot fully appreciate the poem.

Anacrusis: The opposite of *truncation,* anacrusis occurs when an extra unstressed syllable is added to the beginning or end of a *line,* as in the line: "their shoul/ders held the sky/suspended." This line is described as iambic tetrameter with terminal anacrusis. Anacrusis is used to change a rising meter to falling, and vice versa, in order to change the reader's emotional response to the subject.

Anapest: One of six standard rhythmic units in English poetry, the anapestic foot associates two unstressed syllables with one stressed syllable, as in the line, "With the sift/ed, harmon/ious pause." The anapestic foot is one of the three most common in English poetry and is used to create a highly rhythmical, usually emotional, line.

Approximate rhyme: The two categories of approximate rhyme are assonance and half rhyme (or slant rhyme). Assonance occurs when words with identical vowel sounds but different consonants are associated. "Stars," "arms," and "park" all contain identical *a* (and *ar*) sounds, but because the consonants are different the words are not *full rhymes.* Half rhyme or slant rhymes contain identical consonants but different vowels, as in "fall" and "well." "Table" and "bauble" constitute half rhymes; "law," "cough," and "fawn" assonate.

Assonance: See *Approximate rhyme*

Ballad: The ballad stanza, a type of *quatrain,* may alternate its rhyme scheme as *abab* or *abcb.* If all four lines contain four feet each (*tetrameter*), the stanza is called a "long ballad"; if one or more of the lines contain only three feet (trimeter), it is called a "short ballad." Ballad stanzas, which are highly *mnemonic,* originated with verse adapted to singing. For this reason, the poetic ballad is well suited for presenting stories. Popular ballads are songs or verse which tell tales, usually impersonal, and they usually impart folk wisdom. Supernatural events, courage, and love are frequent themes, but any experience which appeals to common people is acceptable material. A famous use of the ballad form is *The Rime of the Ancient Mariner* (1798), by Samuel Taylor Coleridge.

Ballade: The French "ballade," a popular and sophisticated form, is commonly (but not necessarily) composed of an eight-line stanza rhyming *ababbcbc.* Early ballades usually contained three stanzas and an *envoy,* commonly addressed to a nobleman, priest, or the poet's patron, but no consistent syllable count. Another common characteristic of the ballade is a refrain that occurs at the end of each stanza.

Base meter (or metrical base): Poems in English and in most European languages which are not *free verse* are written in one of four base meters (*accentual, accentual-syllabic, syllabic,* or *quantitative*), measured by the number, pattern, or duration of the syllables within a line or stanza. Rhythm in verse occurs because of *meter,* and the use of meter depends upon the type of base into which it is placed.

Blank verse: Although many variations can occur in the *meter* of blank verse, its *base meter* is iambic pentameter. Blank verse lines are unrhymed, and are usually arranged in *stichic* form (that is, not in stanzas). Most of Shakespeare's plays are written in blank verse; in poetry it is often used for subject matter that requires much narration or reflection. In both poetry and drama, blank verse elevates emotion and gives a dramatic sense of importance. Although the base meter of blank verse is iambic pentameter, the form is very flexible, and *substitution, enjambment,* feminine endings, and extra syllables can relax the rigidity of the base. The flexibility of blank verse gives the poet an opportunity to use a formal structure without seeming unnecessarily decorous. T. S. Eliot's "Burnt Norton" is a modern blank-verse poem.

Cadence: The rhythmic speed or tempo with which a line is read is its cadence. All language has cadence, but when the cadence of words is forced into some pattern, it then becomes *meter,* thus distinguishing poetry from prose. A *prose poem* may possess strong cadence, combined with poetic uses of imagery, symbolism, and other poetic devices.

Caesura: When the poet imposes a pause or break in the poem, with or without punctuation marks, a caesura has occurred. The comma, question mark, colon, and dash are the most common signals for pausing, and these are properly termed "caesuras"; pauses may also be achieved through syntax, *lines, meter, rhyme,* and the sound of words. The type of punctuation determines the length of the pause. Periods and question marks demand full stops; colons take almost a full stop; semicolons take a long pause; commas a short pause. The end of a line usually demands some pause even if there is no punctuation.

Cinquain: Any five-line stanza, including the *mad-song* and the *limerick,* is a cinquain. Cinquains are most often composed of a *ballad* stanza with an extra line added to the middle.

Conceit: One of several types of *metaphor,* the term "conceit" is used for comparisons which are highly intellectualized. A conceit may therefore be said to be an extended, elaborate, or complex metaphor. The term is frequently applied to the work of the Metaphysical poets, notably John Donne.

Connotation: Words convey meaning through their sound, through their formal, *denotative* definitions, through their use in context, and through connotation. When a word takes on an additional meaning other than its denotative one, it achieves connotation. The word "mercenary," for example, simply means a soldier who is paid to fight in an army not of his own region, but connotatively a mercenary is an unprincipled scoundrel who kills for money and pleasure, not for honor and patriotism. Connotation is one of the most important devices for achieving *irony,* and readers may be fooled into believing a poem has one meaning because they have missed connotations which reverse the poem's apparent theme.

Consonance: When the final *consonants* of stressed syllables agree but the preceding vowels are different, consonance occurs. "Chair/star" is an example of consonance, since both words end with *r* preceded by different vowels. Terminal consonance creates half or slant rhyme (see *Approximate rhyme*). Consonance differs from *alliteration* in that the final consonants are repeated rather than the initial consonants. In the twentieth century consonance became one of the principal rhyming devices, used to achieve formality without seeming stilted or old-fashioned.

Consonants: Consonants (all letters except the vowels, *a, e, i, o, u,* and sometimes *y*) are among the most important sound-producing devices in poetry. There are five basic effects that certain consonants will produce: resonance, harshness, plosiveness, exhaustiveness, and liquidity. Resonance, exhaustiveness, and liquidity tend to give words—and consequently the whole line if several of these consonants are used—a soft effect. Plosiveness and harshness, on the other hand, tend to create tension. Resonance is the property of long duration produced by nasals, such as *n* and *m*, and by voiced fricating consonants such as *z*, *v*, and the voiced *th*, as in "them." Exhaustiveness is created by the voiceless fricating consonants and consonant combinations, such as *h, f,* and the voiceless *th* and *s*. Liquidity results from using the liquids and semivowels *l, r, w,* and *y,* as in the word "silken." Plosiveness occurs when certain consonants create a stoppage of breath before releasing it, especially *b, p, t, d, g, k, ch,* and *j*.

Controlling image/controlling metaphor: Just as a poem may include as structural devices form, theme, action, or dramatic situation, it may also use imagery for structure. When an image runs throughout a poem, giving unity to lesser images or ideas, it is called a "controlling image." Usually the poet establishes a single idea and then expands and complicates it; in Edward Taylor's "Huswifery," for example, the image of the spinning wheel is expanded into images of weaving until the reader begins to see life as a tapestry. Robert Frost's "The Silken Tent" is a fine example of a controlling image and *extended metaphor*.

Couplet: Any two succeeding lines that rhyme form a couplet. Because the couplet has been used in so many different ways, and because of its long tradition in English poetry, various names and functions have been given to types of couplets. One of the most common is the decasyllabic (ten-syllable) couplet. When there is an *end-stop* on the second line of a couplet, it is said to be "closed"; an *enjambed* couplet is "open." An end-stopped decasyllabic couplet is called a "heroic couplet," because the form has often been used to sing the praise of heroes. The heroic couplet was widely used by the neoclassical poets of the eighteenth century. Because it is so stately and sometimes pompous, the heroic couplet invites satire, and many poems have been written in "mock heroic verse," such as Alexander Pope's *The Rape of the Lock* (1712). Another commonly used couplet is the octasyllabic (eight-syllable) couplet, formed from two lines of iambic tetrameter, as in "L'Allegro" by John Milton: "Come, and trip as we go/ On the light fantastic toe." The light, sing-song tone of the octasyllabic couplet also invited satire, and in the seventeenth century Samuel Butler wrote one of the most famous of all satires, *Hudibras*, in this couplet. When a couplet is used to break another rhyme scheme, it generally produces a summing-up effect and has an air of profundity. Shakespeare found this characteristic particularly useful when he needed to give his newly invented Shakespearean *sonnet* a final note of authority and purpose.

Dactyl: The dactyl, formed of a stress followed by two unstressed syllables ($'\,\smile\smile$), is fairly common in isolated words, but when this pattern is included in a line of poetry, it tends to break down and rearrange itself into components of other types of feet. Isolated, the word "meaningless" is a dactyl, but in the line "Polite/meaning/less words," the last syllable becomes attached to the stressed "words" and creates a *split foot,* forming a *trochee* and an *iamb*. Nevertheless, a few dactylic poems do exist. "After the/pangs of a/desperate/lover," is a dactyllic line.

Denotation: The explicit formal definition of a word, exclusive of its implications and emotional associations (see *Connotation*), is its denotation or denotative meaning.

Depressed foot: Occasionally, two syllables occur in a pattern in such a way as to be taken as one syllable without actually being an *elision,* thus creating a depressed foot. In the line: "To each the boul/ders (that have)/fallen/to each" the *base meter* consists of five iambic feet, but in the third foot there is an extra syllable which disrupts the meter but does not break it, so that "that have" functions as the second half of the iambic foot.

Diction: John Dryden defined diction concisely as the poet's "choice of words." In Dryden's time, and for most of the history of English verse, the diction of poetry was elevated, sharply distinct from everyday speech. Since the early twentieth century, however, the diction of poetry has ranged from the banal and the conversational to the highly formal, and from obscenity and slang to technical vocabulary, sometimes in the same poem. The diction of a poem often reveals its persona's values and attitudes.

Dieresis: Caesuras which come after the foot (see *Split foot* for a discussion of caesuras which break feet), called "dieresis" (although the technical name is seldom used), can be used to create long pauses in the *line*, and they are often used to prepare the line for *enjambment*.

Dramatic dialogue: When two or more personae speak to each other in a poem or a play, they engage in dramatic dialogue. Unlike a *dramatic monologue*, both characters speak, and in the best dramatic dialogues, their conversation leads to a final resolution in which both characters and the reader come to the same realization at the same time.

Dramatic irony: See *Irony*

Dramatic monologue: In dramatic monologue, the narrator addresses a silent persona who never speaks but whose presence greatly influences what the narrator tells the reader. The principal reason for writing in dramatic monologue form is to control the speech of the major persona through the implied reaction of the silent one. The effect is one of continuing change and often surprise. In Robert Browning's "My Last Duchess," for example, the duke believes that he is in control of the situation, when in fact he has provided the emissary with terrible insights about the way he treated his former duchess. The emissary, who is the silent persona, has asked questions which the duke has answered; in doing so he has given away secrets. Dramatic monologue is somewhat like hearing one side of a telephone conversation in which the reader learns much about both participants.

Duration: The measure of quantitative meter is the duration or length of the syllables. Duration can alter the tone and the *relative stress* of a line and influence meaning as much as the *foot* can.

Elegy: The elegy and pastoral elegy are distinguishable by their subject matter rather than their form. The elegy is usually a long, rhymed, *strophic* poem whose subject is meditation upon death or a lamentable theme, while the pastoral elegy uses the natural setting of a pastoral scene to sing of death or love. Within the pastoral setting the simplicity of the characters and the scene lends a peaceful air despite the grief the narrator feels.

Elision: The two types of elision are synaeresis and syncope; they occur when a poet who is attempting to maintain a regular *base meter* joins two vowels into a single vowel or omits a vowel altogether. In the line "Of man's first disobedience, and the fruit" the "ie" in "disobedience" is pronounced as a "y" ("ye") so that the word reads dis/o/bed/yence, thereby making a five-syllable word into a four-syllable word. This process of forming one vowel out of two is synaeresis. When a vowel is dropped altogether, rather than combining two into one, it is called "syncope," as when "natural" becomes "nat'ral" and "hastening" becomes "hast'ning." Less frequent uses of elision are to change the sound of a word, to spell words as they are pronounced, and to indicate dialect.

Emphasis: Through a number of techniques, such as *caesura*, the *line*, *relative stress*, *counterpointing*, and *substitution,* poets are able to alter the usual emphasis or meaning of words. Whenever the meter of a poem is intentionally altered through one of these techniques, certain words or an entire line will be highlighted or emphasized for the purpose of calling attention to the most important parts of the poem.

End rhyme: See *Rhyme*

End-stop: When a punctuated pause occurs at the end of a line, the line is said to be "end-stopped." The function of end-stops is to show the relationship between lines and to create *emphasis* on particular words or lines. End-stopping in rhymed poems creates more emphasis on the rhyme words, which already carry a great deal of emphasis by virtue of their rhymes. *Enjambment* is the opposite of end-stopping.

Enjambment: When a line is not *end-stopped*—that is, when it carries over to the following line—the line is said to be "enjambed," as in John Milton's: "Avenge, O Lord, thy slaughtered saints, whose bones/ Lie scattered on the Alpine mountains cold." Enjambment is used to change the natural emphasis of the *line,* to strengthen or weaken the effect of *rhyme,* or to alter *meter.*

Envoy: Generally, an envoy (or envoi) is any short poem or stanza addressed to the reader as a beginning or end to a longer work. Specifically, the envoy is the final stanza of a sestina or a *ballade* in which all the rhyme words are repeated or echoed.

Extended metaphor: When *metaphors* are added to one another so that they run in a series, they are collectively called an "extended metaphor." Robert Frost's poem "The Silken Tent" uses an extended metaphor; it compares the "she" of the poem to the freedom and bondage of a silken tent. (See also *Controlling image/controlling metaphor*)

Eye rhyme: Words that appear to be identical because of their spelling but that sound different are known as "eye rhymes." "Bough/enough/cough" and "ballet/pallet" are examples. Because of changes in pronunciation, many older poems appear to use eye rhymes but do not. For example, "wind" (meaning moving air) once rhymed with "find." Eye rhymes which are intentional and do not result from a change in pronunciation may be used to create a disconcerting effect.

Falling rhyme: Rhyme in which the correspondence of sound comes only in the final unstressed syllable, which is preceded by another unstressed syllable, is known as a "falling rhyme." T. S. Eliot rhymes "me-tic-u-lous" with "ri-dic-u-lous" and creates a falling rhyme. (See also *Feminine rhyme*; *Masculine rhyme*)

Falling rhythm: A line in which feet move from stressed to unstressed syllables (*trochaic* or *dactyllic*) is said to "fall," as in this line from "The Naming of Parts": "Glistens/like cor/al in/all of the/neighboring/gardens." Because English and other Germanic-based languages naturally rise, imposing a falling rhythm on a rising *base meter* creates *counterpointing*.

Feminine rhyme: Feminine rhyme occurs when (1) a line's final accented syllable is followed by a single unaccented syllable and (2) the accented syllables rhyme, while the unaccented syllables are phonetically identical, as with "flick-er/snick-er" and "fin-gers/ma-lin-gers." Feminine rhymes are often used for lightness in tone and delicacy in movement.

First person: This *point of view* is particularly useful in short lyrical poems, which tend to be highly subjective, taking the reader deep into the narrator's thoughts. First-person poems normally, though not necessarily, signal the use of the first person through the pronoun "I," allowing the reader direct access to the narrator's thoughts or providing a character who can convey a personal reaction to an event. (See also *Third person*)

Foot/feet: The natural speech pattern in English and other Germanic-based languages is to group syllables together in family units. In English, the most common of these rhythmic units is composed of one unstressed syllable attached to one stressed syllable (an *iamb*). When these family groups are forced into a line of poetry, they are called "feet" in the *accentual-syllabic* metrical system. In the line "My mis/tress' eyes/ are noth/ing like/ the sun" there are four iambic feet (˘ ´) and one pyrrhic foot (˘ ˘), but in the line "There where/ the vines/ cling crim/son on/ the wall" there are three *substitutions* for the iamb—in the first, third, and fourth feet. The six basic feet in English poetry are the iamb (˘ ´), *trochee* (´ ˘), *anapest* (˘˘ ´), *dactyl* (´ ˘˘), *spondee* (´ ´), and *pyrrhus* (˘ ˘).

Form: The form of a poem is determined by its arrangement of lines on the page, its base meter, its rhyme scheme, and occasionally its subject matter. Poems which are arranged into *stanzas* are called "strophic," and because the strophic tradition is so old a large number of commonly used stanzas have evolved particular uses and characteristics. Poems which run from beginning to end without a break are called *stichic*. The form of "pattern poetry" is determined by its visual appearance rather than by lines and stanzas, while the definition of *free verse* is that it has no discernable form. Some poem types, such as the sestina, *sonnet*, and *ode*, are written in particular forms and frequently are restricted to particular subject matter.

Found poetry: Found poetry is created from language which is "found" in print in nonliterary settings—on menus, tombstones, fire extinguishers, even on shampoo bottles. Any language which is already constructed, but especially language which appears on artifacts that characterize society, such as cereal boxes, provides the material from which the found poem is created. The rules for writing a found poem vary, but generally the found language is used intact or altered only slightly.

Free verse: A poem that does not conform to any traditional convention, such as meter, rhyme, or form, and that does not establish any pattern within itself, is said to be a free verse poem. There is, however, great dispute over whether "free" verse actually exists. Eliot said that by definition poetry must establish some kind of pattern, and Frost said that "writing free verse is like playing tennis with the net down." However, some would agree with Carl Sandburg, who insisted that "you can play a better game with the net down." Free verse depends more on cadence than on meter.

Ghazal: The ghazal is a poetic form based on a type of Persian poetry. A ghazal is composed of couplets, often unrhymed, that function as individual images or observations but that also interrelate in sometimes subtle ways.

Haiku: Haiku is a Japanese form which appeared in the sixteenth century and is still practiced in Japan. A haiku consists of three lines of five, seven, and five syllables each; in Japanese there are other conventions regarding content which are not observed in Western haiku. The traditional haiku took virtually all of its images from nature, using the natural world as a *metaphor* for the spiritual.

Half rhyme: See *Approximate rhyme*

Heroic couplet: See *Couplet*

Hymn stanza: See *Ballad*

Hyperbole: When the poet deliberately overstates in order to heighten the reader's awareness, he is using hyperbole. As with *irony*, hyperbole works because the reader can perceive the difference between the importance of the dramatic situation and the manner in which it is described.

Iamb: The basic *foot* of English speech, the iamb associates one unstressed syllable with one stressed(˘ ′). The line "So long/as men/can breathe/or eyes/can see" is composed of five iambs. In the line "A cold/coming/we had/of it," a trochaic foot (a *trochee*) has been substituted for the expected iamb in the second foot, thus emphasizing that this is a "coming" rather than a "going," an important distinction in T. S. Eliot's "The Journey of the Magi."

Iambic pentameter: Iambic pentameter is a very common type of poetic *line* in English. It consists of five iambic feet together in a line (a foot is a two-syllable grouping). The following two lines by Thomas Wyatt are in iambic pentameter: "I find no peace and all my war is done,/ I fear and hope, I burn and freeze like ice." (See also *foot*; *iamb*)

Identical rhyme: Identical rhyme occurs when the entire final stressed syllables contain exactly the same sounds, such as "break/brake," or "bear" (noun), "bear" (verb), "bare" (adjective), "bare" (verb).

Imagery: Imagery is traditionally defined as the verbal simulation of sensory perception. Like so many critical terms, "imagery" betrays a visual bias: it suggests that a poetic image is necessarily visual, a picture in words. In fact, however, imagery calls on all five senses, although the visual is predominant in many poets. In its simplest form, an image re-creates a physical sensation in a clear, literal manner, as in Robert Lowell's lines, "A sweetish smell of shavings, wax and oil/ blows through the redone bedroom newly aged" ("Marriage"). Imagery becomes more complex when the poet employs *metaphor* and other figures of speech to re-create experience, as in Seamus Heaney's lines, "Right along the lough shore/ A smoke of flies/ Drifts thick in the sunset" ("At Ardboe Point"), substituting a fresh metaphor ("A smoke of flies") for a trite one (a cloud of flies) to help the reader visualize the scene more clearly.

Interior monologue: A first-person representation of a persona's or character's thoughts or feelings. It differs from a *dramatic monologue* in that it deals with thoughts rather than spoken words or conversation.

Internal rhyme: See *Rhyme*

Irony: Irony is among the three or four most important concepts in modern literary criticism. Although the term originated in classical Greece and has been in the vocabulary of criticism since that time, only in the nineteenth and twentieth centuries has it assumed central importance. The term is used in many different contexts with an extraordinary range of meanings, eluding precise definition. In its narrowest sense, irony is a figure of speech in which the speaker's real meaning is different from (and often exactly opposite to) the apparent meaning. In Andrew Marvell's lines, "The Grave's a fine and private place,/ But none I think do there embrace" ("To His Coy Mistress"), the speaker's literal meaning—in praise of the grave—is quite different from his real meaning. This kind of irony, the easiest to define, is often called "verbal irony." Another kind of irony is found in narrative and dramatic poetry. In the *Iliad* (c. 800 B.C.), for example, the reader is made privy to the counsels of the gods, which greatly affect the course of action in the epic, while the human characters are kept in ignorance. This discrepancy between the knowledge of the reader and that of the character (or characters) is called "dramatic irony." Beyond these narrow, well-defined varieties of irony are many wider applications.

Limerick: The limerick is a comic five-line poem rhyming *aabba* in which the third and fourth lines are shorter (usually five syllables each) than the first, second, and last lines, which are usually eight syllables each. The limerick's *anapestic* base makes the verse sound silly; modern limericks are almost invariably associated with bizarre indecency or with ethnic or anticlerical jokes.

Line: A line has been defined as a poetical unit characterized by the presence of *meter*, and lines are categorized according to the number of feet (see *Foot/feet*) they contain. A pentameter line, for example, contains five feet. This definition does not apply to a great deal of modern poetry, however, which is written in *free verse*. Ultimately, then, a line must be defined as a typographical unit on the page that performs various functions in different kinds of poetry.

Lyric poetry: The two ancient roots of poetry are the narrative and lyric traditions. Narrative poetry, such as the *Iliad*, relates long stories, often historical, which preserve information, characters, and values of a culture. Lyric poetry developed when music was accompanied by words, and although the "lyrics" were later separated from the music, the characteristics of lyric poetry have been shaped by the constraints of music. Lyric poems are short, adaptable to metrical variation, and usually personal compared with the cultural functions of narrative poetry. Lyric poetry sings of the self, exploring deeply personal feelings about life.

Mad-song: The mad-song—verse uttered by the presumably insane—usually expresses a happy, harmless, inventive sort of insanity. The typical rhyme scheme of the mad-song is *abccb*, and the unrhymed first line helps to set a tone of oddity and unpredictability, since it controverts the expectation that there will be a rhyme for it. The standard mad-song has short lines that help suggest benign madness, since "simple" people are associated with uncomplicated sentence patterns.

Masculine rhyme: Masculine rhyme occurs when rhyme exists in the stressed syllables. "Men/then" constitute masculine rhyme, but so do "af-ter-nóons/spoons." Masculine rhyme is generally considered more forceful than *feminine rhyme*, and while it has a variety of uses, it generally gives authority and assurance to the line, especially when the final syllables are of short duration.

Metaphor: Metaphor, like *irony*, is one of a handful of key concepts in modern literary criticism. Like irony, the term "metaphor" is used in such a wide variety of contexts that a precise, all-encompassing definition is impossible. In its narrowest sense, metaphor is a figure of speech in which two strikingly different things are identified with each other, as in "the waves were soldiers moving" (Wallace Stevens). A metaphor contains a "tenor" and a "vehicle." The tenor is the subject of the metaphor, and the vehicle is the *imagery* by which the subject is presented. In D. H. Lawrence's lines, "Reach me a gentian, give me a torch/ let me guide myself with the blue, forked torch of this flower" ("Bavarian Gentians"), the tenor is the gentian and the vehicle is the torch. This relatively restricted definition of metaphor by no means covers the usage of the word in modern criticism. Some critics argue that metaphorical perception underlies all figures of speech. Others dispute the distinction between literal and metaphorical description, saying that language is essentially metaphorical. The term "metaphor" has become widely used to identify analogies of all kinds in literature, painting, film, and even music.

Meter: Meter is the pattern of language when it is forced into a *line* of poetry. All language has rhythm; when that rhythm is organized and regulated in the line so as to affect the meaning and emotional response to the words, then the rhythm has been refined into meter. Because the lines of most poems maintain a similar meter throughout, poems are said to have a *base meter*. The meter is determined by the number of syllables in a line and by the relationship between them.

Metonymy: When an object which is closely related to an idea comes to stand for the idea itself, such as saying "the crown" to mean the king, "metonymy" is being used. The use of a part of an object to stand for the entire object, such as using "heart" to mean a person, is called "synecdoche." Metonymy and synecdoche are used to emphasize a particular part of the whole or one particular aspect of it.

Mnemonic verse: Poetry in which rhythmic patterns aid memorization but are not crucial to meaning is called "mnemonic verse." Ancient bards were able to remember long poems partly through the use of stock phrases and other mnemonic devices.

Mock-heroic: See *Couplet.*

Narrator: The terms "narrator," "persona," and "speaker" are roughly synonymous. They all refer to who is doing the talking—or observing or thinking—in a poem. Lyric poetry most often consists of the poet expressing his or her own personal feelings directly. Other poems, however, may involve the poet adopting the *point of view* of another person entirely. In some poems—notably in a *dramatic monologue*—it is relatively easy to determine that the narrative is being related by a fictional (or perhaps historical) character, but in others it may be more difficult to identify the "I."

Occasional verse: Broadly defined, occasional verse includes any poem written for a specific occasion, such as a wedding, a birthday, a death, or a public event. Edmund Spenser's *Epithalamion* (1595), which was written for his marriage, and John Milton's "Lycidas," which commemorated the death of his schoolmate Edward King, are examples of occasional verse, as are W. H. Auden's "September 1, 1939" and Frank O'Hara's "The Day Lady Died."

Ode: The ode is a *lyric* poem which treats a unified subject with elevated emotion, usually ending with a satisfactory *resolution*. There is no set *form* for the ode, but it must be long enough to build intense emotional response. Often the ode will address itself to some omnipotent source and will take on a spiritual hue. When explicating an ode, readers should look for the relationship between the narrator and some transcendental power to which the narrator must submit in order to find contentment. Modern poets have used the ode to treat subjects which are not religious in the theological sense but which have become innate beliefs of society.

Ottava rima: Ottava rima is an eight-line *stanza* of *iambic* pentameter, rhyming *abababcc*. Probably the most famous English poem written in ottava rima is Lord Byron's *Don Juan* (1819-1824), and because the poem was so successful as a spoof, the form has come to be associated with poetic high jinks. However, the stanza has also been used brilliantly for just the opposite effect, to reflect seriousness and meditation.

Oxymoron: Closely related to *paradox*, an oxymoron occurs when two paradoxical words are placed in juxtaposition, such as "wise fool" or "devilish angel."

Paradox: A paradox is a statement that contains an inherent contradiction. It may be a statement that at first seems true but is in reality contradictory. It may also be a statement that appears contradictory but is actually true or that contains an element of truth that reconciles the contradiction.

Pentameter: A type of rhythmic pattern in which each line consists of five poetic feet. (See also *Accentual-syllabic meter*; *Foot/feet*; *Iamb*; *Iambic pentameter*; *Line*)

Persona: See *Narrator*

Point of view: Point of view may be simply defined as the eyes and other senses through which readers experience the situation of a poem. As with fiction, poems may be related in the *first person*, second person (unusual), or *third person*. (The presence of the words "I" or "we" indicates singular or plural first-person narration.) Point of view may be limited or omniscient. A limited point of view means that the narrator can see only what the poet wants him or her to see, while from an omniscient point of view the narrator can know everything, including the thoughts and motives of others.

Prose poem: The distinguishing feature of the prose poem is its typography: It appears like prose on the page, with no line breaks. There are no formal characteristics by which a prose poem can be distinguished from a piece of prose. Many prose poems employ rhythmic repetition and other poetic devices not normally found in prose, but others use such devices sparingly if at all. Prose poems range in length from a few lines to three or four pages; most prose poems occupy a page or less.

Pun: A pun occurs when words which have similar pronunciations have entirely different meanings. By use of a pun the speaker establishes a connection between two meanings or contexts that the reader would not ordinarily make. The result may be a surprise recognition of an unusual or striking connection, or, more often, a humorously accidental connection.

Pyrrhus: When two unstressed syllables comprise a foot, it is called a pyrrhus or a pyrrhic foot, as in the line "Appear/and dis/appear/in the/blue depth/of the sky," in which foot four is a pyrrhus.

Quatrain: Any four-line stanza is a quatrain; aside from the *couplet,* it is the most common stanza type. The quatrain's popularity among both sophisticated and unso-phisticated readers suggests that there is something inherently pleasing about the form. For many readers, poetry and quatrains are almost synonymous. Balance and antithesis, contrast and comparison not possible in other stanza types are indigenous to the quatrain.

Regular meter: A *line* of poetry that contains only the same type of *foot* is said to be regular. Only the dullest of poems maintains a regular meter throughout, however; skillful poets create interest and *emphasis* through *substitution.*

Relative stress: When more emphasis is placed on one syllable in a pattern than on another, that syllable is said to be "stressed." Once the dominant stress in the line has been determined, every other syllable can be assigned a stress factor relative to the dominant syllable. The stress factor is created by several aspects of prosody: the position of the syllable in the *line,* the position of the syllable in its word, the surrounding syllables, the type of vowels and consonants which constitute the syllable, and the syllable's relation to the *foot, base meter,* and *caesura.* Since every syllable will have a different stress factor, there could be as many values as there are syllables, although most prosodists *scan* poems using primary, secondary, and unstressed notations. In the line "I am there like the dead, or the beast" the anapestic base meter will not permit "I" to take a full stress, but it is a more forceful syllable than the unstressed ones, so it is assigned a secondary stress. Relative to "dead" and "beast," it takes less pressure; relative to the articles in the line, it takes much more.

Resolution: Generally, a resolution is any natural conclusion to a poem, especially to a short *lyric* poem which establishes some sort of dilemma or conflict that the narrator must solve. Specifically, the resolution is the octave stanza of a Petrarchan *sonnet* or the couplet of a Shakespearean sonnet in which the first part of the poem presents a situation which must find balance in the resolution.

Rhyme: Rhyme is a correspondence of sound between syllables within a line or between lines whose proximity to each other allows the sounds to be sustained. Rhyme may be classified in a number of ways: according to the sound relationship between rhyming words, the position of the rhyming words in the line, and the number and position of the syllables in the rhyming words. Sound classifications include full rhyme and approximate rhyme. Full rhyme is defined as words that have the same vowel sound, followed by the same consonants in their last stressed syllables, and in which all succeeding syllables are phonetically identical. "Hat/cat" and "laughter/after" are full rhymes. Categories of *approximate rhyme* are *assonance, slant rhyme, alliteration, eye rhyme,* and *identical rhyme.*

Rhyme classified by its position in the line includes end, internal, and initial rhyme. End rhyme occurs when the last words of lines rhyme. Internal rhyme occurs when two words within the same line or within various lines recall the same sound, as in "Wet, below the snow line, smelling of vegetation" in which "below" and "snow" rhyme. Initial rhyme occurs when the first syllables of two or more lines rhyme. (See also *Masculine rhyme; Feminine rhyme*)

Rhyme scheme: Poems that establish a pattern of rhyme have a "rhyme scheme," designated by lowercase (and often italicized) letters. The letters stand for the pattern of rhyming sounds of the last word in each line. For example, the following A. E. Housman quatrain has an *abab* rhyme scheme.

> Into my heart an air that kills
> From yon far country blows:
> What are those blue remembered hills,
> What spires, what farms are those?

As another example, the rhyme scheme of the poetic form known as *ottava rima* is *abababcc.* Traditional stanza forms are categorized by their rhyme scheme and *base meter.*

Rime royal: The only standard seven-line stanza in English prosody is rime royal, composed of iambic pentameter lines rhyming *ababbcc.* Shakespeare's *The Rape of Lucrece* (1594) is written in this form. The only variation permitted is to make the last line hexameter.

Rondeau: One of three standard French forms assimilated by English prosody, the rondeau generally contains thirteen lines divided into three groups. A common stanzaic grouping rhymes *aabba, aabR, aabbaR,* where the *a* and *b* lines are tetrameter and the *R* (refrain) lines are dimeter. The rondel, another French form, contains fourteen lines of trimeter with alternating rhyme (*abababa bababab*) and is divided into two stanzas. The rondeau and rondel forms are always light and playful.

Rondel: See *Rondeau*

Scansion: Scanning is the process of assigning *relative stresses* and meter to a line of poetry, usually for the purpose of determining where variations, and thus emphasis, in the *base meter* occur. Scansion can help explain how a poem generates tension and offer clues as to the key words. E. E. Cummings's "singing each morning out of each night" could be scanned in two ways: (1) singing/each morn/ ing out/of each night or (2) sing/ing each/morning/out of/each night. Scansion will not only affect the way the line is read aloud but will also influence the meaning of the line.

Secondary stress: See *Relative stress*

Seguidilla: Like the Japanese haiku, the Spanish seguidilla is a mood or imagistic poem whose success hinges on the reader's emotional recognition or spiritual insight. Although there is no agreement as to what form the English seguidilla should take, most of the successful ones are either four or seven lines with an alternating *rhyme scheme* of *ababcbc*. Lines 1, 3, and 6 are trimeter; lines 2, 4, 5, and 7 dimeter.

Shakespearean sonnet: See *Sonnet*

Simile: Loosely defined, a simile is a type of *metaphor* that signals a comparison by the use of the words "like" or "as." Shakespeare's line "My mistress' eyes are nothing like the sun" is a simile that establishes a comparison between the woman's eyes and the sun.

Slant rhyme: See *Approximate rhyme*

Sonnet: The most important and widely used of traditional poem types, the sonnet is almost always composed of fourteen lines of iambic pentameter with some form of alternating rhyme, and it contains a turning point that divides the poem into two parts. The two major sonnet types are the "Petrarchan" (or "Italian") sonnet and the "Shakespearian" sonnet. The original sonnet form, the Petrarchan (adopted from the poetry of Petrarch), presents a problem or situation in the first eight lines, the "octave," then resolves it in the last six, the "sextet." The octave is composed of two *quatrains* (*abbaabba*), the second of which complicates the first and gradually defines and heightens the problem. The sestet then diminishes the problem slowly until a satisfying resolution is achieved.

During the fifteenth century, the Italian sonnet became an integral part of the courtship ritual, and most sonnets during that time consisted of a young man's description of his perfect lover. Because so many unpoetic young men had generated a nation full of bad sonnets by the end of the century, the form became an object of ridicule, and the English sonnet developed as a reaction against all the bad verse being turned out in the Italian tradition. When Shakespeare wrote "My mistress' eyes are nothing like the sun," he was deliberately negating the Petrarchan conceit, rejoicing in the fact that his loved one was much more interesting and unpredictable than nature. Shakespeare also altered the sonnet's formal balance. Instead of an octave, the Shakespearean sonnet has three quatrains of alternating rhyme and is resolved in a final couplet. During the sixteenth century, long stories were told in sonnet form, one sonnet after the next, to produce "sonnet sequences." Although most sonnets contain fourteen lines, some contain as few as ten (the curtal sonnet) or as many as seventeen.

Speaker: See *Narrator*

Split foot: A split foot occurs when the natural division of a word is altered as a result of being forced into a metrical base. For example, the words "point/ed," "lad/der," and "stick/ing" have a natural falling rhythm, but in the line "My long/two-point/ed lad/der's stick/ing through/a tree" the syllables are rearranged so as to turn the falling rhythm into a rising meter. The result of splitting feet is to create an uncertainty and delicate imbalance in the line.

Spondee: When two relatively stressed syllables occur together in a foot, the unit is called a "spondee" or "spondaic foot," as in the line "Appear/and dis/appear/in the/blue depth/of the sky."

Sprung rhythm: If *accentual meter* is taken to its extreme, one can never predict the patterns of succeeding stresses: It is possible only to predict a prescribed number of stresses per line. This unpredictability characterizes sprung rhythm, first described near the end of the nineteenth century by Gerard Manley Hopkins. In sprung rhythm "any two stresses may either follow one another running, or be divided by one, two, or three slack syllables."

Stanza: When a certain number of lines are meant to be taken as a unit, that unit is called a "stanza." Although a stanza is traditionally considered a unit that contains rhyme and recurs predictably throughout a poem, the term is also sometimes applied to nonrhyming and even irregular units. Poems that are divided into fairly regular and patterned stanzas are called "strophic"; poems that appear as a single unit, whether rhymed or unrhymed, or that have no predictable stanzas, are called "stichic." Both strophic and stichic units represent logical divisions within the poem, and the difference between them lies in the formality and strength of the interwoven unit. Stanza breaks are commonly indicated by a line of space.

Stichic verse: See *Stanza*

Stress: See *Relative stress*

Strophic verse: See *Stanza*

Substitution: Substitution, one of the most common and effective methods by which the poet can emphasize a foot, occurs when one type of foot is replaced by another within a *base meter*. For example, in the line "Thy life/a long/ dead calm/of fixed/ repose," a spondaic foot (´ ´) has been substituted for an iambic foot (˘ ´). Before substitution is possible, the reader's expectations must have been established by a base meter so that a change in those expectations will have an effect. (See also *Foot/feet*; *iamb*; *spondee*)

Syllabic meter: The system of meter which measures only the number of syllables per line, without regard to stressed and unstressed syllables, is called syllabic meter.

Symbol: Loosely defined, a symbol is any sign that a number of people agree stands for something else. Poetic symbols cannot be rigidly defined; a symbol often evokes a cluster of meanings rather than a single specific meaning. For example, the rose, which suggests fragile beauty, gentleness, softness, and sweet aroma, has come to symbolize love, eternal beauty, or virginity. The tide traditionally symbolizes, among other things, time and eternity. Modern poets may use personal symbols; these take on significance in the context of the poem or of a poet's body of work, particularly if they are reinforced throughout. For example, through constant reinforcement swans in William Butler Yeats's poetry come to mean as much to the reader as they do to the narrator.

Synaeresis: See *Elision*

Synecdoche: See *Metonymy*

Tenor: See *Metaphor*

Terza rima: Terza rima is a three-line stanzaic form in which the middle line of one stanza rhymes with the first line of the following stanza, and whose rhyme scheme is *aba bcb cdc*, and so on. Since the rhyme scheme of one stanza can be completed only by adding the next stanza, terza rima tends to propel itself forward, and as a result of this strong forward motion it is well suited to long narration.

Theme: Loosely defined as "what a poem means," theme more specifically refers to recurring elements. The term is sometimes used interchangeably with "motif." A motif is any recurring pattern of images, symbols, ideas, or language and is usually restricted to the internal workings of the poem. Thus, one might say that there is an animal motif in William Butler Yeats's poem "Sailing to Byzantium." Theme, however, is usually more general and philosophical, so that the theme of "Sailing to Byzantium" might be interpreted as the failure of human attempts to isolate oneself within the world of art.

Third person: Third-person narration exists when a poem's narrator, or speaker, has not been part of the events described and is not probing his or her own relationship to them; rather, the speaker is describing what happened without the use of the word "I" (which would indicate first-person narration). A poet may use a third-person *point of view*, either limited or omniscient, to establish a distance between the reader and the subject, to give credibility to a large expanse of narration, or to allow the poem to include a number of characters who can be commented on by the narrator.

Tone: Strictly defined, tone is the expression of a poet's attitude toward the subject and persona of the poem as well as about him- or herself, society, and the poem's readers. If the ultimate aim of art is to express and control emotions and attitudes, then tone is one of the most important elements of poetry. Tone is created through the denotative and connotative meanings of words and through the sound of language (principally, *rhyme*, *consonants*, and *diction*). Adjectives such as "satirical," "compassionate," "empathetic," "ironical," and "sarcastic" are used to describe tone.

Trochee: One of the most common feet in English poetry, the trochee associates one stressed syllable with one unstressed syllable ($'\,\smile$), as in the line: "Double/double toil and/trouble." Trochaic lines are frequently *substituted* in an iambic *base meter* in order to create counterpointing. (See also *Foot/feet*; *iamb*)

Truncation: Truncation occurs when the last, unstressed syllable of a falling line is omitted, as in the line: "Tyger,/tyger/burning/bright," where the "ly" has been dropped from bright."

Vehicle: See *Metaphor*

Verse: The term "verse" has two or three different applications. It is a generic term for poetry, as in *The Oxford Book of English Verse* (1939). Verse also refers in a narrower sense to poetry that is humorous or superficial, as in "light verse" or "greeting-card verse." Finally, "verse" is sometimes used to mean *stanza* or *line*.

Verse drama: Drama which is written in poetic rather than ordinary language and which is characterized and delivered by the *line* is called "verse drama." Verse drama flourished during the eighteenth century, when the *couplet* became a standard literary form.

Verse paragraph: A division created within a stichic poem (see *Stanza*) by logic or syntax, rather than by form, is called a "verse paragraph." These are important for determining the movement of a poem and the logical association between ideas.

Villanelle: The villanelle, like the *rondeau* and the rondel, is a French verse form that has been assimilated by English prosody. It is usually composed of nineteen lines divided into five tercets and a quatrain, rhyming *aba, bba, aba, aba, abaa*. The third line is repeated in the ninth and fifteenth lines. Dylan Thomas's "Do Not Go Gentle into That Good Night" is a modern English example of a villanelle.

MASTERPLOTS II

Poetry Series

TITLE INDEX

L

TITLE INDEX

AUTHOR INDEX

LIII

AUTHOR INDEX

TYPE OF POEM INDEX

TYPE OF POEM INDEX

TYPE OF POEM INDEX

TYPE OF POEM INDEX

MASTERPLOTS II